A SOCIOLOGY OF AMERICAN CORRECTIONS

THE DORSEY SERIES IN SOCIOLOGY

Editor **Robin M. Williams, Jr.** *Cornell University*

A SOCIOLOGY OF AMERICAN CORRECTIONS

NEAL SHOVER

The University of Tennessee, Knoxville

1979

 The Dorsey Press   Homewood, Illinois   60430

Irwin-Dorsey Limited   Georgetown, Ontario   L7G 4B3

© THE DORSEY PRESS, 1979

ISBN 0-256-02216-X
Library of Congress Catalog Card No. 78–70012

Printed in the United States of America

1 2 3 4 5 6 7 8 9 0 ML 6 5 4 3 2 1 0 9

For
Wooie and Huey

PREFACE

This book is the result of teaching courses in the sociology of punishment and corrections over the past seven years. In it I have tried to confront three of what I consider to be the major shortcomings of undergraduates when they come to such courses: an uncritical acceptance of the conventional wisdom about corrections and correctional bureaucracies, an overly technocratic approach to correctional problems, and an undernourished capacity for asking what I believe are the most important kinds of questions about corrections. While I have tried in the book to present some of the diversity of American thought and opinion about corrections, I have tried primarily to suggest some critical, possibly alternative ways of looking at corrections and correctional issues. I have tried to avoid accepting very much of what is said publicly about corrections at its face value and in the process I hope the book's stance and content enable undergraduates to move beyond some of their restricted notions about the field. Throughout the book I have emphasized a sociological approach in the hopes of avoiding the managerial-technical emphasis which is characteristic of too much of the correctional literature.

The origins of my interest in and approach to corrections go back a number of years. At the Ohio State University I was fortunate to have Thomas G. Eynon and Samuel P. Daykin as teachers and both of them stimulated my interest in the correctional enterprise. More importantly, they were largely responsible for transforming me into a serious, motivated student after my mediocre and directionless early years as an undergraduate. I am pleased to take this opportunity to thank them for all they have done for me.

After my undergraduate days, both the convicts and my fellow employees at the Federal Reformatory at Chillicothe, Ohio (now closed), and the Illinois State Penitentiary at Joliet taught me some important lessons about corrections, although they may not be aware of that fact. I profited immensely from my nearly three years as a corrector, although it was several years before even I realized it. For instance, as a result of daily contacts with convicts and subsequent reflection on them I eventually came to see and appreciate the importance of the fundamental discrepancy between the way correctors view themselves and their efforts and the way convicts often view these same matters. This discrepancy is too little appreciated by sociologists and others. After my correctional stint I had the good fortune of attending graduate school at the University of Illinois and studying with—among others—Daniel Glaser, David Bordua, and Norman Denzin. A fine group of fellow graduate students, many of whom had previously worked in correctional or mental health agencies, further stimulated me to develop alternative ways of viewing social control processes.

I have now been on the faculty of the University of Tennessee for seven years and I must acknowledge my gratitude as well to officials of the Tennessee Department of Corrections. In their ideologically narrow yet self-assured efforts to promote a type of corrections which has been discredited in other parts of the United States they have caused me to think about corrections in a comparative way. I doubt if this would have occurred to the same extent had I not relocated to the South. But while observing the efforts and pronouncements of Tennessee correctional officials from afar, I have come to see that a certain amount of diversity exists in the correctional thought and efforts of the 50 states and, of course, among the countries of the world. In the process I have begun to realize just how dependent correctional thought and practice are on their underlying economic and political base.

Several colleagues assisted me during the preparation of this book by reading portions of it in draft form. I am grateful to Arlene Sheskin, Ed Pawlak, Chip Hastings, Neil Cohen, and Jim Gobert for their helpful suggestions. Had I followed all of them the book undoubtedly would have been better than it is, but that would have left me nothing to deal with in the classroom. One colleague deserves special mention: BJ the DJ. Throughout the project, BJ was always there when needed. As is customary in these matters, I accept sole responsibility for the book's shortcomings, both small and large.

I am especially pleased to thank my family, Jeanie, Jenni, and Bubby, for their contribution to the book. Their encouragement, assistance, and support made the project possible and worthwhile.

January 1979   NEAL SHOVER

CONTENTS

section one

INTRODUCTION

1

Corrections in the criminal justice context

In the America of the late 1970s the criminal justice system is the topic of much controversy and debate. One group of critics attacks it for being ineffective in the "war against crime," for being so preoccupied with the legal rights and rehabilitation of offenders that the welfare of victims and law-abiding citizens is ignored and jeopardized. These critics—the "new 'realists' " (Platt and Takagi, 1977) —would like to see a renewed emphasis on punishment and incapacitation as a means of dealing with what they believe to be a small group of "serious" or "dangerous" offenders. Another group of critics takes an entirely different position. Generally, they blame the criminal justice system for placing too much emphasis on the very kinds of goals that the first group takes to be desirable. Many in this second group of critics espouse a radical political-economic interpretation of correctional issues. They view the correctional apparatus as a mechanism through which a political-economic elite pacifies and controls a surplus population (for example, Quinney, 1977).

The clientele of correctional agencies have not been idle during this period of ferment. In the past decade or so they have mounted legal challenges to the treatment they have received at the hands of the correctional apparatus. Court decisions in recent years have forced correctional administrators to reexamine some of their previously taken-for-granted procedures for dealing with offenders. In addition, the early 1970s saw a wave of convict rebellions sweep across the American correctional scene, during which a number of offenders and correctional employees alike were killed. Clearly,

3

these are not easy times for those enmeshed in or employed by the criminal justice system.

Turmoil often provides strong incentives to strive for intelligent understanding. So it is with the turmoil within the criminal justice system. Controversy and conflict make it all the more important that we develop an informed understanding of the workings of the criminal justice system. This book aims at an increased understanding of the past, present, and likely future conditions of one component of the criminal justice system: *corrections*.

The name corrections will be used here to refer to *all the officially organized and sanctioned actions to which offenders are subjected as a result of their conviction of crime(s)*, whether these be juvenile offenses, misdemeanors, or felonies. This book deals with the American correctional apparatus and processes. It utilizes sociological knowledge and analysis to understand correctional structures and processes and to highlight some of their apparent strengths and shortcomings.

ORGANIZATION OF THE BOOK

There are 16 chapters in the book, organized into six principal sections. Section one (Chapters 1 and 2) contains introductory materials. Chapter 1 is a brief overview of the correctional apparatus in America, its size and standing in the criminal justice system. Chapter 2 reviews the correctional contributions of social scientists and introduces the reader to the perspective of the sociology of knowledge. Chapter 2 argues that the sociology of knowledge leads us to a more critical and relativistic stance toward correctional scholarship than has been employed in many past studies and analyses of correctional issues.

Section two (Chapters 3 and 4) is a treatment of correctional ideologies and alternative views of the historical process of correctional change. The concept of *preventive ideal* is introduced and two subtypes are discussed: *punishment ideologies* and *rehabilitative ideologies*. Chapter 4 points out the functional similarities of these two types of ideologies. Also, a variety of different rehabilitative ideologies are distinguished and discussed. Chapter 4 compares and contrasts three different perspectives on the process of historical correctional change: *conservative*, *liberal-pluralist*, and *radical-elitist*. Examples are given of how each perspective interprets specific historical correctional changes.

Section three consists of only one chapter (5), which deals with the problems and process of criminal sentencing. Conceptual distinctions are discussed, and criminal sentencing is presented as a type of social process involving interaction between representatives of different offices in the criminal justice system. Problems of sentencing disparity are discussed. Chapter 5 concludes with materials on some of the proposals for sentencing "reform" that have received so much attention in recent years, especially the movement toward determinate sentencing. Some likely consequences of this type of reform are discussed, drawing upon the limited research literature now available.

Section four (Chapters 6–11) summarizes much of what social scientists have theorized and learned about correctional personnel, offenders, and correctional regimens and processes. Chapter 6 is a summary of the characteristics and perspectives of correctional employees and offenders. It points to several areas of differences that are consequential for the correctional process and its impact on offenders. The bulk of Section four is a treatment of jails and detention homes, prisons and training schools, and probation and parole. The final chapter in this section (Chapter 11) briefly indicates some of the ways in which organizational and interactional processes affect the delivery of correctional services. An awareness of these processes indicates that much more than rehabilitative ideologies and good intentions are required to understand the impact of correctional interventions on offenders.

Section five contains four chapters (12–15), all of which deal in some way with the process and results of correctional evaluation. We suggest that at least three different evaluative modes are applied to corrections: *humaneness, legality/due process,* and *efficiency-effectiveness.* An overview of each of these evaluative modes is provided. Chapter 14 is a rather detailed and technical presentation of the elements of evaluative research. Chapter 15 summarizes what evaluative research has thus far concluded about the efficiency and effectiveness of correctional intervention. Chapter 15 also contains a discussion of two different perspectives on the evaluative research process: the *objectivist* and *critical.* The importance of each of them for an understanding of the social process of planning, conducting, and interpreting evaluative research is presented.

The book's final section (Chapter 16) discusses the process of correctional reform and obstacles to it as seen by conservatives, liberal-pluralists, and radical-elitists. This section should give the reader an understanding of the disagreements that surround the process of correctional "reform." Indeed, it is suggested that there is disagreement about the very meaning of *correctional reform.* Chapter 16 should leave the reader better prepared to understand extant reform efforts and proposals and to work for correctional change.

SOME CONCEPTUAL MATTERS

Officially adjudicated offenders are the grist of the correctional system. There are essentially three types of criminal offenders: misdemeanants, felons, and juveniles.

Misdemeanants

A *misdemeanor* is a crime that carries a potential sentence of one year or less in confinement or a fine below a certain specified amount (say, $5,000). Persons convicted of misdemeanors are commonly referred to as *misdemeanants*. Misdemeanor defendants are usually dealt with by the lowest level of criminal courts, including municipal courts. Perhaps a majority of misdemeanor defendants are charged with drunkeness or public order offenses (for example, disturbing the peace, being drunk and disorderly). Misdemeanants ordinarily serve their sentences in local jails or workhouses. Many will have repeated contact with the criminal justice system over a span of many years, especially the so-called chronic drunkeness offenders. Historically, dismissal of charges, small fines, or a sentence to confinement were the only options judges had when dealing with misdemeanants. In the past few years, however, many jurisdictions have established probation programs for them.

Felons

Felonies are crimes for which the law provides penalties of more than one year in confinement or fines over a certain specified amount. *Felons* are persons who have been convicted of felonies. Unlike misdemeanants, felons usually serve their sentences in state prisons or correctional institutions; those felons convicted of violating federal law serve their sentences in federal institutions.

Juvenile offenders

In most states and local communities, juvenile offenders are dealt with by special courts, variously called juvenile courts or family courts. If juvenile offenders are felt to require confinement prior to their "hearing" (a euphemism for a trial), they are detained in a juvenile detention home, although there are still many locales that confine juveniles in their county jail along with older offenders.

Juveniles arrested by police are most likely to be detained in the detention home prior to trial. However, juveniles come to the attention of the juvenile court via other avenues. They are often referred by school officials, by their own parents, or by the other social agencies. Those juveniles referred by these sources are less likely to be held in the detention home prior to their hearing.

Should it be determined in their "best interests," juvenile offenders may be placed on probation, placed in some type of part-time residential treatment facility in their home communities, or committed to a state training school. Following release from either of the latter two types of facilities, offenders usually will spend a period of time under parole supervision before being completely discharged by the juvenile correctional subsystem.

THE PLACE OF CORRECTIONS

Offenders do not enter the criminal justice system until they are taken into custody as suspected perpetrators of criminal acts. They do not enter the correctional subsystem unless and until they are convicted of crimes and, under sentence of a court of proper jurisdiction, receive some kind of penalty for their crimes. Prior to reaching the correctional stage of the system, offenders will likely have had contact with its other components: the *police*, the *prosecutor's office*, perhaps the *public defender*, and the *court*.

Depending upon their age and the type of crime they are charged with having committed, offenders arrive at the correctional stage of this process via somewhat different routes. Figure 1–1, which is a schematic overview of the entire criminal justice process, illustrates this point. This chart shows a tripartite flow of criminal cases, one each for felons, misdemeanants, and juvenile offenders. As can be seen, there are numerous points in the criminal justice process at which offenders may be dropped out so that they do not progress to subsequent stages. What Figure 1–1 does not show is the extremely high degree of attrition of criminal cases as they proceed through the criminal justice system. Those cases (and defendants) that arrive in court for sentencing represent a very small proportion of all those that began the process at the time of arrest. They probably represent an even smaller proportion of all those offenders whose crimes are even reported to the police in the first place. According to a U.S. Census Bureau survey, in 1973 only 28 percent of the victims of personal crimes in the United States reported the crimes to the police (U.S. Dept. of Justice, 1976: 113). Obviously, therefore, those offenders who are arrested and survive the various stages of the criminal justice process until sentencing are a rather small percentage of all *offenders*.

FIGURE 1–1
A general view of the criminal justice system

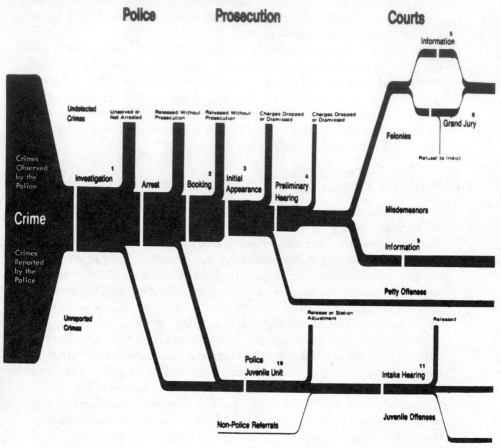

Note: This chart presents a simple but comprehensive view of the movement of cases through the criminal justice system. Procedures in individual jurisdictions may vary from the pattern shown here. The differing line weights indicate the relative volumes of cases disposed of at various points in the system, but are only suggestive since there are no nationwide data of this sort.

[1] May continue until trial.

[2] Administrative record of the arrest. The first step at which temporary release on bail may be available.

[3] Before a magistrate, commissioner, or justice of the peace. Formal notice of charge, advice of rights. Bail set. Summary trials for petty offenses usually conducted here without further processing.

[4] Preliminary testing of evidence against the defendant. Charge may be reduced. No separate preliminary hearing for misdemeanors in some systems.

[5] Charge filed by prosecutor on basis of information submitted by police officers or citizens. Alternative to grand jury indictment. Often used in felonies; almost always used in misdemeanors.

Corrections

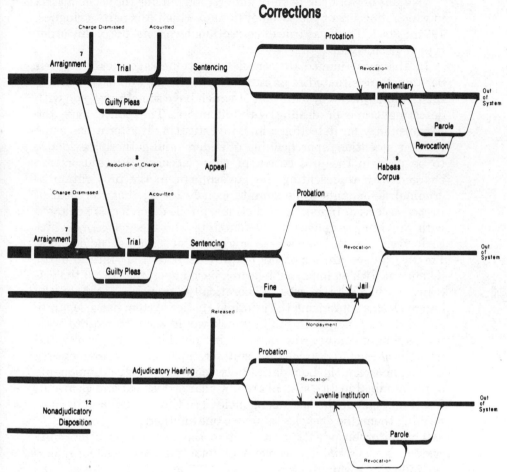

[6] Reviews whether government evidence is sufficient to justify trial. Some states have no grand jury system; others seldom use it.

[7] Appearance for plea; defendant elects trial by judge or jury (if available). Counsel for indigent usually appointed here in felonies; often not appointed at all in other cases.

[8] Charge may be reduced at any time prior to trial in return for plea of guilty or for other reasons.

[9] Challenge on constitutional grounds to the legality of detention. May be sought at any point in the process.

[10] Police often hold informal hearings and dismiss or adjust many cases without further processing.

[11] Probation officer decides desirability of further court action.

[12] Welfare agency, social services, counseling, medical care, and so on, for cases in which adjudicatory handlings is not needed.

Source: President's Commission on Law Enforcement and Administration of Justice. *The Challenge of Crime in a Free Society* (Washington, D.C.: U.S. Government Printing Office, 1967), pp. 8–9.

The criminal justice system

"No line of work can be fully understood outside the social matrix in which it occurs or the social system of which it is part" (Hughes, 1971a: 309). This is as true of correctional work as it is of any other type of occupation.

In the most immediate sense, correctional agencies and their personnel are situated in an interorganizational web of agencies—the criminal justice system—all of which have something to do with detecting crime or dealing with offenders. The police have the responsibility for detecting crime, investigating it after it has come to their attention, apprehending offenders, and gathering evidence to be used in the prosecution of those accused. Prosecutors are charged with representing the government in the prosecution of criminal defendants while simultaneously seeing that the ideal of justice is served. In most jurisdictions, public defenders are charged with providing a defense for defendants who are too poor to hire their own private counsel—a majority of criminal defendants. Finally, judges are supposed to provide both the state and the defendant with an impartial hearing, based upon the law, of the evidence gathered in a case. Theoretically, therefore, each of the organizations comprising the criminal justice system has a separate and distinct function to fulfill, which would seem to require little interaction or contact with one another outside of the officially and formally designated arenas for contact, such as the courtroom. In reality, however, the boundaries between these various components of the criminal justice system are not nearly this neat and clear-cut. The functions of the various agencies tend to overlap and, in performing them, the agencies influence one another.

This interdependence is implicit in the very notion of criminal justice as a *system*. The concept of something as a system makes the following assumptions:

1. That an institution or process which can be viewed as a totality in its own right is, at the same time, made up of distinguishable parts or subsystems.
2. These various components of the larger system exist in a state of interdependence or interrelatedness; the state or condition of any one of the components has implications for the state or condition of the system's other components.
3. Changes in the state or condition of any of the system's components parts will often have predictable, identifiable consequences for the system's other components.

Although Figure 1–1 presents a schematic overview of criminal justice as a system, it does not even begin to suggest the various ways in which this is true. The results of a variety of empirical research on the criminal justice system demonstrate clearly some of the ways in which the activities of the system's various components affect one another. In late 1955 the governor of Connecticut, disturbed by the fact that so many people had been killed in automobile accidents in his state during that year, announced that in the future all persons convicted of speeding would have their driver's licenses suspended. The governor acted in hopes of stemming a mounting highway traffic death toll, and early reports of the impact of the program suggested that it was successful. Later, Campbell and Ross (1968) examined the ways in which the criminal justice system reacted to this attempt to impose harsher penalities on convicted speeders. Despite earlier claims, they found less reason to believe that the crackdown itself had an effect on the highway traffic death rate. Just as important, they found that after the crackdown the police may have been less willing to charge drivers with speeding violations, not wanting them to have to pay "too harsh" a penalty for their violation. Judges apparently reacted to the crackdown by issuing more not guilty verdicts, again as a way of generally vitiating the intended harsher penalties for convicted speeders. The authors conclude that "the courts, and probably also the police, are apparently unwilling to invoke penalties that might seem severe and unfamiliar in context" (Campbell and Ross, 1968: 52). Research on the handling of defendants arrested for criminal offenses during the urban "riots" of the mid-1960s similarly supports the systemic nature of the criminal justice process (Balbus, 1973). During the various riots the police made numerous arrests, which placed a heavy strain on the other components of the criminal process. One of the mechanisms the courts used for dealing with this work overload was offering defendants very light sentences in return for guilty pleas. Had the courts not done this, so many defendants would have demanded trials that the courts would have become hopelessly bogged down in their greatly increased workload. In this case the police activities, which resulted in large numbers of arrests for riot-related crimes, had serious repercussions for the activities of the courts. The correctional subsystem is no different. It, too, is affected by the activities of other components of the criminal justice system. If the courts were to escalate the penalties they impose on some type of offender, corrections necessarily would be affected. For example, the numbers of offenders sentenced to imprisonment would probably increase. In such ways do the various subsystems within criminal justice influence one another.

The moral division of labor

We can also ask about the place of corrections in the general society, especially its place in what Hughes (1971a) referred to as the *moral division of labor*. As he noted, this is a division based on the respectability of the work that various groups or occupations perform. Those occupations that perform a great deal of *dirty work* (Hughes, 1971) tend to be seen as disreputable, largely for that very reason. According to Hughes, the job of dealing with those convicted of crimes is a type of societal dirty work that more respectable elements of the population delegate to correctional workers while, at the same time, not wanting to be told too many of the details of how offenders are treated. In this sense our correctional employees are not unlike the SS guards who ran the Nazi death camps (Hughes, 1971). Like the SS of Nazi Germany, correctional workers are charged with "taking care of" a stigmatized group of persons, a type of societal dirty work. For that very reason they are seen, to some extent, as suspect and their occupation is not accorded very much prestige in the moral division of labor. In a 1967 public opinion poll of a national sample of adults and teenagers, respondents were asked a series of questions about corrections as a career and the degree of confidence they have in correctional workers. The survey concluded that corrections is not generally seen as a desirable occupation (Joint Commission, 1969: 65). Correctional employees seem well aware of the rather low regard in which their line of work is held by others. Complaints about an unappreciative and unsupportive public at large are common among them.

SOME PARAMETERS OF THE CORRECTIONAL SUBSYSTEM

How many persons are employed in corrections in the United States? How are they deployed in the correctional subsystem? In 1975 the U.S. Census Bureau conducted a survey of local, state, and federal criminal justice agencies (U.S. Dept. of Justice, 1977a). The survey found that there were approximately 225,000 full-time employees in corrections. Approximately 5 percent of these were employed at the federal level, 57 percent at the state level, and 39 percent at the local (city and county) level of government.

During fiscal year 1975, correctional agencies at the federal level had a budget of $243 million. State correctional agencies had a combined budget of $2,292 million, and local correctional agencies spent $1,471 million. These figures give an idea of just how large an enterprise corrections really is, and the extent to which it is a source of livelihood for many individuals. Therefore, in terms of its absolute

1. Corrections in the criminal justice context

size, an analysis of correctional agencies and the correctional sub-system is a substantial undertaking, with implications for a rather large component of government. Correctional agencies often make a substantial contribution to the economy of the local communities in which they are located. In this regard, prisons are not unlike military installations, both of them providing the principal source of employment in many communities in the United States.

Now, what can we say about the size of the task correctional workers are called upon to perform? On any given day, how many offenders are within the confines of the correctional subsystem? Complete and reliable statistics are not available; there are only estimates and statistics based on incomplete enumerations. Because the data were not all collected in the same year, the derivation of population parameters is made even more risky. Nevertheless, in Table 1–1 we have indicated the numbers of offenders being "served" by various types of correctional programs, on an average day, for various years from 1965 through 1976. As can be seen in Table 1–1, we arrive at a total figure of approximately *1.25 million offenders* involved in correctional programs on any given day. Given the problems we have already alluded to, there is probably ample reason to assume that the true figure is even higher than this.

TABLE 1–1
Summary estimates of persons under various kinds of correctional programs

Type of program	Number of offenders (and year)	Source of data
State and local jails	82,000 (1972)	U.S. Dept. of Justice (n.d.: 3)
Juvenile detention	13,000 (1974)	U.S. Dept. of Justice (1977)
Adult probation (felony) ..	230,000 (1966)	U.S. Dept. of Justice (1973)
Misdemeanant probation ..	201,000 (1966)	U.S. Dept. of Justice (1973)
Juvenile probation	224,000 (1966)	U.S. Dept. of Justice (1973)
State and federal prisons ...	263,000 (1976)	U.S. Dept. of Justice (1978)
State and private juvenile institutions	77,000 (1974)	U.S. Dept. of Justice (1977)
Adult parole	102,000 (1966)	U.S. Dept. of Justice (1973)
Juvenile parole	60,000 (1966)	U.S. Dept. of Justice (1973)
Total	1,252,000	

In a very real sense, those employed in the correctional subsystem owe their jobs and sustenance to the existence of this offender aggregate. We are reminded of Marx's comment—only half-facetious—that "the criminal . . . appears as one of those 'natural equilibrating forces' which establish a just balance and open up a whole perspective of 'useful' occupations" (1964: 159–60).

CORRECTIONS AS A LIVELIHOOD AND PROFESSION

Recounting these statistics on the parameters of the correctional subsystem does not adequately convey the degree to which corrections has sought to "professionalize itself" in the past decade. Increasingly, individuals are looking to it as a *career*, and governmental agencies and universities are establishing specialized programs and curricula for those interested in pursuing such a career. Therefore, correctional training and correctional employment are becoming more institutionalized and legitimated. The numerous criminal justice programs that have sprung up in American colleges and universities during the past decade are a powerful testimony to the validity of this movement. The time when correctional employees were a small band of isolated and beleaguered *dirty workers* may be drawing to a close. While their work may continue to be treated as "dirty," they are gradually receiving more tangible and ideological remuneration for their labors. Actions by the federal government, involving the expenditure of huge sums of federal revenues, have been especially instrumental along these lines (Quinney, 1973; 1977). With the passage in 1968 of the Omnibus Crime Control and Safe Streets Act and the establishment of the Law Enforcement Assistance Administration (LEAA), the federal government provided a strong impetus to a higher level of crime control and criminal justice organization. The mission of LEAA was stated clearly:

> The mission of LEAA is to reduce crime and delinquency by channeling Federal financial aid to state and local governments, to conduct research in methods of improving law enforcement and criminal justice, to fund efforts to upgrade the educational level of law enforcement personnel, to develop applications of statistical research and applied systems analysis in law enforcement, and to develop broad policy guidelines for both the short and long-range improvement of the nation's Criminal Justice System as a whole (Quinney, 1977: 111).

By 1974 approximately 200,000 students had received $150 million in Law Enforcement Education program funds to finance studies for law enforcement and criminal justice careers (Quinney, 1977: 112).

This movement to upgrade the training and professionalism of correctional personnel has been accompanied by an increased militancy on their part. There are a variety of data to suggest that correctional workers, especially prison guards, have come to see themselves as a beleaguered group. They have gained a new sense of solidarity with one another, and this has helped to spawn and promote the movement to unionize. In corrections, as in other reaches of the welfare state, we seem to be witnessing a revolt of the dirty workers. They "are increasingly caught between the silent middle class, which wants them to do the work and keep quiet about it, and the objects of that work, who refuse to continue to take it lying down" (Rainwater, 1974: 335).

However, this is simply one of several signs that American corrections today is in a transitional state. And while we know where corrections has been, there is much less certainty about where it is headed. It is clear that some of the structures and ideological justifications of the past have been seriously discredited. For instance, sentencing "reform" has dismantled one of the programmatic mainstays of the medical model of corrections: the indeterminate sentence. Faith in corrections' ability to correct has been eroded. Increasingly, the belief in deterrence and incapacitation rather than rehabilitation are cited as justification for punishing offenders. In the present state of uncertainty and disillusionment, some see an opportunity to make fundamental changes:

> ... I believe that we are at a cultural watershed. We are beginning to see that the tools and institutions we have created to solve our social and economic problems no longer work. This recognition may lead in turn to the recognition that we have the opportunity and the resources to recreate ourselves and, in turn, our institutions ... That is my hope (Carlson, 1976: 168–69).

Only time will tell whether this expressed hope will be realized. Clearly, however, these are unsettled times for American corrections. Given such a state, a book such as this one seems a risky venture. At the same time, it seems very appropriate.

2

Social scientists and corrections:
The constriction of inquiry

The insights of the sociology of knowledge provide a convenient starting point for our analysis of American corrections. The sociology of knowledge is a subdiscipline of sociology which, in the broadest terms, explores the relationship between beliefs or ideas and the social context in which they emerge or gain acceptance. The sociology of knowledge begins with the recognition that what people take to be "reality" and "knowledge" is socially relative. Thus, the need for a sociology of knowledge is "given with the observable differences between societies in terms of what is taken for granted as 'knowledge' in them" (Berger and Luckmann, 1966: 3). Fundamental to the sociology of knowledge is a willingness to suspend interest in the truth or falsity of people's beliefs in favor of asking other types of questions about them. In this respect the sociologist is different from the proverbial "man in the street."

> The man in the street does not ordinarily trouble himself about what is "real" to him and about what he "knows" unless he is stopped short by some sort of problem. He takes his "reality" and his "knowledge" for granted. The sociologist cannot do this, if only because of his systematic awareness of the fact that men in the street take different "realities" for granted as between one society and another. The sociologist is forced by the very logic of his discipline to ask, if nothing else, whether the difference between the two "realities" may not be understood in relation to various differences between the two societies. . . . For example, the man in the street may believe that he possesses "freedom of the will" and that he is therefore "responsible" for his actions. . . . What [the sociologist] can

and must do, however, is to ask how it is that the notion of "freedom" has come to be taken for granted in one society and not another, how its "reality" is maintained in the one society and how, even more interestingly, this "reality" may once again be lost to an individual or to an entire collectivity (Berger and Luckmann, 1966: 2–3).

The sociology of knowledge owes much to the work of Karl Marx, especially "its root proposition—that man's consciousness is determined by his social being" (Berger and Luckmann, 1966: 6).

The sociology of knowledge has been particularly fascinated by Marx's twin concepts of "substructure/superstructure." . . . What concerned Marx was that human thought is founded in human activity ("labor, in the widest sense of the word") and in the social relations brought about by this activity. "Substructure" and "superstructure" are best understood if one views them as, respectively, human activity and the world produced by that activity (Berger and Luckmann, 1966: 6).

In following the lead of Marx and others, the sociology of knowledge has concentrated on three types of questions. First, what are the relationships between the characteristics of particular social contexts (for example, historical time periods) and the beliefs that people in that context develop and espouse to make sense of some aspect(s) of their world and experience? Second, what is the relationship between the nature of a group's beliefs and its location within a social structure? For instance, is there a relationship between the nature of beliefs and the location within a social structure of those who develop and promote those beliefs? Third, what is the social and political process by which some beliefs come to be accepted as "true" and others come to be discredited as "false," "misleading," or "trivial?" In sum, the sociology of knowledge usually looks "behind" the beliefs and questions that some group(s) ordinarily take(s) for granted and tries to explain why that is the case.

Taking these brief comments on the sociology of knowledge as a starting point, our principal objectives in this chapter are two. First, we will give a brief overview of American sociologists' contributions to the analysis of correctional agencies and issues. As will be seen, this tradition of work has focused on only a few recurrent problems and has consistently employed a set of assumptions or beliefs about how these problems should best be resolved. Second, we will suggest some possible reasons why sociologists have consistently dealt with these "core issues" and have employed the assumptions they have in their work.

SOCIOLOGISTS AND CORRECTIONS: PROBLEMS AND THEMES

For purposes of convenience, we break the historical involvement of sociologists in corrections into two time periods: the early, formative period of roughly 1890 to 1925, and the more contemporary period of, again roughly, 1926 to the present. Our comments here are primarily applicable to the work of sociologists during the latter time period, although subsequent investigations might reveal that they apply equally well to the earlier time, too.

Actually, little is known about the involvement of sociologists during the period 1890–1925. Existing interpretations of correctional change during the period are shallow and generally lack a critical stance. Changes in correctional structures and practices during the period are cited as evidence of a slow but inexorable advance of humaneness and rationality against the receding forces of ignorance, injustice, and brutality. Such work has tended to sketch the history of corrections as a process of unfolding rationality, usually in the form of a series of "reforms." Perhaps the future will see more historical scholarship on corrections, and the earlier period of American sociologists' involvement in corrections will be scrutinized.

Leaving aside concern with the formative period, however, the correctional contributions of American sociologists during the past 50 years have largely clustered in eight substantive areas:

1. Parole prediction theory and research.
2. Theory and research on the structure and functioning of correctional agencies, primarily prisons and training schools.
3. Theoretical applications of sociological theories to the prevention or control of criminality, usually in urban neighborhoods.
4. Theoretical applications of sociological and social psychological theories to the correction of offenders.
5. Research on some of the social psychological changes attendant to being corrected.
6. Evaluative research on the systemic and social psychological effects of correctional treatment and programs.
7. Research on the exercise of discretion in decision making by correctional personnel.
8. Theory and research on "violent" and "dangerous" offenders and violent behavior, especially in the prison setting.

While these various foci might seem diverse, all have common themes and assumptions. Let's examine some of these assumptions, since this may help us understand the work itself as well as the current state of the sociology of corrections.

Correctional tasks and priorities

Sociologists often lament their assumed lack of significant impact on the operations of correctional agencies. While they may be correct in this assumption, their impact on public discourse and the public's understanding of correctional matters seems more substantial. They have sometimes played a highly visible role in deliberations over correctional issues. Not only have they contributed theoretical and research work to books and journals, but they have served as consultants to departments of corrections, as reviewers of research proposals in the area of correctional research, and as members of governmental commissions that study correctional issues. Carlson (1976: 165) seems to be referring primarily to sociologists when he states that

> researchers can exert a powerful influence on the *debate* about corrections. The renascence of "deterrence" as a viable concept owes much to some dogged investigators who thought the issues were worth exploring. And the erosion of the rehabilitation model, now so visible, is due in large measure to the torrents of criticism launched at it by some researchers. (Emphasis added.)

And we cannot overlook sociologists' impact as educators who have sent forth their students to assume positions in correctional bureaucracies.

It can be argued, therefore, that sociologists' correctional impact has not been as modest as they sometimes think it has. Actually, there has been a great deal of agreement between them and correctional administrators on many issues, albeit these agreements have not always been articulated or recognized. But they have been consequential for our very understanding of correctional regimens and problems. In effect, these underlying agreed-upon assumptions have functioned as a set of unarticulated premises and constraints that have suggested the most fundamental contours and characteristics of correctional tasks, priorities for corrections, and the most "realistic" pathways to reform. In other words, these mutually shared assumptions have served to foreclose or prejudge a variety of alternative conceptions of the same matters.

We see this process at work in sociologists' willingness and readiness to adopt *rehabilitation* as a legitimate and dominant correctional objective. Such an acceptance has both followed from and helped to reinforce an overly simplified view of the nature of *the* correctional mandate. For example, a substantial amount of theoretical and research literature produced by sociologists has juxtaposed "treatment" goals and activities with those of "custody" or "surveillance." This tendency is consistent with what Horowitz and Liebowitz (1968: 280) have dubbed the "welfare model of social problems." Such a model

> has sought to liberalize the visible agencies of social control (the police, judiciary, and welfare agents) by converting them from punitive instruments into rehabilitative instruments. The underlying premise that punishment and rehabilitation are the only two possible responses to deviance yields the conventional tendency to evaluate deviant behavior in *therapeutic* rather than *political* terms. (Emphasis in the original.)

As the authors point out, however, "the social welfare model does not exhaust present options—either on logical or pragmatic grounds." What it *does* do is help prevent serious consideration or discussion of various other alternatives, and suggests that correctional programs are *either* punitive *or* rehabilitative but not both. Clearly, to assume that the two must be mutually exclusive is to ignore the fact that "liberal" correctional programs or reforms can be used for the furtherance of totalitarian ends—what Wright has designated *liberal totalitarianism*. Thus, contemporary prisons

> are institutions which, at least formally, have adopted the liberal goal of rehabilitation, while maintaining totalitarian control over the lives of prisoners. Moreover, they have adopted a variety of liberal programs (the indeterminate sentence, therapy programs) which in practice often serve to further the totalitarian goal of changing prisoners into strict conformists to authority (1973: 152).

But the ideological congruence of sociologists and correctional administrators extends beyond mere acceptance and endorsement of rehabilitative ideologies; it also includes agreement on the fundamental nature of the correctional task. Generally, this has been conceived of as a *technical* problem, implicitly divorced from humanitarian, political, and legal considerations. If only—the argument goes—we can isolate the right set of rehabilitative techniques, it will pay handsome dividends for our ability to correct offenders and convert them into virtuous citizens. Consensus on the desirability and overriding importance of isolating such a set of techniques is taken to be self-evident.

Of course, whatever this ultimate bag of rehabilitative tools looks like, it is assumed that the use of "scientific" strategies will show the way. Social scientists who have been involved in the correctional arena are enamored with the promise of science as an arbiter of correctional issues, and of scientific research findings as guides to restructuring the correctional industry. Indeed, references to the dictates of scientific procedures are assumed to be sufficient rationale for all manner of correctional decisions that those less enamored with science might otherwise regard as much more complex. In the Community Treatment Project, for example, the requirements of a scientific research design resulted in some convicted juveniles being sentenced to prison on the basis of a table of random numbers. This was justified as a means to establish the differential effectiveness of imprisonment versus probation for comparable groups of offenders.

With rare exception, evaluative research aimed at determining the effectiveness of correctional treatment programs simply has not been framed in terms that challenge or contradict the fundamental assumptions of the correctional industry. For example, questions like "which rehabilitative program is most effective?" ignore larger and more important questions, such as "are treatment programs used to create or perpetuate a system of class justice?" or "how do treatment programs produce a sense of injustice in those subjected to them?" In their failure to step outside of the premises embedded in many research questions, sociologists have failed to promote true alternatives.

Whether it be correctional research or the operation of treatment programs, the assumption that "qualified staff" members will remain in control is foremost. So while there is a commitment to finding a workable rehabilitative strategy, the search has gone forward, apparently, with some clear assumptions as to what the final product will *not* be like. It will neither require nor permit the political organization of offenders for pursuit of their own collectively defined interests. Nor will it vest any significant control over their own correctional fate in the hands of offenders themselves. And it will neither require nor deliver comparable treatment for corporate and underclass-offenders.

The trouble with offenders

Offenders have generally been sketched as individuals who have *something* wrong with them. Embedded in nearly all correctional theories is an image of offenders that suggests their "differentness" from the rest of us, or that suggests their deficiency as fully competent, trustworthy human beings. This has reinforced the tendency to think of them almost as inanimate objects or raw material, to be shaped, manipulated, or processed in order to accomplish the correctional mandate. In other words, dehumanization and depolitization are implicit in many approaches to correction. In their defense it must be said that sociologists have not advocated the more extreme or bizarre of these proposals. Schein (1962) has suggested that so-called brainwashing techniques used by the Chinese during the

Korean War might profitably be adapted to correct offenders. Schwitzgebel notes that electronic technology may soon enable us to monitor the movements and activities of offenders. Such an "electronic rehabilitation system" would require that offenders wear "transmitters that permit the continual monitoring" of their location (1971: 17). Schwitzgebel feels that such techniques are superior to many of those we have relied on in the past, making them "remarkably well suited for integration into the criminal justice system" (1971: 63). However, he worries that there may be obstacles to the further development and application of behavior modification techniques.

> Although judicial and legislative opinion is now helpful in setting the outer limits of permissible treatment, restrictive case law and statutes based upon inadequate information are likely to prevent an advantageous development of new knowledge and more effective techniques. . . . There needs to be an opportunity for conceptual changes in the treatment of offenders, at least until a higher degree of therapeutic success is achieved. . . . The vocabulary and definitions of law should not unduly restrict the logical development of the field of behavior modification as they would if they were the predominant terms determining its growth (1971: 65).

Nevertheless, sociologists cannot be excused entirely from advocacy or endorsement of such overly technocratic, potentially totalitarian measures. For instance, Wilks and Martinson (1976) argue for the abolition of parole as it has been structured in the past. In its place the state would establish a network of paid informants to monitor parolees' behavior. Admittedly, these are extreme examples of the lengths to which technocratic thinking can lead, but similar premises are embedded in most correctional theory.

Although varieties of correctional theories have been adapted or developed to date, most of them share another characteristic: an atomistic or micro-sociological focus that either shears away or ignores the relationships between political-economic processes and corrections. In nearly all correctional theories, individuals are seen as the necessary target for change, and the means of accomplishing this consists of tinkering either *directly* with them or *indirectly* with them via manipulation of their immediate interpersonal environment. The example of individual counseling or psychotherapy is an obvious one. The same is true, however, of so-called group-relations approaches, which attempt to harness intragroup processes in order to correct individual members. The much-heralded community corrections movement promises to be little different in this regard.

> To the extent that criminal activity represents a rational response to the absence of opportunities realistically available, community

corrections may be largely irrelevant because it is in a position to generate few new opportunities. . . . If it is true that lack of contact with good schools and adequate housing contribute to criminality and there are no good schools or adequate housing in the community, how can a community corrections center remedy this? It is in no position to improve the schools or bring slum apartments into conformity with housing codes (Greenberg, 1975a: 5).

Now it is obviously in the interest of correctional administrators and employees to attempt ideologically to divorce their handling of offenders from larger political-economic issues. They do not want offenders to perceive any connection between their plight and processes of a political or macro-sociological nature. Typically, prison staff members tell convicts that "we had nothing to do with your being sent here; our only job is to see that you serve your sentence." In such ways they seek to drive a wedge between corrections and the injustices of the wider society. Regrettably, the theories of criminality and rehabilitation produced and supported by social scientists have done little to rectify this situation. Sociologists, for example, continue to produce apolitical, atomistic, and micro-sociological theories in this area. Such theories ignore the effects on offenders of political and economic injustice, apparently assuming that somehow these are of no importance for the correctional industry. (Too few sociologists have recognized the possibility that if offenders do in fact require any kind of melioristic assistance there may be none better than turning them into politically conscious and involved *citizens*. Presumably, the principal obstacle would be to first acknowledge them as competent human beings, fully capable of recognizing, organizing around, and acting in pursuit of their own individual and collective interests.)

It can be argued that by even appearing to accept the priority of rehabilitation as *the* correctional objective, sociologists have helped to reinforce an image of offenders that suggests their pathological natures. Presumably, after all, one feels it necessary to try and *re*habilitate only those whose "habilitation" has made them deficient as human beings. Although correctional personnel are fond of piously proclaiming that offenders are "human beings," their simultaneous pursuit of the ultimate rehabilitative strategy suggests that they view offenders as "diminished, inferior people at best" (Mitford, 1973: 7).

In addition to a micro-sociological bias, most correctional theory and research is founded upon an implicit human-relations model of the correctional process. Like some students of industrial life, many correctional researchers have assumed there is no inherent, structurally given conflict of interests between correctors and offenders. Having assumed this, they then feel compelled to explain conflict and hostility—which are usually attributed to the operation of some peculiar set of structural arrangements (e.g., "total institutions"), problems of communication, the emotional problems of offenders, or deficient training on the part of staff. The possibility that the two groups should naturally be expected to conflict with one another in some form or other is not given serious consideration. Instead, countless hours have been spent trying to determine why offenders engage in collective efforts to thwart their "helpers' " plans for them, or why offenders feel less than grateful to their "helpers."

Dynamics of correctional regimens

In one respect, sociologists have made an outstanding contribution to our understanding of correctional issues through their theory and research on the structure and functioning of correctional agencies, and by research on decision making in these agencies. Certainly this body of works has taught us a great deal about the inherent structural and interactional limitations on the accomplishment of correctional goals. But paradoxically this same work has hindered progress toward a more in-depth and complete understanding of correctional regimens and processes. Too often agencies have been analyzed as self-contained units, with the result that empirical research has failed to probe the relationships between structural or political-economic arrangements and the dynamics of correctional agencies. Although we know a great deal about political and power struggles within individual agencies (for example, studies of "treatment" versus "custody" in prisons), research has generally failed to take account of political struggles within departments of corrections. Such an atomistic focus leaves us poorly equipped to interpret the transformations that some state departments of corrections have undergone in the past decade. We have lacked a systemic view of corrections, even while knowing a great deal about the operations of the separate institutional components of the system. We know virtually nothing, for example, about the effects of an infusion of white-collar personnel into departments of corrections, or about the impact of federal funding programs on the systematic shaping of correctional regimens. More importantly, we should know more than we do about the correctional consequences of economic changes, such as fluctuations in the unemployment rate.

Because research on correctional decision making has generally focused on micro-sociological processes, it has betrayed its grounding in "labeling" theory. It has been plagued by the same failure to come to grips with the relationship between overarching structural arrangements and dynamics and the processes of an interactional or social psychological nature. (To be sure, some of this research predates the appearance of labeling theory, but it is otherwise indistinguishable from research spawned by that body of work.) Admittedly, there is nothing about labeling theory that precludes such a rapprochement with radical structural analyses; in fact, with the exception of isolated works, few sustained or systematic attempts have been made.

In yet another way we have been badly served by accumulated theory and research on the operation of the correctional regimens. Some of it was initially stimulated by an interest in complex organizations or by the development of formal theory rather than by correctional issues per se. In the desire to analyze correctional regimens for these purposes, we have sometimes ignored the *distinctions* between them and other types of complex organizations. For example, Goffman's (1962) analysis of prisons as one type of *total institution* omits concern about the possible significant differences between them and convents and the military or mental hospitals. While such an exercise in the development of more formal sociological theory is highly desirable, it is not done without some cost to other important areas of theory and research. The theory of total institutions has little to say about the possible importance of voluntary versus involuntary admission, which is one dimension where prisons and convents are different.

Correctional research

In discussing a particular type of social research, Blumer (1967: 165) charged that "agency-determined research" characteristically "ignores the interests, rights, and claims of the people who are the objects of inquiry." This seems to be an accurate description of a great deal of correctional research. Indeed, in correctional research we see the operation of a *hierarchy of credibility* (Becker, 1967), where the problems and perspectives of superordinates are more readily adopted than those of subordinates because they are seen as having more merit and credibility. Research that sides with the underdog in such situations is often dismissed as "biased."

> When do we accuse ourselves and our fellow sociologists of bias? I think an inspection of representative instances would show the accusation arises, in one important class of cases, when the research gives credence, in any serious way, to the perspective of the subordinate group in some hierarchical relationship. In the case of deviance, the hierarchical relationship is a moral one. The superordinate parties in the relationship are those who represent the

forces of approved and official morality; the subordinate parties are those who, it is alleged, have violated that morality (Becker, 1967: 240).

It is odd that, when we perceive bias, we usually see it in these circumstances. It is odd because it is easily ascertained that a great many more studies are biased in the direction of the interests of responsible officials than the other way around (Becker, 1967: 242).

The consequences of accepting the correctional hierarchy of credibility are clear: Even after dozens of studies of incarcerated offenders, Irwin justifiably charged in 1970 that most of the problems and perspectives of felons are "either completely unknown, misunderstood or falsely described" (1970: 3). He further charged that "the official image of the felon, the explanation of his acts, the definition of [correctional] programs themselves are quite different than the felon's view of these same things. By the same token, the felon acts according to a set of categories and understandings foreign to the officials" (1970: 3).

There have been exceptions to this general pattern. Research on women's prisons, for example, seemingly has dealt more sympathetically and sensitively with subjects than has been the case with comparable studies of men's institutions. Still, we must recognize that a large amount of correctional theory and research has dealt with issues primarily of interest to correctional administrators or social theorists while generally ignoring topics of presumed critical concern to offenders, or even to lower-level correctional personnel. As Carlson notes, "no Gallup or Harris polls have been taken to reflect inmate attitudes. Most of what we know about the inmate has been based on what has been written by ex-inmates, or on what is occasionally pirated out of the prisons" (1976: 160). Extensive research on "inmate subcultures," which has investigated whether they are indigenous in origin or a diffusion from the outside world, may be of interest to sociologists; but it tells us little about the *experience* of imprisonment. Also, until only recently violence in prison was largely ignored by sociologists.

Another set of difficulties with correctional research stems from the tendency of researchers to rely upon variables defined or produced by the correctional industry. Most sociologists possess at least an embryonic appreciation for the various processes by which social control bureaucracies can shape and create the parameters of the very problems with which they are supposed to deal. Yet despite this, correctional researchers have continued to make heavy use of official records in their studies of correctional issues. It can be argued that, in itself, such a reliance on official records reduces the likelihood of researchers being able to transcend the official reality and to generate or appreciate alternative perspectives on correctional structures and processes.

Generally, the variables selected for analysis in correctional research are both easily quantifiable and primarily of interest to correctional administrators, such as: the rate of recidivism, the total number of days spent in the free world before parole revocation, or the total monetary cost to the state of the parole period. Interest in such things as the fundamental fairness of correctional programs, the feelings of injustice on the part of correctional clients, or the extent to which correctional programs may violate human and legal rights have been given little attention.

A final error in the prevailing image and conduct of correctional research is the notion that it is disinterested, that the sociological expert has "no moral or financial axes to grind" (Young, 1975: 65). Today the largesse of law enforcement and correctional agencies has become an important source of support for empirical research—therefore, an important potential career-escalating consideration for sociologists. It would be inconsistent with common sense to imagine that these agencies are not able, for that reason, to assure themselves of the kinds of research that take seriously their interpretations of problems, and to effectively screen out dissonant interpretations. Moreover, through the effective use of funds to hire consultants from the academic world, correctional administrators can assure themselves of ideological support from fully credentialed "experts." Even those sociologists who are not hired by the correctional industry to lend this kind of legitimacy to their programs may be dissuaded from criticism in yet other ways. Correctional agencies have become an important source of employment for persons with the baccalaureate degree. And those academics, who insist upon "unreasonable" criticism of the correctional industry, may find these jobs closed to students who have been too closely associated with them. In other words, there are a variety of ways by which the correctional industry may use its resources to assure a steady supply of ideological supports (Gouldner, 1968).

Three implications of the foregoing material are immediately evident. First, because of its implicit acceptance of the correctional hierarchy of credibility, sociological research has probably helped define correctional clientele as being inferior and untrustworthy persons whose claims are undeserving of serious attention. Consequently, we cannot agree with Bowker's assertion that "social science research has almost never been damaging to prisoners" (1977: 118). Second, we must develop an ability to analyze correctional theorizing and research as social processes; we must cease to think of them as a purely cerebral activity. That being the case, we must ask ourselves in what way have these activities actually been shaped. We have tried to shed some light on this question. Third, we must be prepared to recognize and correct the situation that, as social scientists, we know a great deal about some aspects of the correctional industry and practically nothing about others. At many places in this book we will be able to draw upon a substantial body of accumulated theory and research. At other places, however, we will be forced to rely upon a more speculative record.

INTERPRETATIONS

To this point we have suggested that sociologists' past involvements in correctional matters has built upon a few recurrent assumptions and has explored certain types of problems to the exclusion of others. How can this be explained or understood? The sociology of knowledge perspective leads us to search for characteristics of the social contexts of sociologists, both individually and collectively, that could make sense of this pattern of involvement. Perhaps an examination of these social contexts and circumstances will help us understand why the sociologists' correctional contributions have employed the assumptions and have focused upon the kinds of problems we have already mentioned.

Interpretations of the type we are interested in, here, range from the analytically neutral to the critical. Let's review several of them, beginning with Mills's important 1942 article on "the professional ideology of social pathologists." Mills noted that the deviance theory of 40 years ago focused on the individual and deviance-producing "situations," rather than on employing a more structural-level analysis. Individuals were deviant because they failed to "adjust" to "norms" that were taken for granted and widely considered appropriate and legitimate. The defining criteria of pathological behavior were "typically rural in orientation and extraction," while "the 'problems' discussed typically [concerned] urban behavior" (1942: 174). Moreover, when rural social problems *were* discussed, they were "conceived as due to encroaching urbanization" (1942: 174–75). Social pathology theorists were committed to social reform, although always the importance of dealing with fragmentary "practical problems" was emphasized. In working for reform, science was to point the way. The theory of cultural lag, which was popular at that time, involved "a positive evaluation of natural science and of orderly progressive change" (1942: 177). Finally, abrupt social change was viewed as disruptive and disorganizing, as opposed to the "slow, 'evolutionary' pace of change," which was considered organized and normal.

How did Mills explain these dominant themes in the social pathology theory of an earlier time? He reasoned that "if the members of an academic profession are recruited from similar social contexts and if their backgrounds and careers are relatively similar, there is a tendency for them to be uniformly set for some common perspective" (1942: 166). Virtually all of the social pathologists "were born in small towns, three-fourths of which were in states not industrialized during [their youth]" (1942: 166–67). They either were members of, or actively mingled with, rising social strata. Thus, there is little wonder that they "saw" an evolutionary trend of social progress, "for notions of progress are congenial to those who are rising in the scale of position and income" (1942: 177). Still, "the common conditions of their profession" also provide important clues for understanding why they employed a common style of thought. The social circles and strata in which they moved were quite homogeneous; many had participated in similar social reform groups. They had married persons of similar social positions and most of them were university faculty members.

Mills's analysis remains one of the better attempts to apply the insights of the sociology of knowledge to the beliefs and theories of sociologists themselves. It is not the only such effort. More recently, Gouldner (1968) has attempted the same thing; this time interpreting the "new" deviance theory of the 1960s.

Gouldner's comments are directed at the societal reactions, or the "labeling" theory of deviance, which created such a stir among sociologists for nearly a decade (say, 1962–72). The two most important characteristics of this work, according to Gouldner, are its identification with the underdog (i.e., prisoners, mental patients, and the like) and its critical stance toward the agencies and organizations that deal with them. Gouldner argues, however, that it is really only *state* and *local* agencies and officials that are criticized, not *federal* agencies or political elites. The new deviance theory is

> essentially a critique of the caretaking organizations, and in particular of the *low level* of officialdom that manages them. It is not a critique of the social institutions that engender suffering or of the high level officialdom that shapes the character of caretaking establishments (1968: 107). (Emphasis in the original.)

In doing so, however, societal reactions theory becomes

> a party to the struggle between the old and the new elites in the caretaking establishments; between the welfare institutions inherited from the 1930's and those now promoted today; and between the "locals" working the municipalities and the "cosmopolitans" operating from Washington, D.C. (1968: 107).

Societal reactions theory is "in each case, injurious to the former and supportive of the latter." Gouldner contends that federal research monies to support these types of debunking studies have become increasingly available today. By adopting an underdog perspective, sociologists—especially younger ones—can secure some of these research monies. And just as important, they can maintain their traditionally liberal political convictions. In summary, Gouldner suggests that "sociologists with liberal ideologies will more likely adopt underdog perspectives when they experience these as compatible with the pursuit of their own career interests" (1968: 108). The new deviance theory is, then,

> a standpoint that possesses a remarkably convenient combination of properties: it enables the sociologist to befriend the very small underdogs in local settings, to reject the standpoint of the "middle dog" respectables and notables who manage local caretaking establishments, while at the same time, to make and remain friends with the really top dogs in Washington agencies or New York foundations (1968: 110).

In Gouldner's opinion, the societal reactions theory is little different in its effects from the earlier social pathology theories. Both types of theory concentrate so exclusively on the "local action" that they represent "an uncritical accommodation to the national elite and to the society's master institutions" (1968: 111).

A third and final example of a sociology of knowledge approach to correctional theory and research, broadly construed, is offered by Platt and Takagi (1977). They are primarily interested in interpreting the appearance of a new conservative strain in criminology and corrections in the past decade by theorists whom they dub the new "realists." Platt and Takagi argue that crime has continued to increase in recent years, and that the reasons for this are political and economic, especially the crises of world monopoly capitalism. Massive governmental expenditures have failed to stem the rising rate of "street crime." This necessitates newer and more severe forms of repression and control. However, such changes in the severity of crime control measures require new ideological rationales and legitimation. Enter the new "realists."

Their theories of deterrence and incapacitation provide the ideological rationale for the new repressive state policies of crime control. According to Platt and Takagi, an important reason for this is simply because "the social sciences in North American universities have *always* legitimated the ruling ideology of monopoly capitalism. . . . Criminology, with its particularly close ties to the state apparatus, was originally developed as a science of repression . . ." (1977:

10). (Emphasis in the original.) However, in recent years this "long-standing collaboration between criminology and the state has been even more strongly cemented . . . with the help of massive investments and subsidies from the federal government and corporate think tanks" (1977: 10).

One other development has made the new "realists" willing to come forward with new "theoretical" justification for increased state repression: their own increasingly precarious class position. The crises of world capitalism, which have produced more street crime, have threatened their own economic security. Platt and Takagi claim that "the ideological repertoire of the new 'realists' is typical of the petty bourgeoisie in crisis. Faced on the one side by an increasingly militant and organized working class, and on the other by the pressures of inflation and rising unemployment in the professional strata, the 'new middle class' feels itself 'beleaguered and pressed from all sides' " (1977: 13).

Implications

We have reviewed three separate attempts to apply the insights of the sociology of knowledge to the theory and research of sociologists themselves, particularly those who write and do research in the area of criminology, deviance, and corrections. All of them illustrate how the work of sociologists can itself be understood as a *social product.* It is important that students understand and appreciate such a perspective. We are not suggesting that any one of the three attempts we reviewed has more validity than the others. We *are* suggesting that it is important to develop and maintain a critical, relativistic stance toward the beliefs and ideas about corrections that are produced or promoted by various groups, including sociologists. Clearly, there are at least two obstacles to the development of such a stance.

To begin with, such a relativistic stance conflicts with the assumption that sociologists, being "scientists," are impartial, objective observers of the correctional scene. Those who maintain this position assume that theoretical ideas in corrections change because of internal dynamics. Put differently, the development and testing of theoretical ideas through empirical research is the most important explanation for theoretical change. We have already given a brief sketch of Platt and Takagi's interpretation for the recent resurrection of interest in deterrence and incapacitation. On the other hand, Carlson's explanation for this is quite different, though very conventional in its approach. He suggests that "the renascence of 'deterrence' as a viable concept owes much to some dogged investigators who thought the issues were worth exploring" (1976: 165). Although there surely is something to be said for this type of explanation for correctional beliefs and changes in them, there is simply too much that it cannot explain. Cross-cultural variation in deviance and correctional theories, abrupt shifts in correctional theory, and the close fit between funding agency interests and the work of social scientists (Galliher and McCartney, 1973) are just some of the issues that such a perspective cannot explain.

Second, students well might ask about the intentions of sociologists whose correctional theory and research is so much a product of social contexts. Are sociologists aware of the connections between their own social circumstances, their intellectual labors, and their ideological productions? Just as important, do they mean or intend to produce beliefs that have the objective consequences that they actually have? The answers to these questions are no. Many sociologists have no real awareness of how their work is shaped by social contexts. In fact, they probably have little interest in such questions, tending to see them as unimportant, misleading, or irrelevant. Nevertheless, it is not necessary for them to intend to develop or promote a style of work that has the social and political effects it has. The social functions of some activity are often something quite different from those its individual promoters ever intended or even desired. Recall Gouldner's charge that societal reactions theory served to legitimate the claims of Washington administrators at the expense of those at the local level. He further notes, however, that "it must not be thought for a moment that [societal reactions theorists] perform this ideological function through any intention to further the ambitions of the upper officialdom or by any intention to conduct [their] research in any narrowly conceived applied manner" (1968: 110). Instead, the social and political consequences of their work can be quite different from what they intended.

The analogy with *institutional racism* is instructive. It is common knowledge now that the standard operating procedures of organizations often have racist consequences. For example, universities that demand certain admission and performance criteria from students may have the effect of preventing blacks from enrolling or, once admitted, completing school. This is true, even though no academic administrator or faculty member may want or intend to discriminate against blacks. We are suggesting that the same distinction between personal, subjective intentions and objective, resultant social consequences can be applied to understand the work of correctional sociologists.

section two

CORRECTIONAL CHANGE AND IDEOLOGIES

3

Historical correctional change:
Differing interpretations

Historically, we can point to particular periods when correctional ideologies and practices underwent fundamental change and transformation. A few examples will suffice to document the validity of this assertion. The early 19th century witnessed the institutionalization of the penitentiary system. During the Reconstruction period in America, southern states established penitentiaries where formerly there had been none. Likewise, in the late 19th and early 20th century, America was swept by the Reformatory movement, which saw numerous states construct a new type of prison called the "reformatory" (Currie, 1973). At approximately the same time, 1880–1920, parole became an accepted part of the correctional policies of many states. Later, as the medical model gained ascendancy as a rationale for various correctional programs, psychiatrists and social workers were hired to work in correctional agencies and to establish classification programs for newly admitted offenders. As this is written, prison populations are rapidly expanding, and many states are simultaneously moving to establish so-called community correctional programs—which are said to be consistent with the most enlightened thinking in correctional circles. Thus, as these few examples suggest, there is little doubt that fundamental transformations and changes in correctional policies and thinking occur.

Both these fundamental transformations of correctional practices, as well as less dramatic short-term changes (for example, fluctuating prison populations), are puzzling to sociologists. We would like to know why they occur when they do, and we would like to have a better understanding of the process by which they take place. Is it possible to apply the insights gained by studying correctional change to contemporary and future reform efforts? Just as important, by examining past or ongoing instances of correctional change can we learn something about the likely future course of correctional development?

The objectives of this chapter are as follow: (1) to define and illustrate what is meant by the concept of *correctional change;* and (2) to review and illustrate three different perspectives on the process by which these changes occur—the *conservative,* the *liberal-pluralist* and the *radical-elitist.* In Chapter 16 we turn to a discussion of the implications of these three perspectives for understanding correctional reform. Chapter 16 will focus on the substance, process, and problems of reform from each of these three perspectives.

THE MEANING OF CORRECTIONAL CHANGE

Some transformations are much more far reaching than others and have significantly greater historical impact. Nevertheless, in the present context, *correctional change* refers to any structural or ideological change that results in one or more of the following: (1) a transformation of the structural arrangements employed to deal with convicted offenders (for example, the establishment of the penitentiary system); (2) a change in the severity of punishments dispensed to offenders (for example, an increase in the average length of time offenders spend in confinement); (3) a change in either the numbers or the proportion of convicted offenders dealt with by various components of the correctional system (for example, an increase in prison population, or assignment of an increasing number of convicted offenders to pretrial diversion programs); and (4) a change in the prevailing ideologies employed to "explain" or make sense of offenders and their involvement in criminality.

Such a fourfold definition of correctional change may seem rather complex at first glance. In truth, changes in each of these four areas often occur together. Thus, the development of community programs for offenders may be accompanied by changes in prevailing ideological interpretations of offenders, by changes in the total number of offenders under correctional supervision, and, presumably, by some change in the severity of treatments accorded to offenders. Still, each type is different and further examples may help to clarify the meaning of each of these different kinds of correctional change.

The first type, structural transformation, has received the bulk of attention and attempts at explanation by social scientists. Yet it is a rather gross indicator of correctional change, which fails to reveal and take into account some significant short-term fluctuations and modifications. Consequently, we do not wish to restrict ourselves exclusively to this kind of change. A fine example of this type of correctional change is the development of the Reformatory movement in America (Currie, 1973). Prior to 1875 there were no institutions of this kind; after the 1890s many American states constructed such places.

The second type of change, severity of punishment, is best illustrated quantitatively. Evidence shows, for example, that offenders sentenced to probation instead of prison, as part of a special experimental community treatment program, were sometimes placed in local jails for short periods when correctional authorities deemed it "appropriate" (Lerman, 1975). Here, then, we see a situation in which offenders ostensibly receiving special rehabilitative treatment were actually punished more severely than if they had not been part of the special program (that is, had received "regular probation").

A further example of what is meant by the second type of correctional change can be seen in Table 3–1, which shows the percentage of all convicted federal offenders who were placed on probation for the years 1945 through 1976 and the average length of imprisonment for those sentenced to prison. The table shows that while the percentage of offenders placed on probation has generally hovered around the 40 percent level, the average prison sentence dispensed to federal offenders has increased steadily over the 28-year period.

The third type of change, rate or numbers of convicted offenders, like the second, is best illustrated quantitatively. Fluctuations in the absolute size of the prison population are an example. Table 13–1 and Figure 8–1 indicate that the total prisoner population in the United States decreased from 220,149 in 1961 to a low of 187,914 in 1968. However, since that time the number of incarcerated individuals has increased steadily and stood at 263,291 at the end of 1976. This is a substantial change in one of the operating parameters of the correctional industry, which all of the three perspectives we will be discussing have made some effort to explain.

An example of changes in correctional ideologies—our fourth type—is seen in the movement during the early decades of the 20th century which resulted in the medical model being adopted as an ideological support for the entire correctional enterprise. Subsequently, many states created "classification" programs, with Illinois establishing a "diagnostic depot" for the "clinical study" of newly sentenced convicts as early as 1933.

38

TABLE 3–1
Dispositions of offenders sentenced in U.S. district courts, 1945–1976

Year	Total number of offenders convicted	Percent placed on probation	Average sentence to imprisonment (years)
1945	36,114	39.8	16.5
1946	32,179	39.4	18.6
1947	32,588	40.9	17.3
1948	30,520	45.9	17.6
1949	33,073	45.8	15.8
1950	34,625	48.0	17.5
1951	38,190	52.0	18.1
1952	36,043	49.1	19.1
1953	34,885	45.3	19.4
1954	39,544	44.2	18.9
1955	35,051	41.6	21.9
1956	28,896	42.8	24.9
1957	27,740	41.2	28.0
1958	28,338	41.0	28.2
1959	28,389	40.1	29.2
1960	28,156	39.4	29.6
1961	28,625	37.4	31.0
1962	28,511	38.9	32.0
1963	29,803	40.4	32.3
1964	29,170	39.9	31.9
1965	28,757	37.5	33.5
1966	27,314	37.5	32.9
1967	26,344	35.8	36.5
1968	25,674	38.2	42.2
1969	26,803	37.3	42.0
1970	28,178	40.4	41.1
1971	32,103	41.3	42.1
1972	37,220	41.4	38.1
1973	34,983	43.0	42.4
1974	36,230	45.9	42.2
1975	37,433	47.9	45.5
1976	40,112	45.4	47.2

Source: Administrative Office of the U.S. Courts. *Federal Offenders in the U.S. District Courts 1974*. Washington, D.C.: Administrative Office of the U.S. Courts, 1977, page H–1.

HOW CORRECTIONS CHANGES: THREE PERSPECTIVES

Discussions and interpretations of correctional change are dominated by three different perspectives. They are conservatism, liberal-pluralism, and radical-elitism. Generally, these three perspectives differ in their conceptions of the causal ordering of the variables that produce correctional change, and their assessments of the relative weights (or importance) that should be assigned to these causal variables. The most fundamental difference in the perspectives, however, lies in their conceptions of the nature of the social and political processes that give rise to correctional changes. In short, each builds upon an implicit though rarely articulated set of beliefs about the nature of the political process, and about the locus of political power and how it is wielded. It is important to probe these differences if we are to fully understand these different perspectives on correctional change and reform.

Certainly, there are several important reasons for including considerations of differences in political philosophies in any discussion of correctional change. First, the punishment of offenders is an inherently political act that is provided for, carried out by, and justified by the state and its representatives. Therefore, any treatment of correctional issues is a treatment of political processes and beliefs as well. Second, any decision to commit the correctional industry to fundamentally different modes of dealing with offenders requires political action by political actors, whether they be administrative, legislative, or judicial in nature. Consequently, correctional change or reform generally requires political action. Those desiring to bring about such change should be informed enough about the political process to employ it for maximum effectiveness in achieving their goals. This is especially true of fundamental structural change in corrections, although it is possible that minor changes could be instituted without any appreciable contact with governmental personnel outside of the corrections bureaucracy itself. Finally, as we indicated in Chapter 2, a complete understanding of extant correctional research and theory itself is aided by an awareness of the background assumptions that are so often embedded in the work and that figure as its silent partners. Consequently, if we want to really understand social scientific work in corrections we should examine these assumptions about the locus of political power and how it is wielded (compare Miller, 1974).

Conservatism

As political philosophy, conservatism is distinguished by several interrelated themes or beliefs that are evident in conservatives' science and historical analyses. This is equally true of their analyses of historical correctional change.

Conservatives place great importance on the necessity for maintaining social order. Any forces or groups that seem in their view to threaten that order are viewed in an unsympathetic light. For the most part, criminal offenders are such a group and receive little sympathy from conservatives. Their writings usually sound a sympathetic note for the victims of crimes and emphasize the necessity to repress criminality.

Conservatives are generally disposed to preserve existing social arrangements and institutions and to favor gradual rather than abrupt change. Existing social arrangements and practices are a reflection of deeply held public sentiments, morality, and a degree of "built in" wisdom or transcendental reason, which to a great extent defies humans' ability to comprehend or explain. Conservatives believe that tampering with social institutions is an inherently risky undertaking, which can easily create more problems or mischief than it solves. Consequently, conservatives do not have much faith in government's ability to solve problems through social planning and welfare programs.

Nevertheless, social institutions and practices do change and conservatives are well aware of this. However, unlike liberals and radicals, conservatives seem to lack a unifying, recurrent, or consistent interpretation for these changes. Unlike liberals—as we shall see—conservatives make no assumptions about unidirectional progress or improvement in history. Rather, they are inclined to be skeptical about historical change and to assume that changes can be retrogressive just as easily as they could be progressive.

Conservatives generally assume that social and political institutions embody and reflect a consensus of deeply held public sentiments and morality. Put differently, the political and governmental process is and should be a mechanism for transforming these deeply rooted public sentiments into institutional practice. Not surprisingly, therefore, changes in the way in which criminals have been treated are attributed to gradual changes in public sentiments about criminals and the kinds of treatment they deserve. Additionally, the assumed leveling of status differences accompanying industrialization and the 18th-century political revolutions (e.g., France) are sometimes cited as the causes of any perceptible humanization of penal policies in the past 200 years.

Although there are recent signs of its growing appeal, conservatism has never been very strong in American sociology. Instead, sociology in the United States has always shown melioristic leanings —which are anathema to conservatives. However, the emphasis on meliorism is one of the mainstays of liberal-pluralism.

Liberal-pluralism

Probably a majority of American sociologists can best be described as liberal-pluralists. Miller (1974: 28) correctly notes that the members of this "large liberal academic majority do proportionately more writing and speechmaking than those of the small conservative minority, so that their impact on the ideological climate exceeds even their large numbers." Therefore, it is especially important that we understand liberal-pluralists' interpretations of correctional change and later—in Chapter 16—their view of the correctional reform process.

Whereas conservatives tend to be obsessed with social defense and the repression of offenders, liberals sympathize with them and want to improve them. And while conservatives subscribe to a moral consensus interpretation of penal practices, and tend to be cynical about the meaning and direction of changes in them, liberals are more likely to see conflict and dissensus as the backdrop for correctional change and to be optimistic about their future development. These differences should become apparent in the comments that follow.

Liberal-pluralism views the entire political process as an *arena* in which private citizens and organized groups compete with one another to influence the governmental process to their advantage or to urge change in a direction consistent with their beliefs. Thus, one group of citizens might urge issuance of a zoning variance to permit operation of a group foster home for juvenile offenders in an urban neighborhood, while another group, perhaps of residents in the area, insists that the variance not be issued. These groups naturally conflict with one another and seek different "expert" testimony of scientists and other governmental officials to support their interpretations of the likely consequences should the government not accede to their wishes. Likewise, they may seek to marshal public opinion in support of their respective positions and stage public demonstrations to dramatize it.

However, this process of group conflict is usually orderly; underlying it is a high degree of consensus on the "rules of the game." All parties to political conflict are mindful of these rules, which prohibit "radical," "extreme," or "violent" means of pressing claims while simultaneously seeking to neutralize one's opponents. A high premium is placed on the value of and necessity for compromise as a method of resolving conflicts and of permitting all parties to salvage at least part of their objectives. Those parties in conflict that refuse to compromise their objectives are derided as extremist, and criticized for placing parochial interest ahead of the public good.

Unfortunately, liberal-pluralism is silent when it comes to explaining the specific sociohistorical appearance of various combinations of interest groups. It tends to ignore the social situation out of which these groupings emerge, or at least it pays little attention to the correspondence between the characteristics of social settings and the characteristics and motives of interest groups. This is a serious flaw in liberal-pluralist interpretations of correctional change.

Because of it, liberals often appear to offer ad hoc, post factum explanations for specific historical changes. These explanations assign causal importance either to the spontaneous historical appearance of specific interest groups or to the workings of such free floating forces as humanitarianism or social progress.

From the perspective of liberal-pluralism the political process is equally open to all. Similarly, the process is not rigged in favor of any particular group or strata of the population. Instead, victory goes to the side whose position is best supported by the "objective facts" (i.e., the group that has "truth" on its side) or that is better organized and thus more effective in pressing its claim(s).

Although no group or strata consistently triumphs in the political arena, it is recognized that the process sometimes gives victory to overly sectarian groups or ideological positions—"moral entrepreneurs" in Becker's terms (1963)—that do not accurately reflect either what is best for the entire community or the objective nature of a problem or situation. But while such a group might triumph in the short run by successfully influencing the process in support of their "biased" and "unobjective" position, such errors will ultimately be rectified and will have little enduring effect on the governmental process. Instead, out of the group competitive process emerges a set of govermental actions and programs which, while not *perfect* for the times, still gives each group at least a partial victory and meets the social needs of the community as a whole.

A major portion of liberals' explanations for historical correctional changes are attributed to the unfolding of some master trend in human history, such as the movement toward greater humanitarianism, rationality, or progress. Liberals, unlike conservatives, tend to be optimistic about the future and humans' collective ability to perfect social arrangements.

For liberals, a critical role in the process of correctional change is assigned to charismatic or innovative individuals. Thus, liberal interpretations of correctional change often amount to a celebration of the importance of the individual and a kind of "great human being theory" of penal history.

Liberal-pluralists adhere to a gradual piecemeal approach to the process of political and correctional change. Specific, limited reforms are sought, usually on the assumption that reform itself is an incremental or evolutionary process and that each of these finite reforms will ultimately help perfect the correctional system. Although there may be occasional short-term retrogressions, the overall trend in the treatment of offenders is one of progress, improvement, and increasing rationality. While maintaining this view of correctional reform, liberal-pluralists tend to be critical of those who would insist upon more fundamental, revolutionary changes in corrections.

Examples of liberal-pluralist interpretations of correctional changes are easily found. Harry Elmer Barnes wrote extensively on the historical development of penal methods and interpreted the emergence and development of the penitentiary in the United States. The assumptions of liberal-pluralism are evident in the results of his analysis:

> There are two sets of influences which constitute the chief phases of the historical background of the reform of the criminal law in America, namely those general forces making for reform and progress of all kinds in the 18th century, and those specific attempts to reform criminal jurisprudence and penal administration during the same period, which center mainly about the writings and activities of Beccaria and Howard and the Pennsylvania reformers, such as Bradford, Rush, Vaux, Lownes, and others (Barnes, 1930: 120).

Regarding the first of these two influences, Barnes suggests that the 18th century saw the emergence of the "firm conviction that social progress and the resulting 'greatest happiness for the greatest number' were possible of attainment through sweeping social reforms carried out according to the dictates of 'pure reason' " (1930: 121). He then asserts: "It is obvious that so barbarous and archaic a part of the old order as the current criminal jurisprudence and penal administration of the time could not long remain immune from the growing spirit of progress and enlightenment" (1930: 121).

Another liberal interpretation of correctional development and change is given by Robert Caldwell. On the emergence of the juvenile court he writes:

> In America, where English jurisprudence was introduced by the early colonists, such tendencies as the increase of the complexity of social relationships, the growth of humanitarianism, and the rise of the social sciences created an atmosphere that was conducive to the expansion of the area in which the child received differential treatment by the law. This manifested itself in the passage of legislation for the protection of the child, in the modification of criminal law and procedure relating to children, in the creation of special agencies and institutions for juveniles, and in the organization of the system of probation. In 1899 the whole development reached a high point with the establishment of the first juvenile court, which began its legal existence in Chicago, Illinois, on July 1 of that year (1965: 386).

Caldwell subsequently notes that punishment practices are "affected by what the people in a particular society feel, want, and believe." Changes in penal practices are the result of "tendencies that exist in various degrees in many countries of Europe and the Western Hemisphere," an important part of which is "the speed of humanitarianism with its emphasis on the value of the individual, the protection of human life, and the reduction of human pain and suffering" (1965: 420).

There are more recent examples of liberal-pluralist interpretations of correctional change. For instance, Rothman (1971) gives us an influential interpretation of the rise of the penitentiary in America during the Jacksonian period. His analysis of the origins of this correctional reform places a heavy emphasis upon humanitarian impulses, a generalized belief among many citizens that the basis of social order was being eroded, and changing conceptions of the nature and causes of crime. Throughout his presentation Rothman assumes the existence of a political process that is responsive to citizen opinion and demand. This is never considered problematic. Thus, given changing public opinion, the inevitable result was the penitentiary movement.

Still in a contemporary vein, Kittrie has interpreted the emergence of the "therapeutic state," which he attributes to the

> "popularization" of government [as a result of which] new classes obtained a voice by which they could proclaim their dissatisfaction with long prison sentences and the harsh treatment of the past. Individualized treatment (which seeks to relieve the offender's shortcomings) was seized upon as being more humane as well as more effective in controlling crime (1971: 33).

What is evident in all these illustrative analyses of correctional change is the liberal's faith in the perfectability of social arrangements and the belief that there is progress in social life.

Radical-elitism

The best starting point for an explication of the radical-elitist perspective on political processes (therefore, correctional change) is to recall what we said earlier about a serious flaw in liberal-pluralism: its failure to adequately deal with the effects of the social setting on the generation of interest groups and on the content of their ideologies of conflict. An insistence that this deficiency must be rectified is an important point of departure for all radical-elitist perspectives. Although we will be discussing several different versions of such a perspective on correctional transformations, they all share the belief that: "The penal system of any given society is not an isolated phenomenon subject to its own special laws. It is an integral part of the whole social system, and shares its aspirations and its defects" (Rusche and Kirchheimer, 1939). Thus, the tendency of liberal-pluralism to study and discuss the correctional system as a self-contained entity is rejected at the outset by radical-elitism.

All radical-elitist perspectives on the political process take their name from the insistence that any analysis of the process must be grounded in an understanding and explication of how it is affected by the most *fundamental* component of the social structure: the political economy. Any analysis of correctional change that does not interpret it in terms of contradictions or modifications in the relations of production is rejected as incomplete, misleading, or misguided.

A second fundamental component of radical-elitism is its rejection of the assumption—so important to liberal-pluralism—that the political process affords all groups an opportunity to share in the exercise of power on equal terms, and that no group or strata consistently triumphs over others in the exercise of power. On the contrary, the social class that owns and controls the means of production represents a ruling elite that employs the governmental process and institutions to maintain its supremacy and to pacify and control the other classes. In Takagi's terms, studies in the sociology of law "reveal how laws originate in response to modifications in the political economy to serve the purpose of legalizing and perpetuating the domination of one class over another. The aim of penal reform is the same" (1975: 25).

Recent radical-elitist interpretations of historical correctional changes have taken the assumed deficiencies of liberal-pluralist explanations as their starting point. Their interpretations lead to conclusions very different from the widely accepted liberal-pluralist assertions. Currie's work (1973) on the American Reformatory movement is instructive in this regard. He rightly notes that

> strong supporters of the treatment ethic in modern penology are generally laudatory and uncritical in their praise of the movement and its leaders. According to this interpretation, the Reformatory movement was a humanitarian and progressive effort, far ahead of its time, that held the key to the problem of crime and punishment, but whose great promise has never been fulfilled—largely because of a lack of public support and understanding. Its leading figures are described as farsighted humanitarians animated by a generous concern for the downtrodden (Currie, 1973: 3).

But Currie suggests a different interpretation—that

> a close analysis of the theory and practice of the Reformatory movement leads to a very different interpretation of its social origins, its character and its historical role. From the beginning . . . it was an

authoritarian and conservative movement, created by upperclass reformers and propelled by the central aim of instilling industrial discipline in the "idle and vicious" masses of the post-Civil War industrial cities (1973: 4–5).

Along these same lines, Scull (1977a) has criticized Rothman's analysis (1971) of the origins of the penitentiary movement in America. According to Scull, in Rothman's account "the rise of the asylum is pictured as the product of a peculiarly Jacksonian *angst* about the stability of the social order—anxiety mixed with a naive and uniquely American utopianism about the value of the well-ordered asylum" (1977a: 338).

> But while Rothman persuasively *describes* this anxiety, he almost entirely neglects to *explain* it—to give us any understanding of why these persons became anxious about these things at this time. The structural sources of the concern with imminent breakdown of the social order remain unexplored and unperceived (Scull, 1977a: 338). (Emphasis in original.)

Smith and Fried have been similarly critical of liberal-pluralist interpretations of correctional changes, especially the tendency to invoke humanitarianism as an explanation: "If humanitarianism is a sufficient cause for social change, we would be living in a Utopia. Since we are not so living, it becomes necessary to ask what the social conditions are within which humanitarian instincts take particular forms and come into play" (1974: 5).

Takagi (1975) has recently suggested an alternative interpretation for the creation of the Walnut Street Jail—which has been widely viewed as the forerunner of the penitentiary in America. He notes that ". . . most of us have been led to believe that the 'gentle and humane' Quakers founded the prison as an alternative to the sanguinary English laws then in effect, and that the idea of a prison was based upon the prevailing theory of humane reason. There are problems with these interpretations" (1975: 18–19). Takagi subsequently argues that establishment of the Walnut Street Jail was, in truth, a penal reform intended to centralize the powers of the state. As these comments indicate, the radical-elitist perspective insists upon tracing reforms and changes back to their structural origins, and then indicating how these structural changes become translated into the political process.

Radical-elitism equally rejects explanations for correctional change that emphasize humanitarian impulses alone and those explanations that assign a primary causative importance to theories of penal reform or offender rehabilitation. In fact, such ideological components of the change process are generally viewed as *accom-*

paniments of the change rather than causes of it. Nevertheless, these theories and the emphasis that they receive are employed in a manner that simultaneously justifies and mystifies the real process of correctional change.

> The new reformers thus create the illusion that a specific penal practice is bound up with a specific penal theory, and that it is sufficient to demolish the latter in order to set the former under way. ... We are actually turning things upside down, however, if we take at its face value the imaginary power of doctrine over reality, instead of understanding the theoretical innovation as the expression of a necessary or already accomplished change in social praxis (Rusche and Kirchheimer, 1939: 141–42).

Scull's recent (1977) analysis of the community corrections movement serves as an example of how "penal theories" are employed to mystify the real reasons behind a correctional reform. As a justification for adopting the programs they favor, proponents of decarceration and other community corrections programs have cited an extensive social science literature on the debilitating effects of imprisonment. This research literature is cited as though, until recently, little was known about the pathologies of imprisonment. Scull indicates, however, that substantially the same things were known about asylums as early as the 1860s, and were widely publicized at the time. Therefore, the existence of a body of literature critical of the prison cannot be a crucial explanatory variable in accounting for the development of community corrections. Instead, decarceration has proceeded for quite a different set of reasons, and research on the self-defeating impact of imprisonment has simply been employed as a gloss on the real process. Between 1860 and 1970

> the arguments [about prisons] had not changed, but the structural context in which they were advanced clearly had. Their contemporary reappearance allowed governments to save money while simultaneously giving their policy a humanitarian gloss. And to take the argument a step further, it is the intensity and extent of such pressures which account for the persistence of this policy [decarceration] despite public resistance to it, and despite the accumulation of evidence that in terms of its *ostensible* goals, community care is substantially a failure (Scull, 1977: 139). (Emphasis in the original.)

According to Scull, it is actually the drive to control the soaring costs of maintaining incarcerated populations that is the primary factor underlying the move towards decarceration. If we generalize these observations, radical-elitism assumes that the ideological "explanations," which politicians, social scientists, and publicists produce for political change, are little more than apologies or justifications selected from the available ideological armaments and have little independent effect except in the minds of the naive and uninformed.

As opposed to conservatism's and liberal-pluralism's view of reform as a piecemeal incremental process, radical-elitism insists that fundamental correctional transformations depend upon a prior change in the relations of production. Remedial tinkering with the correctional system is decried as accomplishing little more than a further systematization and rationalization of the state's controls over offender populations. Equally important, the devotion of reformist zeal to piecemeal reforms drains off the citizen discontent and enthusiasm that might otherwise be devoted to calls for true social justice and a more radical restructuring of the entire correctional industry.

Radical-elitists part company with conservatism and liberal-pluralism over the relative importance they assign to public opinion as an originator of correctional transformations. It will be recalled that the latter is inclined to view public opinion as playing a major causative role in this process. Radical-elitists are much more inclined to view justificatory appeals to public opinion as attempts to ratify decisions already made on the basis of other considerations, or as support for the failure to make any reforms. More important, theoretical and research interest has focused on processes by which elites employ the mass media and public information campaigns for purposes of maintaining ideological hegemony (Shover, 1975). Such work generally builds on the premise that public opinion, while playing some part in the political process, is so manipulated by elites that it is usually supportive of policies they favor.

By necessity these comments on the contrast between conservatism, liberal-pluralism, and radical-elitism have been brief. Consequently, to better illustrate what is distinctive about the latter perspective we will comment on three treatments of the process of penal reform which employ it: Rusche and Kirchheimer's *Punishment and Social Structure* (1939); Smith and Fried's *Uses of the American Prison* (1974); and Richard Quinney's *Class, State and Crime* (1977).

Rusche and Kirchheimer's work, although now nearly 40 years old, still represents a refreshing and pioneering attempt to provide an alternative interpretation of changes in penal methods. They note that it has been common to attribute changing penal methods to the unfolding of a specific idea, progress, or the needs of the war against crime (1939: 4–6). None of these explanations by itself is adequate, however. Instead, "the use or avoidance of specific punishments, and the intensity of penal practices" must be investigated as "they are determined by social forces, above all by economic and then fiscal forces" (1939: 5). What is especially determinative of the "selection" of certain penal methods is the nature of a society's system of production.

> The disappearance of a given system of production makes its corresponding punishment inapplicable. Only a specific development of the productive forces permits the introduction or rejection of corresponding penalities. But before these potential methods can be introduced, society must be in a position to incorporate them as integrated parts of the whole social and economic system (1939: 6).

Rusche and Kirchheimer restrict their analysis to major transformations in penal methods that have occurred since the Middle Ages. Less dramatic short-term changes do not especially interest them. Nor do they devote any substantial attention to changes in the ideological justifications for penal methods (preventive ideals). On the contrary, consistent with a Marxian perspective these are viewed as little more than components of the societal superstructure. Smith and Fried (1974) are different, at least in the latter regard. Moreover, their interpretation is somewhat more complex than Rusche and Kirchheimer's since they interpose an additional step in the correctional change process.

Smith and Fried are critical of Rusche and Kirchheimer because of their assumption "that penal methods change as a direct result in [sic] changes in economic conditions." They charge that "this unilateral model of social change is deceptive since it treats the state, law, and doctrine as mere ideological trappings" (1974: 12–f.n.). Smith and Fried's position throughout *Uses of the American Prison* is that preventive ideals (both punishment and rehabilitative ideologies) are an important independent variable in explaining correctional practices. Preventive ideals play an important part in the political and social process by which particular configurations of penal practices are "selected" and justified in specific historical circumstances. But as they note, there has been—paradoxically—little discussion in the correctional literature on the development of preventive ideals that various groups employ to legitimize their claims. Their own work is an attempt "to show that such theories are, in fact, products of political practices" (1974: 1).

Like Rusche and Kirchheimer, Smith and Fried maintain that changes in the relations of production (that is, economic changes) ultimately produce changes in penal methods. However, unlike the latter, they assert that economic changes first necessitate changes in theories of political obligation and these, in turn, produce changes in the manner in which criminals are interpreted and understood. In their words, "Reclassification of transgressors is then best explained not so much in terms of what they 'really' are—sinners, criminals, or the sick—but in terms of the needs of particular political systems to extract obedience to themselves" (Smith and Fried, 1974: 7). Further, ". . . it is the case that a shift in notions of what constitutes legitimate authority and thus coercion is necessarily accompanied by a shift in justifying the treatment of those charged with transgressing against that authority" (1974: 5).

Smith and Fried believe there may be some time lag between the onset of economic changes which produce new political doctrines and the penal changes which employ and build upon these as premises. In fact, they believe the American penitentiary is currently in the midst of such a disjuncture. "The penal dilemma is increasingly clear: the assumptions of 19th century liberalism contine to be used at the very time the structure of the economy cannot provide the material conditions upon which such assumptions are necessarily predicated" (1974: 25). They charge that the response of the state to this political dilemma has been to employ the medical model to depoliticize the nature of crime and the criminal law. "This effort pervades every aspect of the 20th-century penitentiary" (1974: 25).

Other contemporary writers have offered radical interpretations for correctional change that are generally consistent with earlier analyses of a Marxian nature but go beyond them in certain ways. Quinney (1977), for example, offers an analysis of crime and crime control under capitalist systems of production that permits us to interpret even short-run, less dramatic changes in corrections. While doing so he fleshes out the dynamics of a radical interpretation of the political process and official reactions to crime. Quinney's analysis, however, is restricted to the process of reacting to crime under a late capitalist system of production, which is only one of several possible modes of organization of the productive process. Nevertheless, it is a distinctly radical interpretation, since it relates the process of reacting to crime to the structure and dynamics of the mode of production and the correlative social class structure under capitalism.

According to Quinney, capitalism, especially in its late stages of development, necessarily creates a population aggregate that is essentially superfluous to the production process—a *surplus population*. The criminal justice system is employed to manage and control this surplus population—to prevent it from becoming politically conscious and active and, therefore, a threat to the capitalist class.

Even more specifically, "a way of controlling this unemployed surplus population is simply and directly by confinement in prison" (Quinney, 1977: 136).

The size of the surplus population expands and contracts with the various crises of capitalism, the rate of unemployment being one indicator of these. In its late stages, however, capitalism is particularly prone to these crises, and during these crises the surplus population must be even more closely controlled by an intensified, expanded effort on the part of the criminal justice system. "Control is especially acute in those periods when economic crisis is most obvious—during periods of depression and recession. It is during these times that the surplus population is affected most; and it is during these times that the surplus population grows through unemployment" (Quinney, 1977: 134). And, "As the economic crisis of capitalism grows, the actions generated by this crisis increase. The actions of the surplus population and the actions of the criminal justice agencies are produced by the capitalist system and are increased by the crisis in the system" (1977: 137).

But while prisons are used to control the surplus population, they cannot be used exclusively or too heavily, because the capitalist state is sensitive to the fiscal costs of the control measures it employs. This creates a dilemma for the state since the size of the surplus population grows as capitalism develops, thus necessitating that an ever larger number of individuals be dealt with via the criminal justice system.

> . . . late capitalism is producing a rising crime rate and the social expense of criminal justice is more than the state and the capitalist class can afford. Prisons are already dangerously overcrowded, increasing the number of "trouble-makers" within the prison and strengthening the prisoners' movement. From the standpoint of the criminal justice system, either new prisons have to be built to contain the growing number of people controlled by the system or something has to be done to reduce the size of the prison population at any single time (Quinney, 1977: 138–39).

According to Quinney the capitalist state has adopted a two-pronged strategy to deal with this dilemma. It is planning to build new prisons. Simultaneously, it calls for "sentencing reform"—mandatory and determinate sentences—so that more offenders can be confined in prisons, even if for a somewhat shorter time. Thus, for Quinney, "prison reform actually means that control of the surplus population can be increased, for the time being at least, within the social expense limits of the criminal justice system" (1977: 139).

Quinney, like most radical analysts, rejects the liberal-pluralist willingness to settle for piecemeal "reforms," insisting instead that true correctional reform can only proceed after fundamental changes have been made in the relations and control of production.

CONFRONTING THE OPPOSITION

Proponents of these three contrasting perspectives on correctional change have been unflinching in their criticism of one another. For instance, liberal-pluralists generally have leveled four criticisms at the radical-elitest position.

It is charged that radical-elitism exaggerates the degree to which the criminal justice system discriminates against the criminal behavior of the underclass. Evidence is claimed—and sometimes cited (Newman, 1976)—that there is substantial cross-cultural consensus on the criminality of certain types of behaviors; these are said to be the very behaviors for which individuals are most often incarcerated in the United States. This claim of consensus is cited to rebut the contention that the criminal justice system and the capitalist state act capriciously and willfully to repress those crimes which are most threatening to the capitalist class.

Second, evidence is cited as to the consensus within the United States on the relative seriousness of various types of crimes. By such a rebuttal, liberal-pluralists seek to show that the crimes which are most severely punished by the criminal justice system are those which most people feel are very serious ones. In other words, it is claimed that the criminal justice system, far from being an instrument of repression, is actually an instrument for translating popular opinion into action (Berk and Rossi, 1977).

Third, liberal-pluralists charge that it is poor strategy to imagine that important correctional changes cannot be made in the interim —that is, while we work for a more just social and economic order. In fact, those who insist that correctional and economic reforms must go hand in hand are often times disparaged as being "unrealistic," "extreme," "futile," or "radical and utopian." A recent critic of this more radical view of reform has even charged that ". . . the radical utopian position, arguing that it is ingenuous to try to improve prisons, damning all reformist efforts, and insisting that we concentrate only on the restructuring of society required for social equity, is the ultimate 'cop-out'. It is an abnegation of responsibility" (Morris, 1974: 29).

Finally, liberal-pluralists charge that radical-elitism ignores the extent to which correctional change is a simple response to changes in the volume and nature of crime. It is the recent increase in the crime rate, coupled with changes in the types of offenders who are commiting crimes, which is responsible for many of the recent changes in the correctional system. Calls for more rigorous prison security are viewed merely as the necessary response to the "new kind of offender" who is now being sentenced to American prisons. To the liberal-pluralists, then, it is unnecessary and even foolish to see repression in the actions of the correctional industry when a more convincing and obvious interpretation is readily at hand.

Radical-elitists have not sat idly by while liberal-pluralists have attacked their interpretations of the process of correctional change. They have leveled their own criticisms at liberal-pluralism. Briefly, liberal-pluralists are criticized for being so closely enmeshed in the operations of the correctional industry—as consultants, for example —that they fail to fully appreciate the substance and gravity of the situation which confronts contemporary corrections. This has made them too accepting of the problems and perspectives of those within the correctional industry, to the point that fresh or alternative perspectives are never considered. Also, liberal-pluralism has been attacked for fostering and supporting an apolitical, dehumanized view of offenders, one which is overly conducive to technocratic solutions to correctional problems. Further, radical-elitists have been critical of liberal-pluralism because it eschews comparative analysis, focusing too much of its attention instead on the American correctional experience and failing to learn from the experiences of socialist or third-world countries. Finally, liberal-pluralists have been attacked for being too elitist in their approach to the correctional reform process, for overemphasizing the role of the disinterested expert, and for deemphasizing or ignoring the potential role of offenders.

Wishes to the contrary notwithstanding, there is little likelihood that this debate will be settled quickly or on the basis of so-called scientific evidence. Kuhn (1962), among others, has taught us too much about the practice of science to expect any such resolution. Rather, we must realize that this debate involves three groups or communities of scholars who are probably unlike one another in their backgrounds, training, and career lines. They utilize fundamentally different sets of ideological background assumptions in evaluating scientific work and are preoccupied with different types of theoretical and research problems. Therefore, a resolution of this conflict must await changes in the (1) individual and collective careers of the protagonists to the debate, and (2) social and political context within which social scientists practice their craft.

IMPLICATIONS

For those interested in working to bring about correctional change the programmatic implications of three contrasting perspectives are somewhat different. Liberal-pluralists believe that reform efforts should concentrate on those changes which appear, on the basis of expert opinion and research, to be most needed and most likely to enhance the capability of the correctional industry to achieve its mission(s). Citizen groups should be enlisted in the reform process, both to maximize pressure on governmental leaders and to build a constituency of informed concerned citizens whose assitance can be utilized in future correctional reform efforts. In seeking to bring about correctional change, reformers should work closely with correctional administrators and personnel since they are intimately familiar with the problems corrections faces.

Despite feeling that significant correctional changes cannot occur in the absence of a prior restructuring of the political economy, radical-elitists do not completely eschew interest in short-term reformist efforts. However, their objectives and motives are more complex and different than are the motives and objectives of liberal-pluralists. When radical-elitists engage in small-scale skirmishes to bring about correctional change, they view them more as instruments of political education, in order to produce an altered political consciousness, than as tactical operations intended solely to bring about correctional reform. These short-run reform efforts are considered useful because they may hasten the development of the political consciousness and institutional contradictions which will eventuate in more far-reaching fundamental changes of the correctional industry. Further, public education is viewed as an important step in bringing about a new, different awareness of how the correctional system is used to maintain a portion of the population in subjugation.

4

Correctional ideologies

Officially labeled criminals are commonly believed to suffer from some malady of psyche, character, or intellect which produced their criminal behavior. Understandably, therefore, it has been a persistent dream of those claiming the license and mandate to deal with offenders to modify these assumed deficiencies in order to prevent further criminality. We refer to such a set of beliefs about the causes of crime and the corresponding derivative intervention strategies to prevent further criminality as a *preventive ideal*. In this chapter two broad subtypes of preventive ideals will be distinguished and discussed: *rehabilitative ideologies* and *punishment ideologies*. We will discuss some of the different versions of each of them. Further, we will provide an interpretation for changes in them that goes beyond the typical interpretation—that attributes them to advancing humanitarianism, to the progression of rationality and scientific knowledge, or to shifts in public opinion.

REHABILITATIVE AND PUNISHMENT IDEOLOGIES

For analytic purposes only, it is useful to distinguish between ideas which provide justification for punishing offenders (that is, punishment ideologies) and those which provide justification for giving them special treatment, because this should improve them and thereby prevent further criminality (that is, rehabilitative ideologies). While such a distinction can be made hypothetically, in reality it is virtually impossible to maintain. Punitive and rehabilitative actions are both examples of *social control*, irrespective of the intent underlying them. There are several reasons for such an assertion. First, the clients of correctional treatment often feel that what they are required to submit to is *really*, underneath all the rhetoric and good intentions, a form of punishment. "The first difficulty in meshing treatment with a correctional effort is that the treatment can be forced on offenders" (Lerman, 1975: 11). Therefore, treatment may prove to be subjectively indistinguishable from punishment. This, of course, is not a problem outside of a correctional framework, where individuals are free to choose such programs as tutoring, counseling, or remedial classes. But

> in correctional practice, treatment and punishment generally coexist and cannot appropriately be viewed as mutually exclusive. Correctional activities (treatments) are undertaken in settings established as places of punishment. Restriction of freedom is a punishment, no matter whether it is imposed by physical confinement (jail or prison) or by surveillance of movement in the community (probation or parole) (Robison and Smith, 1971: 80).

Second, rarely do officials punish offenders without believing that they will be improved by it in some way. Put differently, punishment itself is generally thought to have a rehabilitative effect on offenders. Third, the responses of correctional personnel to noncompliance with treatment requirements is frequently a punitive one. For instance, some probation departments periodically require attendance at a group meeting, in order to discuss mutual problems. And fourth, correctional programs whose ostensible purpose is *either* treatment *or* punishment sometimes include elements of both in their operation. For example, a part of the treatment given to youths in the Community Treatment Project is a series of graded punishments. Those youths in the program who do not behave or disobey their youth officer are temporarily confined. Such a mixing of treatment and patently punitive measures within the same program makes it even more difficult to maintain a clear distinction between them. Instead, both should be seen as types of social control activities. "The real choice in correction, then, is not between treatment on one hand and punishment on the other but between one treatment-punishment alternative and another" (Robison and Smith, 1971: 80).

By an ideology of punishment we refer to any set of ideas which provides a justification for the use of punishments or restrictive controls and, typically, a set of standards for determining when these punishments have been used appropriately or inappropriately. A rehabilitative ideology provides a justification for modifying the conditions of offenders' lives in the belief that this will help them—

even if the process of "helping" proves to be coercive, unpleasant, and experientially indistinguishable from punishment by those subjected to the help.

Punishment and rehabilitative ideologies can be thought of as partially overlapping circles, as in Figure 4–1. For while both circles have a distinctive nature, represented by their unshaded portions, still they share something: both provide a justification for the state's intervening in the lives of offenders and in imposing constraints on their lives which they would not have had to endure had they not been convicted of crimes. In Figure 4–1, this common component in rehabilitative and punishment ideologies is represented by the shaded portions of each circle.

FIGURE 4–1
The relationship between punishment and rehabilitative ideologies

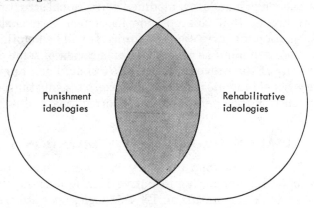

AN ILLUSIONARY SEQUENCE?

In the Marxian view, the term *ideology* is used to refer to a set of ideas or beliefs that are inextricably linked to a particular socio-historical context, even while the promoters or supporters of the ideas remain ignorant of this linkage. In other words, an ideology can be viewed as a set of beliefs that is socially determined and relative, though it is often viewed as being objective and possessing a transituational validity and application.

In Chapter 3 we discussed three different perspectives on the significance of preventive ideologies in the modification of correctional practices and structures. It has been our experience that most employees of the correctional industry subscribe to what might be called a "popular sovereignty theory" of correctional change. This theory attributes the role of stimulant or retardant of correctional reforms to developing scientific knowledge and changing public opinion. Thus, changing preventive ideals can only produce comparable modifications in corrections if scientific knowledge and public opinion are supportive. According to this position, a misinformed and unsupportive public is largely responsible for the persistence of archaic correctional practices. Accordingly, failure to "educate the public" to desirable changes is likely to doom them to failure.

However, from the radical-elitist perspective, public opinion and changes in the correctional knowledge base are almost entirely epiphenomenal in efforts to understand historical transformations of correctional structures and practices. Instead, changes in public opinion and scientific knowledge are "discovered" whenever necessary, that is, when changes in some fundamental structure, such as the economy, mandate a modified correctional structure. In Chapter 3 we argued that this position has much to recommend it as an explanation for correctional reforms. It will be helpful to keep those comments in mind as we embark on a review of some of the different versions of the preventive ideal. We should ask ourselves whether these beliefs and ideas have in fact exerted a substantial independent influence on the operations of the correctional industry.

CRIME CAUSATION THEORIES AND INTERVENTION STRATEGIES

There is a common tendency to assume that a theory of crime *prevention* (that is, a preventive ideal) must be derived from a theory of crime *causation*. By this logic, once we have discovered which variables produce criminality in individuals or collectivities we can intervene to manipulate them for preventive purposes. While at first glance this might seem not only reasonable but necessary, it is important to dispel this notion that preventive actions cannot succeed until the causes of the "disease"—in this case, crime—have been isolated. For example, even though considerable ignorance remains about the initial cause(s) of cancer, a variety of treatment modalities have been developed, some with reasonably high success rates. Moreover, ignorance of the initial cause(s) of cancer has not deterred researchers or medical practitioners from developing knowledge of the developmental process of cancer which can be used to short-circuit the process. So, while there is no necessary reason why a preventive ideal must be linked to a theory of crime causation, it seems to be true that most do link them—offering both a full-blown theory of crime causation and a set of prescriptive intervention strategies.

PREVENTIVE IDEALS

Occasionally, it must seem as though every day brings word of some new correctional treatment theory or technique. For example, just within the last few years correctional literature has become filled with references to and discussions of "reality therapy," "transactional analysis," "community treatment," and "behavior therapy." Nevertheless, despite this illusion of incessant progress and change, nearly all the major versions of the preventive ideal can be grouped into three principal types: (1) those which focus their change efforts upon the individual offender, (2) those which focus upon the small social groups to which the offender belongs, and (3) those which focus upon the local community from which the offender comes.

The individual offender

Defective humans

One major species of the preventive ideal which focuses upon isolated individuals does so on the assumption they are suffering from some type of deficiency or defect that makes them unlike the remainder of the—assumedly law-abiding—population. In short, there is some defect of character, intellect, or psyche which predisposes some individuals to engage in criminality. Once this defect has been identified and appropriately dealt with, the remainder of the population can be confident of no further mischief from offenders.

The precise nature of the defects from which offenders suffer has been variously depicted. And they are believed to be differentially amenable to correctional intervention. Some versions of the preventive ideal take a rather pessimistic view of the prospects for modifying the offender's defects, while others are much more optimistic.

An especially pessimistic view of offenders represents the point of departure for the preventive ideal known as *incapacitation*. The concept of incapacitation is simple: Offenders cannot commit further crimes—at least crimes against people outside of prison—while they are in prison or after they have been executed. The reason for this unmincing approach to incarceration and other forms of punishment is equally simple: Certain types of individuals are believed to be especially prone to engage in crime, and there is little that can be done about it other than to isolate them until they have passed through (that is, aged through) this period of crime susceptibility.

It may be noted in passing that most people who believe in the merits of incapacitation also seem to believe in the value of *deterrence* as a justification for state sanctioning. Deterrence is simply

60

BREAKING THE CRIMINAL CYCLE

Thanks to a program being funded by the Law Enforcement Assistance Administration, at least several thousand potential crimes will not be committed during at least the next several years.

The program is an effort to crack down on "career criminals" by assisting local prosecutors to identify repeat offenders as they are arrested for new crimes, to speed such cases through the courts and to obtain stiff prison sentences.

Begun in 22 cities in May 1975, the program resulted in the identification of 5,107 career criminals through August 1, 1977. More than 4,700 of them were convicted of a variety of crimes, mostly serious, and were given prison sentences averaging 14.3 years.

About half of these career criminals were free on bond or were on probation or parole for previous offenses. Indeed, the 5,107 criminals had a total of 30,000 prior convictions.

James Gregg, acting administrator of the agency, calls the program "one of LEAA's most worthwhile undertakings." We agree.

So effective has the approach been, in fact, that many cities and counties are financing their own programs with their own money.

More and more people involved in the justice system are coming around to the belief that there is such a thing as the career criminal and that there really isn't a great deal that can be done to rehabilitate him. Some studies have indicated that merely growing older is the surest cure for criminal tendencies.

It follows then that the best thing both for society and for the repeat offender is to keep him out of circulation as long as possible.

The nation's war on crime finally may have found the enemy.

Source: *Knoxville News-Sentinel* (Tennessee). November 26, 1977, p. 6.

the belief that punishing offenders for their misdeeds will reduce both the likelihood of their repeating the act and the likelihood of others ever commiting the same act. A blend of both deterrence and incapacitation appears to make the latter more palatable because, until recently, it was rather difficult to align oneself with incapacitation alone; it seems to conjure up visions of a placid social system beset by a "dangerous class" of people. So recent versions of incapacitation generally parade under a belief in both it and deterrence (sometimes with retribution thrown in). Such a position does not embody quite so pessimistic a view of offenders, since it suggests that they can be dissuaded from their lawless ways by a judicious use of punishments.

There is a fetching simplicity to the notion of incapacitation which makes it appealing to many. For example, implicit in it is the tendency to attribute most of our "serious" crime to an identifiable group of persistent and usually intractable offenders. Once these offenders have been identified we can reduce the crime rate by isolating—or executing—them. The appeal of incapacitation is increased by scientific assurances that this group of hard-core criminals is actually quite small and could, therefore, be permanently segregated without undue economic drain on the remainder of the population. There always seem to be properly credentialed experts willing to testify that this is the case (for example, Wilson, 1975). Unfortunately, as we shall see in Chapter 15, the incapacitative effects of imprisonment are very difficult to establish via empirical research. At least two recent studies (Greenberg, 1975; van Dine, Dinitz, and Conrad, 1977) conclude that this effect is quite modest. Nor is there good reason to believe that selective long-term confinement of offenders who are considered to be serious or dangerous would significantly improve the incapacitative effectiveness of imprisonment.

Nevertheless, in recent years the appeal of incapacitation has been increased even further by the widely trumpeted results of evaluative research on the ineffectiveness of correctional treatment techniques. Repeatedly today, the charge is heard that rehabilitation "does not work." In their efforts to retrench, social scientists have shown more of a willingness to draw upon notions of deterrence and incapacitation as justifications for punishment.

Perhaps the most popular version of the preventive ideal, which builds upon a view of the offender as a defective human being, is the *medical model* (or, *individual treatment model*). Although many have argued that the medical model has been discredited and is gradually being eclipsed by newer rehabilitative ideologies, there is no denying its long standing as probably the most influential set of beliefs about offenders and what should be done with them. Because of this fact, contemporary obituaries for the medical model may be premature.

The following assumptions seem to be basic to the medical model:

1. Criminal behavior is symptomatic of something wrong with the emotional makeup or psyche of the offender.
2. The nature of the underlying deficiency or problem can be determined by an intensive, expertly conducted examination of the kinds of symptoms the offender manifests.
3. Identifiable external symptoms and identifiable underlying pathologies co-vary in patterned, predictable ways.
4. It would be foolish to concentrate one's preventive or treatment

---

A CONVICT'S COMMENTS ON THE MEDICAL MODEL

We quickly learned we were expected to view this journey through prison as a quest, and the object of our quest was to discover our problem. It was assumed we were here because of psychological problems, and our task now, by which we could expect to be judged, was to isolate and come to terms with them. Boys who had stolen cars were thought to be acting out a symbolic return to the womb and once they had been helped to understand their true motivation and recognize its utter futility they would be free of the compulsion. I mock this now, even if I didn't mock it then, but it's not the most basic notion at which I will invite you to laugh with me, but simply at the grotesque extensions which sometimes flourished here in the California Department of Corrections. And no matter what your private opinion, when the Adult Authority, the remote body authorized to grant parole, asked in tones of high seriousness if you had come to grips with your problem, you were willing to concede you might have a problem even if you had to invent one on the spot.

Source: Malcolm Braly. *False Starts.* Boston: Little, Brown, 1976, pp. 157–58.

---

efforts on these external symptoms; action instead must be directed toward the underlying deficiency or pathology (that is, the underlying causes).

5. Therapeutic efforts that concentrate only on the symptoms of a problem, while leaving the problem itself unaffected, will only result in the appearance of another form of symptomatic behavior. (The principle of the interchangability of symptoms.)

6. There are appropriate treatments for particular kinds of underlying problems or pathologies.

7. Diagnosis (or "classification") is the first step in the treatment process (that is, identification of the offender's underlying problem).

8. Because it is impossible to specify in advance just how long it will take for the offender to respond to treatment, rehabilitative experts must be permitted an extended, indefinite period of time (that is, an indeterminate sentence) in which to work their cures.

Uncommitted humans

Preventive ideals that are premised on a deficiency view of offenders have held a special appeal for the correctional industry. They have either given rise to or provided belated support for many correctional programs which are accepted as standards fare today. For instance, both classification programs and correctional counseling were spawned by the medical model of the preventive ideal. And the indeterminate sentence, which emerged along with the Reformatory movement as part of a view of the offender as an undeveloped human being, later was adopted as an indispensable part of the medical model.

Still, there have always been some social scientists who persisted in viewing the offender as a much more rational actor than deficiency views would allow. A belief in deterrence has been the mainstay of those who maintain such a position. As recently as 15 years ago nearly all discourse about deterrence had disappeared from the social science literature. Allen accurately observed in 1964 (1964: 95–6) that

> . . . we are abysmally ignorant about the deterrent effects of legal sanctions in general. We are ignorant, not only because an investigation of this problem presents formidable difficulties, but because, apart from studies made as contributions to the death penalty debate, serious empirical investigation has rarely been undertaken. This is in itself a remarkable fact. Rightly or wrongly, most criminal statutes become law on the assumption that their enactment and enforcement will eliminate or minimize the conduct for which sanctions are provided. Yet in a half-century of empirical criminological investigation this important assumption has been largely untested.

The same indictment could not be returned today. In the law and order climate of the past decade there has been a burgeoning of interest in issues of deterrence (for example, Zimring and Hawkins, 1973; Tittle and Logan, 1973; Gibbs, 1975). Surprisingly, this renewed interest in deterrence as a justification for the punishment of offenders has united into one camp individuals and groups we ordinarily would not find consorting with one another; for example, both the conservative social philosopher Ernest van den Haag (1975) and a working party of the American Friends Service Committee (Bacon et al., 1971).

The deterrence preventive ideal is two-edged in its approach to the prevention of criminality. It promises not only to prevent a relapse into crime by those individuals who have previously been punished for a crime, but also to minimize the crime *rate* generally; by doing so, it promises to reduce the total social cost of crime. Corresponding to these dual foci is an important conceptual distinction in the deterrence literature—the distinction between the *general* and *special effects* of a threatened punishment. The special effects of a threatened punishment are the effects upon those who have actually been punished by the imposition of that sanction. General effects are the effects on those who have not previously been punished with the threatened punishment. This is but another way of saying that the deterrence preventive ideal may concern itself with the effects of correctional intervention on both those who actually are subjected to it and those who only observe it from afar. Moreover, analytically the special effects of a correctional measure or punishment may be minimal even while the general effects of the same may be considerable. Thus, recidivism rates alone cannot be cited as evidence that imprisonment presumably does not deter crime, since those who have spent time in prison are an atypical group of individuals; evidence would also have to be adduced on the general effects of imprisonment before such a conclusion would possibly be warranted. The remainder of our brief comments here will focus upon the claimed special preventive effects of punishment (i.e., the claim that punishment prevents recidivism).

The deterrence preventive ideal insists that offenders be seen as rational calculating actors—little different from the rest of us—who choose to engage in criminal behavior under certain conditions. But if offenders are similar to all of us, what makes them choose to commit crime? The answer, it seems, is that they are not *exactly* like the rest of us. At least two slightly different answers have been given to the question of why offenders choose to engage in crime. One answer emphasizes that their commitment to legitimate others and to legitimate lines of conduct is so weak that these represent no real control on their behavior (Hirschi, 1969). Their "stake in conformity" is so low that they, in a sense, exist at the margin of society (Zimring and Hawkins, 1968). Given these weak, ineffectual controls, illicit behavior simply "busts out" whenever it appears propitious to the offender. A second answer to the question of what makes offenders choose to engage in crime emphasizes their social psychological and personality differences from the law abiding portion of the population. For example, because their "risk perception" may be different, their calculus of hedonism makes criminality appear to be less of a risk than it does to others (Claster, 1967; Zimring and Hawkins, 1973: 96–128).

Regardless of which of these views one adopts, supporters of the deterrence preventive ideal believe it is the state's inefficient responses and ineffectual punishment that prompts individuals to opt for a criminal solution to their various personal—usually financial—problems. Therefore, if we would deter them from criminality we must judiciously employ punishments which are swift, sure, and sufficiently severe.

There is scarcely any evidence to support the proposition that would-be criminals are indifferent to the risks associated with a proposed course of action. Criminals may be willing to run greater risks (or they may have a weaker sense of morality) than the average citizen, but if the expected cost of crime goes up without a corresponding increase in the expected benefits, then the would-be criminal—unless he or she is among that small fraction of criminals who are utterly irrational—engages in less crime (Wilson, 1975: 175–6).

The careful use of punishments will not only dissuade offenders from engaging in further criminality but it will deter others who see what has happened to them. If the offender is subjected to correctional treatment programs while incarcerated, so be it; but it is the fact of imprisonment itself, with its attendant deprivations, which must be primarily relied upon to prevent crime and recidivism. Correctional treatment may be all well and good but it is not considered necessary.

From the vantage point of the deterrence preventive ideal, the tasks ahead for social scientists are clear: to conduct research on the deterrent effectiveness of various types and levels of punishments, and to develop theoretical knowledge about deterrence which can be used by policy makers to maximize both the general and special deterrent effects for particular types of crime.

Undeveloped humans

A view of offenders as essentially undeveloped human beings once enjoyed great currency in the United States, even though it has fallen into disuse in the past several decades. This view of offenders suggested they had not had the discipline and training to adequately develop their higher faculties and, as a result, they committed crimes because of not having developed to the point where they could employ other means for solving their problems or meeting their needs. Perhaps the heyday of this kind of ideology of rehabilitation occurred between the end of the Civil War and 1900. For example, writing in 1893, the economist Carroll D. Wright declared that the criminal

> is an undeveloped man in all his elements, whether you think of him as a worker or as a moral and intellectual being. His faculties are all undeveloped, not only those which enable him to labor honestly and faithfully for the care and support of himself and his family, but also all his moral and intellectual faculties. He is not a fallen being; he is an undeveloped individual (quoted in Currie, 1973: 22).

In 1888 another writer declared that the criminal is less than whole.

He

is what he is, not primarily in virtue of that which he has acquired, but of that which he has missed. The fundamental truth regarding him is not that he has become a criminal, but that he has not become, in the full sense, a man. All that he has been is but the vicious exhibition of that which he has failed to be (quoted in Currie, 1973: 28).

This type of rehabilitative ideology played a major part in the intellectual armament of the American Reformatory movement. And yet, importantly, the development of these new theoretical ideas "seems to have come *after* the emergence of a demand for new and more effective means of dealing with criminals"—which culminated in the reformatory as a new type of penal institution (Currie, 1973: 16). (Emphasis in the original.)

As with preventive ideals generally, the thing which offenders have been felt to need to make them whole has been variously depicted; there has been no shortage of prescriptions for rectifying their undeveloped state. In an earlier period, military drill and calisthenics were a standard part of the correctional program in many institutions, on the assumption that they could instill the discipline and orderly habits which had led offenders to transgress in the first place. And, of course, religious instruction has at various times been pointed to as the key to offender restoration. In more recent times, however, it has been academic and vocational training which have been seen as pregnant with rehabilitative potential.

The small social group

Two different versions of a small group approach to the prevention of criminality will be distinguished and discussed here: *group dynamics* and *behavior modification*. Although they share certain premises, they are very different in the specifics of their approach to offender treatment, and they have enjoyed very different receptions by the correctional industry. The heyday of group dynamics, if it ever had one, is at least temporarily over, while behavior modification has attained great popularity as a justification for all types of correctional programs. The two are alike in emphasizing that the criminogenic distillate is found in the relationships which individuals establish and maintain with significant others in their everyday life. There, however, nearly all similarity ends.

Group dynamics

With few but occasionally spectacular exceptions (for example, in the California Department of Corrections) group treatment versions of the preventive ideal have not enjoyed much success as official rationales for correctional programs in America. Nevertheless, they have long been a strong dissenting position within the correctional community.

Precursors of the group treatment approach can be seen in some of the pioneering research of Kurt Lewin and his students (Cartwright, 1951). In various studies they found that the behavior and attitudes of individuals could be most effectively changed if they were dealt with as members of small groups rather than on a one-to-one basis. For instance, they found that women could be induced to change their dietary practices more often if they were informed of the advantages of the new practices in group settings and permitted to discuss them than if they were lectured and simply advised of the advantages of the newer methods.

As with other versions of the preventive ideal, early discussions of the promise of group treatment methods with offenders were quite optimistic, even containing a note of urgency. Like others, Clinard noted that "individual clinical methods of treating potential or actual delinquency . . . have not demonstrated any marked success" (1949: 260). He felt this was because the etiology of criminal behavior lies not primarily in "the conventional individualistic, early childhood explanation of psychiatry and psychoanalysis, but may develop out of a much more extensive process of group interaction" (1949: 260). Noting that group treatment methods had been used by the military during World War II (Abraham and McCorkle, 1946) and later in the New Jersey prison system, Clinard claimed (1949: 261):

> The limited literature indicates that these groups objectively examine their experiences and the reasons for their confinement rather than relying upon prison rationalizations, that there is growth in the capacity of the individual and the group to adjust, and that frequently an *esprit de corps* develops, particularly in the realization that they are helping others. Even personality characteristics appear to be modified for "the belligerent, over-assertive, antisocial rehabilitee is brought into line by his fellows and the asocial, shy, withdrawn person is drawn into the conversation."

These optimistic comments were echoed by Cressey, who inveighed against the medical model of treatment while pointing out that criminal behavior is a product of the individual's group memberships:

> The person or personality is seen as a part of the kinds of social relationships and values in which he participates; he obtains his essence from the rituals, values, norms, rules, schedules, customs, and regulations of various kinds which surround him; he is not

separable from the social relationships in which he lives. The person behaves according to the rules (which are sometimes contradictory) of the social organizations in which he participates; he cannot behave any other way. This is to say that criminal or noncriminal behavior is—like other behaviors, attitudes, beliefs, and values which a person exhibits—the *property of groups*, not of individuals. Criminal and delinquent behavior is not just a *product* of an individual's contacts with certain kinds of groups; it is in a very real sense "owned" by groups rather than by individuals, just as a language is owned by a collectivity rather than by any individual (Cressey, 1965: 51). (Emphasis in the original.)

By implication, therefore, "if behavior of an individual is an intrinsic part of groups to which he belongs, attempts to change the behavior must be directed at groups" (1955: 117). Noting that "opinion is almost unanimous that group therapy is an effective technique for treating mental patients" (1965: 55), Cressey urged criminologists to develop a theory for using group treatment methods in corrections which would draw upon and employ the expertise of ex-offenders. This was felt to be "the most difficult and crucial task that criminologists will face during the remainder of this century" (1965: 50).

Although there are a variety of approaches to the group treatment of offenders, advocates of such methods generally point to the following as background justifications for their approach.

1. Individual treatment methods have proven to be ineffective in the rehabilitation of offenders. But even more important, there are not enough professional personnel available to provide such services on a large scale and it is unlikely that there ever will be.
2. Social psychological research clearly suggests that individuals

---

... the official big gig offered by the authorities in their modern penology bag is Group Therapy. Spell that in capitals and color it sacred.

For me there was never any escape from group therapy, since I was always quite candid in admitting that I was a thief because I enjoyed the stimulation of crime and because I had a marked aversion to the 40-hour week. This didn't go over at all well in a system geared to the premise that a thief is never a thief through preference, but through the workings of a warped id. Nature's abhorence of a vacuum, I tell you, is as nothing compared to the psychologist's loathing of a simple and direct explanation.

Source: John MacIsaac. *Half the Fun Was Getting There.* Englewood Cliffs, N.J.: Prentice-Hall, 1968, p. 69.

are more tractable if sociometric forces within the groups to which they belong are used to change them.

Beyond these, the following assumptions are often cited as some of the special rehabilitative advantages of group treatment methods (Kassebaum, Ward, and Wilner, 1967).

1. An open, permissive group setting is an excellent one for individuals to learn what effect they have on others and how others perceive them. This knowledge can lead to a more accurate and realistic understanding of self.
2. The permissive nature of small groups and the processes of group development and interaction are such that members may feel a degree of uncritical acceptance that they have not experienced before.
3. In the process of discussing and trying to resolve the problems of others within the group, each member necessarily assumes a therapeutic role and learns to view himself differently.
4. Because the members of the group have had similar backgrounds and problems, they are best able to deal with similar problems in others. Moreover, the similarity of the members serves as a check on the behavior of individual members because the group will not permit the individual to play "treatment games" with the group leader.
5. In the process of group interaction and discussion, the individual may learn more constructive means of handling personal problems by learning from the experiences and suggestions of others.

Behavior modification

The behavior modification (or behavior therapy) version of the preventive ideal may be the most chic current approach to offender rehabilitation on the correctional market. Certainly, there seems virtually no correctional practice or program which has proven impossible to rationalize as consistent with principles of learning/ behavior therapy. In the words of one enthusiast, "behavior modification techniques are remarkably well suited for integration into the criminal justice system" (Schwitzegebel, 1971: 63). Among the types of correctional programs which are justified as being consistent with behavior modification are token economies in entire correctional institutions, contract programming for convicts and parolees, and a variety of other, more unusual programs, some of which have been successfully challenged in court as violations of the Eighth Amendment—which prohibits cruel and unusual punishment (see Chapter 12).

Behavior modification is usually depicted as the confluence of experimental psychology and psychological learning theory. Behavior therapists view behavior as learned and controlled by the nature of individuals' interactions with others in their interpersonal environments. Behavior of any kind, whether prosocial or antisocial, is learned; it is a function of positive and aversive reinforcements (i.e., the effects it produces in the environment). Once this simple fact is recognized and accepted—the story goes—knowledge of how behavior is learned can be systematically employed to unlearn undesirable behavior. In short, punishments and rewards are to be used to modify offenders' behaviors so the likelihood of their acting in criminal ways again is reduced or eradicated.

Behavior therapy enthusiasts generally contrast their approach to therapy with that of traditional evocative or psychoanalytically based therapy. In contrast to the latter, behavior therapy is said to be more scientific, because it deals only with observable phenomena (units of behavior) rather than hypothesized internal, psychic, or emotional problems and processes. Behavior therapists deal, therefore, with quantifiable variables, which are subject to independent observation and verification, instead of relying upon the unique observational skills of individual therapists. Moreover, behavior therapy can be conducted using lay citizens as therapists, with short periods of specialized training. This means that the therapy is not dependent upon the use of personnel with many years of advanced training—a stricture which makes therapy unavailable for most persons. These and other contrasts are evident in the following explication of the assumptions which underlie behavior therapy:

1. Criminal behavior is not symptomatic of anything disfunctional within the offender's psyche. In fact, it is not *symptomatic* of anything.
2. There is no truth to the belief in the interchangability of symptoms. Put differently, if rehabilitative efforts successfully change the offender's overt observable criminal behavior, no new symptom (i.e., aberrant behavior) such as bedwetting will appear.
3. Criminal *behavior itself* is the target of change, not something within the offender.
4. Offensive behavior is learned according to the laws of operant learning. It can be unlearned by employing the same knowledge; the same principles are involved. Behavior is a function of the results it produces in the environment (that is, the result of environmental contingencies); modify these and you can modify behavior.

Behavior modification's scientistic posturing and extravagant claims of effectiveness, coupled with its amazingly flexible concepts, have proven to be immensely appealing to correctors. The long-term effects of this remain uncertain, but many of those groups and individuals most concerned about the human and legal rights of offenders have deplored this development. Correctly or not, many see this as signaling an increasing willingness to ignore fundamental offender rights in the quest to achieve the ultimate rehabilitative strategy. From this vantage point, behavior modification programs evoke surrealistic images of a world of behavior control and the tyranny of behavioral experts—a world of *Clockwork Orange*. The proposals and programs of behavior therapists have done little to allay these suspicions and fears. Proposals for dealing with offenders range from the imposition of garden variety deprivations through some unique forms of "treatment" (drugs which induce prolonged vomiting) to the manipulation of entire communities. In fact, new social environments that inhibit the development of social problems by incorporating appropriate contingencies, role models, and incentives are the envisioned ultimate results of this growing emphasis on behavior modification. It is ironic that this infatuation with behavior modification techniques in the correctonal industry has gained momentum with apparent unawareness of concern for the fact that among psychologists there has been a heated debate over the validity of many of the claims made by its supporters. Even the claimed greater effectiveness of behavior therapy has been questioned (Durkin, 1974). Even these questions, of course, may prove to be largely irrelevant to the ultimate acceptance of behavior therapy. For

> Behavior therapy's claims to objective success alone do not seem to justify its emergence and rapid acceptance. From the standpoint of the sociology of knowledge, the question is what factors in the surrounding cultural context have determined the preference by those involved, therapists and patients alike, for the image of man conveyed by behavior therapy over competing ones (Portes, 1971: 311).

The local community: The community corrections movement

A belief in the criminogenic and rehabilitative powers of the local community currently enjoys much popularity in American corrections. The *community corrections* version of the preventive ideal has captured the imagination of correctional personnel and publicists in much the same way that the belief in therapy, religious instruction, or vocational education did in earlier eras. The irony of this fact has been wryly noted by Wilson (1975: 170): "Today we smile in amusement at the naivete of those early prison reformers who imagined that religious instruction while in solitary confinement would lead to moral regeneration. How they would now smile at us at our presumption that conversations with a psychiatrist or a return to the community could achieve the same end."

"Decarceration" and community corrections have become synonymous. Many states have moved to legitimize wholesale changes in their correctional bureaucracies and institutions by employing the rhetoric of community corrections. In Tennessee, for example, the state department of corrections plans to build at least six new prisons over the next decade; but since these are to be called "regional prisons," they are said to be consistent with the latest correctional thinking (community corrections).

What is this body of ideas and practices that has so captured the imagination of correctional personnel? Although it is very difficult to know just what its components are, because of the vacuity of some of its claims and the aura of holiness that has surrounded it, the following seem to be some of the assumptions of the community corrections preventive ideal:

1. Empirical research, most of it conducted in the past 15 years, has shown that prisons are a type of social institution which creates forces and problems which assure that it cannot function as an instrument of rehabilitation. Prisons are bad.
2. One of the worst aspects of prisons is the high degree of segregation from the free world (the elusive "community"). This segregation simultaneously creates artificial social and emotional conditions within the prison and makes it impossible to utilize community resources in the rehabilitation of offenders.
3. The badness of imprisonment in traditional prisons is directly related to the distance that prison is from one's home. Put differently, if offenders can be confined in newer prisons, closer to their homes, a greater rehabilitative impact can be achieved.
4. In fact, any kind of program that reduces the degree of segregation from the free world which the offender experiences will automatically produce greater likelihood of rehabilitation.
5. The greatest rehabilitative potential is achieved when offenders are kept within their home communities and the resources of that community are used to help them.
6. Community correctional programs are more efficient than traditional modes of dealing with offenders (i.e., incarceration).
7. Community correctional programs and treatment are more effective than treatment in traditional institutions.

The community corrections preventive ideal has breathed new fires of justification into some very traditional correctional programs (probation; parole), has taken over some recent innovations as its own (halfway houses) and has created some entirely new ones (community correctional centers; volunteers in probation).

Although community corrections advocates make powerful claims for the increased effectiveness and efficiency of treatment in the community, only recently have some of these claims come under critical scrutiny. Scull (1971: 1) has roundly attacked the charge that treatment in the community is more effective:

> The contention that treatment in the community is more effective than institutionalization is an empty one. There is massive ignorance about what "community treatment" actually involves, and about the likely effects of abandoning institutional controls. The claims that leaving deviants at large "cures" or "rehabilitates" them is just that—a claim. Little or no solid evidence can be offered in its support. Instead, it rests uneasily on a cloud of rhetoric and wishful thinking.

Another critic has suggested that "despite manifestly high hopes for corrections in the community, evaluations suggest that most such programs are no more effective than those conducted in prison." The same critic goes on to inquire: "One might ask why, if the community is so therapeutic, the offender got into trouble there in the first place" (Greenberg, 1975a: 4–5). Finally, Lerman (1975) has challenged the claim that community corrections alternatives to incarceration are necessarily more efficient. Using data from two highly publicized experimental community corrections programs in California (the Community Treatment Project and the Probation Subsidy Program) he has shown that the monetary costs of these programs was much greater than program advocates had claimed; numerous other unintended consequences of the programs were uncovered that not only increased the programs' costs but also vitiated some of their intended treatment effectiveness.

In view of the substantial popularity of the community corrections preventive ideal, these critiques would seem to be deserving of more systematic and sustained attention than they had thus far received. Taken together they amount to a serious indictment of the putative benefits of community treatment programs. If community corrections were to continue to grow despite the searching questions which have been raised, then we would seem to be justified in concluding that reasoned criticisms and the results of evaluative research actually have little impact on correctional programming unless political and economic exigencies make the times ripe for the "discovery" of such counter arguments.

Actually, at least one observer suggests that the community corrections movement has already run its course. According to Irwin, by 1970 the growing criticism of other rehabilitative ideologies took full shape and spread among criminologists and criminal justice experts. For a short period of several years there was an intense effort to quickly substitute a new ideology—community corrections—for the old, which would leave most of the basic structures, particularly the discretionary decision-making systems, intact. However, flaws in this system were quickly recognized, and the same type of criticisms which were aimed at the [other rehabilitative ideologies] were turned toward it. . . . The movement toward community corrections still continues, but it has had its rationale seriously damaged and will probably not succeed in supplanting the dying [rehabilitative ideologies] (1977: 31).

If Irwin's assessment is correct, the way has been left clear for the unrivaled ascendancy of punishment ideologies of deterrence and incapacitation in the late 1970s and 1980s.

THE DISCOVERY OF CORRECTIONAL MANAGEMENT

In 1960, Myrl Alexander, later to become director of the Federal Bureau of Prisons, addressed a gathering of criminal justice professionals on changes that corrections could anticipate during the coming decades. He chose to emphasize five points, one of which was the necessity for "vastly improved management practice."

More and more, the sound principles of management practiced in industry and explored and taught in universities throughout the country are being applied to government. And as government in the United States moves toward efficient methods of management, longer and harder looks will be taken at our correctional programs.

In Alexander's view, "the best management practice is one which integrates the total activities and services toward the goal of curing criminality." Further, "I am convinced that during the next decade this concept of correctional management will develop rapidly and find widespread support throughout the country" (1960: 348). The author's comments were prophetic. The ensuing years have witnessed a development which can only be described as the "discovery of correctional management," a movement which will be discussed at greater length in Chapter 6.

Today much is being written about the application of sound management practices to the field of corrections (e.g., National Advisory Commission, 1973: McConkie, 1975). What makes this development relevant to a discussion of preventive ideals is the belief by some that certain types of management practices or styles may prove to have rehabilitative impact. *Participatory management* in particular is thought to have merit along these lines. One observer claims "there is evidence to indicate that there are some real, measurable, positive effects resulting from involving the participants in their own destiny" (Murton, 1976: 31). The reasoning underlying such a belief is easy enough to grasp. If offenders must eventually live their lives as self-directing responsible participants in a democratic political community, then perhaps the best rehabilitative experience for them would be training in the skills required to become this.

As this is written it is still too early to know whether current discussions of correctional management practices will result in another full-blown version of the preventive ideal. All that seems clear today is that, as the fiscal crisis of the state has grown (O'Connor, 1973) and as correctional bureaucracies have become larger, pressure has intensified to assure an adequate return for every dollar spent in corrections.

PREVENTIVE IDEALS AS IDEOLOGIES

Social scientists have written extensively on the concept of *ideology*, the original formulation of which owes much to Karl Marx. An understanding of preventive ideals as one type of ideology, and an analysis based on that recognition, will tell us much about their origins, fundamental nature, and social and political functions. These are issues and processes that heretofore have not especially interested correctional theorists and practitioners. Instead, we have become accustomed to asking only a few—and perhaps the wrong—questions about preventive ideals. Traditionally, we have examined them with an eye toward determining conclusively whether and to what extent they are "scientifically valid" or "supported by research literature." When we restrict our interest in preventive ideals to these types of questions, there is little time or inclination for the pursuit of other questions that may prove to be sociologically more significant.

Plamenatz (1970: 15) correctly notes that the concept of *ideology* is generally used "to refer to a set of closely related beliefs or ideas, or even attitudes, characteristic of a group or community." This definition leads us to three fundamental characteristics of ideologies: (1) they tend to be reflective of the social and political contexts in which they are formulated or "discovered"; (2) their content is to some extent a function of the personal, social and economic characteristics of those who create and espouse them; and (3) they are instruments by means of which identifiable groups of individuals pursue their collective interests. Put differently, ideologies are used to try to convince others of the validity of an interpretation of a situation or problem that is compatible with the position taken by the members of interest groups. In using ideologies in this fashion, the members of the group hope to profit both individually and collectively—though not necessarily intentionally—from successful persuasive appeals. Ideologies are *weapons* and are the means by which groups attempt to *advance their interests* in wealth and prestige. Surely by the mid-1970s there is no one left who cannot see this process at work in the public relations pronouncements of, say, the American Medical Association. All that is required, therefore, is that we be alert to the same process at work in the activities of many other groups, whether these be social scientists, members of the news media, or correctional workers.

An awareness of the collective nature of ideologies suggests a host of questions that might aid us in understanding their origins, how they are used in correctional discourse, and how they change. We should always try to identify the groups that are supportive or resistive of particular preventive ideals. What are the characteristics of these groups? To what extent do their ideological differences reflect differences in social class, prestige, and interests? Since different ideologies tend to be spawned in different social contexts, we should inquire whether changes in social and economic contexts do not lead to a "need for" and, therefore, a discovery of new ideologies. It was Max Weber who pointed out that "the structure of basic socioeconomic relations among men does not lead directly to intellectual orientations; its influence lies in producing differential receptivities to the various intellectual systems" (Portes, 1971: 311). There is no shortage of preventive ideals; the problem is one of explaining why some come to be accepted as more valid than others.

In suggesting that we might examine the social context in which some preventive ideology gains ascendance, we are not arguing for a one-sided political-economic explanation of these matters. Our position is closely akin to the one taken by Currie (1973: 5) in his analysis of the American Reformatory movement.

> In emphasizing the social and economic context surrounding the rise of the Reformatory Movement (and its alteration after 1900), I do not mean to imply a crude "economic determinism." I will not be suggesting that the political economy of post-Civil War capitalism somehow directly elicited in mysterious fashion, an appropriate ideology of penal treatment. I *am* suggesting that the post-war political economy formed the general framework within which the theorists of the Reformatory Movement worked, and that their acceptance of that framework both stimulated certain lines of thought and excluded others. (Emphasis in the original.)

Bringing such an interpretational stance up to more contemporary times, is the recent resurgence of interest in the deterrence preventive ideal indicative of some recent and fundamental change in political and economic circumstances? Traditional answers to such questions—when they were even asked—tend to emphasize the causative role of purely intellectual variables, such as accumulating research findings or theoretical breakthroughs. We are suggesting, however, that such explanations for changing preventive ideals are incomplete, misleading, and illusionary. In fact, they may be viewed as one type of ideology, by means of which the members of an intellectual/educational elite maintain their claims to specialized expertise, honorific treatment, and lucrative positions as consultants to correctional agencies.

section three

SENTENCING

5

Sentencing:
Entering the correctional system

In 1974 the 50 federal district judges of the Second Circuit (New York, Vermont, and Connecticut) took part in an unusual study of differences in sentencing (Partridge and Eldridge, 1974). Copies of 20 presentence reports were mailed to the individual judges and each was asked to decide upon a sentence for the defendants described in the reports. The 20 hypothetical defendants were selected from actual cases that had previously been sentenced by judges in the Second Circuit, and were selected so as to be representative of the kinds of cases typically handled by the courts. The study's results reveal substantial disparity in the sentences meted out in the 20 cases. For purposes of the study, disparity was defined as "dissimilar treatment by different judges of similarly situated defendants." In 16 of the 20 cases there was no unanimity on whether any incarceration was appropriate. Moreover, even when prison sentences were imposed there were large differences in the lengths of the terms imposed in the same case. These findings can hardly be called surprising. They only lend support to one observer's claim that "whatever their intention, whatever their purposes, disparity exists at an incredible rate and is documented anew with each new researcher in each new generation" (Gaylin, 1974: 13).

Nor is sentencing disparity the only problem with the sentencing process; systematic *discrimination* against particular classes, age and ethnic groups, and sexes is another serious problem. For instance, between 1930 and 1975 a total of 3,859 persons were executed in the United States for the commission of capital crimes. Of this total, 53.5 percent were black. Of the total number of 455 persons executed for rape, 89 percent were black (U.S. Dept. of Justice, 1976). Although social scientists seem unable to agree on the nature and extent of racial discrimination in criminal sentencing, these extreme racial imbalances in the use of the death penalty are taken by many to be prima facie evidence of such discrimination. "The death sentence is disproportionately imposed and carried out on the poor, the Negro, and the members of unpopular groups" (President's Commission, 1967: 143). Eventually, even a majority of the U.S. Supreme Court was persuaded by this evidence and argument. In *Furman* v. *Georgia* [408 U.S. (1971) 238]—which struck down the death penalty—Justice Douglas observed:

> We know that the discretion of judges and juries in imposing the death penalty enables the penalty to be selectively applied, feeding prejudices against the accused if he is poor and despised, and lacking political clout, or if he is a member of a suspect or unpopular minority, and saving those who by social position may be in a more protected position (p. 255).

Other examples of possible sentencing discrimination are easily cited.

Several pieces of evidence suggest that males and females are not dealt with equally by the criminal justice system. Rather, females tend to be punished more severely and more often for some offenses than are boys. Status offenses are those for which juveniles can be tried and convicted, even though they would not have been crimes if committed by an adult. Examples are running away from home, "incorrigibility," or being "habitually wayward." The very existence of such offenses attests to a degree of age discrimination—since they apply only to juveniles. Just as important, girls are disproportionately sentenced to confinement for these rather benign forms of misconduct. According to an LEAA census of children in custody, in 1974 there were 31,270 "adjudicated delinquents" confined in public juvenile detention and correctional facilities in the United States (U.S. Dept. of Justice, 1977). Offense data were available for only 16,949 of these offenders. Of the 13,891 boys, 11.1 percent were confined for status offenses, but 48.5 percent of the 3,058 girls were confined for these offenses. Besides this discriminatory treatment, there is evidence to show that, on the average, girls are confined for longer periods than boys (Singer, 1973; Wooden, 1976: 119). In some cases, discrimination of this type is written into the substantive law. In some states, statutes enable courts to sentence women to longer terms of confinement than men convicted of the same offenses (Temin, 1973).

On the other hand, females receive more lenient treatment than males for some kinds of offenses. For instance, of the 3,859 persons executed in the United States since 1930, only 32 were women (U.S. Dept. of Justice, 1976). Consequently, sex discrimination appears to work both ways, against females for some offenses and in their favor for others.

> . . . I think that men are discriminated against with proportionately higher arrests and convictions because they are *considered* more dangerous, not because they *are* more dangerous. People are more afraid of being hurt by a man than of hurting him. This is not so true with women.
>
> I think that people in general, including law enforcement personnel, judges and prosecutors, are more reticent about hurting women . . . [Consequently] women who appear to be moral by conventional standards or who seem "proper," warm, and soft, can and probably do get away with behavior men serve time for.
>
> On the other hand, women who appear to have different moral codes or who have stepped far enough out of line to be arrested are no longer protected by stereotypes. When they appear to be living disintegrated lives or violating their roles as "ladies" or mothers in a way considered socially harmful, they are often subject to a great deal of additional disdain and abuse based on subjective definitions and moral judgments. Stereotypes work both ways.

*   *   *   *   *

> Women who are caught and sentenced are often scorned as "tramps" or "cheap women"—basically as "anti-mothers" (Burkhart, 1976: 78–79). (Emphasis in the original.)

There are other reasons for looking askance at the entire sentencing process. With rare exception, the limited ethnographic research that has been conducted in our criminal courts points to a general disregard for procedural rights in these courts (Robertson, 1974). This seems to be especially true of those lower-level courts that routinely process the least powerful members of our society (for example, chronic drunkenness offenders). Noting that these problems have long been known, the President's Crime Commission observed in 1967 that "the inescapable conclusion is that the conditions of inequity, indignity, and ineffectiveness previously deplored continue to be widespread" (President's Commission, 1967a: 29).

IMPLICATIONS

"There is no decision in the criminal process that is as complicated and difficult as the one made by the sentencing judge" (President's Commission, 1967: 141). There is also no decision that is more important to the defendant. The fact that it is often made hastily and with little attention to the circumstances of his particular case is not lost on the defendant. The inequities, discrimination, sentencing disparities, and general indifference of the personnel who make the sentencing decision have grave implications for the entire correctional operation. For these reasons, no adequate treatment of the correctional industry and its problems can ignore the process of conviction and sentencing, the offender's feelings about them, and the serious constraints they pose for the correctional process generally. In short, the sentencing process directly affects numerous aspects of the correctional process.

To individual offenders the sentence they receive directly determines the degree of unpleasantness they must suffer for having been convicted; it also determines, indirectly at least, the amount of time they must spend in confinement since parole eligibility is directly tied to the nature and length of one's sentence. Just as important, their perceptions of the manner in which the criminal process deals with their cases and arrives at a decision on just sentences affects their beliefs about the legitimacy of the process itself. Rossett and Cressey (1976: 46) remark about their hypothetical defendant, Peter Randolph, that he

> was offended by what happened in the courthouse, to say nothing of what happened to him in jail. The problem was not the matter of his guilt. It was his discovery that he was a case to be processed by a mindless machine. The system treated him as less than a person, as an annoyance to be gotten rid of. Nobody was interested in who he was and how he got into trouble.

To the body of convicts collectively, the various sentences each has received helps to determine collective perceptions of the justice or injustice of the entire criminal justice system. To this extent these shared perceptions influence individual offenders, and it may make the task of dissuading them from further law violation that much more difficult. To the correctional system as a whole, the configuration of sentences that its clientele receive determines the total amount of drain on system resources and in other ways constrains the actions of its personnel. For example, if an inordinately large number of offenders receive lengthy prison sentences, this may make for an unusually recalcitrant prison population—since long-term offenders may feel they have little to gain by being overly cooperative with prison authorities. This may produce an increase in the total cost of custody measures within penal institutions. Furthermore, if increasing numbers of offenders are funneled into any particular part of the correctional system, there may be serious repercussions for other components of the correctional system. Since

The only thing I resent and resent deeply is that I was promised by my
lawyer and the DA that if I copped a guilty plea I'd get probation. I
waived all my rights before the court—they say "no one promised you
anything . . . this or that" . . . and you swear to it. When I went to court
for the sentencing, the judge sentenced me to prison, not to probation.
I have cancer of the abdomen and need radium treatments. The judge
stipulated I get whatever I need in here . . . but I haven't yet. The judge
said he figured I had cancer when I committed the crime, so I should
have considered it.

Source: Kathryn Watterson Burkhart. *Women in Prison*. New York: Popular
Library, 1976, p. 24.

1972, the prison population in the United States has increased substantially (see Table 13–1), putting severe strains upon the prison
systems of the various states. Finally, a number of writers have
argued that one effect of the use of indeterminate sentence has been
to make for reduced convict solidarity, thereby making it easier for
prison officials to manage their convict populations. For instance,
Irwin (1970: 65) claims that the indeterminate sentence "has [had]
an important impact upon the convict in respect to his prison behavior. Generally, the convict desires to present a favorable view of
his progress in prison and/or remain largely inconspicuous to the
prison administration. This, among other things, has driven a wedge
into convict solidarity."

THE VARIETY OF CRIMINAL SENTENCES

Sentencing codes

That portion of a state's criminal law stipulating the range and
types of sentences a judge may impose for violation of various statutes is commonly referred to as the *sentencing code*. In many states,
the sentencing code has been enacted piecemeal, and over the years
the resulting grading of offenses in terms of seriousness is replete
with anomalies and inconsistencies. A decade ago the President's
Crime Commission (1967: 142) noted these examples—which in
no way are unusual or unique:

A recent study of the Colorado statutes disclosed that a person
convicted for first-degree murder must serve ten years before becoming eligible for parole, while a person convicted of a lesser
degree of the same offense must serve 15 years or more; stealing a

dog is punishable by ten years' imprisonment, while killing a dog carries a maximum of six months. Under Federal law, armed bank robbery is punishable by fine, probation, or any prison term up to 25 years, but in cases involving armed robbery of a post office, the judge is limited to granting probation or imposing a 25-year prison sentence.

This is not the only defect of some sentencing codes. Many also provide very severe mandatory minimum sentences for certain offenses and forbid the granting of probation or parole to those convicted of such an offense. This unrealistic rigidity makes the law impossible to apply to many cases where individualization is clearly required, and thus only assures that covert bargaining between the prosecutor and defendant will mitigate the sentence severity. In other cases, when the judge feels such a sentence is inappropriate, she may simply dismiss the case or acquit the defendant.

Another defect of many sentencing codes is the extremely high maximum sentences provided for many offenses. Maximum sentences of 20 or 25 years are not uncommon, and many offenses even provide for life imprisonment. Judges may choose penalties that range from probation to these lengthy prison terms. Not only does this grant broad discretionary powers to judges, parole boards as well frequently have wide discretion as to how much of his sentence a prisoner serves. In recent years the parole mechanism has been under heated attack, with some proposing that parole be eliminated altogether. Responding to this criticism, a former member of the U.S. Board of Parole charges that many of the inequities of the parole process actually have their origins in the sentencing process. Indeed, "the fairness of the parolee process depends almost directly on the fairness of the sentencing process" (Sigler, 1975: 48).

Given the broad discretion that is permitted judges in determining criminal sentences, a final defect of sentencing codes is their failure to set forth criteria for circumscribing this discretion. A federal judge has charged that "the almost unchecked and sweeping powers we give to judges in the fashioning of sentences are terrifying and intolerable for a society that professes devotion to the rule of law" (Frankel, 1973: 5). Although the process is complicated and laborious, there is a clear need to frame explicit grounds for the imposition of sentences of differing degrees of severity.

While sentences can and do vary greatly in their severity, the *types* of sentences imposed upon those convicted of crimes are few.

Determinate or "flat" sentences

Determinate sentences are simply those for which a defendant is sentenced to a fixed term of confinement, such as five years or one year and one day. Such sentences make it possible for defendants to know at the time of sentencing how much time they will actually have to be imprisoned. Ordinarily, they enable them to calculate their release dates just a few moments after receiving their sentences.

In most jurisdictions a fixed sentence does not mean that a defendant must actually spend as much time in prison as the sentence stipulates, say, five years. Instead, the workings of *good time laws* must be taken into account. These are legal formulas that provide that convicts are to have their sentences reduced a certain amount for each year of the sentences, as long as their conduct is good. A typical law might provide that a convict must serve three years and nine months in prison on a 5-year sentence, or 11 years and 3 months on a 20-year sentence.

Indeterminate sentences

As the name implies, indeterminate sentences are those that make it impossible for offenders to know at the time of sentencing exactly when they will be released from imprisonment. There are varying degrees of indeterminateness. The epitomy of a truly indeterminate sentence would be one day to life, or possibly one day to five years. Such sentences are rare. In most states indeterminate sentences specify a longer minimum, say, two years, and a maximum far short of life, such as ten years. Under such sentences, parole eligibility is provided for by law. Usually, convicts may be paroled at any time after serving their minimum term of imprisonment.

In some states, considerably greater discretion and power over sentencing has been vested in the parole board. In such states—until recently California was the outstanding example—the judge in effect gives offenders provisional maximum sentences, and the parole board is empowered to meet with them after their arrival in prison and make whatever reductions in the maximum sentences it deems desirable. An offender might, therefore, go to prison under sentence of five years to life only later to have the parole board cut the maximum sentence to 15 years.

Sometimes a sentence that is technically an indeterminate one may actually function as a flat sentence. In such cases, the time between the minimum and maximum terms of imprisonment is so short as to effectively preclude any possibility of parole before the expiration of the sentence itself. A sentence of ten years to ten years and one day would be such a sentence. In such a case, the convict's parole eligibility date would probably arrive only a few days before the date on which she would be released from imprisonment at the end of her sentence.

Concurrent and consecutive sentences

Many defendants appear in court charged with multiple offenses or with multiple counts of one offense. In such cases, the prosecutor and judge have great discretion in deciding how to sentence. Often all charges but one will be dismissed and the defendant sentenced for only that one remaining crime. At other times the defendant will be sentenced for more than one offense. The court could impose *concurrent* or *consecutive* sentences at that time. Consecutive sentences are those that must be served "back to back"; only after one sentence has been served does the offender begin serving the next one. Consequently, an offender who is sent to prison with consecutive sentences of two to five years and one to three years would have to serve at least three years before release on parole. Concurrent sentences are those that are served together, or at the same time. In the example cited here, the offender's sentence of one to three years would be "eaten up" by her two to five year sentence and she would be eligible for parole after serving two years.

Juvenile and adult sentences

Not only are adults and juveniles ordinarily sentenced by different types of courts, but the types of sentences they receive vary as well. Because of the state's extension of its *parens patriae* powers to the realm of juvenile justice, it has been claimed that juveniles do not even have a "trial" in the literal sense of that term. Instead, a "friendly hearing" is held to determine what is in the best interests of "the child." It is widely believed that since rules of evidence and procedure and guarantees of due process could easily prove to be an interference with this process, they are abbreviated or dispensed with entirely. The judge is permitted to proceed in a "fatherly fashion" to probe for the facts and to arrive at a decision that meets the "needs of the child."

Until recently, this view of the juvenile justice process, when challenged in court, met with little success. However, since 1965 the state's arbitrary powers to deal with juvenile offenders without protection of due process rights has gradually been abrogated. This does not necessarily mean that juveniles are now receiving a greater measure of justice than had previously been the case. In fact, research seems to suggest that at least one of the changes wrought by the extension of legal rights to juveniles—the right to counsel—has made rather little difference in the proceedings in juvenile courts (Lemert, 1970). The presence of counsel in juvenile court hearings has not produced any significant amount of advocacy in the proceedings.

Differences between the adult and juvenile justice processes begin even before offenders' appearance in court. Juveniles can be charged with and convicted of offenses for which adults cannot be charged or convicted. As noted, such offenses are commonly called *status offenses*. We have already indicated that a substantial percentage of juveniles who are confined in public institutions in the United States are confined for having committed such offenses.

Juveniles are usually sentenced by a juvenile court to an indefinite term of confinement that is not to exceed their minority. Once having been sentenced, they then become wards of a state department of corrections (or youth commission), which retains custody of them until they are for some reason discharged. While they are wards of the state, juveniles may spend one or more periods of time in confinement, interspersed with other periods under community supervision (parole).

Ordinarily, juveniles must be tried in a juvenile court. However, there are certain crimes for which adult criminal courts have concurrent jurisdiction with juvenile courts, and juveniles beyond a certain age who are charged with any of these crimes may, at the discretion of the court, be tried as adults in the regular criminal courts. In a jurisdiction in which an offender ordinarily could not be tried as an adult until age 17, a juvenile of 15 who was charged with murder or rape, for instance, could possibly be tried as an adult.

SENTENCING AS A SOCIAL PROCESS

The myth of trial by jury

Although adults charged with a felony are guaranteed the right to a trial by their peers (a jury trial) and detective shows on television invariably show a defendant locked in a dramatic courtroom battle, few real-life defendants enjoy such a privliege. For them the question of guilt or innocence is moot once they reach the trial stage of the justice process. In 1973, 82.8 percent of all defendants convicted of crimes in the federal district courts were convicted on pleas of guilty or *nolo contendere* (Administrative Office of the U.S. Courts, 1976: 14). The precise percentage varies considerably from one district to another, and it is even higher in some states and state courts. The President's Crime Commission (1967a: 9) found that the percentage ranges from approximately 65 percent to 95 percent among the states.

Once defendants have been arrested and indicted for crimes, a variety of pressures and motivations often operate to induce them to avoid a trial and, instead, to "cop a plea." Both pressures and inducements come into play. Among the pressures are the fact that they probably do not have adequate funds to hire a private and competent lawyer, so must settle for a public defender or assigned counsel. They may be forced to lie in jail for a protracted period before their cases actually come to trial, and the time they spend there may not even be counted as a part of their sentences in the event they are convicted and sentenced to imprisonment; it could simply be "dead time." Should they insist upon having trials, the state, through the prosecutor, may threaten them with lengthy sentences should they be found guilty. At the same time, any or a combination of the following inducements may be offered:

AN EXPERIENCE WITH THE PUBLIC DEFENDER

Our P.D. was a kindly and fatherly man who approached us with apparent sympathy. Yes, he acknowledged, you might beat them in a trial, but why take the chance when you could lose? Then they'll jam it into you. Take the middle course. Cop out. Save time, theirs and yours, save money. Cop out and do it the way that's easiest for everyone. There was, he said, little chance, considering the time we had already served, we would be sent to San Quentin.

Bob was convinced, and, with some reluctance, I agreed. As soon as we entered our pleas of guilty, we were routinely processed and swiftly sentenced to the California Department of Corrections at San Quentin for a period of not less than one year and not more than life.

This official process was marked by another irony. We had been sentenced and returned to the crowded bull pen to await return to our tanks. Bob seemed stunned. "San Quentin isn't Carson City," he told me. I knew that. Everyone had heard horror stories set in San Quentin. But I had also heard they had a school there, and I was telling myself how hard I would study, how much I would learn, how hard I would try, and what was another year or two. I was still young.

The P.D. came in to say a few consoling words to us, but he happened to sit down next to two other kids, even younger, and began to father away at them, telling them of the opportunities to be found in Quentin, and one of the boys burst into tears. They were juveniles who had not yet been sentenced. They were sitting there waiting to go home and here was this strange man telling them they were being sent to San Quentin.

The P.D. rose in some confusion and finally recognizing his mistake began to look around for us. I turned away and rested my head on my arms. He had advised us badly, failed his promise, cost us several years of our lives, and now he didn't even remember what we looked like.

Source: Malcolm Braly. *False Starts*. Boston: Little, Brown, 1976, pp. 147–48.

1. A recommendation to the judge for shorter sentences, or even for probation.
2. In the case of multiple charges, concurrent sentences instead of consecutive sentences.
3. A promise to drop any other charges that might be pending against the defendant.
4. A reduction of the charged offense to a lesser offense, such as reducing the charged offense from armed robbery to unarmed robbery.

The flexibility of the entire process, and the informal bargaining that is so much a part of it, place a real premium on advance knowledge of how the system operates. Professional offenders, because of their past experience with the criminal justice system, are one of the few types of offenders who possess such knowledge. Because they know that an insistence upon a jury trial can be disruptive to the process, they realize they, too, hold some cards in the game. Consequently, they are often able to extricate themselves from the situation with much shorter sentences than either their crimes or their extensive criminal records would otherwise indicate. As a result, the criminal justice system, paradoxically, least protects citizens from one of the types of offenders that represents a serious threat to them.

The controversy over plea bargaining

The pervasive practice of plea bargaining remains the topic of great controversy among lawyers and social scientists. Those who defend it claim there is no other way that vastly understaffed and overloaded criminal courts could effectively deal with the volume of criminal cases that comes before them. In this view, plea bargaining is an inevitable and necessary mechanism for dealing with a staggering work load.

It is also charged that plea bargaining, far from being an abridgement of offenders' legal rights, is actually a mechanism by which they can avoid the expensive and risky trial process. Especially for those defendants who have little chance at trial of winning a not-guilty verdict, plea bargaining enables them to emerge from the whole process with a better deal than they perhaps would have gotten had they insisted on their "legal right" to a jury trial.

Finally, defenders of plea bargaining contend that it provides a degree of flexibility in the sentencing process which is often necessary. It imports a degree of certainty and flexibility into a rigid, yet frequently erratic system. The guilty plea is used to mitigate the harshness of mandatory sentencing provisions and to fix a punishment that more accurately reflects the specific circumstances of the case than otherwise would be possible under inadequate penal codes (President's Commission, 1967: 135).

Critics of plea bargaining tend to see it as a potential threat to defendants who insist upon exercising their right to a trial. Such defendants are often threatened with sentences that are considerably more severe than the ones they would have received had they not bargained with the prosecutor in return for a plea of guilty.

The threat of a jury trial is one of the subtleties employed by the prosecution to reduce a defendant's resistance. Jury trials are discouraged in any event, because they are time consuming, expensive, and introduce an altogether cumbersome dimension into a system which is otherwise characterized by regularity, supreme rationality, and efficiency. Indeed, at the time of sentence, whether one was convicted after a trial or by way of a plea becomes a basis for invidious comparison (Blumberg, 1967: 31).

Such critics charge that the overwhelming reliance upon plea bargaining in the courts of our largest cities has fundamentally altered our adversary system, producing in its place a system of justice by negotiation—a *bureaucratic due process* (Blumberg, 1967).

The excessive reliance upon plea bargaining as a mechanism for managing the courts' workload is criticized for leading to haphazard, sloppy investigative work and case preparation by both the police and prosecution. When these worthies know that a defendant may be induced to plead guilty in return for favorable treatment by the court, it makes them less likely to put forth the kind of rigorous and thorough efforts that would be required were the case to go to trial.

The myth of the judge as a solitary decision maker

It would be a serious mistake to think of the sentence as a product of the efforts of only one person, the judge. In truth, the sentence is a product of a complex network of relationships between representatives of different offices, including the police, prosecutor, and court, with the judge being called upon merely to ratify a sentencing decision that has already been made in private. Taken together, these offices make up what is commonly referred to as the *criminal justice system;* but each of them has interests and goals that are only partially like those of other offices in the system. Each is also an *organization*, and the characteristic goals and activities of its various personnel are affected by this fact as well. Consequently, the criminal justice system is actually a largely routinized series of working relationships between representatives of bureaucratic organizations.

Various writers and researchers have called attention to this phenomenon, and to its consequences. According to Blumberg (1967) there are actually two models of the criminal process. "One is couched in constitutional-ideological terms of due process and rule of law; it is the one we think we have, or ought to have." But, he argues, this model has gradually been displaced by another model, one that emphasizes efficiency and rationality in the handling of criminal cases. This other model is an "administrative, ministerial, rational-bureaucratic one" (1967: 189).

> The official goals of the criminal court, based on ancient values, remain; due process, justice, and rule of law are necessary ideologies. But concerns of secularism and rationality, based on modern values of efficiency, maximum production, and career enhancement, have deflected and perhaps displaced those goals (1967: 78).

Similarly, Packer (1964) has discussed two models of the criminal justice process: the Crime Control Model and the Due Process Model. He suggests that: "The criminal process as it actually operates in the large majority of cases probably approximates fairly closely the dictates of the Crime Control Model. . . . The real-world criminal process tends to be far more administrative and managerial than it does adversary and judicial" (1964: 61). However, unlike Blumberg, Packer argued that the criminal process is moving closer to the other model, where greater emphasis is placed on the protection of defendants' due process rights. Unfortunately, events of the past 15 years suggest that Packer's predictions generally have failed to materialize.

A variety of research tends to show that the real-life criminal process works quite differently from what high school civics textbooks would lead one to expect. Mileski (1971) conducted an observational study of the handling of 417 cases in one lower criminal courtroom. She began this study of courtroom encounters by noting: "The processing of defendants through court can be seen simply as a task for courtroom personnel—the cases presenting not only occasions for moral outrage or legal acumen but also presenting problems for the legal bureaucracy as such" (1971: 473). Thus, "the control of crime is as much a bureaucratic as it is a moral enterprise" (1971: 533). During her courtroom observation Mileski noted that judges occasionally engaged in "situational sanctioning" of defendants, that is, by lecturing, chastising, or by manifesting a firm or harsh demeanor. In part, judges appeared to use these sanctions as a mechanism for maintaining the informal rules of the court. Defendants who created minor disruptions in the courtroom, or who showed disrespect for its personnel, were likely to be situationally sanctioned. There was little relationship between the seriousness of defendants' charges and whether or not they were the object of situational sanctions. The use of such sanctions is one mechanism that court personnel—in this case the judge—employ to reinforce and maintain its organizational integrity.

Isaac Balbus (1973) studied the responses of the criminal courts in three cities—Chicago, Detroit, and Los Angeles—to defendants arrested during the urban "riots" of the 1960s. He found that, during the early stages of processing them, the courts generally took a hard line and seemed to be concerned with helping maintain order in the streets. Extremely high bail was set in many cases—in an apparent effort to "keep them off the streets." However, during the latter stages of processing, especially at sentencing, the courts became much more preoccupied with managing the flow of cases smoothly, so they would not overwhelm and in other ways disrupt the courts' efficient operating procedures. In all three cities, by the time the defendants arrested during the disturbances came to trial, the "sheer volume of cases" compelled court authorities "to offer lenient sentences in return for the assurance of a predictable and efficient disposition of cases" (1973: 239). In other words, those defendants who were willing to plead guilty, often to reduced charges, received very light sentences in return for their cooperation.

> We are left, then, with the seemingly paradoxical conclusion that a participant in a full-scale ghetto revolt involving widespread participation and destruction of life and property is likely to incur *less* concrete deprivation from the criminal courts than one arrested for a comparable offense during "normal" conditions . . . (1973: 252). (Emphasis in the original.)

What emerges clearly from research of this type is that the sentencing decision, as noted earlier, is the outcome of a process of negotiation between representatives of the defendant and one or more of the various offices that comprise the criminal justice system. In return for a plea of guilty, the defendant usually is given some consideration in sentencing.

It should not be supposed that control over the sentencing decision is used only to promote the goal of efficiency in case handling. There are other ways in which leniency in sentencing can be used to promote the objectives of one or more of the organizational components of the criminal process. Thus, the negotiated plea of guilty "is frequently called upon to serve important law enforcement needs by agreements through which leniency is exchanged for information, assistance, and testimony about other serious offenders" (President's Commission, 1967: 135). During the trial of the Watergate burglars, federal Judge John Sirica used his control over the sentencing process to pressure defendants to reveal more about the offense than they previously had been willing to divulge.

Once a bargain has been struck between the defendant and the prosecutor's office, the sentencing process turns into a charade. In most jurisdictions, the law requires that defendants who are pleading guilty must be questioned by the judge and asked to affirm that they are pleading guilty on the basis of an informed evaluation of their situation, and that no promises or deals of any kind were made to them to induce them to plead guilty. All parties to such a performance are aware of the falseness and absurdity of the defendant's assurances that all conditions have been met. Whereupon the prosecutor usually recommends to the judge that a sentence of, say, three to five years "seems just in this case" and the judge usually proceeds to give the defendant the "recommended" (bargained-for) sentence.

As we have seen, the significance of bureaucratic influences and concerns on the sentencing process cannot be denied. Nevertheless, the personal characteristics of judges are also an important influence. Their background characteristics, political philosophies, and demographic characteristics have all been shown to have an effect on their sentencing behavior. In an illustrative study, Wheeler, Banouch, Cramer, and Zola (1966) found that Boston juvenile court judges who identified with a treatment doctrine tended to commit children to institutions more frequently than those primarily concerned with punishment. In Canada, Hogarth (1971) employed personal interviews and an attitude questionnaire to collect data on

---

THE CRIMINAL JUSTICE SYSTEM: AN OFFENDER'S VIEW

[Dealing] is the backbone of American justice. It doesn't matter if you've killed your kindly old parents, robbed the orphans' fund, or criminally molested an entire Sunday school class; if you have something to deal with, you can disentangle yourself from the law without earning a single gray hair behind bars. . . . The whole thing is marvelously flexible.

Source: John MacIsaacs. *Half the Fun Was Getting There*. Englewood Cliffs, N.J.: Prentice-Hall, 1968, pp. 204–5.

70 magistrates. These data were used to examine and explain variation in the magistrates' sentences in a sample of 2,500 criminal cases from the years 1965–67. Differences in the attitudes and social and background characteristics of magistrates were shown to be related to their definitions of "the facts" in criminal cases. In turn, variations in definitions of the facts were related to differences in sentencing severity. Further, Hogarth found that magistrates appeared to use information in sentencing selectively, so as to maintain their original attitudes intact. "Magistrates tended to seek information consistent with their preconceptions (which are the essence of their attitudes). At the same time, they tended to avoid information which was likely to present a picture of the offender that was in conflict with their expectations" (1971: 374).

ISSUES IN CRIMINAL SENTENCING

The accumulated literature on criminal sentencing consistently points to several problem areas. We shall briefly comment on these and close this chapter with some remarks on proposals for dealing with them.

Sentencing disparity and discrimination

There may be few issues in criminology and corrections that have been studied so little yet indicted so much as sentencing disparity. Noted earlier, sentencing disparity may be defined as "dissimilar treatment by different judges of similarly situated defendants." Disparity is a problem for a variety of reasons, not the least of which is the impact it has upon defendants who receive quite different sentences when both their crimes and personal circumstances would seem to be very much alike. Disparity is of concern to correctional personnel as well, because it generates inmate feelings of bitterness and hostility toward the legal system, feelings that may make the correctional task much more difficult.

Nevertheless, disparity would seem to be less of a problem than *discrimination*. The latter we define as dissimilar treatment by the judiciary of different sexes, races, and socioeconomic, religious, or ethnic groups. While disparity has an individual referent, discrimination has a collective one. It is assessed, for example, by comparing the average length of prison sentences imposed on black and white offenders of otherwise similar circumstances who have committed similar crimes. The differences between disparity and discrimination can be analogized to the difference between *error* and *bias* in the realm of statistics. Errors are assumed to be random, to have diverse origins and to generally cancel one another out. Bias, on the other θ hand, is assumed to be systematic and unidirectional.

Evidence for the existence of systematic discrimination by the criminal justice system is mixed and difficult to summarize or use as a basis for generalization. On one hand, there are well-known examples of rather massive discrimination in the imposition of criminal sanctions. As we indicated at the beginning of this chapter, the death penalty is one sanction that is employed in a highly discriminatory fashion against the poor (Swigert and Farrell, 1976). Similarly, it is well known that juvenile justice authorities deal much more harshly with girls suspected of sexual misconduct than with boys suspected of similar activities. On the other hand, studies of the sentencing process in the more routine, day-to-day handling of criminal cases raise serious questions as to the existence of discrimination against blacks and other minorities. Hagan (1974) reviewed the findings from 20 earlier studies of sentencing discrimination, which had sought to determine the extent to which extralegal offender characteristics, such as race, age, and socioeconomic status, were determinative of sentencing severity. He concluded that, "while there may be evidence of differential sentencing, knowledge of extra-legal offender characteristics contributes relatively little to our ability to predict judicial dispositions" (1974: 379). In fairness, however, it must be pointed out that the absence of discrimination at the sentencing stage of the criminal process says nothing about its possible existence at earlier stages, or the extent to which the criminal process reacts differently to the crimes of the poor and minorities. It is possible that the system in its entirety discriminates so much against them that by the time of sentencing it is simply least visible. An analogous situation would occur if we were studying the relationship between height and the ability to play basketball among high school students. Suppose a sample of students was drawn and all those over 5'6" were excluded from the study at the outset. The study then concludes there is no appreciable relationship between height and basketball excellence. This may be true for the sample studied—but only because the sample contains no taller persons.

The influence of treatment ideology and personnel

Whatever the origins and extent, it might be supposed that sentencing disparity and discrimination are partially the result of poorly trained judges who are overly punitive in their orientation toward offenders because of a lack of training in the behavioral disciplines. By such reasoning, we would expect judges who are more treatment-oriented to be less punitive in their sentencing behavior and their sentences to show no relationship to the extralegal attributes of defendants. By the same token, those courts that maintain and use a professional probation staff would be expected to show less disparity and no relationship between sentence severity and the extra-legal attributes of defendants. To what extent is this true? To what extent do so-called professional staff either ameliorate or contribute to sentencing disparity? Carter and Wilkins (1967) produce data to show that, both in the federal courts and in the California superior courts, there is a close relationship between probation officers' recommendations and the sentence of the court. In short, when probation officers recommend defendants for probation, the court usually complies with this recommendation; when probation officers recommend against granting probation, judges usually sentence to imprisonment. Carter and Wilkins next examined the characteristics of criminal defendants that seemed to be associated with the decisions of both probation officers and judges. "These data indicate that there is considerable agreement between probation officers and judges as to the significance of certain factors and characteristics for decisions relating to probation or imprisonment recommendations and dispositions" (1967: 511). Both groups assigned major importance to such factors as the defendant's prior criminal record, the nature of the offense he or she had committed, and the number of previous times of arrest. These two findings led Carter and Wilkins to conclude that "disparities in sentencing are supported, at least in terms of recommendations, by the parole officer member of the judicial 'influence group'" (1967: 514). Put differently, probation officers contribute to the problem of disparities in sentencing.

These findings are supported and carried one step further in a recent study by Hagan (1975) of the presentencing behavior of probation officers in 17 cities in a western Canadian province: Questionnaires containing descriptions of hypothetical defendants were mailed to the probation officers, who were asked to complete a presentence report on each defendant. A total of 765 questionnaires were returned by the probation officers. Hagan found that probation officers tend to be somewhat influenced in their decisions by extralegal attributes of offenders, and this is especially true in those courts where judges specifically request the probation officer's recommendations on the sentence. In other words, "the organizational arrangements that give the probation officer an advisory role in the court process may also introduce a channel of extralegal influence" (Hagan, 1975: 635). Hagan speculates that "the more traditional judges seem to be serving the interests of offenders best by resisting the expanding role of the probation officer" (1975: 635).

These findings are interesting in light of Max Weber's distinction between two types of rationality in law: *formal* and *substantive.*

Rationality here refers to the nature of the reasoning process by which legal decisions are reached. A formally rational decision is one that is reached in accordance with formal, logical rules; it is *logically* "correct." A substantively rational decision is one reached on the basis of ethical or technical considerations; it is *substantively* "correct." According to Weber, there tends to be an inevitable tension and conflict between these two types of rationality in law. Decisions that are formally rational often prove to be substantively irrational (that is, violative of ethical or technical principles). Similarly, decisions that are substantively rational sometimes appear to be formally irrational. A son who intentionally killed his aged and terminally ill mother in order to spare her further suffering, though guilty of homicide, would probably not be sentenced to life in prison. To do so would be formally logical (that is, consistent with the logic of the criminal statutes) but it would probably be seen as a substantive injustice, as a violation of ethical principles.

Weber argued that an emphasis upon one or the other of these two types of rationality is characteristic of legal systems. Further, over a period of time they tend to succeed one another in a cyclical fashion. Periods in which there is much emphasis on formal rationality give rise to criticism on substantive grounds. This eventually produces a situation in which substantive rationality is ascendant.

Judicial decision making, which draws upon the supposedly arcane behavioral knowledge of treatment experts, may lead to sentencing practices that are abhorred on formal grounds. Somehow, extended periods of confinement for relatively minor infractions, though supposedly in offenders' "best interests" and intended to "meet their needs," strike many as legally indefensible. The recent move in many states to reform the sentencing process may be seen as an example of the process to which Weber pointed. It may confidently be predicted that in time these reforms, if they actually produce more rigidity and severity in the sentencing process, will be attacked for the substantive injustices they have produced.

What is a just sentence?

To this point we have said a great deal about the issues of sentencing disparity and discrimination. Under the ideological assumptions of the individual treatment model (that is, the medical model), for the past 100 years judges have been encourged to dispense unequal sentences. These disparities were justified on the basis of defendants' different "needs" and the likelihood that they would commit further crime in the future. Sentencing statutes gave judges great latitude in arriving at appropriate sentences, and they were permitted to take into account various nonlegal characteristics. Probation officers conducted presentence investigations to assist judges to arrive at appropriate sentences. As we have suggested, there is some reason to believe that probation officers have exacerbated the problem of sentencing disparity and discrimination.

In the past decade, several groups of liberals put forth proposals for sentencing reform (for example, Bacon et al., 1971). These liberal proposals were aimed at (1) the destruction of the individual treatment model of corrections, (2) the creation of a system of shorter, mandatory sentences, and (3) the extension of the sanction of imprisonment to a wider range of crimes—so that corporate and white-collar offenders also would face the threat of confinement. The purpose of these suggested reforms was to seriously reduce or even eliminate disparities and discrimination in the use of criminal sentences.

Today it appears doubtful that this movement has enjoyed the kinds of success it had hoped for (Greenberg, 1977a). The movement's objectives were eminently defensible, but they were put forth at a time when many people were obsessed with the establishment of "law and order" in America. It is also possible that these reformers were overly naive about the prospects for creating a system of a just criminal sentencing in a society where there are such gross inequities in the distribution of wealth and all that this entails. In any case, their goals were worthwhile, even though some have suggested that their proposals were utopian in nature (Platt and Takagi, 1977). Nevertheless, partly as a result of their labors, many people have been moved to consider the whole issue of criminal sentencing. Unfortunately, no definitive answer can be given to the question of what constitutes a just sentence. Liberals believe sentences are entirely too long, and that they are used too exclusively against the poor and disadvantaged. Conservatives feel sentences should be longer and that there should be less emphasis on the rights of defendants. Radicals believe the entire criminal justice apparatus is used to pacify and control the underclass. They believe criminal sentences are too long, and they generally express amazement that others believe it could be otherwise in a capitalist system of production. Given this state of affairs, the likelihood of any consensus on the issue of how long criminal sentences should be, and how they should be employed, seems remote.

PROPOSALS FOR SENTENCING REFORM

The recognized shortcomings of the sentencing process, along with increased criticism in recent years, has led to various proposals

A SUMMARY OF CALIFORNIA'S DETERMINATE SENTENCE LAW

In this section we will address the scope of changes made by the determinate sentence law. This section will also provide an introduction to the terminology used in the new law, and a general overview of the new law's organization.

A.   Dispositions Not Affected

In order to understand the scope of the new law, it is important to realize that not all provisions of the old law have been changed. For example, neither misdemeanor sentences nor alternative dispositions for felonies, such as probation, are directly affected by the new determinate sentencing scheme. The new law also does not affect the sentences for the most serious felonies, such as first degree murder. The sentences for these felonies remain life terms; however, new paroling procedures are provided for inmates convicted of these offenses.

One of the most notable changes engendered by the determinate sentence law is the requirement of computing prison terms. In this area, the mechanics become somewhat complex and it is important to understand the terminology that the new law introduces. A prison term under the new law is determined by adding the *base term* and any *enhancements* that are pleaded and proved.

B.   Base Terms

Except for crimes with life terms and several others of little consequence, all crimes punishable as a felony carry sentences of a determinate "range." Each range specifies three possible periods of incarceration. The judge must choose the middle term in the range as the base term unless circumstances in aggravation (upper term) or mitigation (lower term) are found to be true by a preponderance of the evidence and are stated on the record. Once the base term is chosen, enhancements may be added to arrive at the prison term that will actually be imposed.

C.   Enhancements

For purposes of discussion, it is convenient to divide enhancements into two categories, specific and general. *Specific* enhancements are those specifically relating to the crime, such as use of weapons. *General* enhancements relate to other crimes committed by the offender for which the offender has served prior prison terms or will now serve consecutive sentences.

There are four specific enhancements which, if pleaded and proved, must be imposed by the judge unless circumstances in mitigation are found to be true and are stated on the record. These specific enhancements are imposed for: (1) arming with a firearm or use of a deadly weapon; (2) use of a firearm; (3) intentionally causing great bodily injury; and (4) causing great loss of property.

There are two general enhancements. The first general enhancement, for prior prison terms actually served by the criminal, if pleaded and proved, must be added by the judge unless circumstances in mitigation are found to be true and are stated on the record. The second general enhancement results from consecutive sentences which may be imposed at the discretion of the court. If a consecutive sentence is imposed for multiple crimes, the reasons must be stated in the record.

D.   Limitations

There are several limitations on the use of enhancements to increase the base term. In general, the same fact used to add an enhancement cannot also be used to impose an upper base term, and the enhancements for arming with or use of weapons or for causing great bodily injury do not apply if the facts justifying the enhancement are an element of the underlying offense. There are also three additional limitations. First, there is a five-year limitation on total enhancements for consecutive nonviolent offenses imposed by Penal Code Section 1170.1(a). Second, there is a "double the base term" limitation imposed by Penal Code 1170.1(f). The total term cannot exceed twice the base term unless the crime is a violent one, or there is a specific enhancement, or a consecutive sentence is being imposed because the crime was committed while in prison or subject to reimprisonment for escape. Last, there is a "stacking enhancements" limitation imposed by Penal Code Section 1170.1(d). Only the largest enhancement for arming with or use of weapons or for causing great bodily injury shall be added if more than one of these enhancements is found to be true for the same crime.

E.   Sentence Hearing

Under the determinate sentence law, the court now has a new and expanded role in the sentencing process. At the time set for sentencing, many factors must be taken into consideration by the court to determine the length of the sentence to be imposed. The court: (1) receives any additional evidence if either side has filed a statement citing circumstances in aggravation or mitigation or if the court on its own motion wishes to hear further evidence; (2) decides whether to grant or deny probation; (3) if probation is to be granted, decides whether to suspend imposition of sentence or to suspend execution of sentence —the former will require that sufficient facts be set out in the record to allow a prison sentence to be later determined should probation be revoked; (4) if a prison sentence is to be imposed, stays punishment of any counts that would result in multiple punishment proscribed by Penal Code Section 654; (5) decides whether the upper, middle or lower term is to be imposed on the principal offense, and on any offense which will be concurrent; (6) imposes any specific enhancements that were pleaded and proved, or finds circumstances in mitigation that justify staying the enhancement; (7) imposes any enhancements for prior prison terms that have been pleaded and proved, or finds circumstances in mitigation that justify staying the enhancement; (8) imposes any consecutive sentence, giving the reasons for doing so; (9) applies any limitations on enhancements, staying any punishment that exceeds the limits; and (10) advises the defendant that he is subject to release on parole after completion of the prison term.

F.   Good-Time Credits

All determinate sentences can be reduced by one-third as a result of good-time credits. These include credit for refraining from specified misbehavior, and credit for participating in prison work or prison programs. These credits may be denied or taken away in specified amounts under specified procedures.

G.   Community Release Board

The Community Release Board, a new parole board, is created to consider parole for life prisoners, to review each determinate sentence for disparity, to revoke parole, and to apply the new law retroactively. It will also perform additional functions regarding review of the length and conditions of parole and denial of good-time credits by the Department of Corrections.

H.   Parole

Release from prison is *mandatory* (after reduction for good-time credits) for determinately sentenced prisoners, but *discretionary* with the Community Release Board, for life prisoners. New procedures are provided to guide the Community Release Board in considering and reviewing parole for life prisoners.

Once released, determinately sentenced prisoners must serve one year on parole, unless waived or shortened by the Community Release Board. Life prisoners must serve three years on parole, unless waived or shortened by the Community Release Board.

Reincarceration after revocation of parole by the Community Release Board is limited to six months, and time spent in custody for revocation of parole does not count toward the period of parole.

I.   Retroactivity

The Community Release Board is to apply the new law retroactively to all prisoners and parolees who committed their crimes before July 1, 1977. Penal Code Section 1170.2 provides a mechanical method for calculating the retroactive sentence, but allows the Board to conduct a hearing with counsel and impose a longer sentence than that which would be imposed under the mechanical calculation. Regardless of the retroactive sentence imposed, the prisoner is entitled to the benefits of the old law, including the procedures previously in effect and parole dates set. The prisoner will be released on the earlier of the retroactive term or the parole date set under the indeterminate sentence law procedures.

This summary gives the reader an overview of a system that is tremendously complex.

Source: April Kestell Cassou and Brian Taugher. "Determinate sentencing in California: The new numbers game." *Pacific Law Journal* 9 (January 1978), pp. 22–26. (Footnotes omitted.)

for reforming it. One or more of these proposals have been adopted in various states. As yet rather little is known about their impact on the problems that led to their adoption.

Sentence review mechanisms

One proposed reform for dealing with the problem of sentencing disparities and injustices calls for the establishment of mechanisms for review of offenders' sentences. Appellate review of sentences and sentence review boards are two such mechanisms.

Traditionally, appellate courts in only a few states have had the power to review and modify criminal sentences. Some, including a federal district judge, believe the role of review should be expanded: "I stump here for appellate review of sentences as one step toward the rule of law in a quarter where lawless and unchecked power has reigned too long" (Frankel, 1973: 85). At present, approximately one-third of the states permit such appellate review of sentences.

A more popular proposal calls for the establishment of administrative boards for the review and modification of criminal sentences. While a number of states have adopted this reform, little is known about the practical effects of it. The establishment of sentence review boards has gone hand in hand with overhauls in the parole system. It has often been argued that one of the principal advantages of the parole system has been the parole board's de facto function in equalizing and making more just our criminal sentences.

> A parole system allows us to advertise heavy criminal sanctions loudly at the time of sentencing and later reduce sentences quietly. ... In a system that seems addicted to barking louder than it really wants to bite, parole (and "good time" as well) can help protect us from harsh sentences while allowing the legislature and judiciary the posture of law and order. ... One function of parole may be to even out disparities in sentencing behavior among different localities (Zimring, 1977: 7–8).

In short, parole boards historically have functioned to some extent as sentence review boards.

Sentencing councils

Sentencing councils consist of several judges of a multijudge court who meet periodically to discuss sentences to be imposed in pending cases. Sentencing councils are in use on a regular basis in at least three U.S. district courts. As it works in the Eastern District of Michigan,

> the arrangement is that not only the judge who is charged with the particular case but two of his fellow judges as well will receive copies of the presentence report. Each of the three studies the report and notes the tentative sentence he might base upon that reading alone. The three men then meet, usually with a probation officer in attendance, compare their preliminary estimates, and discuss the case. Upon the basis of that session the judge responsible for the case may or may not, as a matter of his exclusive judgment, revise his own initial appraisal (Frankel, 1973: 70).

Supporters of the sentencing council proposal claim that they promote a consensus on sentencing standards and, eventually, a reduction in sentencing disparity.

Modifying plea bargaining

Another proposal for reforming the sentencing process calls for modifications in the negotiated plea of guilty. To one group of observers, the overriding defect in plea bargaining is the clandestine manner in which it is carried out. This produces misunderstandings between the parties, abuse of prosecutorial discretion, and feelings of having been unjustly pressured on the part of defendants. To this group, plea bargaining should be reformed by bringing it into the open. Defendants and prosecutors would each be informed of their options and defendants would not be coerced into pleading guilty. Plea bargaining agreements would be written and submitted to the court. Judges would no longer be required to play a game of charades, to act as though plea bargaining had not taken place. Instead, the judge could accept the agreement, giving the defendant the agreed-upon sentence, or she could decline to do so; in such a case, the defendant would be given reasons for the judge's disinclination to honor the agreement, and he would have an opportunity to reach a new agreement with the prosecutor.

A second group of critics would eliminate plea bargaining altogether. This would be accomplished by drastically curtailing the workload of the courts while simultaneously increasing their resources in budget and personnel. To this second group, plea bargaining is undesirable because it permits criminals having inside knowledge of how the criminal process operates to extricate themselves with very light punishment for their crimes. Put differently, professional criminals and repeat offenders are able to use their knowledge of the process to avoid paying sufficient penalties for their crimes.

Substantive law reform

Presumptive sentences

Recently a number of observers have called for a drastic reduction in the use of imprisonment generally, while maintaining that it should be used primarily for offenders who have committed serious offenses. The Committee for the Study of Incarceration put it this way: "Incarceration, being a severe punishment, must never be used except for that narrow range of offenses that qualify as serious" (von Hirsch, 1976: 110). Consistent with at least one part of proposals such as this, a number of states have recently changed their sentencing codes to remove some of the inconsistencies and other shortcomings that have plagued them in the past. A typical reform calls for the grading of all felonies into three categories on the basis of their seriousness and the statutory provision of presumptive minimum and maximum terms of imprisonment for each type. Then, to further reduce judicial discretion, judges are given statutory guidelines specifying factors that may be considered as mitigating or aggravating ones in arriving at an appropriate sentence in individual cases. The nature and length of a defendant's previous criminal record, and whether violence was employed in the commission of the offense, are two such factors written into sentencing guidelines.

> To illustrate: Suppose a defendant were convicted of armed robbery for the second time. Were no special circumstances of aggravation or mitigation shown, he would receive the disposition which the guidelines specify as the presumptive sentence for a second armed robbery. Were there several participants in the robbery and his role in the crime a peripheral one, however, this could be a mitigating circumstance permitting a limited reduction below the presumptive sentence (von Hirsch, 1976: 101).

By the use of such procedures many hope that some of the disparities and injustices of sentencing in the past will be reduced.

Mandatory sentences

As part of a state's sentencing code, mandatory sentence provisions stipulate that offenders convicted of certain specified offenses must be sentenced to specified terms of confinement. Mandatory sentencing provisions are supported by people of quite different political persuasions, albeit for different reasons. Conservatives support them as a means of assuring that "criminals are gotten off the streets." Mandatory sentences are seen as a way of limiting judicial discretion to place serious offenders on probation or to dismiss charges. Assumedly, by incarcerating and incapacitating a larger percentage of serious offenders, the community will see a reduction in the rate of crime.

Liberals, too, have called for mandatory sentences. However, they have suggested that terms of incarceration be shortened and applied more uniformly to *all* those convicted of particular crimes. By such proposals they seek to accomplish two objectives. First, they desire to reduce judicial discretion and the sentencing disparity and injustice which flows from it. And second, they see mandatory sentences as a means of eliminating the indeterminate sentence and the embittering, deleterious effects these sentences have upon offenders. Under the proposals put forth by the Committee for the Study of Incarceration,

> Penalties will be scaled down substantially. Incarceration will be restricted to offenses that are serious— and most prison sentences kept relatively short. . . . Severity would thus be substantially reduced, but we emphasize: these suggested punishments would not be so easily avoided (von Hirsch, 1976: 140).

Several states have recently enacted mandatory determinate sentencing provisions (e.g., Maine, Indiana, and California) and many others are considering them.

The impact of sentencing reform

What have been the consequences of these movements toward determinate and mandatory sentences? Given the recency of the changes, it is difficult to say, but a few tentative generalizations can be made. First, it appears that the switch to a system of determinate sentences will not eliminate all elements of indeterminacy from criminal sentences; "good time" will be manipulated as a method for controlling convicts' behavior, much as they were controlled under the former system of indeterminate sentences (Clear, Hewitt, and Regoli, 1977). There also is reason to believe that prisoners may actually serve longer prison terms under the new system of mandatory determinate sentences. Finally, a system of mandatory determinate sentences probably will not reduce official discretion in handling criminal defendants; it will simply shift the discretion from one office to another and, in the process, the total amount of discretion may actually be increased. Thus, in seeking to limit judges' sentencing discretion, it appears as though the new laws have given even more discretionary powers to prosecutors to decide what charges to file against defendants. Prosecutors may find the new mandatory sentence laws much more effective than older sentencing statues for wringing guilty pleas from defendants (Zimring, 1977; Clear et al., 1977). In these, and perhaps other ways as well, recent changes in sentencing statutes may prove to have consequences quite different from what their supporters had anticipated. Greenberg has charged that the whole movement toward sentencing reform has been coopted for repressive purposes, even though it was originally proposed as a mechanism for promoting justice in sentencing.

> . . . The changes we can expect to see in the next few years, and perhaps longer, are likely to bear only a superficial resemblance to the principles of justice. While some of the changes may bring limited benefits to some defendants or prisoners, these benefits are likely to be compensated by other provisions which are detrimental to prisoner interests. Primarily, these changes are designed to rationalize and thereby restore legitimacy to a system that has come under sharp criticism for its irrational and discriminatory practices (1977a: 20).

In the next few years we should learn a great deal more about the effective impact of sentencing reform. It will be interesting to see if these predictions are borne out in practice.

section four

CORRECTIONS: STRUCTURES AND PROCESS

6

The characteristics and perspectives of correctors and offenders

Having discussed three views of the process of correctional change, in this chapter we will focus on variables and processes that are temporally and sociologically more bounded, which will aid us in understanding the dynamics of correctional agencies and some of the distinctive qualities of the interaction between correctors and offenders within these agencies. In our attempt to understand the dynamics of correctional agencies, three different types or levels of causal variables can be distinguished: (1) the characteristics and perspectives of correctors and offenders, (2) the organizational or managerial characteristics and processes of the agencies, and (3) the situational aspects of interaction between correctors and offenders. In this chapter we will discuss primarily the first of these, leaving the others for a subsequent chapter.

BACKGROUND

Formal organizations of all types are generally created to achieve some goal(s) and, whenever they fail to do so, the blame is often placed on their personnel. Their presumed social or psychological shortcomings are cited as the culprit. The field of corrections, and the assumed shortcomings of correctional agencies, are no exception to this pattern. According to Haney, Banks, and Zimbardo (1972: 70), many people believe that

> a major contributing cause to despicable conditions, violence, brutality, dehumanization, and degradation existing within any prison

can be traced to some innate or acquired characteristic of the correctional or inmate population. Thus, on the one hand, there is the contention that violence and brutality exist within prison because guards are sadistic, uneducated, and insensitive people. It is the "guard mentality," a unique syndrome of negative traits that they bring into the situation, that engenders the inhumane treatment of prisoners. Or, from other quarters comes the argument that violence and brutality in prison are the logical and predictable result of the involuntary confinement of a collective of individuals whose life histories have been characterized by disregard for law, order and social convention and a concurrent propensity for impulsivity and aggression.

We need not search far for an example of this type of explanation for correctional failure. The New York State Special Commission on Attica concluded that prior to the 1971 uprising "the relationship between most officers and inmates was characterized by fear, hostility, and mistrust, nurtured by racism." The commission went on to charge that "the relationship was probably inevitable when predominantly poor, urban, black and Spanish-speaking inmates were placed under the supervision of white officers from rural areas equipped with only three weeks of training" (1972: 80). More important, the commission declared that "racist attitudes in the institution were an undeniable factor among the tensions leading to the uprising" (1972: 82).

While recognizing the validity of such interpretations or assertions, we must at the same time be aware of a danger in them, the danger that Haney, Banks, and Zimbardo (1972) have labelled the *dispositional hypothesis*. This is the tendency to attribute too many of the pathological aspects of an organization's functioning to the assumed deficiencies of *individuals*. Such explanations fail on at least two counts. First, they ignore the fact that employees of organizations often employ group or collective (that is, shared) perspectives in their work performance, that their attitudes and behavior have their origins in an occupational or institutional *culture*. Consequently, if we would understand the individual, we must look to the collective as well. Second, they do not take sufficient account of the *structural* elements that shape and give rise to particular kinds of behavior. These structural and cultural components represents emergent levels of analysis when individuals are brought together and given some task to perform, or are required to share a common fate which results in their interaction over a period of time.

A recognition of the structural component in behavior represented a critical point of departure for the famous Stanford study of a simulated prison (Haney, Banks, and Zimbardo, 1972). By populating and staffing the prison entirely with "normal-average" undergraduates, the experimenters ought to create an environment in which any observed pathological conduct could be attributed solely to situational components of "prisonness." In Chapter 8 we will discuss *sociologically functional* explanations for the distinctive nature of the prison's social structure and culture, for which simulation research on imprisonment provides some supporting evidence.

CORRECTIONAL EMPLOYEES

The task we face is one of assaying the research literature for data on the personal characteristics of both correctors and offenders. We must then attempt to extrapolate from these data to an understanding of some of the dynamics of correctional agencies. In presenting materials on the characteristics and perspectives of correctional employees, we will distinguish between *administrators* and *supervisors, line workers* (primarily custodial personnel), and *functional specialists* (primarily white-collar employees, such as school teachers, counselors, probation officers). When presenting materials on offenders, we will distinguish between adults and juveniles at places where the data permit it, and where this will enhance interpretation.

Administrators and supervisors

Until recent years little systematic information was available on correctional administrators. Since the mid-1960s, however, we have witnessed the "discovery of correctional management," and today a great deal is being written about them. Reflecting this trend, in Chapter 4 we discussed ideologies of correctional management as an emerging version of the preventive ideal. This dramatic increase of interest in correctional administration is the result of at least three, largely independent, developments. First, social scientists studying correctional agencies in the 1960s began to ask different types of questions about them than had previously been asked. *Organization for Treatment* (Street, Vinter, and Perrow, 1966) was an initial effort in this direction because the researchers studied six different juvenile institutions and examined administrative strategies as one of the critical variables which operationalizes organizational goals. In earlier research on correctional agencies, administrative strategies and practices had been largely ignored. This piece of research was indicative of a perceptible shift during the past decade toward concern with administrative behavior and its consequences for correctional organizations (for example, Duffee, 1975). Second, as states have increasingly moved to establish unified departments of corrections, these agencies have for the first time had to rely more upon administrators who were indigenous to the field itself. Previously, many correctional agencies had operated as largely autonomous units within state administrative departments whose tasks were diverse and broad. In Illinois, for example, prior to 1966 juvenile and adult correctional agencies were in separate departments of state government. Adult corrections was a part of the Department of Public Safety, which also included such diverse agencies as the Illinois State Police and the Division of Fire Inspection. Top-level administrative personnel in the Department of Public Safety had sometimes come from one of these other agencies; occassionally corrections was treated as a stepchild. In 1966 the state established a Department of Corrections, thereby consolidating all its correctional services into one agency. As these large departments of corrections have sprung up, the task of running them has placed a new emphasis and a premium on administrative skills. Third, the federal government, through its granting policies and study commissions, has directed attention to the critical importance of correctional administration. Of special significance in this regard is the *Report on Corrections* (1973) of the National Advisory Commission on Criminal Justice Standards and Goals. Appointed by Richard Nixon, this commission was largely made up of management experts—which differed from earlier comparable commissions that were generally staffed by social scientists. The commission's report on corrections stressed the development and application of "sound management procedures" as an answer to the various problems of correctional bureaucracies (see Conrad, 1974). The commission's report thus gave impetus to the movement that had gotten underway several years earlier.

Characteristics

One of the few sources of data on the characteristics of correctional employees is the final report of the Joint Commission on Correctional Manpower and Training (1969), which presents data from a national sample survey of such personnel. Because these data were collected a decade ago, they may not sufficiently reflect the changes that have accompanied the professionalization of correctional management.

As might be expected, correctional administrators and supervisors tend to be slightly older than other categories of correctional employees. Whereas the median age for all correctional employees is 42.8 years, the median age of administrators and supervisors is approximately 43.5 years (estimated from Joint Commission, 1968: table 40). Only 5 percent of administrators and 17 percent of supervisors are women, compared to 12 percent women for all corrections employees. Blacks are underrepresented, not only among correctional employees generally, where they account for 8 percent, but especially among administrators and supervisors, among whom less than 1 percent are black. Again, as might be expected, correctional administrators and supervisors have been employed in corrections longer than other correctional employees with median years of employment of 16.4, 11.4, and 8.8, respectively.

Entrance requirements and personnel screening

Traditionally, correctional administrators and supervisors worked their way up through the ranks of correctional agencies, having started at lower-level positions and progressing eventually to administrative positions. Although this probably remains the predominant pattern, there is a recent trend toward developing a nationwide pool of experienced correctional administrators who can and do move between various states and correctional agencies as opportunity permits—or as necessity requires. Again, this would seem to be one more change accompanying the professionalization of correctional employment. Little else is known about the process of selection and screening for administrative positions in corrections. Top-level administrators, unlike middle managers, tend to be political appointees of the governor but, increasingly, these appointment decisions are made without regard to candidates' political loyalties.

The administrator's world

Corrections appears to be one of the last areas of governmental services to be professionalized and subjected to the "managerial revolution." As this movement has gained momentum the world of the correctional administrator has necessarily been transformed. Whatever it may have been like in the "good old days," today's correctional administrators are finding it increasingly necessary to become expert in the rhetoric and techniques of public administration and accounting. At first it was PPB (Planning, Programming, and Budgeting) and, later, MBO (Management by Objectives) (McConkie, 1975) that appeared on the correctional scene, both necessitating that correctional administrators modify their traditional ways of thinking about the process of management and cost accounting. There is every reason to assume that these currents of change will continue, bringing even further change in the role of the correctional administrator.

Line workers

The centrality and importance of custodial officers in any analysis of the correctional mandate has long been recognized. Empirical research has confirmed what common sense would suggest: In correctional institutions, custodial personnel have the most contact and interaction with offenders and, therefore, the greatest impact on them.

> They may be the most influential persons in the institutions simply by virtue of their numbers and their daily intimate contact with offenders. It is a mistake to define them as persons responsible only for control and maintenance. They can, by their attitude and understanding, reinforce or destroy the effectiveness of almost any correctional programs. They can act as effective intermediaries or become insurmountable barriers between the inmates' world and the institution's administrative and treatment personnel (President's Commission, 1967: 96–7).

Echoing these remarks, Jacobs (forthcoming: 1) states that "prison scholars and reformers have, from the beginning of the penitentiary movement, emphasized the decisive importance of the line officer for carrying out penological goals." In perhaps the best documentation of this belief, Glaser's study (1964) of federal prisoners "found, on questioning inmates about their staff preferences and prejudices, that 'custodial officers are very frequently the most liked, in addition to being more often than others the most disliked staff members' " (Hawkins, 1976: 88).

An anecdotal observation may prove instructive here. While employed in corrections we observed that offenders who had spent time in other prisons earlier in their lives usually could not recall the names of the counselors or caseworkers with whom they had had contact. On the other hand, many of them were able to recall the names and personal idiosyncracies of the custodial officers under whom they had been employed. In being able to recall the names of custodial officers, but not treatment personnel, these offenders may have also been telling us which group of correctional employees had the greatest impact on them.

Given the well-recognized importance of custodial personnel in the correctional process, one might think that a great deal would be known about them. Regrettably, this is not the case.

> Prison scholarship has focused, almost exclusively, on the culture and social structure of prisoners. Countless studies report prisoner attitudes toward themselves and their fellow inmates, prison staff and society in general. But there exists hardly any research on the demographic characteristics, attitudes, values and ideology of cor-

rectional officers (as the guards have come to be renamed) (Jacobs, forthcoming: 1).

In fact, this is true of all correctional *employees*. By necessity, therefore, the materials we present in this chapter will be sketchy, possibly even erroneous in some details or respects. The picture we present may not do justice to the intrainstitutional and individual differences among correctional employees and offenders. We run the risk of overgeneralizing and suggesting more unanimity on these matters than actually exists. For instance, one study claims that

> Unlike the picture of the Hollywood formula guard, his real life counterpart does not lend himself to a capsule portrait. There is no national model. There is none even within a single state or, for that matter, within different prisons under the jurisdiction of the same department (May, 1976: 4).

Nevertheless, the study goes on to adopt the position we are taking here:

> But if there are disparities within and among individual corrections systems, there are similarities that transcend departments in large and small states alike. They are the similarities of attitudes, worries and, often, frustrations (May, 1976: 12).

The Joint Commission's survey revealed that nearly 70 percent of all correctional employees are employed in institutions (primarily prisons and training schools). Of these 75,000 institutional employees, 65 percent are line workers (guards and cottage parents). In terms of their sheer numbers, as well as their significant impact on offenders, line workers are an extremely important component of the correctional work force.

The same survey found that line workers in adult correctional institutions tend to be overwhelmingly white (95 percent), male (95 percent), older (26 percent over age 50; median age 40.8) and experienced at their jobs (36 percent have over ten years experience). By comparison, line workers in juvenile institutions include more members of minority racial groups (26 percent) and females (34 percent) although they are still older (25 percent over age 50) and 30 percent have had over ten years work experience in corrections. These demographic data are substantially similar to data on the line workers in individual state institutions and correctional systems. Jacobs (forthcoming) surveyed 929 Illinois prison guards and reported an average age of 45 years; the average time on the job was 66 months, with 16 percent of the guard force having two years of experience or less and 23 percent having more than ten years experience; 85 percent of the guards were white.

The fact that so few line workers in corrections are from minority racial groups results from complex causes. Historically, no doubt, the corrections bureaucracies of the various states have been affected by the institutional racism that is such a pervasive aspect of American life. But more benign reasons can be found. Since many correctional institutions are located in remote rural areas of the states and draw their employees from the surrounding environs, few blacks or Hispanics have been employed. New York's Attica prison, for example, is located in rural upstate New York and, prior to the 1971 rebellion, did not have a single black correctional officer (New York State Special Commission, 1972: 24). A common complaint among convicts is that "rural guards from the small towns where prisons generally are located do not understand the inmate who generally comes from the city" (May, 1976: 40). In recent years many state departments of corrections have made special efforts to recruit minority correctional officers, since the absence of such persons was sometimes cited as a contributory cause of the uprisings of the early 1970s. In Illinois, "despite substantial efforts in the last several years to increase minority representation 85 percent of the guards are white" (Jacobs, forthcoming: 2).

How do these data on the demographic characteristics of line workers compare with what is known about offenders? Data on adults confined in state prisons are available from the *1974 Survey of Inmates of State Correctional Facilities* (U.S. Dept. of Justice, 1976c). A more complete presentation of the data can be found in Table 8–1. In 1974 there were approximately 190,000 adults confined in state correctional institutions in the United States (including the District of Columbia). Of this total, 47 percent were classified as black; 38 percent of all convicts were age 24 or younger, and only 5 percent were age 50 or older. Ninety-seven percent of all state prisoners were male. Sixty-one percent of the prisoners had less than a high school education and 42 percent had preincarceration incomes of $3,999 or less.

Actually, the fact that 47 percent of all state prisoners were black in the United States masks a great deal of interstate variation on the racial variable. While some states had practically no black prison inmates—for example, only one each in the states of Vermont and New Hampshire in 1973—others had a heavy concentration—74 percent in Maryland and 71 percent in Louisiana, again in 1973 (U.S. Dept. of Justice, 1976). In states that have a significant percentage of blacks in their population, they tend to be overrepresented in the prison population as well. Everywhere, however, the poor and economically disadvantaged, whether white or black, make up the bulk of the prison population. In this respect they are probably more like their keepers than many would suspect, since guards also appear to be drawn primarily from the economically disadvantaged portions of the population. Indeed, for most states, Jacobs' observation seems undisputably true: "One thing is clear. Guards continue to be recruited from the lower levels of the work force. Very few have been exposed to higher education, even with the opportunity provided by the Law Enforcement Education Program" (Jacobs, forthcoming: 10).

Many have long believed that the job of prison guard attracts persons who are emotionally warped or sadistic. Interestingly, therefore, an earlier study of guards in a maximum security penitentiary reported that

> Our impression is that new applicants for the custodial force represent a random sampling from the ranks of the unskilled and semi-skilled labor force. There is no indication that one type of individual, in terms of personality makeup, is attracted to seek employment in the penitentiary. . . .
>
> There is no evidence that the popular stereotype of a guard is applicable to even a small number of officers in this particular institution (Motivans, 1963: 189).

Entrance requirements and personnel screening

> Entry requirements for correctional officer jobs are minimal and vary from state to state. Many now demand a high school diploma. In Ohio, however, the minimum is a fourth-grade education or its equivalent. In some states an applicant must be 21, in others only 18. Many now give standard state civil service examinations, some don't (May 1976: 40).

Apparently, very few people aspire to be prison guards and many do so only under the pressure of unemployment or because the job offers employment security. In a succinct and probably accurate statement, Fogel (1975: 104) claims that "wherever prisons were built, men came to work at them but not usually as a first choice. The prison was close, sometimes the only industry around, and sometimes it was sought out by the unemployed." In his survey of Illinois guards, Jacobs (forthcoming: 2) found that 35 percent of them had grown up on farms, 9 percent in moderate-size cities, and only 7 percent in metropolitan areas. More than one-half (57 percent) of the 929 guards surveyed gave reasons for choosing the job of guard that had "nothing particularly to do with corrections; they 'just needed a job' and this was available. Forty-one percent report being unemployed at the time they joined the force" (forthcoming: 3).

Throughout corrections—and especially at the level of recruitment for line workers—a rather haphazard recruitment policy prevails. Most states appear to require nothing more than that an applicant be a high school graduate and not have a previous criminal record. No doubt this is partially responsible for the fact that the Joint Commission found in its national sample survey of correctional employees that 16 percent of line workers had less than a high school education, 52 percent were high school graduates, and the remaining 32 percent had some college education (Joint Commission, 1968: 28). Apparently, most states also have minimal physical requirements for the position of prison guard (for example, height and weight) and may require that applicants be residents of the state. But beyond these rather minimal standards for recruitment, little is known about prevailing practices.

It has often been asserted that, because of the sensitive nature of their work, prison guards should be screened for psychological and emotional fitness. Those who persist in believing that the job of guard appeals to and attracts sadistic or emotionally unstable individuals have been especially supportive of such proposals. In order to learn more about the use of procedures for screening guard applicants on these dimensions, the American Bar Association (Goldstein, 1975) surveyed personnel directors of the District of Columbia and 50 state departments of corrections in the United States. Usable responses were obtained from 46 of the departments. The survey found that more than 90 percent of the departments claim to do some screening for emotional suitability, but the thoroughness and appropriateness of the procedures employed seems open to question. Thirty-eight of the 46 departments employed an oral interview to assess applicants' emotional suitability, 25 departments use the standard medical interview as a device for assessing fitness, and only eight states appear to routinely use personality tests. Even the states that do so seem to be uncertain as to exactly what they are searching for in the testing process. Thiry-eight departments indicated they use a police and background information search as a technique for assessing emotional suitability, although the relevance of this procedure would seem to be unclear. On the basis of this survey, therefore, it may be concluded that very little effort is currently being made to employ sophisticated and research-grounded procedures in screening guard candidates for emotional suitability.

Admittedly, the process of developing and using adequate screening mechanisms is handicapped by the absence of sufficient consensus on the qualities that a guard should *not* possess, such as racial prejudices or negative attitudes toward offenders. It should be possible, even given the present state of knowledge, to develop screening procedures that would help to eliminate guard candidates who are unsuited for the task of supervising incarcerated offenders, in close contact, for eight hours each day (Hawkins, 1976).

If progress in personnel selection is handicapped by lack of knowledge of what constitutes the "good guard," the same is even more true of the training process. There continues to be substantial disagreement over what should be the method and substance of the training given to correctional officers. Until recent years, correctional officer candidates in most states were given little more than a brief rudimentary training experience, with the stress being on-the-job training. In the past decade, however, "correction academies" have been established in many states, with the apparent intention of systematizing what has previously been conveyed to guard recruits in the form of folklore, ideology, and ritual. Although little is known at present about these academies or their impact, some have heartily endorsed them as an unquestionable and distinct improvement over what prevailed in the past (Jacobs, forthcoming).

The line worker's world

It is a hazardous undertaking to speak in overly general terms about the world of the prison guard. The research, though limited, suggests there may be some important differences in different types of correctional institutions. Therefore, most of our remarks here will be confined to what is known about guards in traditional maximum security penitentiaries—the type of institution in which most adult convicts are confined in the United States. Regrettably, we will have less to say about the staff in juvenile institutions because less research has been conducted on them.

The persistent and yet changing problems of correctional officers as they go about their job are powerful testimony to the structural locus of prison problems, and an historical legacy of how their job has been modified to take account of the theories and dreams of reformers. Historically, prison guards have been organized along paramilitary lines, and have been expected to employ rigorous rule enforcement and coercion, if necessary, to maintain institutional security. Despite these articulated expectations, their superior officers judged their work performance on the basis of how "quietly" their work assignments were run or how few problems the guards created for them. The inherent contradiction between these two sets of expectations has been one of guards' principal problems. It has left them with the feeling that they are very much on their own when it comes to carrying out their job assignment and dealing with convicts.

Traditionally, neophyte guards learned quickly that in many respects they were every bit as much captive as their charges. They were far outnumbered by inmates, confined in the same close quarters with them, and completely unarmed—unlike the convicts who had ready access to numerous crude but effective homemade weapons. Adding to the feeling of captivity is the unavoidable proximity to and the necessity for interaction with some convicts who are considered to be unstable and even dangerous. "Tension continually looms over the prison threatening to explode into assault or even riot. This is drilled into the recruit during his first training classes. The guard's manual stresses the need for vigilance and alertness lest the unexpected take one unaware" (Jacobs and Retsky, 1975: 22). The chances are very good that during the normal day

> a correctional officer or other employee will be involved with an incident whose origin, location, timing and duration are unpredictable. This type of repetitious uncertainty takes as great a toll in strain and apprehension among staff as the more episodic occasions when notorious inmates become assaultive, get inebriated on homebrew or burn out another prisoner's cell. Incidents that reinforce staff beliefs about the capriciousness of prisoners occur almost daily (Guenther and Guenther, 1976: 518).

Nevertheless, guards tend to be dependent upon convicts for successful work performance, meaning that they must gain and maintain inmates' acquiescence—if not their active cooperation (Sykes, 1956). Recognizing this perverse form of dependence, convicts expect guards to be "reasonable" and consistent and not engage in overly strict rule enforcement. Consequently, cut off from consistent and clear support from their superiors, while expected to run a "tight," trouble-free work assignment, necessitating that they engage in reciprocity behavior with inmates, it is little wonder that guards have been described as feeling "on the spot" and in the middle of conflicting groups, demands, and pressures. A study of prison guards in six states notes simply that "the lack of clarity and, particularly, consistency regarding what is expected of them is a frustration that links officers from one part of the nation to the other" (May, 1976: 12).

Two recently published studies of prison guards suggest that one of the dominant aspects of their work world is danger and uncertainty (Guenther and Guenther, 1976; Jacobs and Retsky, 1975). Guards realize they must deal routinely with individuals whose cooperation they must gain, individuals who are considered to be unpredictable and even dangerous. Guards' problems are exacerbated by the fact that they are increasingly called upon to define themselves as rehabilitative personnel and to counsel and assist inmates, rather than supervise them and enforce rules. These pressures have intensified in recent years as treatment personnel have gained administrative authority in state departments of corrections. One result of this change has been the promulgation of treatment or rehabilitative theories, which leave guards without precise guides for dealing with inmates. Consequently, many guards seem to yearn for a return to the "good old days" when they were expected to be nothing more than rule enforcers and disciplinarians, to a time when guidelines for action were believed to have been unambiguous.

The guards' responses to their work problems appear to be of two types. First, they often retreat into an exaggerated reliance on and belief in strict rule enforcement and vigilance. On the basis of participant observation research at the federal penitentiary at Atlanta, Guenther has dubbed this the "stick man" ideology.

> Those subscribing to the "stick man" ideology—about two-thirds of the custodial staff—supported the view that they should expect the worst from the inmate population and would be well-advised to adopt a style which minimizes uncertainty: "Learn all about the inmates who are 'hot' "; "Be nosy: check the unusual *and* the usual"; "Give an order and then enforce it at all costs"; and "Say what you mean; mean what you say" (Guenther and Guenther, 1976: 522).

Second, and in contrast to these guards, the other one-third of the staff seemed to thrive upon the nonrepetitive, unsystematic features of correctional work.

> These officers look forward to quarterly job changes, the introduction of new treatment programs, new regulations affecting inmate conduct and a fluid, upwardly-mobile staff. This is not to suggest that they are foolhardy adventurers; on the contrary, they have as great a distaste for disarming an assaultive inmate, coping with a food strike, in short, unstable or dangerous situations, as the others. Their distinctive preference, though, is for a job in which initiative, challenge and ingenuity are required, and they are likely to tailor decisions about inmates individualistically rather than categorically (Guenther and Guenther, 1976: 532).

Other types of research suggest further that at least in traditional maximum security prisons guards and convicts tend to hold rather negative, stereotypical views of one another. Chang and Zastrow (1976) administered questionnaires to 220 convicts and 80 correctional officers in several midwestern state prisons. Each group was asked to rate 13 groups of persons on each of 20 bipolar, semantic differential scales. Of the 13 groups, prison guards assigned the lowest ranking to prison inmates, and inmates assigned the next to the lowest ranking to guards. (Convicts ranked convicts at the bottom of their rankings!) The authors conclude that: "Apparently security officers have fairly negative perceptions of inmates. . . . [S]ecurity officers may view inmates as being law-violating, unpredictable, sneaky, untrustworthy, dishonest, undependable and lazy" (Chang and Zastrow, 1976: 96).

The negativism, danger, and unpredictability that seem to be a pervasive part of guards' perceptions of their work may account for the extremely high rate of turnover among neophyte guards. This will probably continue to be true until significant changes are made in the administration of correctional institutions, until guards are compensated at higher levels, and until attempts are made to treat guards with the degree of importance and respect which their job deserves.

In recent years convict uprisings and the actions of appellate courts have combined to make line workers feel that they are insufficiently appreciated and generally under attack. Also, in some states, special efforts have been made to recruit minority guards and this has led to friction between old-line guards and the newer, younger, and black recruits (Jacobs, forthcoming). The responses of prison guards have paralleled those of other governmental employees faced with similar problems, for example, the police. Perhaps the most obvious change has been the growth of the union movement among correctional officers. This alone promises to make the future work of the prison guard different in some personal, critical respects from what it has been like in the past.

Sociological research suggests a relationship between managerial style and workers' feeling of alienation and dissatisfaction in the workplace (Etzioni, 1964). Traditionally, prison guards have been organized on a paramilitary model, and correctional administrators have relied heavily upon the manipulation of monetary and other punitive sanctions as a means of securing compliant predictable behavior from them. In fact, prison guards have been managed in much the same way in which inmates have been dealt with by prison administrators. But this appears to be the most alienative style of management. Not surprisingly, therefore, it is not only the lack of support from their superiors that disturbs line officers. The *manner* in which they are supervised and managed is another irritant to them. Presumably, this helps explain why guards in at least one study (Jacobs, forthcoming) listed difficulties with their superior officers as one of the "main disadvantages" of their job. Further evidence for assuming lack of trust for guards' superior officers comes from findings that guards generally feel "who you know" is more important in determining who is promoted than is competence on the job (Jacobs, forthcoming). However, at this time there is some doubt about the ability to generalize these findings, since another

A CONVICT'S OBSERVATIONS ON PRISON GUARDS

For a prisoner, of course, a guard is possibly the lowest imaginable form of humanoid life, a species somewhere about the level of the gorilla and often rather easily mistaken for one. He's called a bull, a pig, a wethead or a screw, and it's understood he'd rather shoot you than give you the time of day, stick you in the back rather than give you a crust of bread. . . .

The intriguing aspect of this view of guards, however, is that no inmate I've ever met came by it through his own experience—at least not initially. It's an opinion a prisoner automatically picks up at the door, along with his issue of prison clothes and his government-issue toothbrush, and from that point on he simply looks for incidents to *confirm* the view. Without even having to discuss it, he understands instinctively that such an opinion goes along with his khaki shirt and his cheapo boots, that it's wise to establish one's loyalties clearly and that guard-hating is an act which clearly confirms such a loyalty to the inmate cause. It's expressly part of the function of being a prisoner.

The unflattering guard profile is mostly untrue, but for an inmates [sic] there are, nevertheless, a number of signal advantages to subscribing to it. For one thing, the designation of a common enemy helps considerably to ensure inmate solidarity, which in turn tends to reduce the incidence rate of informers. For another, a vigorous hatred or anger is a remarkably dependable source of strength for an underdog; most inmates rely on it to carry them through the frustration of imprisonment to a far greater extent than they can probably afford to realize. Because no matter how justified or unjustified our practice of imprisoning malefactors may be, it has always been true that everything in a human being revolts against being stuffed into a cage, and *that* becomes the major issue once he or she is behind bars, not (or very much less) the question of *why* he is there. A prisoner will play along with the rehabilitative gobbledygook he's fed Inside for obvious reasons, but what he really wants is simply to get the hell out of there, and the actions of the guards provide a handy outlet for his resentment and irritation at being unable to do so. . . .

Most guards, unlike police officers or narcotics agents, never intended to become prison security personnel in the first place; for one thing, the pay is too low and the working conditions rather less than delightful. Most simply blundered into the job because they could find no other, and most are constantly on the lookout for better work somewhere else. The qualifications for becoming a prison guard are so low as to be almost nonexistent, which doesn't exactly attract the brightest minds and the most highly motivated humanitarians. . . . But above all else, it is simply a fact that most guards didn't become guards in order to satisfy some latent sadism or other perversion in their characters; they simply answered all the want-ads and Corrections gave them a job.

Source: Andreas Schroeder, *Shaking It Rough.* Garden City, N.Y.: Doubleday, 1976, pp. 151–53.

study (Joint Commission, 1968) did not find guards to be particularly dissatisfied with their relations with supervisors. Nevertheless, organizational theory and research suggest that one of the surest ways to modify the feelings—and presumably the behavior—of prison guards would be to overhaul the mechanisms by which they have been managed by their superiors. A more open, participative style of management, in which less reliance is placed upon the use of negative sanctions and more reliance is placed on the use of internalized professional standards, perhaps could produce dramatic changes in the attitudes and behavior of prison guards.

To this point our comments on the world of prison guards have stressed primarily the negative aspects of the work and the dissatisfactions that they experience. We would be unjustified, however, in assuming there are no rewarding and satisfying aspects to guards' work. One survey (Joint Commission, 1968) asked a national sample of line workers the question: "Do you find your job satisfying?" Responses are given for four different categories of correctional workers. Although line workers proved to be the least satisfied of all four groups, they are only slightly more dissatisfied than functional specialists. While 94 percent of the latter responded that their job is either "almost" or "usually" satisfying, 92 percent of the line workers responded similarly. When asked what they most liked about their job, line workers gave these answers: (1) the opportunity to work with and help people (mentioned by 54 percent of the respondents); (2) the work is interesting and satisfying and gives a feeling of accomplishment (mentioned by 37 percent); and (3) the chance to see results—to watch improvement (mentioned by 30 percent). When asked to rate them, the two most important job attributes for line workers were "job security" and "the chance to help others."

> Everywhere *Corrections Magazine* interviewed officers, they defined the "worthwhile" aspects of their jobs in highly personal anecdotes of inmates they believe they may have helped: Unscrambling administrative snarls for an inmate who may not have received what was due him . . . the isolated success stories of those who "made it on the street," job assignments they urged for a man who later used the newly learned skill "on the outside" (May, 1976: 47).

Research also suggests that prison guards may be more liberal in their attitudes toward the purpose of incarceration than many would think. The Joint Commission survey (1968) found that 98 percent of line workers felt "rehabilitation" should have primary or secondary emphasis in correctional agencies, while 48 percent felt "protection of society" should be emphasized. Only 12 percent thought that "punishment" should be a primary or secondary goal. Another study of guards in one state reached similar results: "Forty-six percent of the guards believe that 'rehabilitation' is the purpose of imprisonment, although a quarter of the force believes that punishment 'is the main reason for putting the offender in prison'" (Jacobs, forthcoming: 8). The author further notes that "with the recent trend toward embracing a punitive justification for imprisonment, the guards may be in the anomalous position of holding higher expectations about the prison's capacity to rehabilitate than academic and professional penologists" (forthcoming: 9).

Our comments to this point have focused entirely on line workers in the prison setting. Less is known about line workers in juvenile institutions. However, a study by Bartollas, Miller, and Dinitz (1976) gives a revealing glimpse of the subculture of youth leaders in one state's end-of-the-line maximum security institution for males. (In this institution, youth leaders are the lowest-level custodial personnel, roughly comparable to guards in the prison setting.) Unlike prisons, most of the youth leaders in this particular institution were black. The authors suggest that youth leaders "go through a series of stages or 'plateaus' during their careers" and that their relations with inmates "vary with the plateaus reached and the promotions received" (1976: 197).

> Of equal importance is the staff code which provides the guidelines for acceptable and unacceptable behavior. This code is divided into two sections, one of which is concerned with staff orientation to other staff, who will "make it" in the institution, what kinds of behavior to accept from others while on the job, and the acceptable attitudes toward various components of their work. The second part of the code concerns staff's approach to the youths, and consists of a series of tenets which are ranked from acceptable to unacceptable from the viewpoint of the staff (1976: 197–99).

The following are some of the significant components of section one of the staff code:

1. "Only Blacks 'Make it' Here":   Staff believe that white youth leaders are resented by black inmates, are often socially impotent for that reason, and consequently do not last as long as youth leaders.
2. "Unless You Have Been There, You Don't Know What it's Like": Youth leaders must come from the same social background as the inmates if they are to work effectively with them.
3. "Be Secure":   Youth leaders should maintain good security practices and be eternally vigilant about escapes.
4. "There Is a Certain Way to Inform on Staff":   Informally established procedures should be followed when youth leaders criticize

one of their own or register a formal complaint about a youth leader's performance.

5. "Don't Take No Shit": Staff members should not show hesitation in asserting their power in any confrontation with inmates.
6. "Be Suspicious": Youth leaders should always be suspicious because inmates will try to manipulate them at every opportunity.
7. "Be Loyal to the Team": Cottage employees should stick together, should assist one another, should not permit inmates to create dissention among them, and should try to settle all disputes internally, going to administrators only in cases of serious staff misconduct.
8. "Take Care of Yourself": Within certain limits it is permissible to exploit one's job and the institution itself for personal reasons.
9. "Stay Cool, Man": Do not lose your "cool" and overreact to emotional situations.
10. "The Administration Will Screw You": Administrators will try to exploit youth leaders in every possible way. Do not trust administrators.
11. "Don't Listen to Social Workers": Social workers are believed to be naive, easily manipulated by inmates, inclined to make poor decisions about inmates, and using their present position as a stepping-stone to a better job. Consequently, they should be pressured and co-opted to youth leaders' values so they do not interfere with the cottage functioning.
12. "Don't Do More than You Get Paid for": Youth leaders should not do work unless it is stated in the job description (1976: 200–6).

The second part of the staff code focuses on negligence in their work, exchange relations with inmates, and exploitation of inmates. Youth leaders should not be overly negligent in their duties because this may lead to serious incidents that bring "flack" from supervisors. It is permissible for youth leaders to use threats of bad reports and unsanctioned privileges to do their work and maintain a smoothly run cottage. Finally, while youth leaders are permitted to employ deception as a means of controlling inmates, other practices are impermissible: (1) encouraging victimization of one inmate by another, (2) physical brutality, (3) aiding escapes, and (4) exploiting inmates for sexual purposes (1976: 206–15).

Functional specialists

Functional specialists are the white-collar employees in correctional institutions and community programs (probation and parole). Included are social workers, psychologists, school teachers, and probation and parole officers. According to the Joint Commission (1969), functional specialists make up approximately 30 percent of the total number of correctional employees in the United

States. By far the majority of these are employed in community settings.

Characteristics

Whereas the median age of all correctional employees is 42.8 years (with only 25 percent under age 35) and the median length of time employed in corrections is 8.8 years (with 20 percent having three or less), among functional specialists the comparable statistics are 37.2 years (with 42 percent under age 35) and 4.6 years (with 38 percent having three years or less). The ranks of functional specialists also include more women (16 percent, as opposed to 12 percent for corrections generally) but only an infinitesimally larger percentage of blacks (1 percent, as compared with less than 0.5 percent for corrections generally). Only 17 percent of functional specialists have less than a B.A. degree, the lowest percentage for any category of correctional workers; among functional specialists, field settings have more college graduates than do institutions. Bachelor's degrees are mainly in the fields of sociology, psychology, and education. Fifteen percent of functional specialists have an M.A. degree and 1 percent have the Ph.D.

Entrance requirements and personnel screening

Little is known about the process of recruitment and screening for functional specialists. Apparently, in most jurisdictions both a college degree and a passing score on a civil service examination are required. The extent to which personal interviews are employed, and to what ends, is not clear.

The functional specialist's world

We have already indicated that little is known about the workaday experiences of prison guards; unfortunately, not much more is known about the workaday experiences and perspectives of functional specialists. Those recruited to the ranks of functional specialists apparently feel that they have a special rehabilitative mission to fulfill, and special skills for doing so. The limited empirical research suggests the contrary—that their impact is minimal and that they spend much of their time doing paperwork of limited importance for offenders and their concerns. Of course, here again we run the risk of overgeneralizing and thereby doing an injustice to the diversity that may actually exist on these matters. Certainly, there has been speculation about the differences among one type of functional specialist—the probation and parole officer (Glaser, 1964; Ohlin, Piven, and Pappenfort, 1956; Dembo, 1972; Irwin, 1970; Studt, 1973).

Functional specialists employed in institutional settings tend to be a dissatisfied group of employees. Much of their time is spent bemoaning their perceived lack of significant impact on the day-to-day operations of the institution and on the fates of offenders. Historically, these matters have been largely the purview of custodial staff members, and the daily reality of this fact is not lost on functional specialists. They deplore what they see as the institution's lack of a real commitment to the goals of treatment, and they console themselves with the collectively held belief that if only they were in real positions of authority things would be different (assumedly better).

Blau and Scott (1962), among others, have shown that persons who consider themselves to be "professionals" often chafe under the rules and regulations of the organizations employing them. This conflict has been shown to exist in a variety of organizations involving a variety of occupations; corrections is not immune to it. "Thus, the conscientious, professionally minded parole officer, particularly if educated as a social worker, is painfully aware of the conflicts between his professional values and the goals and practices of the parole organization" (Stanley, 1976: 130). Such personnel tend to see a conflict between loyalty to the organization and compliance with its regulations and to providing services for their clients on the basis of established or presumed professional norms. Also, Jacobs (1976) has argued that the marginality and demoralization of a group of counselors newly introduced into one maximum security prison setting stemmed from their belief that their job responsibilities did not meet their self-definition as professionals. Their marginality was further increased by "the absence of an extra-institutional professional reference group with which to identify and professional expertise upon which they could claim charismatic authority" (Jacobs, 1976: 139). Finally, a study of probation officers noted that "their lack of genuine professional status in the court is a constant source of personal anxiety, work alienation, and general dissatisfaction" (Blumberg, 1967: 130).

A common complaint among functional specialists states they are so overworked that insufficient time is left for adequate, "meaningful" work with offenders. The volume of paperwork which their jobs entail and seemingly require is another favorite complaint; this, too, is seen as leaving little time for counseling with offenders. The focus for all these perceived problems with treatment work, especially in institutional settings, becomes complaints about their salaries. This is an enduring topic of complaint, and one which is often cited as a principal reason for leaving correctional work. That many functional specialists plan to leave as soon as possible is a well-known fact. Indeed, turnover among correctional functional specialists is among the highest of any other group of correctional employees. The Joint Commission (1968) found that 14 percent of specialists surveyed were planning to make their career outside of corrections. The most often cited reason for why "people are leaving correctional work" was "economic reasons—low pay," which was mentioned by 63 percent of those who were surveyed. In terms of their general orientation to correctional work, functional specialists tend to bifurcate. There are those who find it possible or convenient to submerge their idealism and desire to work with offenders (*agency-identified* employees) and those who find it impossible to do so (*agency independents*). During the early years of their correctional employment, the first group increasingly comes to scale down their original hopes for correctional employment and becomes more "realistic" (i.e., more willing to accept agency definitions of the limitations of their work). The second group proves unable to make this adjustment, and many if not most of them resolve to leave correctional employment.

Our personal experience of working in correctional institutions suggests that these two groups of employees probably differ on basic demographic characteristics. Specifically, the group, which we have chosen to call "agency-identified," are older when they begin their correctional employment, probably have families, and have previously held at least two or more jobs. By contrast, the "agency-independents" are younger, more begin their correctional employment immediately after receiving their bachelor's degree, and they do not have as many family commitments. Their younger age, coupled with a lack of familial obligations, makes them able to be more independent in their stance toward the agency. Unlike their colleagues, they need not and do not permit themselves to become trapped in correctional employment (Shover, 1974).

Those functional specialists who are employed in field settings apparently differ from their institutionally employed counterparts in several critical aspects, although here again we are seriously handicapped by the absence of sufficient research. The Joint Commission (1968) found the former to be more satisfied with their work and generally more optimistic about the effectiveness of corrections. In other respects, however, they seem similar to their institutional counterparts. Studies (Wahl and Glaser, 1963; Stanley, 1976; Comptroller General, 1977) suggest that much of field workers' time is spent doing paperwork, too. A study of California parole officers noted that:

> . . . most had experienced struggle, change, and diversion from
> original career goals before reaching parole.
> For many of the agents, parole or a job in corrections was not a
> first career choice. Quite simply, parole offered the best-paying job
> with security and personnel benefits available at a critical choice-
> point in their work lives (Studt, 1973: 46).

These parole agents were remarkably uniform in reporting the satis-
factions of their jobs. "Almost without exception they listed these as
(1) enjoyment of the power they exercised in people's lives; (2)
their freedom from direct supervision in the field; and (3) the drama
and variety of the human situations to which they were exposed"
(Studt, 1973: 47).

Earlier we noted that there is no real evidence to support the contention that prison guards are particularly sadistic. This conclusion
is echoed by the research on correctional workers in field settings:

> In only the very rare instance did the Study's interviewers observe
> an agent evidencing in either words or actions, the need to hurt or
> punish that is often so glibly imputed as motivation to those who
> enter correctional work, although many of the agents interviewed
> appeared insensitive to the more subtle expressions of human feel-
> ings (Studt, 1973: 47).

These California parole agents were also consistent in reporting the
aspects of their work that they found irritating.

> For all of them, impatience with "red tape" and "meaningless"
> instructions from above was chronic. As in most bureaucracies,
> these bottom level workers felt unrecognized and unappreciated
> by upper administration; in the agents' view the people "at the top"
> had little awareness of the real nature of the agent's job (Studt,
> 1973: 47).

The study found remarkably little commonality among parole
agents in how they organized their work and planned the use of their
time. Parole agents in the sample

> gave minimal attention to the systematic analysis and planning for
> individual cases, and almost none to the examination of their total
> caseloads in terms of types of needs represented.
> Instead, most agents' work revealed an ad hoc, reactive approach
> to problems solving, at least in part a response to the somewhat
> conflictual pressures in their assignments (Studt, 1973: 50-1).

Blumberg's (1967) study of probation officers in New York City
presents a generally consistent picture. He notes that the 60 probation officers studied "had envisioned other jobs than those in which
they find themselves," but they "have surrendered earlier illusions

to accept the realities of limited career opportunities" (1967: 154). Blumberg's sketch of the probation officers in this particular court stresses their preoccupation with writing presentence reports, the incredible vacuity of their reports, and their anxiety over lack of recognized professional status. These probation officers make heavy use of hostile, stereotypic labels and vituperative words to describe their clients, a practice that is one part response to the strains and pressures of their work and one part response to their fear of being manipulated by administrators and clients. Further, "Frustrated as professionals, stripped of real decision-making power, lacking a genuine career motif, and assigned relatively low status by the community, it is not surprising that probation workers often develop a high degree of cynicism" (1967: 158). Blumberg's study differs from the California study in finding a generally more hostile and cynical stance toward clients. In other respects, however, the two studies are quite consistent.

OFFENDERS

Despite the vast accumulation of research on offenders, surprisingly little of it has sought to determine the nature of offenders' perspectives on the correctional system and particular groups of employees within it. Nevertheless, this is the type of material we require for present objectives. The rationale for this is quite simple: If one group of people would change another groups' attitudes or beliefs, then the first group must know something about how the target group views the entire operation, how they view the process of being the objects of change efforts. We take this to be a fundamentally important type of data for anyone seriously committed to the goal of corrections. The essential validity of this point has been clearly recognized in an English study of a residential treatment center:

> Perhaps the most important aspect of the lack of systematic information regarding residential treatment in this country is that we know little or nothing about how the young offenders themselves perceive it. The perception of the nature of residential establishments is changing in the minds of those who administer the system but there is as yet little evidence to suggest that it is changing in the minds of the boys for whom it is designed. Possibly an important factor in the apparent "failure" of our residential schools is the fact that those who run the system and those who are subject to it define the situation in different ways. . . . More generally the regime and purpose of the school may be interpreted in significantly different ways by boys and staff (Gill, 1974: 318).

And we regard it as equally important on the grounds that since offenders are human beings and are the objects of the most severe sanctions at the disposal of the state we should inquire as to how they feel about the treatment to which they are subjected and incorporate this knowledge into correctional programs.

Characteristics

We have made passing reference to the fact that in most respects, besides social class background, offenders differ from any group of employees in the correctional system. Offenders are generally younger, poorer, more poorly educated, and representatives of minority racial groups. These differences alone are serious enough to cast some doubt on the ability of the correctional system's employees to constructively influence the lives of their clients. When the involuntary nature of correctional servitude and treatment is added to the fact that much of what passes for "treatment" in corrections is seen by offenders as irrelevant to what actually happens to them, we have the makings of two separate perspectives on the correctional experience and the world, jogging along side by side with only occasional points of contact.

Offender's perspectives

During our period of employment at the Illinois State Penitentiary, a common saying among convicts when referring to treatment workers was "those guys can't help you but they sure can *hurt* you." By this, convicts meant that treatment personnel had no real control over any of the important decisions that affected their daily lives; they certainly couldn't guarantee that a convict would be paroled on a particular appearance before the parole board. However, treatment personnel could, by saying sufficiently negative things about a convict, assure that negative decisions would be made by others. The upshot of all this was that convicts generally felt that they had much to lose and little to gain from seeking out and talking with treatment personnel.

Apparently, offenders do not take exception or quarrel with the right of the correctional system to have them within its grasp. Most of them realize and accept the fact that they have broken the law, that the laws they broke were legitimate, and that persons who break these laws should pay some kind of a penalty. Studies seem agreed on this point. What offenders *do* object to is the *way* in which they are treated, the objectification which accompanies their movement through the system, and the fact that they are dehumanized and treated inhumanely in the process.

The defendant sees himself as an object in the hands of a "they" that really doesn't care very deeply about *him;* he sees in the substance of the law itself a set of principles for behavior whose morality and virtue he accepts; in the enforcement of the law he sees not principles but work—a variety of men doing their jobs (Casper, 1972: 168). (Emphasis in the original.)

Offenders appear to expect that they will have to suffer some unpleasantness as a result of conviction. They are unprepared, however, for what they see as the petty, gratuitous and systematic nature of the oppression that they sometimes must endure. Because they expect to pay with unpleasantness, they are often pleasantly surprised when something better is forthcoming. Their feelings of appreciation must not, however, be interpreted as evidence that they are changing themselves or are amenable to treatment. It simply means that they react warmly as human beings to being treated in a manner which affirms their essential humanity. This explains why they often feel real gratitude and even warmth toward particular correctional employees while continuing to feel generally negative toward the system as a whole (Berman, 1976). Having expected to find universal hostility or indifference, they are pleasantly surprised occasionally to find the opposite—and they react in kind.

Offenders take exception with the feeling that the correctional system exists on their succorance; that they are essentially playing functional roles within a gigantic bureaucracy which is primarily concerned with assuring itself of continued existence—if not growth. For example, a parole violator told Irwin (1970: 173): "They have that parole system set up to make you fail. I guess they have business going in this state and once they get you hooked into the system they don't want to let you go. They release you from the institution with a line on you and after a while they give it a jerk and you find yourself back."

Other components of offenders' perspective toward corrections

---

The only quality we admired in any bull was consistency. So he was a total prick, who would beef you for an overdue library book, that was fair enough, we knew him by his rattles and behaved accordingly. But if one day he let us slide on a major beef and the next day wrote us up for jerking off, we knew we were dealing with a dangerous man, who was, in addition, no more principled than ourselves.

Source: Malcolm Braly. *False Starts.* Boston: Little, Brown, 1976, p. 195.

generally, and treatment programs specifically, have been discussed (Irwin, 1974). Many offenders appear to feel that the entire correctional system is shot through with hypocrisy, that they are treated unjustly, and that they are made to suffer more in the name of rehabilitation than would have been the case if they had simply been "punished" for their crimes. A great many offenders view the entire development and impact of rehabilitative programs as having mixed blessings.

The fact that correctional confinement and treatment are involuntary is an important aspect of the way offenders view these things. Those offenders who wish to participate in a treatment program would prefer to not have this seen as something they were coerced to do; they would rather see it as something they elected to do as competent human beings, not because they are deficient in some way. In fact, this entire aspect of the involuntary nature of correctional confinement and treatment colors every aspect of offenders' reactions to it. As an English study of a residential treatment program noted:

> ... to talk about the "family life" of the school and to look at White-gate as anything other than an abnormal society is to evade the problem. *To the boys for whom it operated Whitegate was a place where young offenders were sent.* Heated swimming pools, floodlit playgrounds, late television and relaxed staff-boy relations were of course important, but their effects were superimposed onto this more fundamental definition (Gill, 1974: 333). (Emphasis ours.)

Offenders generally do not want to be rehabilitated; *they want out* of the correctional system. As a result, their interactions with correctional employees will reflect their fears that something they do or say will prolong their stay—whether within an institution or "on paper" (parole). This makes for a very guarded quality to many of the contacts between staff and offenders. Staff contributes to this quality of guardedness by often assuming that offenders are trying to manipulate them for some private advantage. Consequently, the resulting interaction is a shallow caricature of the interaction that staff members would like to have with offenders. An ethnographic study comments on the interaction between parolees and parole agents—that

> parolees are, in general, not actively hostile toward the agents as persons, tending instead to blame "the system"; that they often find agents more decent as persons than they expected; and that personal antipathy is not the ubiquitous block to helping relationships that it has sometimes been described as being. On the other hand, the Study's evidence suggests equally strongly that most agent-parolee

relationships are superficially friendly; and that the ambiguous structure in which interaction occurs, together with the critical jeopardy inherent in it for the parolees, tends to press both agents and parolees toward (1) the maintenance of an interaction relationship that is bland and diffuse, and (2) the avoidance of confronting tough issues until a problem situation becomes openly critical (Studt, 1973: 109).

In other words, parolees tend to feel that the conditions and terms of parole make "honest interaction with an officer impossible" (Citizens' Inquiry, 1975: 123).

Interestingly, findings very similar to these are reported in an English study of parole. Morris and Beverly (1975) studied 69 men from pre-release through their first six months on parole. The subjects were interviewed three times during this period. According to the parolees, while they were in prison parole "was a topic of endless discussion, but it [only resulted] in a great deal of speculation and guesswork, a reinforcement of the general air of mystification surrounding the decision-making process, and in consequence breeding strong feelings of resentment" (Morris and Beverly, 1975: 83). During interviews with parolees and parole officers it became apparent that some fundamental discrepancies existed between the two groups' perceptions of one another and the nature of their relationship. For instance, parole officers

> considered they had given much more help than was thought to be the case by the parolees themselves. . . . More significant is the fact that the perceptions of parolees and [parole] officers as to the *nature* of the help given differed markedly. Where parolees interpreted the [parole] officers' remarks as 'general chat' the latter often saw themselves as giving advice on the parolees' social and domestic life (1975: 134). (Emphasis in the original.)

Further, parole officers "were apt to consider many aspects of their clients' lives as problematic which were not perceived as such by the parolees themselves." Also, matters such as

> debt, marital problems, drink, unemployment and ill-health were often not felt to be problematic by the parolees because they were "normal" conditions of life for many who suffered them. They were also known to be problems experienced by most of their friends and relatives—even those never convicted of an offence—so that had they not been parolees they might never have been defined as having "problems" (1975: 99).

Importantly, as the parolees probably realized, many of their "problems were, in any case, intractable and were related to wider aspects of the social structure. [Parole] officers could only hope to deal with the more transitory ones ..." (1975: 139).

The authors seem surprised to find these discrepancies in officers' and parolees' perceptions, for they subsequently note that "little is known about how they [parolees] feel regarding the values that are imposed upon them." But, "the findings cast doubts upon the positive treatment value of [parole] supervision" (1975: 164).

Despite these findings, there is little evidence of animosity between parolees and their parole officers. The authors note:

> There is little doubt that for the most part [parole] officers were seen by the parolees as reliable people who treated them as adults, even in some cases as friends ... They sought a relationship devoid of paternalism, authoritarianism and even of professionalism. Very few complained of feeling badly treated, by which they meant feeling that the [parole] officer regarded them as incompetent, and/or treated them like children.
>
> Nevertheless the most overwhelming impressions to emerge from the interviews with parolees were of the irrelevance and superficiality of supervision. Most parolees thought that the understanding [parole] officers had of them as people, and of their life-style, was very limited, and such views persisted throughout the six months follow-up period (Morris and Beverly, 1975: 137).

In short, the relationships between parole officers and parolees is generally shallow and not especially helpful to the parolee. However, there is little hostility between them; in fact, in some cases there is even mutual respect and liking for one another.

7

The regimens of correctors: Jails and detention centers

A diverse set of agencies and dispositions is clustered under the umbrella term *corrections*. Some have been the object of extensive theorizing and research, while others have received much less scrutiny. Relatively neglected are some newcomers on the correctional scene, such as community correctional centers, but paradoxically, some of the historically oldest correctional regimens (for example, jails and workhouses) also have been little studied. On the other hand, prisons and training schools have held a special fascination for sociological research. Such agencies have been examined, partly because of their intrinsic appeal but also because they are "extreme" examples of more inclusive categories, such as complex organizations. Thus, many studies of the prison have been conducted with an eye toward what they can tell us about complex organizations or "total institutions."

The systematic omissions characteristic of past correctional theory and research extend beyond a mere lack of coverage of the entire range of existing correctional agencies and processes. In addition, as we suggested in Chapter 2, there have not been sufficient studies of alternative questions and issues. While much attention has been paid to some problems—such as the effectiveness of rehabilitative programs—our knowledge and understanding of correctional problems, processes, and alternatives is incomplete. To some extent, these problems can be rectified by drawing upon an accumulation of theory and research developed by other social scientists on such processes as the validity of clinical diagnoses, the accuracy of clinical predictions, and the self-fulfilling processes in the provision of services to offenders. We will be able to employ this body of theory and research as it pertains to the structure and functioning of correctional regimens.

In this chapter, and in the three that follow, we review what is known about a variety of correctional regimens. However, because of the systematic omissions of the past, our knowledge of some agencies and processes is necessarily sketchy. Chapter 8 will concentrate on prisons for adult males. Chapter 9 will discuss training schools and women's prisons, and Chapter 10 will deal with community correctional programs and agencies, primarily probation and parole.

A NOTE ON SOCIAL CLASS, CRIMINAL JUSTICE, AND CORRECTIONS

Most types of humanly and socially injurious conduct are unevenly distributed in the social class structure. In turn, this unevenness reflects the differential distribution of the volume and quality of resources available to persons at different positions in the class structure. Because of their positions of affluence and organizational domination, members of the economic elite are able not only to perpetrate socially injurious acts that members of the underclasses could never commit, but also to constrain others to commit injurious acts "for" them. Given the resources controlled by members of the elite, it would be a most unlikely and indeed irrational act for them to take another person's money with a threat of bodily harm. It is more likely that members of the economic elite would engage in conduct that leads to the adulteration of packaged food, pollution of the environment, or violation of their employees' rights to be free from unsafe or unhealthy working conditions. The same cannot be said about members of the underclass. Their resources are so limited that their socially injurious conduct is usually committed by them *personally* and involves the use of guile, threats of bodily harm to victims, or frontal assaults on others' property.

All types of socially or humanly injurious conduct do not have an equal probability of being designated as "criminal" by the state. While sociologists have not been able to agree on the reasons for this, its validity seems uncontested. The modally injurious conduct of the underclasses has a much greater likelihood of being condemned by criminal law than does the harmful conduct of an elite. The elite's behavior, if noticed at all by the state, is likely to be circumscribed by civil or administrative regulations, not the criminal law.

This differential response to the injurious behaviors of members of different social classes is continued into the realm of organized reactions to those behaviors. We have one set of ideologies and institutions for dealing with the crimes of the underclasses, and an entirely different set for dealing with the dangerous and harmful conduct modally engaged in by elites and those who do their dirty work. Social scientists have generally shied away from conducting research on elites and the agencies that deal with their misconduct. There are a variety of ideological and methodological reasons for this omission, but an important upshot of it is that we know more about the structure and functioning of those agencies that deal with underclass crime than those that supposedly are charged with reacting to crimes and other dangerous conduct of elites. We know a great deal about the police, criminal courts, and prisons, but rather little about the various administrative and regulatory agencies.

JAILS

Historical

The jail is an exception to the assertion that we know a great deal about agencies that react to underclass criminality. There has been little systematic research on the jail and much of it is of recent origin. This is paradoxical because the jail has the longest history of any type of penal institution; it can be traced to the earliest forms of civilization and government. Some of its predecessors were the unscalable pits, dungeons, suspended cages, and sturdy trees to which prisoners were variously chained or confined pending trial on criminal charges (Mattick, 1974).

> The history of the American jail is firmly rooted in Anglo-Saxon society, from which we have derived most of our social institutions. The American jail is a curious hybrid between the 10th century gaol with its principal function being to detain arrested offenders until they were tried, and the 15th and 16th century houses of correction with their special function being punishment of minor offenders, debtors, vagrants, and beggars (Flynn, 1973: 49).

Historically, the jail has served multiple purposes and these generally continue today. Jails confine in one facility such diverse groups as those persons awaiting trial, inmates serving misdemeanor sentences, suspected mental patients, alleged parole violators, felony prisoners in transit, and chronic drunkenness offenders in the process of "drying out." And some jails continue to serve as a place of pretrial detention for juveniles.

Since the time of its adoption in America, the jail has remained a peculiarly local institution that manifests all the variation in financing, structure, and operation characteristic of local communities and government in the United States. The majority of American jails are located in rural areas, usually in the county seat. They were built from 50 to 80 years ago, hold small numbers of inmates, and are dirty and dilapidated. Although far fewer in number, the second major type of jail is located in large urban areas. These jails hold as many as several thousand inmates, and collectively they confine more than 50 percent of the nation's jail population. The typical city or county jail is under the control of the local police, either the county sheriff, a duly appointed deputy or warden, or the chief of police.

Current conditions

Although sparse, sociological research and writing on jails has generally emphasized a few recurrent themes: the squalidness of physical facilities, the frequent indiscriminate mixing of all types of inmates, the poor training of staff, the absence of recreational or supposedly rehabilitative programs, and the presence of a junglelike atmosphere in which stronger and institutionally experienced inmates dominate the institutionally inexperienced and weak. Sociologists have not studied the jail with nearly the degree of theoretical interest or analytic acumen they have brought to studies of the prison and training school.

In 1970 and again in 1972, the U.S. Bureau of the Census conducted a survey of facilities, services, programs, and inmates in American jails. The data, although now more than five years old, give us the most complete and current picture of the jail. A *jail* was defined in the survey as any locally administered institution that has authority to retain adults for 48 hours or longer. The 1972 National Jail Census (U.S. Dept. of Justice, 1975a) located 3,921 such facilities operating in the United States. The Census Bureau also conducted personal interviews with a sample of 4,300 jail inmates throughout the United States in June and July 1972. Inmates were asked their age, marital status, educational attainment, work experience, confinement status, and income before incarceration. Questions were also asked concerning length of sentence, most serious offense with which they were charged or sentenced, bail status, participation in rehabilitative programs, and past criminal record. Estimates for the total American jail population of approximately 141,600 persons are based on responses given by this sample of inmates.

Table 7–1 is a summary of selected characteristics of jail inmates in the United States. The reality of the assertion that the jail exists to deal with underclass conduct could not be any clearer than it is

TABLE 7–1
Selected socioeconomic and legal characteristics of jail inmates in the United States, June–July 1972

Race	Percent
White	56.4
Black	41.6
Other	2.0
Sex	
Male	95.0
Female	5.0
Prearrest annual income	
Less than $2,999	55.0
$3,000–$7,499	31.0
$7,500 or more	11.0
Not available	3.0
Educational attainment	
Elementary only (0–8)	23.0
Some secondary (9–11)	43.0
Completed secondary (12)	24.0
College (more than 12)	10.0
Marital status	
Never married	50.0
Separated, divorced or widowed	26.0
Married	24.0
Confinement status	
Awaiting trial	35.9
Serving sentence	42.5
Other stages of adjudication	21.5

Source: U.S. Department of Justice, Law Enforcement Assistance Administration, *Survey of Inmates of Local Jails: Advance Report.* Washington, D.C.: National Criminal Justice Information and Statistics Service, n.d.

in Table 7–1. In no way could the profile of jail inmates be said to approximate that of the general population. Instead, jail inmates are disproportionately black and impoverished, and in other ways disadvantaged. Further, the heterogeneity of the jail population is apparent from an inspection of the category "confinement status" in Table 7–1. Data such as these have led one critic of the jail to refer to it as "the ultimate ghetto of the criminal justice system" (Goldfarb, 1975).

An interesting revelation in the Census Bureau report is the substantial variation between states in the number of jail inmates per 100,000 population. Ignoring Vermont's unusually low rate (0.4) and confining our attention only to the 48 contiguous states, Iowa had a jail population in 1972 of 18.6 inmates per 100,000 population, while the comparable rate for Georgia was 131.9. (Table 7–2.)

The personnel, size, physical facilities, and program offerings of local jails show considerable variation as well. Of the total 3,921 jails

TABLE 7–2
Jail populations for the 50 states, June–July 1972

State	Number of jails	Number of jail inmates	Inmates per 100,000 population
Total	3,921	141,588	68.0
Alabama	107	2,972	84.4
Alaska	7	87	26.8
Arizona	38	1,754	89.4
Arkansas	104	941	46.9
California	152	25,348	124.2
Colorado	76	1,427	60.4
Connecticut*	—	—	—
Delaware*	—	—	—
Florida	164	8,104	131.9
Georgia	239	6,243	131.9
Hawaii	4	124	15.2
Idaho	59	411	54.4
Illinois	103	4,894	43.5
Indiana	90	2,017	38.2
Iowa	90	537	18.6
Kansas	123	870	38.4
Kentucky	137	1,896	57.4
Louisiana	98	3,340	89.4
Maine	14	247	24.1
Maryland	22	2,218	54.8
Massachusetts	16	1,847	31.9
Michigan	89	4,148	46.0
Minnesota	76	1,071	27.6
Mississippi	98	1,498	66.4
Missouri	141	2,246	47.3
Montana	66	281	39.2
Nebraska	100	742	48.6
Nevada	24	656	123.1
New Hampshire	11	283	36.6
New Jersey	33	3,517	47.9
New Mexico	39	899	83.6
New York	76	15,190	82.7
North Carolina	98	2,455	47.0
North Dakota	47	125	19.7
Ohio	161	4,804	44.8
Oklahoma	107	1,808	68.7
Oregon	65	1,185	54.2
Pennsylvania	77	6,274	52.7
Rhode Island*	—	—	—
South Carolina	97	2,424	90.2
South Dakota	57	295	43.4
Tennessee	115	3,372	82.8
Texas	318	9,802	84.5
Utah	33	475	42.1
Vermont	4	4	0.9
Virginia	96	3,119	65.5
Washington	76	2,410	70.5
West Virginia	59	1,054	58.7
Wisconsin	76	1,767	39.0
Wyoming	33	192	55.5

* No locally operated jails.
Source: U.S. Department of Justice, Law Enforcement Assistance Administration. *The Nation's Jails: A Report on the Census of Jails from the 1972 Survey of Inmates of Local Jails.* Washington, D.C.: National Criminal Justice Information and Statistics Service, May 1975.

THE TOMBS [NEW YORK CITY]

The cell—five by eight, with a seven foot ceiling—was constructed of steel plate, with the usual bars on the front. I had a cot without a mattress, a toilet without seat, a diminutive wash basin with a single cold water spigot, a steel seat and a table, hinged to the wall. I was locked in the cell 19 hours a day. It was hot in the Tombs in August—and it smelled. No air moved near the ventilator opening in the wall. After breakfast I was permitted out of the cell for two hours, when I could walk up and down the aisle in front of the cell. After lunch I could promenade for three more hours.

*   *   *   *   *

Theoretically this was a jail, a facility for holding men for a short time prior to trial. Thus it had no yard, and no indoor recreational facilities. There were some old battered decks of cards around, and occasionally someone would produce a checker set out of nowhere. That was it. Somehow the men were supposed to pass the time doing absolutely nothing.

*   *   *   *   *

When I first arrived I ate everything indiscriminately. In fact, after Laredo it tasted good. But after about a month my stomach rebelled; luckily I was able to buy a couple of containers of milk from the commissary cart, drinking one with my lunch and the other at supper. Somehow I managed. Everything was so flat, I wondered that salt was not available. An investigation revealed that the salt did indeed come up from the kitchen with each meal, but the "runners," the men who were in charge of dishing out the food, put the salt aside and peddled it for cigarettes. I paid my pack of cigarettes and got a container of salt, enough to last at least a month. However, on the following weekly shakedown, the hack who inspected my cell picked up the container and emptied it down the toilet. After this happened a second time I realized this was part of a petty conspiracy between the runners and the guards. The guards depended on the runners for the orderly maintenance of the institution, and this was their payoff.

The runners, unlike all of us on the fourth floor, were sentenced prisoners. They slept in dormitories and did not mingle with the unsentenced prisoners, whom they considered subjects for prey. On weekends the runners would sell cigarettes, for three times the regular price. Or if a new arrival came in after suppertime, they might bring him a sandwich for an appropriate price. The runners rationalized such peddling on the grounds that, since they were not paid, this was the only way they could get smokes.

Source: Morton Sobell. *On Doing Time.* New York: Charles Scribner's Sons, 1974, pp. 96, 100, 102.

in the United States, 74.0 percent held fewer than 21 inmates, 23.1 percent held from 21 to 49 inmates, and 2.9 percent confined more than 250 inmates. Overall, only a small proportion of the total jail population had access to any social or rehabilitative services and programs. These programs, where they existed at all, were far more likely to be offered in large jails than in small ones.

> Approximately six out of every ten jails provided facilities for religious services, but no other single type of program was found in a majority of jails. Alcoholic treatment programs were available in only about one-third of the jails and drug addiction treatment programs in approximately one-fourth. Programs of inmate counseling, remedial education, vocational training, and job placement were found in slightly fewer than one-fifth of all jails . . . In all, only about one-tenth of the inmate population of the Nation's jails participated in federally and locally sponsored programs, religious services excepted (U.S. Dept. of Justice, n.d.: 9).

In 1972 only 8 percent of all sentenced jail inmates in the United States were participating in a work-release program.

> A related practice, namely, allowing selected sentenced inmates to serve their time on weekends, was permitted by nearly half the Nation's jails, including almost three out of every five of the large jails. Only about 900 inmates were serving their sentences on weekends, however (U.S. Dept. of Justice, n.d.: 10).

Generally, the daily routine in our jails is one of the unrelieved idleness. Card playing, conversations, meditation, and occasional television viewing are the only options available.

The general public only becomes aware of jail conditions through the misfortune of family members or acquaintances, or whenever a scandal or media exposé occurs. The latter occurs with predictable regularity, especially in the larger cities. Confinement in filthy, dilapidated facilities and deprivation of adequate food and medical care are common. So, too, are violence and various forms of predation among jail inmates. Beatings, extortion, and sexual assaults are commonplace occurrences in America's jails. Supervision is weak or absent, inmates are housed in large heterogeneous groups, and jails are run in such a way as to provide minimal problems and disruptions for custodial staff. This leaves the inmates free to work out their own internal order. Under such conditions, individuals experienced in crime and accustomed to life in jails and penitentiaries assume positions of informal leadership and control. Glaser notes that "control over inmate behavior usually can be achieved by other inmates more immediately, directly, and completely in jails than in

---

A CONVICT'S EXPERIENCE IN A SUBURBAN COUNTY JAIL

My first night in jail, after sentencing, was one I shall never forget! After witnessing all the crying and carrying on of my family, relatives, and friends just hours before, I was in no mood to laugh and joke with the rest of the inmates on our tier in the County Jail that night. As you might expect since our county is less known for violence than most, those in our county were less violent. In fact they were fairly decent fellows, as far as convicts go. All were not convicts, however, naturally we had our share of petty thieves, traffic violators, and drunks which made up over half of the population. My stay of ten days in the county jail was actually quite pleasant.

Source: Dae H. Chang and Warren B. Armstrong, eds. *The Prison: Voices from the Inside.* Cambridge, Mass.: Schenkman, 1972, pp. 225–26.

---

other types of confinement institutions, such as penitentiaries or State Hospitals" (1971: 239). A glimpse of the extreme abuses which can result under such conditions is provided in a report of sexual assaults in the Philadelphia city prison system (Davis, 1968). The study found that sexual assaults are epidemic, and went on to state that "virtually every slightly built young man committed by the courts is sexually approached within a day or two after his admission to prison. Many of these young men are repeatedly raped by gangs of inmates" (Davis, 1968: 9).

Reform proposals

The jail has been a disgrace to every generation since its inception. Each has called for its reform. However, succeeding generations have sometimes rejected the pet reforms of earlier ones, seeing them as misguided and foolish. Certainly, there is no shortage of contemporary proposals for jail reform. Most of them emphasize the same themes and all stem from the currently popular litany of the jail's shortcomings.

The fact that jails are locally controlled has long been seen as a problem and a fundamental impediment to reform. "Jails are left in a paradoxical situation: localities cling tenaciously to them but are unwilling or unable to meet even minimal standards. 'The problem of American jails, put most concisely, is the problem of local control' " (National Advisory Commission, 1973: 274). Four reforms have been proposed to deal with local governments' refusal or fiscal inability to provide clean, safe, and adequately staffed jails with

even minimal recreational and rehabilitative programs: (1) the issuance of minimum standards for the construction and operation of
jails, (2) state inspection of local jails, (3) the development of regional jails, and (4) the development of diversified institutions for
the jail's heterogeneous population.

At least two organizations, the Federal Bureau of Prisons and the
American Correctional Association, have made past attempts to develop and publish minimum standards for the construction and operation of jails. Proposals of this type will be discussed at greater
length in Chapters 12 and 13. It will suffice now to point out that
such efforts have met with little apparent success in mitigating the
problems of jails in America. Some of the reasons for this are also
discussed in Chapters 12 and 13.

In the past decade a number of states have established procedures for state inspection of local jails. The objective of such endeavors is to use state expertise and fiscal incentives to bring about
improvements in local jail conditions. The principal difficulty with
such efforts is their frequent failure to include any mechanism for
enforcement of jail standards. "At the last tally there were 21 states
without legislation which provides for enforcement and 34 states
without legislation requiring any kind of jail inspection" (Matheny,
1976: 139).

Regional jails serve multiple cities or counties in one geographical
area of a state. The development of such facilities provides a mechanism through which fiscally poor counties that otherwise could not
afford nor need a modern jail can pool their resources and operate
such a facility.

A final proposal for overcoming some of the problems of the jail
calls for the creation of diversified facilities, each of which would
serve one or more of the types of individuals now housed together in
the jail. The juvenile detention home represents an earlier and successful effort to establish a more specialized facility for such purposes. More recently, detoxification centers have been established
in many American cities to provide an alternative disposition for
drunkenness offenders who formerly would have been placed in jail.
A number of people have suggested that this movement toward diversified facilities be carried one step further by creating a special
place of detention for those awaiting trial on criminal charges (for
example, Goldfarb, 1975) They believe it is an injustice to confine
those who have not been convicted of any crime with those who are
serving penal sentences. Too often the former are subjected to in-
timidation and abuse from the latter, or receive the dubious benefit
of their criminal experiences and attitudes.

The impetus to reform the jail has probably gained momentum in

THE COOK COUNTY [CHICAGO] JAIL

When I entered the Cook County Jail I was assigned to cell Block H-4. This was intended for "young offenders" but it was a mad house. There were over 140 inmates in a cell block intended for 84. Inmates slept on every inch of floor space available, and fighting was an hourly occurrance. In the Cook County Jail only the strong survive as men—the weak are used for the sexual expression of the strong, the weak do the work.

Each Cell block was run by three inmates, the strongest, and no officer ever came inside the cell block. During the time I was on H-4 (two months) no officer ever came inside. The officers allowed the count to be taken by the three strongest inmates, the food was distributed by these inmates, the cells assigned when they became available, etc.

The three inmates who run the cell block or tier have titles as follows: the "Barn Boss," who is in charge of disipline [sic] among the inmates—the "Assistant Barn Boss" who, as his title implies, assists the "Barn Boss" in keeping disipline [sic], and the "Tier Clerk," who keeps the count and assigns the cells, and handles the commissary orders (a very lucrative job).

While I was "Tier Clerk" on H-4 I also assisted the two "Barn Bosses" in keeping disipline [sic] because we were so very overcrowded, thus overworked. Usually, if someone got out of line on the tier it was necessary to give them only a warning. However, if this warning was ignored, he didn't receive a second warning. He got his skull cracked. At night, after everyone was locked in their cells (the three men—the barn bosses and clerk's cells were never locked) the officer would open the offender's cell, and the three of us would go in on him. When we beat an inmate we used clubs, refered to as "shit-sticks," and the injuries were usually serious enough to require hospital treatment. After the inmate had been beaten he was dragged to the front of the tier, thrown into a bullpen, and picked up by an officer. They never came back to that tier again, and they knew better than to act up on the new tier they were sent to after being released from the hospital. I beat one inmate before I became "Tier Clerk," and helped beat several others while "Tier Clerk."

I would also like to add that if a man wishes to survive in comfort in the Cook County Jail he must obtain a position of authority on his tier. These three positions are often fought for, the strongest holding them. I remember that Murphy, the "Tier Clerk," and the "Barn Boss" at the time, a fellow named Simms, used to practice boxing everyday. It was necessary and they became quite good.

Source: Dae H. Chang and Warren B. Armstrong, eds. *The Prison: Voices from the Inside.* Cambridge, Mass.: Schenkman, 1972, pp. 49–50.

recent years because of jail inmates' efforts to improve their plight through court action. For example,

> in a case involving the Jefferson Parish Jail in Louisiana, the court was concerned about specific situations in the jail, particularly the many mentally disturbed people who are housed there and the physical conditions of the place which the court called "a combination medieval dungeon and zoo," used simply to "stow people" (Goldfarb, 1975: 436).

Jails have not escaped the inmate rebellions of the 1970s, and these, too, have shed light on the problems of the jail. As Goldfarb (1975: 372) notes,

> The protesting inmates' lists of grievances are remarkably alike. Fundamental to them all is a desire to be treated with some measure of personal dignity. The most damaging part of imprisonment, prisoners say, is the demeaning and dehumanizing stripping away of personal identity that begins when they enter the institution's receiving room. Such treatment is especially enraging when it is applied to pretrial detainees, who compose the majority of most jail populations, and who have been convicted of nothing.

DETENTION CENTERS

Detention centers are the juvenile analogue of the jail for adults. They are used to confine juveniles awaiting court action and a variety of others who are placed there because local authorities and agencies have no other place to put them (for example, those youths considered dependent and neglected). On June 30, 1974, there were 331 detention centers in the United States, all but 50 of them at the local governmental level (U.S. Dept. of Justice, 1977: 22). These institutions confined 11,010 juveniles, of which 69.9 percent were males and 30.1 percent were females (U.S. Dept. of Justice, 1977: 34).

Detention centers are a product of the juvenile reform movement of the last decade of the 19th century. One of the principal rationales for building them was to remove juveniles from local jails where, it was believed, they were exploited by adult inmates and exposed to criminalizing influences. Although detention centers have gradually become more commonplace during the past 70 years, there are still many localities that confine juveniles in their jails. A March 1970 survey of local jails in the United States found that juveniles were 4.8 percent of the jail population (U.S. Dept. of Justice, 1971: 10). "About 2 percent of jails, however, fail to separate juveniles from adults" (Matheny, 1976: 137).

Although there is no easy way to determine the percentage of all juveniles who are confined awaiting court action and lodged in local jails, we can compute an estimate. In June 1974 there were 11,010 juveniles in detention centers; in March 1970 there were 7,800 juveniles in local jails. Those confined in jails represent 41.5 percent of all juveniles confined. This means that local jails, the juvenile justice reform movement notwithstanding, continue to confine a large percentage of those youths who are awaiting action by local courts. However, there is considerable variation among the states in the extent to which local jails are used to confine juveniles (Sarri, 1974).

Besides their functional equivalence, jails and detention centers are alike in other ways. Detention is a significant phase in the juvenile justice process because it constitutes the initial, critical contact with the system for many youths. It seems likely that those youths routed through detention centers may develop an indifference and bitterness from the way they are treated and generalize those feelings to the entire juvenile justice system. Sarri (1974: 14) speaks of the "overwhelmingly negative results of most juveniles' experiences with detention." The architectural design of detention facilities

---

THE DETENTION HOME

The first time I was in juvie, I was 12. . . . Mom and Pop Moriana was there. I really loved them. Like they were my parents, you know. I really dug it.

Oh, I can remember the first night I went in, though. I was in a room by myself. And they had a window in the door. And the next morning—this is when I was 12—they'd go walking by—the oldtimers—and they'd be lookin in the window. They'd go "Umm, nice in there. How are you, baby?" The other inmates would always do this to new girls. But see, that's how they scare you. I was so scared after being searched and everything. You don't know what the fuck's going on, but these are older people telling you what to do, so you just get right in there and take off your clothes and whatever. So you sleep it through, and then you wake up and all's you see is these faces in the door, you know, yelling at you and telling you, "You better watch it, bitch." I was thinking, "They're going to kill me. What did I do? I don't know anybody—they're going to kill me." So when I came out of my room, I was high-stepping, hanging on the wall. How funny it is we become adjusted so fast . . . because two days later, I was looking in someone else's window, "Hey, bitch."

Source: Kathryn Watterson Burkhart. *Women in Prison.* New York: Popular Library, 1976, p. 57.

may be partly responsible for this negative impact. They often resemble jails, many are located next door to a jail, and staff may be used interchangeably (Pappenfort et al., 1970). Finally, detention centers have been largely ignored by researchers, and little effort has been directed toward change or innovation. Detention practices appear to have changed little over the past half century, despite overwhelming criticism in most regions of the United States.

What are the characteristics of those confined in America's detention centers? Reliable nationwide data are not available, so we must rely upon several different sources of varying age and completeness for a picture of juvenile detainees. We have presented such a picture in Table 7–3. Despite the fact that some of these data are now more than 12 years old, there is little reason to believe that a different picture would emerge today. Juvenile detainees are predominantly male, approximately 15 years of age and spend less than one month in detention. Although data on their racial and social class backgrounds are not available, we would probably be safe in assuming that blacks and other economically impoverished groups are overrepresented among detainees.

Reliable offense characteristics are not available, but according to Sarri (1974: 45) "only a minority of detainees are charged with

TABLE 7–3
Selected demographic and legal characteristics of detention center inmates in the United States, varying years (1966–1974)

Sex*	Percent
Male	69.9
Female	30.1
Age†	
Under 2 years	1.0
2–5 years	2.0
6–11 years	9.0
12–15 years	60.0
16 and over	28.0
Median age	14.7
Average length of stay (in months)†	
Less than 1	86.0
1–3	12.0
3–6	1.0
6–12	1.0

Sources: * U.S. Department of Justice, Law Enforcement Assistance Administration. *Children in Custody: Advance Report on the Juvenile Detention and Correctional Facility Census of 1974.* Washington, D.C.: National Criminal Justice Information and Statistics Service, February 1977.

† Rosemary C. Sarri. *Under Lock and Key: Juveniles in Jails and Detention.* Ann Arbor: University of Michigan, National Assessment of Juvenile Corrections, December 1974.

felonies. . . . Nearly 75 percent of the females held [are] charged with status offenses. The comparable percentage for males [varies] between 20 and 30 percent."

The rate of juvenile detention, like the rate of jail use, varies greatly among the states. Sarri (1974: 75–6) shows that the combined rate of jail and detention use for juveniles ranges from a low of 2.28 per 100,000 population (ages 5 to 19) in North Dakota to a high of 114.62 in California. As with state variation in jail and prison population, the reasons for this are not entirely clear.

When compared with scholarship on jails, little is known about conditions in detention centers and the social organization and culture of their inmates. However, it is doubtful that the extremely poor conditions characteristic of many jails are as common in detention centers in the United States.

8

The regimens of correctors:
Men's prisons

As of December 31, 1976, a total of 263,291 persons were confined in state and federal penal institutions in the United States, serving sentences of at least 366 days (U.S. Dept. of Justice, 1978). This does not include juveniles confined in detention centers, training schools, and other types of facilities. This is the largest number of prisoners held in America's prisons since the annual count of convicts was begun in 1926. Figure 8–1 shows the trend in prison populations since 1925; as can be seen, the general trend has been one of continued growth, to some extent reflecting the growth of the population. Two marked downturns in America's prison population occurred, during World War II and the 1960s.

Various demographic, social, economic, and legal data on state prison inmates are provided in a 1974 survey conducted by the U.S. Bureau of the Census. Some of these data are in Table 8–1; as can

TABLE 8–1
Selected demographic, socioeconomic, and legal characteristics of state prison inmates in the United States—1974

Sex	Percent
Male	97
Female	3
Race	
White	51
Black	47
Age	
Under 18	1
18–24	37
25–34	37
30 and over	38

TABLE 8–1 (continued)

Level of educational attainment
Eighth grade or less 26
1–3 years of high school 35
4 years of high school 28
1–3 years of college 8
4 years or more of college 1
Marital status
Married 24
Separated or divorced 25
Never married 48
Personal income (year prior to arrest)
No income 5
Less than $2,000 19
$2,000–$3,999 18
$4,000–$5,999 18
$6,000–$9,999 18
$10,000 or more 14
Employment status (month prior to arrest)
Employed (full or part time) 68
Unemployed 31
Occupation at time of arrest
Professional and technical workers 3
Managers and administrators 6
Salesworkers 2
Clerical workers 4
Craftsmen and kindred workers 23
Operatives 29
Nonfarm laborers 17
Service workers 11
Whether released on bail
Released 38
Not released 61
Whether jail time credited toward sentence
Credited 65
Not credited 27
Don't know/not reported 8
Maximum sentence length
Less than 2.99 years 11
3–4.99 years 15
5–5.99 years 14
6–9.99 years 11
10–15.99 years 22
21 or more years 8
Life 12
Death .... *
Don't know/not reported 1

* Less than 0.5 percent.

Source: U.S. Department of Justice, Law Enforcement Assistance Administration. *Survey of Inmates of State Correctional Facilities 1974.* Washington, D.C.: National Criminal Justice Information and Statistics Service, 1976, pp. 24–5.

FIGURE 8–1
Number of sentenced prisoners in state and federal institutions at year end, 1925–1976

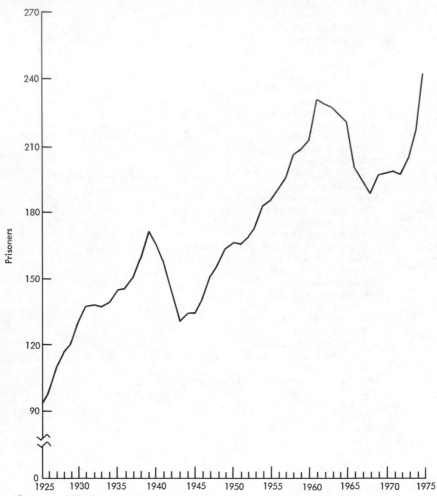

Source: U.S. Dept. of Justice, Law Enforcement Assistance Administration. *Prisoners in State and Federal Institutions on December 31, 1976,* Washington, D.C.: National Criminal Justice Information and Statistics Service, 1978, p. 14.

be seen, America's state prison inmates are overwhelmingly male and drawn from economically impoverished groups. They are disadvantaged in a variety of other ways as well (for example, educationally), and following arrest a substantial majority could not even make bail.

The most serious offenses for which state prison inmates in 1974 were confined are contained in Table 8–2. A slight majority of pris-

TABLE 8–2
Most serious offense of state prison inmates in the United States—1974

Offense	Percent
Robbery (all types)	23
Burglary	18
Homicide (all types)	18
Drug offense (all types)	10
Larceny	6
Assault (all types)	5
Sexual assault	5
Forgery, fraud, or embezzlement	4
Motor vehicle theft	2
All other offenses	9

Source: U.S. Department of Justice, Law Enforcement Assistance Administration. *Survey of Inmates of State Correctional Facilities 1974.* Washington, D.C.: National Criminal Justice Information and Statistics Service, 1976, p. 28.

oners were confined for property offenses, with the remainder generally confined for assaultive or drug offenses.

EARLIER SOCIOLOGICAL STUDIES OF THE PRISON

The bulk of sociological research on correctional institutions has been conducted on those that confine adult male felons. Theory and research on institutions for other types of offenders (juveniles and women) has generally taken this work as a starting point and has sought to determine how closely it applies to the newer settings. In this chapter we will discuss sociological research on prisons for adult males. Chapter 9 will discuss theory and research on institutions for juveniles and women.

Convict social organization and norms

The earliest sociological theory and research on the prison developed many of the themes that subsequent observers were to follow. First, individual prisons were studied as *self-contained* entities; they were studied in isolation from the external world and little mention was made of the possible influence of general societal currents or conditions on the prison world. Second, studies presented a picture of the prison world that emphasized its *consensual* nature, as evidenced, for example, by the existence of a single overreaching inmate code and status hierarchy. Third, while convicts and the prison staff obstensibly existed in a state of barely controlled warfare, there were in fact complex *accommodative* relationships between them. These themes should become apparent as we briefly review prison scholarship.

When social scientists began studying the prison they found a rich sub rosa economy, social organization, and culture among convicts. This convict world existed in a state of tacit, if tenuous, accommodation with the world of officials and guards. Among convicts there was a complex web of social roles or *social types*, which served to provide scarce goods and services and also as models of proper and improper conduct. "Real men" and "right guys" were figures of approbation in the prison world while "gorillas," "square johns," and "merchants" were scorned and held up to varying degrees of ridicule. This picture proved to be generally consistent in a large number of prisons, with only the labels showing significant variation.

There were 47 of us on that tier, two to a cell and you couldn't trade, but I was amazed how quickly we all banded together. We were an improbable bunch, everything from failure to pay alimony to attempted murder, we were Indians, Chinese, Hungarians, East Indians, Italians, you name it. We would probably never have given each other the time of day if we'd met on the Outside.

In here, it was a different story. It was us against them, not active warfare but a cold war, each side keeping as much to itself as it could. If communication was necessary you kept it short and loud; loud because secrets were dangerous commodities to have in prison. To be labeled a rat was the kiss of death; rats were stool pigeons and they had something to hide. So the apparent antagonism between inmates and guards was rarely anything but impersonal, each person simply maintaining the party line for his own safety and comradeship. And if comradeship was essentially a pact between strangers to agree extravagantly on one or two items and forget the rest, we certainly had it made; a simple settling back on one's haunches and baying at the institutional moon, at the injustice, the oppression, the outrage, etc., invoked an instant clamor of agreement all around; one sat marvelously bathed in the wash of so much concord.

Even our speech reflected this will to solidarity. Cursing and general foul language was no accidental characteristic of prison jargon. When an inmate kicked irritably at an uncooperative piece of machinery and announced succinctly that "the fuckin fucker's fucked, fer fuck sakes!" he had neatly sandwiched two separate statements into one outburst; one direct (the machine malfunctions), one implied (jail is hell). He could always count on unanimous agreement because at least one of those statements was always correct, automatically ensuring safe passage for the other.

Source: Andreas Schroeder. *Shaking It Rough.* Garden City, N.Y.: Doubleday, 1976, pp. 19–20.

Social relationships among convicts were marked by an under-current of fear and suspicion. Convicts were expected by staff and peers alike to "do their own time" and neither interfere nor act in concert with one another. Prison staff promoted this "do your own time" philosophy as a means of keeping convicts isolated from one another, thus preventing any collective response to their common condition. It was quite successful. Most convicts did their time while not forming any, or only one or two, friendships with other convicts.

The convict belief system (the convict "code") prescribed how convicts should do time and relate to one another and to the prison staff. By one account (Sykes and Messinger, 1960), the chief tenets of the convict code were classified into five major groups: (1) *Don't exploit convicts.* Included in this maxim are several other directives, such as "don't break your word," "don't steal from other cons," and "pay your debts." (2) *Don't weaken.* Put differently, the ideal con should "be tough, be a man." He should show courage, strength, and integrity in the face of privation and threats from others. (3) *Don't lose your head.* This places an emphasis on "playing it cool" and do-ing "your own time." The convict should curtail affect, minimize emotional frictions, and generally ignore the irritants of daily life. (4) *Don't interfere with convict interests.* The most inflexible direc-tive in this category is "never rat on a con." Other directives include "don't be nosey," "don't have a loose lip," "don't put a guy on the spot," and "be loyal to your class—the cons." And (5) *Don't be a sucker.* Prison officials should be treated with constant suspicion and distrust. And in situations of conflict between convicts and prison employees, the latter should automatically be considered in the wrong.

Partly as a result of this maxim, interaction between convicts and prison officials showed many of the elements of interaction within any castelike system of stratification. There was a heavy emphasis on the maintenance of interactional ritual—such as convicts always standing in the presence of staff and never referring to staff mem-bers by their first names—which only served to reinforce and high-light the caste distinctions. The convict belief system required con-victs to generally avoid any unnecessary communication with staff; required interaction was to be polite but brief. Although honored in the breach, convicts could not entirely escape the pull of this and other aspects of the convicts' normative system.

Among convicts there was a complex stratification system for the allocation of prestige. The type of crime one had committed, pre-vious criminal experience, the degree of one's commitment to anti-social values, ethnicity, and background all played some part in the determination of one's place in the prisoner hierarchy. Those con-

And there was another phenomenon, which, concurrent with all our abandon, I could already see becoming increasingly defined: a hierarchy, a rigid pecking order was already relentlessly sorting itself out, eventually floating an elite to the surface which few challenged and even fewer successfully defied. By the time I had been Inside for a week, I had already developed an uncannily sure sense of where a newcomer would eventually come to rest on the social scale; in fact, most of us had done so. There was no distinct pattern to the selection, but one characteristic was unquestionably a major asset: if you clearly didn't *care,* if you could convince inmates and guards that you had absolutely nothing to lose and that your countermeasures to even the most trivial provocation would be totally unrestrained and pursued to the utmost of your abilities—then you were given respect and a wide berth, and people looked to you for leadership and advice. "He's crazy," they'd say admiringly, even longingly, when the name came up. "He's just totally, completely insane."

Source: Andreas Schroeder. *Shaking It Rough.* Garden City, N.Y.: Doubleday, 1976, p. 23.

victs who were looked up to by others were permitted more access to staff without risking the suspicion this would otherwise entail. Order was maintained in the prison by a tacit alliance between these elite convicts, whose high status gave them a vested interest in maintaining the status quo, and prison officialdom.

Research consistently noted that convicts do not have favorable attitudes toward the criminal justice system, the prison, its staff, or its supposedly rehabilitative programs. Indeed, convicts' beliefs and attitudes in these areas were negative and often oppositional. Having thus determined that convicts do not feel gratitude or warmth but rather alienation and hostility toward their keepers, and that they engage in collective actions to thwart their keepers' plans and to provide themselves with amenities otherwise denied them, research pursued two lines of further investigation in the prison: (1) studies of convict socialization, and (2) theoretical explanations for the nature of convict social organization and beliefs.

Socialization research

There have been many studies of socialization in the prison community (see Bowker, 1977, and Leger and Stratton, 1977). Most started with the assumption that adoption of the dictates of the convict code and involvement in efforts to thwart the plans of correctors is an indicator of how thoroughly the convict has been *criminalized*. Clemmer not only coined the concept of *prisonization* but also provided a statement of this argument:

> If I have one thought to offer it is that "by their prisonization shall ye know them." This is to say, in my judgment, that the conventional criteria customarily pondered in determining parole selection can have added value if authorities also have some judgment as to the depth to which the prison culture has penetrated the inmate personality (Clemmer, in Evjen, 1962: 226).

Studies of socialization in the prison world consistently demonstrated that there is a U-shaped curve of expressed conformity with the convict code. As a rule, prisoners in the first six months and the last six months of their imprisonment tend to be more pro-staff in their expressed beliefs, while those in between tend to be more pro-prisoner in their beliefs. Importantly, despite all this research one critic has rightly noted that "it has yet to be established that anti-prison attitudes and behaviors are predictive of post prison antisocial attitudes or behaviors" (Tittle, 1974: 390).

Because prisoners appear to consistently develop collective responses to frustrate the plans of correctors, prison administrators have dreamed of somehow manipulating the sociometric processes of the inmate world for rehabilitative purposes. Hartung and Floch (1956), for example, after attributing the prison riots of the early 1950s to the earlier destruction of inmate leadership and "self-government" by reform administrators, suggested that while

> it was correct to destroy that self-government . . . it was incorrect not to use at least some of its personnel afterwards, for the attaining of a good end. . . . There is at least one way of minimizing the possibility of the collective type of riot recurring, assuming that the fortress-type of prison will be retained for the great majority of prisoners. This is by exploiting inmate-leaders *under official direction* so that they will once again have incentives for a stake in a smoothly-operating, peaceful prison. It may of course be necessary for prison administrators to take an active although unobtrusive part in the development of inmate leaders (1956: 56–7). (Emphasis in the original.)

This stance reflects the manipulative human-relations approach to the correctional mandate that has been so strong in previous sociological work. It has led to research aimed at demonstrating that the convict social and belief systems in thoroughgoing rehabilitative institutions can indeed be won over to prosocial norms and conduct (for example, Street, Vinter, and Perrow, 1966).

Some of the most imaginative sociological work on prisons has

---

THE CONVICT CODE CIRCA 1930

The code of the good hoodlum, while rigorous, is basically simple. Its cardinal tenet is the single commandment: Thou shalt not beef. Under no circumstances whatsoever must an adherent of the code turn to constituted authority. Beefing is the imparting to the authorities in any way whatsoever, directly or indirectly, of information detrimental to anyone.

* * * * *

Finking [need not] be direct and straightforward. It may be done indirectly. For example, a fink may say to a fellow inmate within earshot of a screw, "Gee! Didn't Hank look funny coming out of the Bake Shop with those pies under his shirt!" Or, in casual conversation with a screw, he may let slip some remark conveying information about another prisoner. . . . The real hood, however, shuns these methods as completely as he does outright squawking. While he may be polite and courteous to screws, he doesn't spend too much time chatting with them; the con who talks a great deal with the screw, who "sits on the screw's lap," is suspect among his fellows.

* * * * *

The good hood minds his own business. He may disapprove very much of what some other con is doing; but unless it directly affects him adversely, he merely shrugs and walks away.

The hoodlum code is stringent enough; the fellow who tries to live up both to it and the code of the gentleman has his work cut out for him! Unfortunately the hoodlum code, like the code of the gentleman, is often honored in the breach.

Source: Nathan F. Leopold, Jr. *Life Plus 99 Years*. Garden City, N.Y.: Doubleday, 1958, p. 141.

---

come from efforts to develop theoretical explanations for the distinctive nature of convict social organization and beliefs. Let's briefly review some of these.

Theoretical explanations

Three different, though easily interrelated, perspectives have been put forward to account for the oppositional nature of the convict culture and the social organization which emerges among convicts: (1) psychologically functional, (2) sociologically functional, and (3) cultural importation.

In 1954 McCorkle and Korn presented the rudiments of what we have called the *psychologically functional* explanation for convict culture and social organization. Briefly put, their thesis is that these represent functional responses by convicts to the rejection they experience as they are processed through the criminal justice system.

> Observation suggests that the major problem with which the inmate social system attempts to cope center about the theme of social rejection. In many ways, the inmate social system may be viewed as providing a way of life which enables the inmates to avoid the devastating psychological effects of internalizing and converting social rejection into self-rejection. In effect, it permits the inmate to reject his rejector rather than himself (1954: 89).

It is the problems that convicts experience individually that gives rise to the "inmate social system." This system acts to mitigate those problems. This interpretation has not really been followed up with systematic research by social scientists and has generally received little attention. To this day, it remains an idea that has produced few supporters, despite whatever merits it might possess. Instead the dominant interpretation has been one that we have elected to call *sociologically functional.*

A number of sociologists have presented explanations for convict culture and social organization which, like the work of McCorkle and Korn (1954), sees them as functional adaptations to *something* inherent in the structure and experience of confinement. A peculiar set of structural arrangements characteristic of the prison is usually pointed to as the causative agent. Yet, the structural argument has shown some variation from one observer to another, and few attempts have been made to systematically reconcile them.

Sykes (1958) and Sykes and Messinger (1960) argue that the critical aspect of the structure of the prison is that it imposes the *pains of imprisonment* upon convicts. These pains result from the deprivation of (1) liberty, (2) goods and services, (3) heterosexual relationships, (4) autonomy, and (5) security. To the extent inmates endorse and abide by the dictates of the inmate code, and demonstrate a solidarity with one another, these pains are lessened; to the extent the code is ignored, and inmates prey upon one another, the pains experienced are more intense.

Goffman's (1961) functional interpretation stresses the causative significance of a different set of variables. He identifies the prison—along with the military, convents, and "mental" hospitals—as one type of *total institution.* Presumably, any institution possessing the characteristics of "totalness" would generate similar responses on the part of its "inmates."

A basic social arrangement in modern society is that the individual tends to sleep, play, and work in different places, with different co-participants, under different authorities, and without an over-all rational plan. The central feature of total institutions can be described as a breakdown of the barriers ordinarily separating these three spheres of life. First, all aspects of life are conducted in the same place and under the same single authority. Second, each phase of the member's daily activity is carried on in the immediate company of a large batch of others, all of whom are treated alike and required to do the same thing together. Third, all phases of the day's activities are tightly scheduled, with one activity leading at a prearranged time into the next, the whole sequence of activities being imposed from above by a system of explicit formal rulings and a body of officials. Finally, the various enforced activities are brought together into a single rational plan purportedly designed to fulfill the official aims of the institution (Goffman, 1961: 5–6).

This explication of the characteristics and consequences of total institutions represents a brilliant attempt at the development of formal sociological categories and theory.

One of the more provocative pieces of research to date that suggests the validity of a structural analysis of the convict normative and social system comes from a study reported by Zimbardo (1972; Haney, Banks, and Zimbardo, 1972). Zimbardo used paid college student volunteers in an effort to simulate a prison structure and atmosphere. The students were arbitrarily divided into groups designated as either "guards" or "inmates." The latter were confined in close quarters under a set of rules and regulations similar to those used in real prisons. A simulated parole system was also employed as a part of the experimental prison. Zimbardo found that it was necessary to terminate the study prematurely when he observed the emergence of various kinds of behavior by both guards and inmates that he considered too realistic (i.e., too much like what appears in real-life prisons). Specifically, some of the guards had begun to display extremely authoritarian conduct, and some of the inmates begged to be permitted to terminate their involvement prior to the projected end of the study and their agreed-upon term of service as subjects. Zimbardo seemed unprepared for these various forms of pathological behavior and equally at a loss to interpret them. Eventually, he suggested that "with regard to prisons, we can state that the mere act of assigning labels to people and putting them into a situation where those labels acquire validity and meaning is sufficient to elicit pathological behavior" (1972: 7).

If we ignore this rather ambiguous interpretation then we can analyze the problem in the light of a functional interpretation of

---

HUSTLES IN A WOMEN'S PRISON

"I worked in the garment shop work with all the hassles just because I wanted that twenty dollars a month to buy my coffee and cigarettes . . ." said a woman who had been confined at Terminal Island, a federal division for women in California. "I did it even though I used to pass out from the heat. Just bonk—I'd pass out. They'd give me smelling salts and bring me some water and I'd go back to work. It's so insane when I look back on it—I just can't believe I did it. But it was some kind of need; I had to do some of those little extra nice things for myself since I didn't have no outside source of funds. Not many people did have any outside source of funds.

"The people there that really needed a trade or skill besides the streets, something useful, are the same ones who go into the garment shop to work because they don't have a source of funds. But they can't learn anything useful in there—it's just a way to survive inside. Then they go back out in the street and hustle some more.

"I had to hustle a lot at prison—you know, like do people's ironing or cleaning for them. For about two dollars' worth of commissary a week you can do their laundry and that kind of thing. Even though cigarettes are cheaper without federal taxes and all, you can't earn enough money to support even smoking—let alone all the other little things you want, like extra food or goodies. People do all sorts of things—like maybe you knit sweaters or blankets for people or you do their hair or that kind of thing. If they get money from the outside, that's the way they can share it and get helped out at the same time themselves. It's all like a constant hustle between the women—but there's a lot of co-operation, too."

Source: Kathryn Watterson Burkhart. *Women in Prison.* New York: Popular Library, 1976, pp. 306–7.

---

prison culture and informal social organization. It would seem that it was not the assignation of labels to the two groups of participants so much as the differential allocation of authority and deprivations that perhaps accounts for the "pathologies" Zimbardo observed. One of the more interesting pieces of empirical research to explore this relationship between institutional structure and the informal organization of staff and inmates was conducted by Street, Vinter, and Perrow (1966). Their comparative study of six juvenile institutions found a fairly consistent relationship between the attitudes and social organization of inmates and the nature and severity of the deprivations imposed upon them by the institutional regimen. These findings are consistent with what we would expect on the basis of a sociologically functional interpretation.

The third type of explanation, in effect, suggests that no special explanation is even required for the negativism and social organization of imprisoned individuals. According to this model, those who are confined bring with them to the institution the same beliefs, identities, and group allegiances that they held on the streets. The prison world thus becomes a microcosm of the demimonde existing outside the prison itself (Irwin and Cressey, 1962; Irwin, 1970). To this extent the social organization, beliefs, and behavior of prisoners becomes less a functional adaptation to the problems and deprivation of confinement than a variant of the culture and social organization of the outside world that is imported into the prison. Understandably, this interpretation is designated as the *importation* model of prison social organization and culture.

CURRENT SOCIOLOGICAL VIEWS OF THE PRISON

More recent sociological theory and research on the prison has continued to pursue many of these past themes while providing some new ones as well. Today, many believe that the prison has been analyzed unrealistically as though it were a self-contained entity completely isolated from the outside world. The total institution interpretation of the prison world has been particularly criticized for this reason. There is more interest today in the importation model of prison social organization and convict culture, largely because events of the past decade have made it virtually impossible not to see the relationship between changes in the prison and sociopolitical currents in the society.

Sociopolitical events of the 1960s and early 1970s, coupled with growing prison populations have made the American prison of the late 1970s a different place from what it was 20 years ago. The civil rights movement of the 1960s helped to politicize black prisoners. It gave them a heightened sense of collective identity and stimulated them to interpret their plight in political terms. The prison advocacy movement, which has produced an outpouring of legal challenges from the prisons, has also helped to politicize prisoners. This increase in racial awareness, and the tendency to interpret imprisonment itself as a political act, have generally transformed the American prison. Where the convicts of the past were described in apolitical terms, their counterparts today are politically aware and may employ political interpretations of correctional processes when pressing for changes in their situation.

The prison warden of an earlier time successfully fractionated the convict population by granting privileges and concessions to a conservative convict elite and promoting a "do your own time"

OBSERVATIONS ON PRISON FRIENDSHIPS

It took, I was bemused to note, an astonishingly short time to become a reasonably seasoned jailbird. In no time at all I had learned the language, the prison terminology, the basic assumptions and the basic rules. . . .

Applying all this was a slightly more complex matter, of course, but the school was a rough one and rarely permitted mistakes, so the incentive was there to learn and learn fast. The first thing you needed was allies, and that as quickly as possible. The procedure tended to begin as soon as you were taken from court to the precinct jail, where they gathered the sentenced offenders and handcuffed them two by two for transport to maximum security. You sized up the guy you were handcuffed to and let your instincts do the rest; if he looked like a useful sort, you started up a conversation and established a rapport. You kept this procedure up until you knew enough people to generally cover the territory you were going to run in (e.g., your tier, the exercise yard, your place of work, the gym) and then you chose your friends and chose them carefully, keeping in mind that anything they were involved in would inescapably involve you too. Most of these maneuverings didn't happen as mechanically as this may sound, but the rationale behind them was unavoidably clear and few could afford to ignore the routine. A loner or loser in prison was a goner more often than not.

Source: Andreas Schroeder. *Shaking It Rough.* Garden City, N.Y.: Doubleday, 1976, pp. 29–30.

---

ideology. For the most part, this limited the prison's social organization to a system of economic exchange and fairly small apolitical friendship cliques. In contrast, today's warden must sometimes deal with informally recognized and powerful representatives of various ethnic blocs in the prison (Jacobs, 1974). Blacks have become a significant force within the prison, especially in those states where they now make up a large majority of the prison population (Denfeld and Hopkins, 1975). Where their numbers remain proportionally less, and where they have not been as effectively politicized, their influence remains less significant. Hispanic prisoners have also become an important power bloc in those states where they constitute a significant proportion of the prison population—chiefly New York and California. White convicts generally remain divided; consequently, they seem incapable of sustained or large-scale collective action. Race relations within the prison have become a microcosm of those in the larger society. The level of racial tension and conflict has escalated dramatically in some prisons. According to one observer, by the early 1970s race relations at San Quentin had deteriorated so badly that they amounted to a "war behind walls" (Bunker, 1972). Consequently, Bowker is probably correct in saying that "to ignore racial differentiation in prisoner groups is to seriously distort the reality of the social situation in American prisons in the 1970s" (1977: 71).

Adding to the difficulties of today's correctional administrators are problems with their own personnel. Guards, middle-range staff, and other employees in the prison "are becoming assertive and, in fact, demanding in the pursuit of their own self-interests" (Irwin, 1977: 38). Correctional employees are moving to unionize in many states. Consequently, correctional administrators seem caught between their restive and politically aware prisoners and their own increasingly militant employees.

Today's correctional administrators face growing problems in the ideological realm as well. As rehabilitative ideologies have been discredited, they have lost "a guiding philosophy to give their enterprise justification, meaning and importance. . . . Many administrators are adopting punishment and deterrence as their primary objectives" (Irwin, 1977: 38).

It is increasingly apparent to all that there are a variety of ways by which events in the external society influence the correctional scene—including the prison. Thus, there is more support today for the importation model of prison social organization and culture. For example, Jacobs conducted research on the activities and influence of Chicago street gangs inside the Illinois State Penitentiary (Stateville).

> This exploratory report has highlighted an unusual development within Illinois prisons. It suggests that the inmate organization cannot be understood in terms of "indigenous prerequisities." By emphasizing the *importation* of organization, roles, and norms from the streets of Chicago, support has been offered for the Irwin-Cressey theory of cultural drift.
>
> Within Stateville Penitentiary, gang members remain oriented toward the same membership group and leadership hierarchy as they did before having been committed to prison. Rather than experiencing a collapse upon passing through the gates, they have maintained the same self-identity conception as they held upon the streets. To the extent that adjustment needs to be made to the contingencies of incarceration, the adjustment is a group rather than an individual phenomenon (Jacobs, 1974: 408). (Emphasis in the original.)

Irwin (1977) believes that the tumultuous events of the 1960s have fundamentally altered the prison.

When you're in prison, time stops. You come out with the same problems you go in with—and start all over again with their 12 extra rules of parole in addition. While you're there, you just learn to survive and manipulate any extra pleasure you can. A comparatively honest person who just committed a crime of passion would end up becoming a manipulator in prison. A girl who works in the kitchen takes extra slices of meat and gets cigarettes for them. Cigarettes are money in prison. There's nothing there to foster the qualities society wants. You become dishonest just to make it. All the qualities you're being sent there to get, they forget you won't have when you get back. You wind up doing all those little things just to make life more comfortable for yourself. Sixty percent of what you do is against some rule. If you have more than four slices of bread in your room, it's against the rules. An egg or rice— you get three days in punishment. I know a woman who got 19 days in punishment for refusing two slices of burnt toast. They'd have raids on your room. But they'd only look where you hide things. So I'd leave whatever I had that was contraband out in open view. I never got busted.

Source: Kathryn Watterson Burkhart. *Women in Prison.* New York: Popular Library, 1976, p. 90.

Needless to say, there is no single "inmate culture" or "inmate social system." Nor is there an overreaching inmate code. The variety of cultural and subcultural orientations (ethnic, class, and criminal), the variety of preprison experiences, and the intense, open hostility between segments of the prison population preclude this. The general climate is much more threatening, both to prisoners and staff, and there is more prisoner-to-prisoner and prisoner-to-guard violence (1977: 32).

Nevertheless, a new form of social organization and order has emerged, one that Irwin calls *ordered segmentation*. Most prisoners now form small friendship groups and restrict their social interaction to members of these groups.

[T]hese cliques supply the satisfaction which derives from group interaction, and they are the mechanism for cooperative task performance which cannot be accomplished individually or through other channels. Some of those tasks are the provision of mutual protection from theft and physical assault, the conduct of gambling or other "wheeling and dealing" activities, and the learning of crafts or academic subjects (1977: 32–3).

A state of hostile accomodation exists among the various cliques and categories of prisoners, especially racial categories. Some of the

170

> The hardest part of serving time is the predictability. Each day moves like every other. You *know* nothing different can happen. You focus on tiny events, a movie scheduled weeks ahead, your reclass., your parole hearing, things far in the future, and slowly, smooth day by day, draw them to you. There will be no glad surprise, no spontaneous holiday, and a month from now, six months, a year, you will be just where you are, doing just what you're doing, except you'll be older.
>
> This airless calm is produced by rigid routine. Custody doesn't encourage spontaneity. Walk slow, the Cynic says, and don't make any fast moves. Each morning you know where evening will find you. There is no way to avoid your cell. When everyone marched into the block you would be left alone in the empty yard. Each Monday describes every Friday. Holidays in prison are only another mark of passing time and for many they are the most difficult days. Most of the outrages that provide such lurid passages in the folklore of our prisons are inspired by boredom. Some grow so weary of this grinding sameness they will drink wood alcohol even though they are aware this potent toxin may blind or kill them. Others fight with knives to the death and the survivor will remark, "It was just something to do."
>
> Source: Malcolm Braly. *False Starts*. Boston: Little, Brown, 1976, pp. 181–82.

most extreme and intense forms of violence between groups has decreased.

Martinson (1972) has also suggested some ways in which the prison has been transformed. He feels there has been a transformation in the nature of prison riots. "Clearly, convict disturbances take different forms over time reflecting both prison conditions and dominant attributes of society" (1972: 4). Historically there have been three patterns of prison disturbances, manifested in the mass escape, the prison riot, and the expressive mutiny. The mass escape belongs to an earlier era in American corrections but the remaining two are more recent in origin. Prison riots—

> which dominated the 19th and early 20th centuries—involved a struggle to improve conditions *within* the prison rather than an attempt to escape from it. Within the armed perimeter, power struggles occurred over the meager privileges prison had to offer. Such riots were often nicely timed to provoke the intervention of the prison reform movement and sometimes led to changes in the paroling practices, better food, less punishment for breaking prison rules or fewer rules. (Emphasis in the original.)

Unlike riots of this type, the expressive mutiny of today

is not primarily focused on winning power, maintaining privileges or improving conditions within the prison. It aims to communicate the inmate's plight to the public so far as he understands it. It is a new form of disturbance not merely a temporary reflection of new left influence among a group of politicized black convicts. The prison is used as an arena in which to stage dramatic renditions of inhumanity and rebellious gestures of inchoate despair and apocalypse. Demands for improvements in prison conditions appear side by side with borrowings from the Black Power movement, and the revolutionary sect. The entrepreneurial spirit of the escape artist is replaced by the organizational methods of the militant (Martinson, 1972: 4).

The changes we have referred to have made America's prison wardens and employees a beleagered bunch. The unionization movement has been fed by these developments as correctional employees try to cope with perceived diminution of their power and control. To be sure, there are many states and institutions where these changes have made few inroads, but few if any correctional institutions have been able to escape them completely. The next decade promises to be a time of considerable ferment in American corrections.

One final change in prison scholarship must be noted. Earlier prison theory and research had little to say about violence within the prison. Today, this is an issue of concern to many students of the correctional scene (Toch, 1977; Sylvester et al., 1977). For example, as prisons have become more overcrowded, some have wondered about a possible relationship between decreasing "personal space" and the incidence of violence (Bowker, 1977). Unfortunately, there is a curious one-sidedness to this whole line of inquiry: it generally ignores the violence perpetrated by staff and focuses instead upon convict violence.

The years ahead promise to be interesting ones for prison scholarship. As prison populations grow and the proportion that is black increases, correctional researchers may shed some of their sympathy for convicts. This may be especially true if racial conflict within prisons continues. In one sense, the recent growth of interest in prison violence can be viewed as a reaction to its shifting racial composition. So long as whites victimized each other little research was conducted on the problem. However, now that prison violence crosses racial lines, it has become a "problem."

9

The regimens of correctors:
Institutions for women and juveniles

Institutions for women and juveniles have not been studied as extensively as have institutions for adult males. Nevertheless, the studies that we do have are extremely important for theoretical reasons. The findings from this research help us to see the shortcomings of an exaggerated reliance on only one theoretical explanation for prisoner social structure and culture, whether it be the sociologically functional or the importation model. Studies conducted in juvenile institutions and women's prisons suggest that neither of these explanations by itself is sufficient to make sense of the diversity that exists in total institutions (Bowker, 1977). This will become apparent as we review what is known about institutions for women and juveniles.

WOMEN'S PRISONS

Women's prisons are both similar to and yet different from prisons for males. The evidence leaves little doubt on this point, even though there still are some inconsistencies in the picture which has been sketched of women's prisons. The following are some of the ways in which the two types of institutions appear to differ:

1. Violence and physical aggression are commonplace in men's prisons; they are much less common in women's prisons, where disputes do not usually erupt into violence. Similarly, riots and other forms of collective challenges to prison staff and administration are much rarer in women's prisons.

I was scared when I went to Bedford Hills. But I knew a few things by then. Like if you act quiet and hostile, people will consider you dangerous and won't bother you. So when I got out of isolation and women came up and talked to me, I said, "I left my feelings outside the gate, and I'll pick 'em up on my way out." I meant I wasn't going to take no junk from anyone. I made a promise if anybody hit me, I was gonna send 'em to the hospital.

When you go in, if you have certain characteristics, you're classified a certain way. First of all, if you are aggressive, if you're not a dependent kind of woman, you're placed in a position where people think you have homosexual tendencies. If you're in that society long, you play the game if it makes it easier to survive. And it makes it easier if people think you're a stud broad. I played the game to make it easier so they would leave me alone. I didn't have money to use makeup and I couldn't see going through any changes. You're in there and the women are looking for new faces. Since I was quiet and not too feminine-looking, I was placed in a certain box in other people's mind. I let them think that's what box I was in—'cause it was a good way to survive. My good friends knew better. But I had three good friends and they were considered "my women"—so they in turn were safe, too. You have to find ways to survive. You cultivate ways to survive. It's an alien world and it has nothing to do with functioning in society better. What I learned there was to survive there.

Source: Kathryn Watterson Burkhart. *Women in Prison.* New York: Popular Library, 1976, pp. 89–90.

2.   Homosexual relationships are found in all types of American penal institutions. In men's prisons many times they are the result of violence and coercion, whether real or threatened. They seem to function as a mechanism for some convicts to make public displays of their dominance and masculinity. The nature of homosexual relationships in women's prisons seems somewhat different. Rarely are women's homosexual involvements the result of coercion or force; rather, they are more often entered into voluntarily, and homosexual involvements do not appear to function as a means for expressing domination to the extent they do in male's prisons.

3.   Unlike male prisoners, women prisoners tend to establish extended pseudo-family relationships. These fictitious families consist of not only roles for parents, but also a variety of "relatives." It should be noted, however, that these family structures have not been found in women's prisons as much as in training

PRISON VISITS

It's unquestionably a mixed blessing, this business of visits. Visits probably cost an inmate three times as much as they're worth; a single one-hour visit is often enough to throw a man into a frenzy for a week; a regular weekly visit can keep an inmate unsettled through his entire term. Nevertheless I've rarely met an inmate who would turn down a visit if it was offered, and many use up their entire mail ration (two letters a week) to arrange for them as often as they can. I'm sure I do much harder time as a result of my own visits, but I don't suppose I'd give them up any more readily than an addict would give up a fix.

The trouble with visits is that they won't let you forget. The more alive you keep your memories of the Street, the worse things look and feel to you Inside. The less you know about what you're missing on the Street, the easier it is to imagine you're not missing anything at all. In order to shake easy time Inside you have to rid yourself of all Outside voices. Outside problems (which you can't resolve in any case) and Outside comparisons with Inside life. The sooner you give up trying to live your life in two places at once, the sooner your time eases into that long, mindless lope which makes a year only marginally longer than six months, a fin only slightly more drawn out than a deuce. It's a phenomenon well known to old-timers and lifers, who count on it to get them through sentences that would otherwise probably drive them right into the ground. Visits, however, tend to interfere with all that.

Source: Andreas Schroeder. *Shaking It Rough*. Garden City, N.Y.: Doubleday, 1976, pp. 135–36.

schools for girls; even there they do not appear to be a universal phenomenon.

4. Although there is very little evidence of solidarity among male prisoners, there seems to be even less among incarcerated women. Some evidence suggests that they trust one another even less than do male convicts, and that they do not react as severely to violations of the convict code.

5. When compared with men's prisons, the sub rosa economic system for the production and exchange of scarce goods and services may be less developed and less common in Women's prisons. Some evidence suggests that women prisoners, more often than men prisoners, resort to simple thievery to acquire the commodities they need to ameliorate the pains of imprisonment (Bowker, 1977: 91).

There are also peer rewards in being a rebel. ". . . You live in a whole fantasized world of Miss Bad Girl," said Fran Chrisman, who did time in both New York and California. "And the badder you are the more strength you have because you're looked up to by the inmate population. Also, once you've established yourself, they don't mess with you so much. The guard who says she's not scared of the women is lying. . . . She says 'move' and you say 'make me.' That's why they have male guards put women in the hole. Some male guards can't believe what they see out there. . . ."

For the number of women who play "Miss Bad Girl" there is an equal number who are pushed to the opposite extreme of becoming passive nonentities in response to the pressure. But the majority seem to concede to the power structure and adjust to doing "easy time"— getting prison wise to stealing extra food, trading favors, sneaking to see friends. Superficially, the threat of confinement and a poor behavior record contribute greatly to management and control of the institution for administrative purposes. But in the long run, ironically, the repressive security considerations add to the development of all the qualities prison is supposed to erase, not promote: dishonesty, cheating, stealing, hustling, evasiveness. These attributes are usually necessary for prison survival. They are necessary for co-opting the system, staying out of the hole, getting parole. Honest or direct responses to the conditions—like openly asking for extra food, striking for better work conditions, sticking up for someone else, asserting your rights openly—mean punishment and a poor record. Another irony is that it is just as often the little or insignificant things—not the big issues—that give a woman the "bad" record that denies her parole or commutation.

Source: Kathryn Watterson Burkhart. *Women in Prison.* New York: Popular Library, 1976, pp. 155–56.

6.   Female prisoners appear to be less committed to the convict code than do male prisoners.

With these exceptions, empirical research on women's prisons reveals few important differences from what we know about men's prisons. One point on which there seems agreement is that women's prisons will gradually change and become more like their male counterparts as extrainstitutional gender roles become more alike. At present, it is impossible to say just how far this convergence will go, but there it little doubt that we will see changes in the social structure and culture of the convict group in women's prisons.

RACE RELATIONS IN WOMEN'S PRISONS

Occasionally I heard racial antagonisms from both black and white women. "They're always complaining about how they get the raw end of everything," one white woman said, referring to black women. "But I'm a living testimony to the fact that whites get fucked over just as bad. You can't tell me any different. If you ask me, they got more privileges than I ever had. I get tired of all their bellyaching. I got some black friends, but they're not into that bag all the time. If you lived here, you'd know what I mean. I just get tired of hearing black this and black that and black, black, black. . . ."

"We don't get shit around here," a black woman said. "Don't tell me no white girl has to do time like I have to do time. They get the best and they still be carrying that white thing around on their shoulders, signifying and strutting—like ain't I somethin. . . . You'll see it, they get away with all kinds of shit we get locked for."

Although some racial hostilities give vent to "disciplinary problems," most of the women in the prisons I visited maintain that tensions are created by the staff and staff policies, not by the women themselves. They say staff tactics are used to "divide and rule."

Source: Kathryn Watterson Burkhart. *Women in Prison*. New York: Popular Library, 1976, p. 151.

TRAINING SCHOOLS

A note on private institutions

When we compare the ways in which adult and juvenile offenders are treated, we find a more diversified set of arrangements and agencies for dealing with juvenile offenders. There is greater diversity in juvenile corrections than in adult corrections. One measure of this diversity is the existence of a substantial number of private institutions for juveniles, whereas there is no comparable private sector for adult offenders. Originally, these private institutions confined youths considered dependent or neglected, but in recent times they have increasingly accepted youths with delinquency offenses as well. Little is known about private juvenile institutions.

Public and private facilities differ significantly in the distribution of their inmates by detention status. In the 1975 census of children in custody (U.S. Dept. of Justice, 1977), dependent and neglected children and voluntary admissions accounted for 2 percent of the juvenile population in public institutions, but for 40 percent in private institutions. There were 1,277 privately operated juvenile detention and correctional facilities in 1975—a count 4 percent below the figure (1,337) for 1974. Approximately three of every five detention and correctional facilities operating in the United States in 1975 were privately operated.

The 1975 census enumerated approximately 47,000 juveniles housed in public facilities and about 27,000 in the more numerous, but typically smaller, private institutions. Males accounted for roughly 75 percent of all juveniles held in juvenile facilities in the U.S., the proportion being slightly above that figure in the public sector and slightly below in the private.

There may be greater diversity in the programs and structures of private correctional institutions than in public ones. For instance, one of the private institutions included in a comparative study (Street, Vinter, and Perrow, 1966) of six juvenile correctional institutions described its objectives:

> When a boy comes to us we are primarily interested, not in what he has done, but why he has done it. We are committed to demonstrate to our boys that the community is not hostile to the individual. We must symbolize to them the cooperative forces of our society which are interested, not in avenging aggressive acts, but in preventing them. We therefore inflict no punishment, either corporally or otherwise, in the handling of our boys. Treatment and education are the only tools we have. We are convinced that punishing teaches the child only how to punish; scolding teaches him how to scold. By showing him, by our own example, that we understand, he learns the meaning of understanding; by helping him, he learns the meaning of cooperation (Street, Vinter, and Perrow, 1966: 59).

Contrast this description with one contained in a brochure prepared and circulated by the staff of another private institution, located in the Southwest. (This description of the institution was sent to state departments of welfare, promoting the institution as a possible placement for their youth.)

> Dear Friend:
>
> After these years of operating the _____ Home for Girls, we are more convinced than ever that CHRIST meets every need. When a girl comes to our home, she must look at it as a real spiritual hospital and trust us and cooperate with us as much as she would her family doctor. We have some requirements . . . that have proven best for those who come for help. If for some reason you *cannot* or *will not* submit to these requirements, we can cannot help you. And remember, those of us who lead you live under the same conditions. *Be sure to bring a King James Version Bible.* We receive you with open arms and open hearts and know that by faith that victory can be yours through the blessed Saviour.

REQUIREMENTS

1. No coffee, tea, magazines, TV, radios, cigarettes, newspapers will be brought into the _____ Home.
2. No dresses or skirts above the knee. No pants or pant suits allowed.
3. No eye shadow of any kind.
4. No hippie purses, beads or anything that pertains to a hippie, including excessive jewelry. Girls may wear two rings and an identification bracelet or a charm bracelet, etc. Nothing with the "Peace" symbol on it.
5. Only two letters a week are written out, and those only to relatives or guardians.
6. No *candy, gum* or *cookies* will be sent in to the girls while they are in the home.
7. All bags and boxes will be inspected on entering and leaving.
8. All money sent will be kept by the home and given as needed. No girl will be allowed to have money in her room.
9. If while at the home any girl should run away, her bags, clothes, etc. *will not* be sent home C.O.D. or express—they will be the property of the home.
10. If anyone brings pants, eye make-up or any of the items listed as not allowed, they will be taken up and destroyed.
11. No telephone calls will be made by the girls except in an emergency or of great importance.
12. Phone calls once a month from parents or guardians.
13. During the months of June, July, and August, all phone calls will be received only between 9:30 A.M. and 4:00 P.M. Monday through Friday.
14. During the school months of September through May, phone calls will be received only between 6:30 P.M. and 7:00 P.M. *NO PHONE CALLS ON SUNDAY*
15. Calls will be limited to five minutes unless an emergency.
16. No visiting in the dorm after 5:00 P.M. any day.
17. No visiting in the girls' rooms—all visiting must be in reception rooms or one of the visiting rooms.
18. Any girl that leaves the dorm with parents must have permission from one of the staff when she leaves, and report in when returning.
19. The home will not be responsible for the girls' actions when they are with parents.
20. No girl will be allowed to go off the farm with anyone except parents and/or workers of the _____ Evangelistic Enterprise.
21. All medical, dental, and other personal bills made by your daughter will be mailed to you, the parent or guardian for payment.

Boys' training schools

Empirical investigations of training schools have focused rather heavily upon social structure and culture at the cottage level; there has been correspondingly less attention paid to institution-wide informal organization and norms. Later we shall offer some possible reasons for this tendency to focus on smaller, more restricted social settings. Here we simply note this characteristic of past training school research.

The social life and culture of cottages has been described in several studies. With the following exceptions, the picture presented seems similar to what is known about prisons for adult males:

1. Although fights are common in boys' training schools, lethal violence is not as common as it is in penitentiaries.
2. There may be less solidarity among male juveniles than among male penitentiary convicts. For instance, collective disturbances and rebellions are much less common in males' training schools.

These differences aside, some of the sociopolitical events of the 1960s produced results in training schools similar to those produced in penitentiaries. Perhaps the principal consequence has been the intensification of racial conflicts and the solidification of the black inmate group. This fact, and its social consequences on the daily occurrences in juvenile institutions, has been depicted in a recent study of an Ohio youth institution. Bartollas, Miller, and Dinitiz (1976) describe not only the social roles and sociometric and hierarchical relationships among the boys but also the dynamics of interracial contacts—many of which consist of exploitation of whites by blacks. Boys' experiences within the institution are largely determined by the reputation they acquire during their first three weeks of confinement.

> Once boys were in the intake cottage, the other boys immediately subjected them to tests designed to ascertain whether they could be exploited for food, clothes, cigarettes, and sex. Sexual exploitation was found to be severe, with blacks pressuring whites in most of the encounters. If the new boy looked and acted tough, exploitation was minimized; if any weaknesses were shown, he was immediately misused by the others. . . . Nearly all of the most seriously exploited were white, and most of the exploiter boys were black. As in many adult prisons, the whites were disorganized and the blacks stuck together. Boys were acquainted with the local version of the convict code shortly after arrival. This code had standards for all prisoners but also some that were specific to blacks or Caucasians. The general code items were "exploit whomever you can," "don't kiss ass," "don't rat on your peers," "don't give up your ass," "be cool," "don't get involved in another inmate's affairs," "don't steal squares" (cigarettes), and "don't buy the mind f—king." Additional norms for blacks were "exploit whites," "no forcing sex on

blacks," "defend your brother," and "staff favor whites." For whites, the additional norms were "don't trust anyone" and "everybody for himself" (Bowker, 1977: 100).

As in all penal institions, the boys had labels for the various social types. Bartollas, Miller, and Dinitz found that staff members often used these same labels, plus some informal labels of their own, "including 'punk,' 'sickie,' and 'pussy.' They often made open bets on a boy's future adjustment after release in front of him. Even worse, they sometimes used labels to pass on a boy's sexually exploitable status to the other prisoners, thereby inadvertently setting up a sexual attack" (Bowker, 1977: 101). Although this study provides a wealth of empirical data, the picture it presents does not differ significantly from the one presented in other studies of boys' training schools. An inmate code—probably honored primarily in the breach, collectively defined and recognized social roles, and exploitation and scapegoating among the boys seem to be near universal aspects of the training school. As noted, however, what does seem to be more recent is the phenomenon of black domination, at least in those institutions in which blacks comprise a substantial proportion of the inmate group.

Girls' training schools

The social organization and culture of the inmates of girls' training schools appears to have more in common with what is known to be true of women's prisons than of institutions for males. Sociological research suggests that girls frequently create pseudo-marital and pseudo-family structures, and that homosexual relationships are both common and noncoercive. Generally, girl's training schools are not as violent as boys' training schools are; like boys, however, there is little evidence of solidarity among incarcerated girls, except perhaps along racial lines.

ACCOUNTING FOR THE SIMILARITIES AND DIFFERENCES

Given these similarities and differences in the social organization and norms of incarcerated men, women, and juveniles, how can we account for them? Are there important differences between the institutions themselves that might explain them? Or are they so similar that we would expect incarcerated males and females to organize themselves and behave in similar ways? Certainly, one very important institutional similarity comes to mind: Prisons and training schools, whether for males or females, are all total institutions as Goffman (1961) used that concept. All impose a high degree of segregation from the free world; all are socially, materially, and psychically depriving places of involuntary confinement. In view of these similarities, we should be not surprised that there are so many similarities in the social organization and culture of prisons and training schools—as a functional argument would lead us to expect. Nevertheless, there are some major differences, too.

The first difference is the smaller size of training schools and women's prisons. Rarely does one of them confine more than 400 inmates. By comparison, there were 2,350 convicts at the Illinois State Penitentiary at Menard when Clemmer conducted his classic study of the prison community (1958), and there were 1,200 convicts at the New Jersey State Prison when Sykes researched *Society of Captives* (1958). Contrast these population figures with the 650 convicts at the Federal Reformatory for Women (Alderson, West Virginia), which Giallombardo studied (1966), the 800 convicts at Frontera—an exceptionally large women's institution—during Ward and Kassebaum's research (1967), and the 190 juveniles at the Training Institute for Central Ohio (Bartollas, Miller, and Dinitz, 1976). So although women and juveniles, like male convicts, conduct their daily activities en masse, the masses are not as large as in traditional men's prisons. The average number of convicts confined in men's prisons is substantially higher than the average number of inmates in women's institutions (Arditi et al., 1973).

Training schools and women's prisons also differ architecturally from their adult male counterparts. Whereas the latter type of prison usually features cellblock housing—in which as many as 1,000 men live together—the former tend to be spatially more dispersed. Because many of them feature the so-called cottage system, rarely will women or juveniles live in groups of larger than 30 to 50. These living units often are self-contained and, therefore, do not require a large proportion of the entire convict body to come together as often at any one time, as is the case in male prisons.

A third difference—this one between training schools and prisons for both males and females—is age. The average age for confined juveniles is approximately 16 years (Vinter, 1976), whereas the average age for imprisoned men and women in 1974 was approximately 29.8 years (estimated from U.S. Dept. of Justice, 1976: Table 1). The approximate median age for incarcerated adults in the United States in 1974 was 25 years.

A final difference—here again, between training schools and penitentiaries for both sexes—is in the average length of stay. Although we do not have reliable data, it seems likely that juveniles are confined for shorter periods than are adults. If this is true, we would not expect to find as much solidarity in juvenile institutions since the population is more mobile, thus not permitting the longer-term contacts that could give rise to higher degrees of convict solidarity.

But while these differences might be expected to produce variations in the social organization and culture of training schools and prisons, they do not tell the whole story. There is good reason to believe that some of the differences in the reactions to the pains of imprisonment by males and females and by adults and juveniles are the result of factors imported into the institution. Let us briefly review this line of argument.

The external world and prisoner organization

Recall that female prisoners tend to be less violent, less cohesive, less committed to the convict code, more accepting of homosexual liasions, more likely to create pseudo-marital and family structures, and less likely to develop extensive sub rosa economic networks than male prisoners. How can we account for these differences? Most prison researchers seem agreed that the explanation lies in (1) differences in the preprison criminal experiences of men and women, and (2) traditional sex role differences. Traditional sex roles, especially, function as latent roles and identities that prisoners bring to prison with them. As a result male prisoners, both individually and collectively, respond to the pains of imprisonment in typically masculine ways while females respond to them in typically feminine ways.

Traditionally, women have functioned as wives and mothers, in emotionally supportive roles to others. Females' socialization experiences prepared them for dependent roles as marital partners rather than occupational roles and careers in the labor force. Consequently, women derived much of their personal satisfaction from supportive involvements with others, while men were encouraged to be more independent and to pursue occupational roles outside the home. Women were less aggressive and less prone to violence, another reflection of their traditionally dependent status. Indeed, even in their criminal involvements women acted less independently, playing supporting roles to men, and were less actively involved. Finally, because women traditionally have been oriented to the marriage market, they have tended to see other women as rivals.

All of these components of the traditional feminine role are reflected in females' response to the pains of imprisonment. When females are confined they reportedly experience the loss of close supportive social relationships more acutely than do males. Homosexual liasions and pseudo-family groups represent attempts to create surrogate relationships that mitigate these deprivations. Moreover, women prisoners tend to be less committed to the convict code, and there is little emphasis on solidarity and collective opposition to prison staff. Among females, solidarity seems undermined by their tendency to see other women as rivals, and by their lower rate of involvement in criminal groups in the free community. (The convict code is similar in content to the norms of criminal groups in the free world.) The traditionally nonviolent behavior of females and their socialization to be nonaggressive—except perhaps on a verbal level—finds characteristic expression in the relative absence of violence in women's institutions. Finally, the traditional deemphasis of the breadwinner role for women makes them less likely to engage in entrepreneurial activities in the institutional setting, and makes the economic underlife of women's prisons less developed than in male institutions (Williams and Fish, 1974).

On the other hand, men traditionally have been less socialized to be independent, aggressive, and occupationally oriented. When they are confined they involve themselves in the kinds of activities that gave meaning to their lives in the free world: activities that earn them a livelihood. In the prison this finds expression in the production and exchange of scarce goods and services, many of which are contraband (for example, sexually explicit pictures and books, loan sharking, or drugs). The traditional male emphasis on aggressiveness and machismo pervades the world of incarcerated men. It makes them inclined to see every dispute or altercation with others as a character contest, with even lethal violence a justifiable response if the stakes are high enough.

Much less attention has been paid to explaining why the social worlds of imprisoned juveniles and adults are different. It seems possible, however, that many of the characteristic interpersonal and social dynamics of training schools for males are an attempt by adolescent males to prove their mettle and establish an identity for themselves. In any event, what is known about the differences among total institutions lends strong support to the cultural importation model of inmate social organization and culture. There now seems to be little doubt that prisoners bring with them to the total institution certain latent roles and identities which influence their adaptations to the pains of imprisonment.

SEXISM IN PRISON PROGRAMS

The rehabilitative programs and services that American prisons offer their convicts may be viewed as historical tracings of the rehabilitative ideologies of the past 100 years. Religious programs, vocational training, academic education, individual counseling, group counseling, and even prison disciplinary practices are justified in terms of some particular set of ideas about the deficiencies of offenders. In a tour of virtually any contemporary prison, officials will proudly show off these programs and brag about them—even when they're not asked about the programs. Visitors leave with the impression—which the prison rarely discourages—that a large proportion of the inmates participate in them. Extravagant claims are sometimes made about these programs' success, usually on the basis of anecdotal or methodologically suspect findings. Little or no regard is shown for the results of evaluative research, which calls into question the usefulness of most of these programs.

The reality of prison programs is often very different from what is presented on prison tours. Although there are exceptions, rehabilitative programs in most American prisons touch the lives of a minority of convicts. Most convicts spend their time on a prison industry job or are engaged in maintenance work that assures the smooth running of the institution itself (clerk in the school, electrician, janitor). For such convicts, time is spent with little regard for rehabilitative programs. Not until their impending appearance before the parole board—when suddenly everyone seems concerned with whether they have been "rehabilitated" and are "ready for release" —does anyone seem to care whether they are participating in institutional programs. Instead, the most important thing is that they do their time quietly and without any disruption of the institutional routine. However, some convicts "elect" to take part in rehabilitative programs. They do so for a variety of motives: (1) a sincere desire to learn something that may prove helpful after release, (2) to relieve the boredom of confinement, or (3) to be able to show something to the parole board as evidence of a desire to change.

Recently we have learned something about the differences in facilities and rehabilitative programs in men's and women's prisons. It is apparent that incarcerated men and women do not have access to equivalent prison programs. Arditi et al. (1973) interviewed officials of 47 male prisons and 15 female prisons in 15 states, collecting data on prison rehabilitative programs, services, and facilities. Regarding physical facilities, they found that gun towers, double fences, and concrete walls are rare in women's prisons. Furthermore, women's prisons afford their inmates more privacy and individuality than is found in men's prisons. Even inmate uniforms, which are almost universally mandated in men's prisons, are rare in women's institutions, and the staff at men's prisons are more likely to wear uniforms than their counterparts in women's prisons.

The study found that medical/dental, recreational, and religious services and programs were much more developed in male prisons. Also, there are some differences in the academic education available to men and women prisoners, with women generally disadvantaged in the number and types of programs that are offered. On the other hand, women's prisons tend to have better teacher/convict ratios than men's prisons.

The greatest differences between male and female institutions were found in the areas of vocational training programs and industries. As Table 9–1 shows, male prisons consistently offer a greater variety of vocational programs than are offered in women's prisons. Men seem to be given programs in mechanical skills and physical labor, while women are offered training in clerical skills and personal services. Table 9–2 shows that male prisoners also have access to a much greater variety of industrial job opportunities than female prisoners.

How can we account for these differences in prison programs? Arditi et al. suggest that because women's prisons tend to be smaller it is economically more difficult to justify as extensive a range of programs there as would be found in men's prisons. A much more important explanation, they believe, is the influence of sexual stereotypes, which create disparities especially in vocational and industrial opportunities in male and female prisons. They conclude that

> male and female inmates face markedly different prison experiences: Neither has an exclusive claim to "better" treatment. . . . [M]any inmates of *both* sexes are disadvantaged by being treated according to stereotypes applied to all members of their sex in a segregated correctional system (Arditi et al., 1973: 1244). (Emphasis in original.)

There is additional support for these conclusions, especially the ways in which sexual stereotypes effect programs in women's prisons. A national study (Glick and Neto, 1977) of women's correctional programs found that prison administrators hold distinctive views of the "special needs" of the female prisoner:

1. Her social role in society is homemaking; she needs a homelike setting, even in prison (this is why women inmates turn to homosexuality) she needs stronger ties to family and better relationships with her children; she needs to learn how to care for her children.
2. Being "head of household" is a big problem for many women inmates.
3. Women inmates are unmotivated; they need more counseling and positive social involvement; they need to acquire problem solving skills; women inmates have low self-esteem because of societal stigma.
4. Women have difficulty dealing with institutionalization.

TABLE 9–1
Vocational programs in men's and women's prisons in the United States—1973

Vocational programs

Male Prisons	Air cond. rep.	Arts and crafts	Auto body	Auto mech.	Baking	Barbering	Bookbinding	Brick masonry	Build. maint.	Build. trades	Cabinetmaking	Carpentry	Carpet laying	Chemistry	Computer maint.	Cooking	Data proc.	Diving	Drafting	Electronics	Eng. and appl. rep.	Farming	Farm equip.	Forestry	Furniture mfr.	Graphics	Horticulture	Laundry	Leatherwork	Machine shop	Meat cutting	Metalwork	Off. mach. rep.	Optics	Painting	Plumbing	Printing	Radio/TV rep.	Recreation aide	Silk screening	Shoe repair	Steam fitting	Tailoring	Watch repair	Welding	Clerical	Cosmetology	Dental tech.	Floral design	Food service	Garment mfr.	Housekeeping	IBM keypunch	Nurses' aide	Total
Frank Lee (Ala.)		x	x	x				x												x	x	x																							x										9
Atmore		x	x	x				x													x	x																							x										5
Draper		x	x	x			x	x												x	x						x														x				x										9
Holman																																																							0
Cal. Corr. (Cal.)	x		x	x	x				x		x										x						x						x												x						x				12
Cal. Inst.			x	x	x							x				x		x	x											x	x	x								x	x														7
Folsom		x					x													x										x	x	x	x							x	x				x										7
San Quentin		x	x	x							x						x	x		x	x						x			x	x	x	x					x		x	x				x	x		x							13
Cheshire (Conn.)		x	x	x		x				x		x			x		x				x					x							x				x							x	x	x			x	x					6
Osborn		x	x	x		x				x					x		x																													x			x	x					7
Somers			x			x				x																																			x										3
Menard (Ill.)		x	x	x	x	x													x							x				x	x	x			x	x	x			x			x	x	x									9
Pontiac		x	x	x	x	x													x											x	x	x	x		x	x	x			x	x				x									7
Statesville		x	x	x	x	x					x								x	x	x						x			x	x	x			x	x	x			x	x				x									7
State Farm (Ind.)		x	x	x						x									x		x			x	x																				x										3
State Pris.		x	x	x		x		x	x										x	x				x	x				x	x	x	x					x	x							x										8
State Ref.		x	x	x		x		x		x									x	x				x	x				x	x	x	x	x				x								x										9
Ionia (Mich.)		x	x	x						x																			x	x	x	x	x		x	x	x							x	x										5
Jackson		x	x	x													x												x	x	x	x			x	x	x								x										6
State Pris. (Minn.)		x	x	x	x											x	x		x	x			x	x			x			x	x	x			x	x	x			x	x				x	x									11
State Ref.		x	x	x	x							x				x			x											x	x	x	x		x	x	x				x				x	x									17
Parchman (Miss.)		x	x	x						x		x													x										x	x					x				x										9
Int. Ref. (Mo.)		x	x	x													x			x										x	x	x	x		x	x	x	x							x										9
State Pen.		x	x	x																x	x									x	x	x	x								x											x			7
Training Center																				x	x												x				x	x							x							x			9
Lincoln (Neb.)		x	x	x				x			x	x							x		x				x					x	x	x	x				x				x				x	x								x	9

Institution	Total
Clinton (N.Y.)	2
Elmira	12
Green Haven	9
Wallkill	11
Chillicothe (Ohio)	5
Lebanon	9
Marion	5
So. O. Cor.	3
State Ref.	10
State Cor. (Ore.)	15
State Pen.	8
Rockview (Pa.)	18
Camp Hill	39
Dallas	29
Graterford	11
Huntingdon	34
Pittsburgh	24
Reg. Cor.	2
Monroe (Wash.)	12
Shelton	13
Walla Walla	6

Female Prisons

Institution	Total
Tutwiler (Ala.)	3
Cal. Inst. (Cal.)	3
Niantic (Conn.)	2
Dwight (Ill.)	2
Women's Pris. (Ind.)	2
Det. Cor. (Mich.)	3
Women's Pris. (Minn.)	3
Parchman (Miss.)	1
Cor. Cent. (Mo.)	3
York (Neb.)	2
Bedford Hills (N.Y.)	3
Women's Pris. (Ohio)	6
Women's Cor. (Ore.)	2
Muncy (Pa.)	3
Purdy (Wash.)	3

Source: Ralph R. Arditi et al. "The sexual segregation of American prisons." *Yale Law Journal 82* (May 1973), pp. 1269–71.

TABLE 9-2
Industries in men's and women's prisons in the United States—1973

Male Prisons	Auto rep.	Bookbindery	Cabinetmaking	Cloth mfr.	Coffee roasting	Concrete	Dairy	Data proc.	Dental	Detergent mfr.	Farming	Flag mfr.	Furniture mfr.	Heavy equip. opr.	Library	License plate	Machine shop	Metal shop	Printing	Road sign mfr.	Shoe mfr.	Engine rep.	Tailoring	Twine mfr.	Upholstery	Wax, brush mfr.	Canning	Food service	Garment mfr.	IBM keypunch	Laundry	Total
Frank Lee (Ala.)																																0
Atmore											x																					1
Draper											x																					1
Holman											x					x																2
Cal. Cor. (Cal.)												x																	x			2
Cal. Inst.							x								x	x											x		x			5
Folsom															x	x																2
San Quentin													x	x						x												3
Cheshire (Conn.)	x												x				x	x														4
Osborn																																0
Somers								x					x	x					x	x		x			x	x						6
Menard (Ill.)				x							x							x	x	x									x			6
Pontiac				x																												1
Statesville		x																x	x							x			x			5
State Farm (Ind.)						x	x			x	x																		x			5
State Prison							x			x			x			x													x			6
State Ref.												x	x					x		x	x		x									6
Ionia (Mich.)																	x												x		x	3
Jackson													x	x			x	x											x			5
State Prison (Minn.)														x		x								x								3
State Ref.																x	x															2
Parchman (Miss.)																													x			1
Int. Ref. (Mo.)		x																														1
State Pen.									x	x	x		x			x	x	x	x	x											x	9
Training Center		x								x			x																		x	4
Lincoln (Neb.)							x			x			x			x		x		x						x						7

Institution	Count
Clinton (N.Y.)	2
Elmira	0
Green Haven	2
Wallkill	0
Chillicothe (Ohio)	4
Lebanon	3
Marion	3
So. O. Corr. Inst.	4
State Ref.	2
State Cor. (Ore.)	0
State Pen.	5
Rockview (Pa.)	3
Camp Hill	3
Dallas	4
Graterford	7
Huntingdon	5
Pittsburgh	4
Reg. Cor.	0
Monroe (Wash.)	5
Shelton	1
Walla Walla	4

Female Prisons

Institution	Count
Tutwiler (Ala.)	3
Cal. Inst. (Cal.)	1
Niantic (Conn.)	1
Dwight (Ill.)	1
Women's Prison (Ind.)	1
Det. Cor. (Mich.)	2
Women's Prison (Minn.)	0
Parchman (Miss.)	1
Cor. Center (Mo.)	0
York (Neb.)	1
Bedford Hills (N.Y.)	3
Women's Prison (Ohio)	2
Women's Cor. (Ore.)	0
Muncy (Pa.)	2
Purdy (Wash.)	0

Source: Ralph R. Arditi et al. "The sexual segregation of American prisons." *Yale Law Journal* 82 (May 1973), pp. 1272–73.

5. Women inmates need to learn to stand alone (many are looking for knights in shining armor).
6. They need more medical help (because they're women).
7. The women have few skills; they have employability problems.

"Most of the program emphasis in prisons reflected administrator's views that the inmates need to strengthen their ability to perform in traditional supportive roles as mother and homemaker, rather than as worker" (1977: 39). Another study states that the literature on women's corrections is full of such assumptions, which are "coupled with blatant expressions of the archaic presumptions which such administrators foist upon the individuals committed to their care" (Rogers, 1972: 244). Rogers's comparative study examined two public training schools in Connecticut: the Long Lane School for Girls and the Connecticut School for Boys. She found that the latter institution "has bungled its way (albeit ineptly) into the 20th century while Long Lane School still prepares women to reenter the community as 19th century domestics" (1972: 223). These findings seem typical. Traditionally, as we have seen, institutions for females have offered programs that emphasize domestic skills, personal service, volunteer activities in the free world, and preparation for vocationally supportive roles.

A LOOK AHEAD

Much of what we have said here about women's institutions probably will not stand the test of time. In fact, there is already sufficient evidence to argue that women's institutions are changing and will continue to do so. They are becoming more violent places and women, like male prisoners, are becoming more insistent and vocal in pressing their claims for better treatment. All in all, the years ahead should witness some interesting, perhaps even dramatic, changes in women's institutions.

10

The regimens of correctors:
Probation and parole

Although probation and parole differ in their legal status, they are sufficiently alike as social processes to justify discussing them together. *Probation* is the release to supervision of a person who has been convicted of a crime, *rather than* placement in confinement. On the other hand, *parole* is release to supervision *following* a period of confinement. Offenders are placed on probation by a judge; they are placed on parole by the action of an administrative board typically designated a "parole board." The person who allegedly violates the terms of probation can only be sentenced to confinement by a judge; the alleged parole violator can be returned to confinement by the decision of parole authorities, usually the parole board itself. Despite these differences, both probation and parole supervision are provided by one group of personnel (called U.S. Probation Officers) where violations of federal law are concerned; many states have similarly merged these two processes and responsibilities into a single agency and set of personnel.

This chapter will review statistics on the use of probation and parole and present an overview of sociological research and writing on these two traditional community correctional programs. We will examine some of the controversy surrounding probation and parole and close the chapter with a brief review of some proposals for parole reform.

Extent of use

As we saw in Table 1–1, in 1966 there were 431,000 adult felons and misdemeanants and 224,000 juveniles on probation in the

United States (U.S. Dept. of Justice, 1973). There were 102,000 adults and 60,000 juveniles on parole. Thus, of an estimated 1,252,000 persons under correctional supervision, 52.3 percent were on probation and 12.0 percent were on parole.

Just as the rate of jail and prison use (that is, number of inmates per 100,000 population) varies greatly from one jurisdiction to another, so does the use of probation and parole. However, excepting the federal courts, less is known about the variation in the use of probation than in the use of parole, and our data are most limited in the areas of *juvenile* probation and parole. Table 10–1 shows the state variation in the use of parole during 1976. As can be seen, for

TABLE 10–1
Adult felons paroled from state and federal prisons—1976

	Total number of convicts released during the year	Percent of releasees paroled	Total number released on parole
United States	119,191	64.8	65,962
Federal prisons	12,263	28.2	3,457
State prisons	106,928	68.9	73,724
Alabama	2,621	42.3	1,109
Alaska	112	58.9	66
Arizona	1,283	37.9	486
Arkansas	1,539	89.1	1,372
California	8,058	91.8	7,426
Colorado	1,255	82.5	1,036
Connecticut	1,411	67.5	952
Delaware	289	67.1	194
District of Columbia ...	1,615	51.7	835
Florida	5,659	50.0	2,831
Georgia	4,057	36.1	1,463
Hawaii	115	74.8	86
Idaho	476	46.8	223
Illinois	3,187	90.5	2,886
Indiana	2,038	82.5	1,682
Iowa	670	73.9	495
Kansas	959	83.4	800
Kentucky	2,344	56.9	1,333
Louisiana	1,518	41.0	622
Maine	722	89.0	643
Maryland	3,442	70.8	2,424
Massachusetts	1,021	81.9	836
Michigan	4,306	88.7	3,821
Minnesota	1,109	74.4	825
Mississippi	1,515	73.7	1,117
Missouri	2,002	52.6	1,053
Montana	315	79.0	249
Nebraska	703	54.6	384
Nevada	395	78.2	309
New Hampshire	209	94.8	198

TABLE 10–1 (continued)

	Total number of convicts released during the year	Percent of releasees paroled	Total number released on parole
New Jersey	3,468	93.3	3,237
New Mexico	554	94.6	524
New York	7,274	68.5	4,980
North Carolina	6,730	66.6	4,484
North Dakota	165	77.6	128
Ohio	6,261	72.0	4,510
Oklahoma	1,714	46.4	795
Oregon	1,290	73.6	949
Pennsylvania	3,049	80.2	2,446
Rhode Island	175	57.8	101
South Carolina	2,937	61.9	1,819
South Dakota	223	55.6	124
Tennessee	2,650	58.1	1,540
Texas	8,816	58.2	5,133
Utah	242	90.5	219
Vermont	159	92.5	147
Virginia	2,700	68.6	1,851
Washington	1,500	99.0	1,485
West Virginia	524	70.4	369
Wisconsin	1,413	75.9	1,073
Wyoming	144	37.5	54

Source: U.S. Department of Justice, Law Enforcement Assistance Administration. *Prisoners in State and Federal Institutions on December 31, 1976.* Washington, D.C.: National Criminal Justice Information and Statistics Service, February 1978, Table 7.

the 48 contiguous states the use of parole ranged from a low of 36.1 percent in Georgia to a high of 99.0 percent in Washington. There is probably just as much county and state variation in the use of probation in the United States; some states and local communities have poorly developed probation services, which probably results in fewer persons being placed on probation than would be the case if probation services were more fully developed. In 1977, 38.9 percent of all offenders sentenced in the U.S. district courts were placed on probation (Administrative Office of the U.S. Courts, 1977).

The Uniform Parole Reports

Only in the past decade have correctional administrators and social scientists had available nationwide descriptive data on the operation of parole and parolees. In October 1964 the National Council on Crime and Delinquency initiated the Uniform Parole Reports program. This program, which is similar to the FBI's Uniform Crime

REACTIONS TO A PRISON FURLOUGH

After four months in prison they gave me a weekend out. I hadn't felt in such turmoil since I was a child, when I seem to recall feeling fear or happiness far more intensely than after my teens. It took an entire day to be cleared through the Haney Correctional Centre's labyrinth of offices, checkpoints and gates. When I finally passed through the last, the Main Gate, it was almost evening and half my weekend had already evaporated. She was waiting in the parking lot in the dented little Japanese car she drove, asleep. She'd been there for seven hours.

I was so tense, I just stood there for a while, watching her breathing. This world outside the gates had become so unfamiliar, some idiot part of me just wanted to walk back in and escape the emotional furor involved in dealing with it. By Sunday noon it had abated only slightly; we were sitting in a small Greek restaurant on Twelfth Avenue, and I was still having difficulty suppressing the urge to counterattack when somebody reached too abruptly for the salt. These people all around me, carelessly laughing, thoughtlessly waving their arms about and casually leaving their backs exposed, had become complete strangers; they reeked of freedom and paid absolutely no attention to it. Somehow, I can't say exactly how, the entire scene seemed dangerous, as if a crowd of children were playing ball with live hand grenades.

I couldn't snap out of it. In one way or another, everything I encountered became simply an extension of prison; the only thing that came to mind at the sight of the superbly prepared salad was that it wasn't like the cabbage we ate Inside. Between silences, I talked of prison life until I realized I was surrounding myself with it, then subsided. Finally we gave it up, walked back to the house and made love slowly, wordlessly, until it was time to go.

It was as close as I got to "being out." On the way back I was already so busy thinking ahead about how to negotiate the upcoming bureaucratic hurdles that the ride became tedious and I wished it were over more quickly. I said my goodbyes hurriedly in the parking lot and hastened through the Main Gate to join a knot of other inmates who had also returned from similar leaves. It was like a fraternity reunion, and we didn't even know each other. When I reached the main courtyard, which first affords a complete view of the whole prison complex, I suddenly realized with a mixture of embarrassment and dismay that for the first time in 36 hours I felt relaxed and back in my skin, and that the bastards had caught me too, goddamn them, and I hadn't even felt the net come down.

Source: Andreas Schroeder. *Shaking It Rough*. Garden City, N.Y.: Doubleday, 1976, pp. 142–43.

Reporting program, has created a uniform system of parole data collection and reporting for the states (Neithercutt, Moseley, and Wenk, 1975). A majority of the states now voluntarily provide data on their parolees to the *Uniform Parole Reports*. The resulting publications provide reliable nationwide statistical data on parole that are based upon (1) the uniform definition of items, and (2) individual persons paroled.

Probation-parole outcome

Numerous studies of probation outcome show that a clear majority of offenders placed on probation successfully complete it without new criminal convictions. For instance, an early study by England (1955) of 490 federal offenders found that only 17.7 percent had new convictions after placement on probation. These findings are typical; upwards of 80 percent of probationers usually are successful when recidivism is used as a criterion measure. So although there continues to be disagreement and uncertainty, as to exactly what (if anything) it is about probation that accounts for its relative success, the success itself is uncontested. Not all types of offenders do equally well on probation; success rates vary, depending upon certain background characteristics of offenders and their crimes.

What is true of probation is also true of parole: The vast majority of parolees successfully complete their parole period without new criminal convictions, and the degree of success varies considerably depending upon the personal and offense characteristics of parolees. This can be clearly illustrated with data from the *Uniform Parole Reports*. In the 1972 period, 20,576 felons (19,540 males and 1,036 females) were paroled by those states that subsequently provided three-year follow-up data (National Probation and Parole Institutes, 1976). The results of this follow-up are presented in Table 10–2. At the end of three years, 74 percent of the males and 82 percent of the females either were still on parole or had successfully completed it. The failures had absconded from parole supervision (4 percent of the males and 5 percent of the females), had been returned to prison for technical violations of parole rules (15 percent and 10 percent respectively), or had been returned to prison with a new major criminal conviction (7 percent and 3 percent, respectively). Consistent with much previous research, Table 10–2 also shows that homicide offenders had very high success rates (82 percent for males and 88 percent for females), while the success rates for forgers (64 percent and 68 percent, respectively) and auto

TABLE 10–2
Percent of parolees successful in first three years for males and females
paroled in 1972

	Percent successful	
	Males	Females
Commitment offense		
Homicide	82	88
Aggravated assault	76	90
Rape	75	n.a.
Armed robbery	68	77
Auto theft	67	—*
Larceny/Theft	74	70
Forgery	64	68
Narcotics	80	81
Parolees with prior prison sentence (s)	67	76
Parolees with prior nonprison conviction (s)	72	76
Parolees whose commitment to prison was for probation or parole violation	69	72

* Not enough cases.
   Source: National Probation and Parole Institutes. *1972 Parolees, Three Year Follow-up and Trend Analysis.* Davis, Cal.: National Council on Crime and Delinquency Research Center, December 1976.

thieves (67 percent for males—with no comparable rate for females, due to an insufficient number of cases) were much lower. There are no comparable data for juveniles. In fact, very little research has been conducted on the juvenile parole process and the problems of juvenile parolees (an exception is Arnold, 1970).

SOCIOLOGICAL WORK

Much of the speculation and research on probation and parole has sprung from liberal political convictions and from the belief that, because probation and parole are rehabilitative in intent, they could not simultaneously be punitive. Probation and parole are assumed to be more humane, effective, and efficient than incarceration; consequently, their merits have been taken for granted. Largely for these reasons, parole research has taken administrative ends as researchable problems. Only recently has there been sufficient detached interest to investigate seriously and systematically some of the long-held conventional wisdoms about probation and parole.

Probation-parole prediction

Social scientists have been conducting parole prediction research for nearly 50 years. (More recently the same type of research has been extended to the area of probation prediction.) The objective of parole prediction research is the development of *experience tables* that can be used by parole boards and other decision makers. Using official records as data and actuarial methods of analysis, this research sorts offenders into groups that have known—or presumably known—risks of violating parole by the commission of new crimes. A variety of statistical procedures have been employed, from rather crude early ones to contemporary multivariate approaches (Gottfredson, 1970; Wilkins, 1971).

The traditional importance of prediction theory and research can be seen by the amount of space devoted to it in earlier sociological textbooks on corrections. For example, of 738 pages devoted to courts, sentencing, and corrections in the second edition of *Sociology of Punishment and Correction* (Johnston, Savitz, and Wolfgang, 1970), 100 pages, or 14 percent, deal with the process of prediction. Critics have charged that this type of research illustrates clearly how supposedly detached scientists have aided the correctional establishment, helped to promote an individualistic conception of the nature of "the" crime problem, and mystified the real nature of crime control in the U.S.

> The administrative problems of parole boards [have been] seen as problems for criminologists. The bulk of their research focused on "prediction," and asked the question, "Is the parole board using the right factors for selection?" . . . The problem was seen as one of having to identify features about an individual that correlated with his or her ability to stay out of prison, expressed in terms of a prediction of "risk." The focus was on the individual's psychological makeup or immediate social environment, and not on the social order itself (Schmidt, 1977: xv).

This research has uncovered a variety of factors which, taken singly or in combination, have proven to be correlated with parole success (O'Leary and Glaser, 1972). We already have seen that parole violation rates tend to be lower for those offenders convicted of homicide or rape, crimes which, unlike property offenses, least often serve as vocations. Research suggests the validity of two other generalizations: (1) parole success increases with the age of prison releasees, and (2) parole success decreases as the length of releasee's previous criminal record increases (the longer the previous criminal record, the lower the success rate).

Parole boards and judges have been urged to employ information of this type as an aid in decision making. Nevertheless, questions remain as to whether they *should* be guided by it and precisely how much use they make of it.

The trouble with prediction is simply that it will not work—that is, it will not work for individuals, only for groups. A parole board may know that of 100 offenders with a certain set of characteristics, 80 will probably succeed and 20 will fail on parole. But the board members do not know whether the man who is before them belongs with the 80 or the 20 (Stanley, 1976: 56).

Despite these and other criticisms, probation-parole prediction research continues. As we shall see in Chapter 14, one type of parole prediction approach—base expectancy—may have some value as a method for the quasi-experimental evaluation of correctional programs.

Probation-parole decision making

The origins of parole in America can be found in the late 19th century. Parole became an integral part of the reformatory movement and has generally continued today as an important type of correctional disposition and program. Along with the indeterminate sentence and prison classification, it is a basic part of several different preventive ideals, although its justifications are most clearly evident in the medical model of criminality. According to this version of rehabilitative ideology, informed and accurate decisions can be made concerning which offenders require varying degrees of state intervention—in the form of "treatment." It is felt to be possible and desirable to sort offenders into homogeneous categories on the basis of (1) their underlying problem or "need," (2) the appropriate treatment strategy, and (3) predictions about their likely future conduct, especially in the absence of therapeutic intervention. However, it is impossible to specify in advance precisely how much time will be required to "cure" the offender's "disease." Therefore, flexibility and discretion are required so that offenders can be treated as long as necessary—but no longer. Release on parole should occur at the point where they have received the maximum benefit from their treatment and pose no substantial threat to the free community.

Obviously, such a scheme can only work effectively if it is actually possible to make accurate diagnoses of offenders and reliable predictions of their behavior. A variety of evidence suggests this cannot be done. (Here we disregard the important ethical and legal questions posed by any scheme of punishing persons for what they might do in the *future*, or for what they are alleged to *be* instead of what they have already *done*.)

Hakeem (1961) asked ten parole officers and ten laymen to read ten standardized correctional case summaries and to predict whether the subjects of the reports would violate the terms of their parole. He found no appreciable difference between the two groups in the accuracy of their predictions (which he already knew, since real cases were used). Takagi and Robison (1969) asked 316 parole agency employees to read ten actual case histories involving suspected violations of parole and to make a decision as to whether the alleged parole violators should be continued on parole or returned to prison as a parole violator.

> Judgments of the 316 agency staff members varied wildly. Among them were five who recommended ten returns to prison, and one who recommended one return. About half the staff members would have returned either six or seven of the parolees—however, even those who would have returned the same *number* of cases were not in agreement about *which* cases they would return. Agents who came from a background of prison work would have returned many more alleged violators to prison than those who came from some outside social work position (Mitford, 1973: 221). (Emphasis in the original.)

Research conducted on *correctional* decision making is not the only relevant research here. For example, there is a great deal of accumulated research conducted by psychologists that calls into question the ability of clinicians to reliably diagnose behavioral afflictions. There seems to be little doubt that many of the signs that clinicians use as evidence of personality pathology are themselves highly unreliable, and perception of them varies greatly from one diagnostician to another. In an interesting piece of research, Rosenhan (1973) arranged to have eight persons with no history of psychological pathology admitted to a psychiatric hospital as pseudo-patients. *All eight of the volunteers were diagnosed as being mentally ill,* and even after they elected to inform hospital authorities of their pseudo-patient status they were not believed. Instead, their accounts of their activities (as participants in a scientific study) were interpreted as further evidence of their "illness." Clearly this suggests that purported experts are unreliable in their diagnoses of pathological behavior.

The extreme ambiguity of alleged psychopathological symptoms and the bias evident in the diagnostic process are only two of the reasons why it is important to maintain a skeptical stance toward the claims to expertise made by correctional workers. When these problems are coupled with an extremely low probability of occurrence for many of the kinds of behavior that they attempt to predict, the potential for injustice becomes very great. During the early 1970s, for example, there was much talk about the "preventive detention" of persons thought to have a high potential for violent behavior. However,

> . . . the indications are that any system of predicting future [violent] crimes would result in a vastly larger number of erroneous confinements—that is, confinements of persons predicted to engage in violent crime who would not, in fact, do so. Indeed, all the experience with predicting violent conduct suggests that in order to spot a significant proportion of future violent criminals, we would have to reverse the traditional maxim of the criminal law and adopt a philosophy that it is "better to confine ten people who would not commit predicted crimes, than to release one who would" (Dershowitz, 1971: 32).

Follow-up studies of mental patients and prisoners ordered released as a result of U.S. Supreme Court decisions have shown very graphically just how unreliable expert predictions of future behavior can be—while also suggesting that the presence of treatment after release can be quite irrelevant for offenders (Eichman, 1966, cited in Orland, 1975: 114–15; Steadman and Kveles, 1972).

The same appears to be true of clinicians' *predictions* of behavior. Meehl (1954) reviewed previous studies that compared the accuracy of behavioral predictions made by clinicians with those made on the basis of actuarial methods. The latter proved overwhelmingly to be more accurate than the former. These findings are not unusual.

> In the ability to classify a large proportion of parole applicants into favourable categories which experience demonstrates have markedly above average success rates, and into unfavourable categories which prove to have markedly below average success rates, statistical prediction methods have been shown to be clearly more accurate than prognoses by psychiatrists, psychologists, sociologists, prison wardens or prison unit officers (O'Leary and Glaser, 1972: 189).

The implications of this are clear: it is extremely difficult for clinicians—whether in or out of corrections—to reliably diagnose and predict behavior. This fact cannot be ignored by those committed to an ideology of correctional treatment.

Still another body of research literature casts doubt on the claims of people-changers because of what it reveals about the actual decision-making process they employ. The substance of this process, *a priori*, seems to diverge from what we would expect to be true if there was any validity to rehabilitative ideologies as guides to decision making. Whereas we have previously argued that correctional personnel—and clinicians generally—cannot make reliable and valid diagnoses or predictions, here we suggest that the manner in which they make decisions itself undermines their ideological position.

We begin with research that examines decision making in a "pure" fashion (without the intrusion of bureaucratic or interpersonal considerations). Carter (1967) has reported the results of a simulation of the decision-making process among probation officers. Using a methodology employed in an earlier study by Wilkins (1965), Carter asked 14 U.S. probation officers to read a series of pieces of information about five different defendants and to come to a decision whether to recommend for or against probation. The information was presented in such a way that subjects could only view one piece at a time; consequently, the experimenter could note the order in which different pieces of information were examined in the decision-making process. The procedure also permitted Carter to determine if and when subjects changed their minds about their recommendation and, if so, the type of information which influenced their decision. If there is any substance to the claims of correctors, presumably we would expect to see a high degree of similarity in the process by which they make decisions, and in the kinds of information they employ in doing so. Carter actually observed only minimal similarity in the probation officers' decision-making process.

> A brief examination of the "decision-making" of the probation officers indicates that each officer develops his own style. . . . None of the officers selected information at random; instead they followed a common basic pattern that was still somehow unique to the individual (Carter, 1967: 209).

Just as important, Carter found that probation officers make decisions relating to presentence report recommendations with relatively small amounts of information—an average of 4.7 items of information prior to the decision. Moreover, the receipt of additional information after the recommendation has little effect upon the recommendation in most cases, except to serve as confirmation of a decision already reached. Given this variation in probation officers' decision making, and the fact that they rarely change their decisions, even with the receipt of additional information, we must necessarily ask whether this doesn't call into question their employment of a body of arcane "expert" knowledge.

Gross (1967), too, sought to determine what kinds of information probation officers find most useful in decision making. In a mail questionnaire, he asked 70 Minnesota juvenile probation officers to rank the various sections of the presentence report in terms of their usefulness for appropriate or accurate recommendation of disposition. The data do not permit an examination of the variation among officers; but Gross does present the subjects' mean rankings for ten different types of information usually contained in the presentence report. "The probation officers ranked as *most* important (1) the child's attitude toward the offense, (2) family data, and (3) previous delinquency problems" (1967: 214). (Emphasis in the original.)

What is especially significant about these rankings is the relative *unimportance* of those kinds of information which, presumably, probation officers would be expected to rank highly on the basis of the ideology of rehabilitation (for example, psychological test data, psychiatric examination results). In fact, a consideration of the kinds of data the subjects find most useful suggests they are less oriented toward the psychodynamics of offenders than they are toward rather straightforward commonsensical notions, such as whether the offenders are repentant. Again a discrepancy exists between the kinds of information we would expect to weigh heavily in the decision-making process and those kinds that ultimately receive emphasis. Another study (Reed and King, 1966) employed a questionnaire methodology to study probation officers' decision making. The researchers found a basic split between rural-conservative and urban-liberal officers in decision-making styles. In situations where the probation officers had to decide whether to revoke probation, rural-conservative officers more often opted for taking official action against probationers. When they did so, they typically rationalized their decisions by citing the need to maintain social order. Urban-liberal probation officers less often favored probation revocation, opting instead for unofficial methods of handling violative behavior. Moreover, they rationalized their decisions as being in the best interests of the probationers.

Parole procedures and parole decision making

As is true of virtually all aspects of the correctional process, formal procedures for releasing felons on parole vary considerably

---

THE PAROLE BOARD AND CONVICTS

We had our body of wisdom and our intuitions as to how they must function, but they also had learned something about us. They had been subjected to the most artful and elaborate cons until now they took nothing on faith. They knew we would say anything to get out. Every man who came before them sat there with a single purpose—to somehow leave that room with his freedom restored. Few cared how.

Source: Malcolm Braly. *False Starts*. Boston: Little, Brown, 1976, p. 253.

among the states. Such variation is found not only in the composition of parole boards—their size and the qualifications of their
members—but also in their formalized procedures for conducting
hearings and notifying convicts of hearing results. Table 10–3 summarizes the results of a 1972 survey of parole board procedures

TABLE 10–3
Methods of parole hearings for felony offenders in United States—January 1972

Jurisdiction	Persons conducting hearing	How inmate informed of decision	Prison staff recommendation
Alabama	Full board	In person§§	Yes
Alaska	Varies†	After hearing¶¶	Yes
Arizona	Full board	In person	Some
Arkansas	Full board	After hearing	No
California	At least 2-person panel‡	After hearing	No
California Women	Full board	In person	Yes
Colorado	At least 2-member panel	After hearing	No
Connecticut	3-member panels§	In person	No
Delaware	Full board	After hearing	Yes
District of Columbia	At least 2-member panel¶	After hearing	Yes
Florida	1 member or rep.	After hearing	Yes
Georgia	No hearings	—	Yes
Hawaii	No hearings	—	No
Idaho	Full board	In person	Some
Illinois	3-member panels	After hearing	Yes
Indiana	Full board	In person	Yes
Indiana Women	Full board	In person	Yes
Iowa	Full board	In person	Yes
Kansas	Full board	After hearing	No
Kentucky	3-member panels	After hearing	No
Louisiana	Full board	In person	Yes
Maine	Full board	After hearing	No
Maryland	2- or 3-member panels	In person	Yes
Massachusetts	3-member panels	In person	Yes
Michigan	2-member panels	In person	Yes
Minnesota	3-member panels	In person	Yes
Mississippi*	Full board	After hearing	No
Missouri	2-member panel	After hearing	Yes
Montana	Full board	After hearing	Yes
Nebraska	Full board	In person	Yes
Nevada	Panels of 2 persons‡	After hearing	Yes
New Hampshire	Varies#	In person	Yes

TABLE 10–3 (continued)

Jurisdiction	Persons conducting hearing	How inmate informed of decision	Prison staff recommendation
New Jersey	Full board	After hearing	Yes
New Mexico	2- or 3-member panels	After hearing	Yes
New York	3-member panels	After hearing	No
North Carolina*	2-person panel**	After hearing	Yes
North Dakota	Full board	After hearing	No
Ohio	2-member panels	After hearing	No
Oklahoma	Panels of at least 3	After hearing	Yes
Oregon	Panels of at least 2	In person	Yes
Pennsylvania	Varies††	After hearing	Yes
Rhode Island	At least 3-member panel	After hearing	Some
South Carolina	Full board	In person	Yes
South Dakota	Full board	After hearing	No
Tennessee	Full board	After hearing	Yes
Texas	No hearings	—	Yes
U.S. Parole Board	1-member or rep.	After hearing	No
Utah	Full board	In person	Yes
Vermont	2-member panels	In person	Yes
Virginia	Varies‡‡	After hearing	Some
Washington	2-member panels	In person	Yes
West Virginia	Full board	In person	No
Wisconsin	2- or 3-member panels	In person	No
Wyoming	Full board	After hearing	Yes

* Cases are screened and selected for hearing.

† One member only may hear for federal cases and outlying areas; otherwise, full board hears.

‡ Any combination of hearing representatives and board members may be used.

§ Chairman is always present as part of panel.

¶ A hearing officer or a member of the parole staff may sit in place of a board member.

The full board sits on cases with minima of two years or more; otherwise, the state parole officer will hear alone.

** Panel consists of one board member and one case staff worker.

†† One or more board members will hear cases.

‡‡ One member hears cases in smaller institutions; two members hear cases in larger ones.

§§ "In person" indicates that the decision is given personally to the inmate by the persons conducting the parole hearing.

¶¶ "After hearing" means that the parole decision is delivered to the inmate either by mail or someone other than the persons conducting the parole hearing.

Source: O'Leary, Vincent, and Joan Nuffield. *The Organization of Parole Systems in the United States.* Hackensack, N.J.: National Council on Crime and Delinquency, October 1972, pp. xxxii–xxxiii.

among the 50 states, the District of Columbia, and the federal government.

Research on parole board decision making has produced inconsistent results. On the one hand, various studies show that parole board members spend only a few minutes on convict hearings. The data in Table 10–4 show that most parole boards hear a rather large number of cases on a typical day. Another study suggests that they spend an average of fifteen minutes interviewing each convict, with an approximate range of from four to 30 minutes (Stanley, 1976: 38–39). This does not seem to be adequate time to make a very thorough appraisal of the convict's strengths, weaknesses, and readiness for parole—even if this were possible. (Parole boards respond that they spend a great deal more time studying the convict's records, and this is ignored by studies that concentrate only on the amount of time spent on hearings.) Further, O'Leary and Nuffield (1972a) surveyed 51 parole boards in the United States and found that 40 do not even record the reasons for their decisions to release or not release on parole. While this by itself does not necessarily lead to the conclusion that parole boards rely upon ad hoc, commonsensical criteria in reaching their decisions, other research does suggest such a conclusion. Dawson (1966) and a team of Yale Law School researchers (Genego et al., 1975) found in their observations that a whole host of variables extraneous both to the convict's "condition" and the likelihood of recidivism effect the release decision. Reasons for which parole boards often deny parole include: (1) poor institutional adjustment—which serves to reinforce prison disciplinary practices; (2) a perceived obligation to protect the public from those who have shown themselves capable of assaultive behavior (that is, "serious" crimes); (3) the belief that a convict may have served too little time for the institution to "get to know her"

TABLE 10–4
Average number of parole hearings per day: 51 jurisdictions, felony offenders (1972)*

Average number of cases heard per day	Number of parole boards
1–19	11
20–29	15
30–39	14
40 and over	11

* Excludes Georgia, Hawaii, and Texas, where no parole hearings were conducted in 1972.

Source: Vincent O'Leary and Joan Nuffield. *The Organization of Parole Systems in the United States.* Hackensack, N.J.: National Council on Crime and Delinquency, October 1972, p. xxx.

One of the great games we played in the joint was to imagine what we would do our first night out. I'm going to get a good room, take a big healthy shit and a long hot shower, catch a shave and go out to the best restaurant I can find and order the biggest steak on the menu. This is possible if you want to spend all your gate money the first night, but soon fantasy slips in, and the waitress is a fine chick, and you come on to her and discover she's really a jazz singer, weathering a dry spell between gigs, and you arrange to pick her up when she gets off, and the two of you hit the after-hours spots, dig the sounds until dawn, when you walk arm-in-arm up Telegraph Hill to the very top where her pad overlooks both bridges and most of the bay, and there on the coffee table are *The Prophet* by Kahlil Gibran and Walter Benton's *This Is My Beloved*. She pours wine, rolls a joint and puts Bird on the record player. You kiss and she sighs and says, You must of really been lonely, baby. And when you make it, you don't come immediately as you will for weeks, but ride on and on, Oh, Lord, as her apartment windows slowly turn bright with the sun.

Nothing like this happens. I was too shy to speak to anyone. I wandered down into North Beach and went to a jazz club where I sat at the bar and stared at myself in the mirror. A male Cinderella, already a little too old for the part.

Source: Malcolm Braly. *False Starts.* Boston: Little, Brown, 1976, pp. 264–65.

and her case; (4) to give the convict time to benefit from prison programs; (5) the belief that the convict has not served enough time for the type of crime he committed; and (6) to avoid criticism of the parole system should the convict commit a new crime—especially one that is widely publicized (Schmidt, 1977: 123). Scott (1974) did a computer analysis of the relationship of various factors considered by the parole board to the number of months convicts were actually imprisoned in one midwestern state. He found that the seriousness of the crime was the best predictor of the severity of punishment. Schmidt (1977) conducted similar research on a sample of 7,286 convicts who appeared for a parole hearing before the U.S. Board of Parole in the period from November 1970 to June 1972. The population from which the sample was chosen consisted of all cases considered for parole during that period. The data consisted of information regarding the background characteristics and past and present performance of the potential parolees. Schmidt sought to determine whether parole decisions were made on the basis of the three factors that the U.S. Board of Parole had said were the basis for its decisions (that is, offense severity, normal amount of time to be served for such an offense, and salient-factor score). Her computer analysis suggested that "the predictive power [for the parole decision] of knowing the offense severity, the score on the nine salient factors, and the time served is not great. It would appear that other criteria are operating in the parole decision-making process" (1977: 53). Further analysis revealed that three variables, in combination, had the greatest overall effect on the parole decision: (1) the amount of time the convict had served, (2) the length of her sentence, and (3) her prison custody classification (i.e., minimum, medium, or maximum). Studies such as these can be interpreted in different ways.It can be argued that parole boards are actually engaged in a process of trying to assure that convicts who have committed so-called serious crimes are sufficiently punished for their crimes. Alternatively, the kindest interpretation from the parole boards' perspective would be that "the nature of the crime, the prisoner's past, his demeanor, the suitability of the parole plan, and other considerations are used with varying emphasis in different decisions" (Stanley, 1976: 60). In either case, such research findings raise questions about not only the expertise and true nature of the parole decision, but its fundamental fairness as well.

Still, there is some research suggesting that parole boards are not so unpredictable as sometimes alleged in their decision making or necessarily overly concerned with punitive considerations. Questionnaires were sent to all state parole board members in the United States, with approximately half of them responding (N = 139). In these questionnaires the members were asked their estimate of how often, in the preceding year, they considered various items in their decisions to grant or to deny parole. The results reveal that

> no matter how one designates or tabulates it, the leading preoccupation of most parole board members, in their decisions to grant or to deny parole, was their judgement on whether or not the prisoner was likely to commit a serious crime if paroled (O'Leary and Glaser, 1972: 138).

Probation-parole officer types and differential effectiveness

Research of the type we have been reviewing casts doubt on the reliability and validity of clinical judgments generally. Nevertheless, such research often finds that some clinicians perform much better than others in that their predictions are more accurate. Partly for reasons such as this, some social scientists have endeavored to construct theoretical probation-parole officer types, much as efforts have been made to isolate different types of offenders. Ultimately, it is hoped, certain types of probation-parole officers will prove to be better suited and, therefore, more successful with certain types of probationers-parolees. In such a case, we will be able to match offenders with officers to achieve maximum probation-parole effectiveness.

Most efforts to distinguish types of officers begin with a recognition of the different purposes of parole and the resulting dual functions of parole officers. They are combination police officers and social workers, simultaneously providing assistance to parolees and controlling and monitoring them to prevent the commission of new crimes. The manner in which the parole officer reconciles these often conflicting demands varies considerably from one officer to another. Several writers have attempted to distinguish extant differences in the personal style and orientation of parole officers as they actually carry out their tasks. For instance, Ohlin, Piven, and Pappenfort (1956) distinguished three styles of officer performance and related these to three conceptions of parole work:

1. The "punitive officer" is the guardian of middle-class community morality; he attempts to coerce the offender into conforming by means of threats and punishment and his emphasis is on control, protecting the community against the offender, and systematic suspicion of those under supervision.
2. The "protective agent" . . . vacillates between protecting the offender and protecting the community. His tools are direct assistance, lecturing, and praise and blame. He is recognized by his ambivalent emotional involvement with the offender and others in the community as he shifts back and forth in taking sides with one against the other.
3. The "welfare worker" . . . [has as his] ultimate goal the improved welfare of the client, a condition achieved by helping him in his individual adjustment within limits imposed by the client's capacity. He feels that the only genuine guarantee of community protection lies in the client's personal adjustment since external conformity will be only temporary and in the long run may make a successful adjustment more difficult. Emotional neutrality permeates his relationships. The diagnostic categories and treatment skills which he employs stem from an objective and theoretically based assessment of the client's situation, needs, and capacities . . . (1956; quoted in Glaser, 1964: 430).

Glaser adopted and modified this scheme by adding a fourth type—the "passive agents" who see "their jobs as sinecures, requiring only a minimum effort"—and changing the label and description of the protective agent to the "paternal officer." His resulting fourfold typology is derived logically by cross-classifying two variables: em-

"What kind of parole officer have you got?"

"A hope-to-die asshole. Man, he's so square—one of those edu-cated fools. Got book learnin' up the ass, but doesn't know a fuckin' thing about life or people. He's one of those guys that lived in a neat white house with a picket fence and pretty lawn and went to Sunday school every day until he was 16. He never stole anything in his life—never had to steal anything. Him and his wife both teach Sunday school. I know he doesn't give her any head . . . probably didn't ball the broad until they were married. He acts like his job is some kind of missionary work among the heathen parolees."

The crude description was funny in a way, yet Willy's difficulties were vivid. There'd be no communication between someone like Willy and the personality he described.

"He should be happy you're not hooked and stealing," I said.

"He wants everyone to be like him. People are different. I know that, and I'm just an illiterate dope fiend. I'll show you what an asshole he is. If he knew I was driving a car he'd throw me in jail and write a report to the parole board. He'd feel bad, but to him it would be his responsibility. Can't he understand that being without a car in L.A. is like being in Death Valley without water? It'd take me four hours to ride a bus to work."

Source: Edward Bunker. *No Beast So Fierce.* New York: W. W. Norton & Co., 1973, p. 46.

phasis on control and emphasis on assistance, as shown in Table 10–5. Paul Takagi devised another scheme of parole officer types:

1. The "rebels" who dissipate most of their energies fighting the agency. These workers find themselves in conflict with the agency rules and their supervisors. Such agents believe that the organizational rules and procedures are silly and hamper their best efforts, and they criti-cize the supervisors for lack of knowledge and competence.

TABLE 10–5
Types of parole officers (Glaser, 1964)

Emphasis on assistance	*Emphasis on control*	
	High	*Low*
High	Protective agent	Welfare worker
Low	Punitive agent	Passive agent

2. The "accommodator" also experiences severe frustrations and conflicts, but primarily in the area of providing services to the client. This is the agent who is committed to his profession and to the ideology of treatment which he believes can be implemented in an administrative structure . . . [and] attempts to work within the framework of organizational policies and administrative relationships.

3. The "noncommitted" whom parole agency administrators refer to as "bodies filling positions in the organization." His work style is guided by task objectives and ignores the goals of the organization. He is neither oriented toward the needs of the client nor the needs of the supervisor. He is thoroughly familiar with the routines of the job; and he can be depended upon to do the minimum; that is, eight hours of work for eight hours of pay.

4. Finally, the "conformist" who does not find himself in conflict with agency rules and procedures. He works within the framework of the administrative structure to achieve task objectives as well as the officially stated goals of the organization (Takagi, 1967; quoted in Irwin, 1970: 129–41).

Surprisingly little research has examined differences in the job behavior of different types of parole officers. Among federal proba-

---

. . . I began to have a series of curious collisions with my current parole officer. When I had first transferred to the Hollywood office I had been assigned to the caseload of the sort of officer I was familiar with—you didn't give him trouble, he was willing to leave you alone. If you seemed to be going along reasonably well, he was willing to put you on "hold" in his mind and concentrate on those who were obviously failing. If you sent your reports in on time, lived quietly, didn't collect a wreath of traffic tickets, beat the shit out of your old lady or get picked up for D and D, you could wear out your parole with a minimum of interference.

But you were also, not infrequently, transferred from one caseload to another without notice, and this is what happened to me. For months the parole office had shown no interest in me, no one had even taken the trouble to come by to confirm I actually lived at the place where I reported my address. Then twice, ten days apart, I found the card of a new P.O. under my door. He had called, found me not home, and left his spoor. I called the parole office, asked for him, but he wasn't in. I left a message, but he didn't call back. I thought of going by to see him. It was a small ploy some of us used. Invent or exaggerate a problem, ask for advice, let him imagine he's helped you, and, meanwhile, he's reassured and isn't likely to drop by your home unannounced.

Source: Malcolm Braly. *False Starts.* Boston: Little, Brown, 1976, pp. 342–43.

tion-parole officers Glaser found some differences in the personal backgrounds of his four types. Using questionnaires, he also found some interesting differences in parole officer responses to various kinds of hypothetical parolee-problem situations (1964: 437–42). Dembo (1972) developed a twofold typology of parole officers and examined variations in the behavior of the two types. Ninety-four New York State parole officers were interviewed, and agency files were examined to determine variations in their actual case handling procedures. He found a relationship between parole officer orientation and their recommendations to return parolees to prison as technical parole violators.

> The results . . . show the existence of two parole officer groups, originally uncovered by Reed and King (1966) in their study of North Carolina probation officers: (1) an urban-liberal, probationer-oriented group favoring unofficial actions short of revocation and (2) a rural-conservative group, with a preference for officer-oriented, or social-order rationalizations favoring revocation (1972: 209).

Pursuing this line of thought, Dembo further suggests that

> apparently, the experience of living in the cosmopolitan, urban culture sensitizes officer awareness and fosters reintegrative concern for the antisocial products of indigenous slums. And, conversely, prolonged life experience in the predominantly white, Protestant, rural culture does not stimulate concern and involvement in antisocial persons, making it conducive to punishment orientations (1972: 209).

Research of this type, which examines and attempts to explain differences in the decision making of probation-parole officers, is extremely important and should be continued. It begins with the recognition that probation-parole officers have some discretion in the way they perform their work and in the kinds of information they choose to report to their superiors. Any serious attempt to understand parole supervision and parole violation must somehow incorporate an understanding of the forces that influence probation-parole officer decision making. In this respect the parole-violation-production process is similar to the crime-rate-production process; it necessitates an understanding of police decision making and the forces which effect it. Further studies of the parole-violation-rate process will overcome the traditional tendency to regard parole outcome "as simply the function of parole behavior to the neglect of the parole agent as decision maker" (Martinson, Kassebaum, and Ward, 1964: 37).

There seems to be little doubt that different types of parole officers can be identified via empirical research. It is also quite likely that future research will demonstrate differences in the personal backgrounds and work behavior of these types. It is questionable, however, whether this type of research will aid us in understanding differences in the behavior of *parolees*.

> This is because these types are constructed from variables which (1) result in differences in parole-agent behavior which are not visible to the parolee and (2) are related to differences in agent behavior which though visible to the parolee are not important to him. For instance, in their actual performance in regard to the parolee it has been pointed out that persons with a "social-worker" orientation are in effect more "punitive" than "cop-oriented" parole agents. . . . An officer who is concerned primarily with the welfare of the parolee and has a treatment orientation to parole work can still be very intolerant of deviant behavior. Persons trained in social welfare usually have middle-class orientations and have often had much less contact with deviant subcultures than, say, an ex-policeman. Furthermore, other writers have suggested that authority can be a "treatment" tool. . . . Consequently, the treatment-punishment dichotomy does not make a meaningful division in parole-agent behavior relative to the parolee (Irwin, 1970: 165–66).

An even more important shortcoming of decision-making research is its failure to give adequate recognition to the way in which bureaucratic structures and processes effect decision makers. Decision-making research must recognize that the parole agent, like the police officer, does not have unlimited discretion. Instead, the parole agent's discretion is constrained by "the complex limits set by operations manuals, by district officer supervision, and by career concerns" (Martinson et al., 1964: 36). This is a theme we will explore in more detail in Chapter 11.

PROBATION-PAROLE: DEVELOPMENTS AND ISSUES

The subtitle of a recent analysis of the parole system is "the problem of parole" (Stanley, 1976). It is a revealing choice of words. Until recently, when parole was discussed, any problems that were identified were assumed to be problems *in* parole. Many now seem willing to believe that parole itself is a problem. In this respect, the recent fate of parole is different from that of probation, which has been praised and its merits extolled as a form of community treatment. Given the substantial similarity of the two types of programs, this different reception seems strange indeed. While the blessings of an expanded use of probation are taken for granted, the same is true for the assumed shortcomings of parole.

Probation subsidy

In 1965 California initiated a probation subsidy program, which has since been copied by several other states. Legislation empowered the state to provide fiscal subsidies to county probation departments if they reduced commitments to state adult and juvenile institutions. In other words, the basic principle of probation subsidy is to reward counties for *not* sentencing offenders to state penal institutions.

> The benchmark by which a county's earnings are computed is its own past commitment performance over a five-year period beginning in 1959 and continuing through 1963, or the two years 1962–63, whichever is higher. This five-year or two-year average commitment rate becomes a never changing "base commitment" rate for the county.
>
> Annually, this rate is applied against the county's population to determine its "expected number of commitments." A county is entitled to subvention if its total commitments for any given year are less than its "expected number of commitments." The amount of subvention is dependent upon a formula that provides varied amounts from $2,080 to $4,000 per case, with the larger amounts taking effect as counties increase their percent of reduction (Saleeby, 1972: 4–5; quoted in Lerman, 1975: 108).

The designers of this program argued that county correctional programming was at least equal if not superior to state institutionalization and parole. The goals of probation subsidy involved a decrease in the rates of first commitments to state penal facilities and the growth of local probation services. As it has worked out in practice, the California probation subsidy program has had some unintended and, presumably, undesirable consequences. Lerman notes that many more youths were locked up at the *local* level in 1970 than in 1965, although fewer youths were being locked up at the *state* level. Those confined in state institutions were having their length of stay and parole stay increased. Thus, "the amount of local youth lockups more than compensated for the fewer state lockups of juveniles" (1975: 209). At present we do not know whether other states that have established probation subsidy programs have had similar experiences; nor do we know what the overall system impact of probation subsidy has been.

Parole under attack

We have pointed to several problems with the assumptions and operation of parole, problems that would seem to be endemic to it.

They have probably been present as long as parole itself. Nevertheless, until recent years few people "chose" to see these problems or to take them seriously. This has now changed drastically. Parole is under attack from radicals, liberals, and conservatives alike, and there are proposals for reform from every quarter. We will comment briefly on some of these criticisms and proposals.

As we shall discuss at greater length in Chapter 13, prisoners and parolees have mounted numerous and sustained legal attacks on the fairness of traditional correctional practices, including parole. The courts have called for closer compliance with constitutional guarantees, and correctional administrators have been forced to change some of their operating procedures. The secrecy and apparent arbitrariness, which have long been a part of the parole process, are now under increasing attack.

As convicts have become more vocal and unwilling to tolerate correctional injustice, others have also "discovered" it. At the same time, parole has been attacked for its ineffectiveness, that is, for having little demonstrable effect on recidivism rates. The net result of these two charges of injustice and ineffectiveness has been a series of reform proposals and programs. (Interestingly, although probation shares many of the assumptions and shortcomings of parole, no one seems particularly anxious to either "discover" this fact or reform it.)

The charge of correctional injustice has fed the movement to abolish the indeterminate sentence in favor of a system of mandatory determinate sentences. As we indicated in Chapter 5, many states have moved in this direction. For instance, California's complex new sentencing law makes changes in the structure and operation of parole. These types of sentence reforms have been supported by liberals and conservatives, though for different reasons. Another reform has been parole board issuance of decision-making guidelines, which are intended to remove some of the uncertainty and disparities that have characterized parole decision making in the past. In Chapter 13 we will review the changes in organization and operation of the U.S. Board of Parole—now called the U.S. Parole Commission.

The charge of parole ineffectiveness is based on evaluative research findings as well as the belief that service to parolees and surveillance of their activities cannot be combined in the same agency and personnel. Two reform proposals stem from this belief: (1) contract parole, and (2) the separation of the service and surveillance functions. The provisions of contract parole are that parole authorities should enter into a contractual agreement with prisoners, agreeing to parole them if the prisoner achieves certain agreed-upon objectives (such as a high school diploma or completion of a vocational training program). Contract parole is believed by many to be a way of reducing or eliminating the coercion of treatment—which militates against its effectiveness. Second, many believe that the responsibility for controlling parolees should be lodged in the police and taken away from parole authorities. This would leave parole officers free to concentrate their efforts on helping offenders. Since parolees would no longer have reason to fear them, interaction with parole officers would be more effective than is true under the present system.

What are we to make of these proposals to reform parole? Given the legacy of past correctional reforms, it is difficult not to be skeptical of their ever achieving their stated aims. In light of the rather sudden discovery of the shortcomings of parole, even though they have always been present, it is difficult to ignore completely the charge of radical commentators on these developments:

> What appears to have occurred is the disappearance of rehabilitation as a goal of imprisonment in light of changed material conditions. With this disappearance and reduced emphasis on corrections, the problems and tasks of parole boards have also diminished, along with the need for such agencies (Schmidt, 1977: 140).

This same critic charges that, in truth, parole has always functioned as a means for assuring that offenders served specific minimum periods of time in prison according to the kind of crime they committed. "The practice has not changed but, rather, is now openly declared. . . . The mechanisms of social control are tightening up, illustrative of the way in which intensification of punishment is a response to deteriorating social and economic conditions" (1977: 141).

If such radical critics of parole reform are correct, there is little reason to believe these reforms will achieve the objectives that have caused so many to support them. At present, it is still too early to know what all the consequences of parole reform will be.

11

The delivery of correctional services: Bureaucratic and interactional process

The quality and outcome of contacts between offenders and employees of correctional agencies are of critical importance for any analysis of the dynamics of corrections. Whether we are interested in the outcome of correctional treatment, prison disciplinary practices, or parole violation, ultimately we must devote some attention to what actually transpires between correctional employees and offenders. We propose to discuss some of the determinants of the variable quality and outcome of these contacts.

LEVELS OF ANALYSIS: DETERMINANTS

The varying quality and outcomes of contacts between offenders and correctors, and the nature of the latters' decisions, have at least three different types of determinants: *organizational*, *occupational*, and *situational*. These correspond to three distinctively different sociological *levels of analysis*. The importance of differences in levels of analysis as determinants of decision making can be illustrated with research on the police. (There is much less research on correctional decision making.)

Police officers are vested with a great deal of discretion in their work, especially in the handling of many of their routine duties. In their contacts with citizens who have violated traffic ordinances, for example, individual police officers have a range of options open to them—from doing nothing at all to issuing a citation or even arresting the offender. Similarly, in contacts with minor juvenile offenders, a police officer may choose to lecture them and send them on their way, release them to their parents' custody, or confine them in the local detention home. Research on police decision making has shown that there are distinct differences in the way officers in different police departments exercise discretion in these matters (for example, Goldman, 1963; Wilson, 1968). Put differently, there appear to be organizational "styles" in police departments, and these determine, in part, the way in which individual police officers in different departments carry out their duties. The importance of this is clear: If one is a certain type of offender—say, a traffic violator—the way in which your "crime" is reacted to is a result, in part, of the type of police department your city has. The type of department determines what action is taken in your own case. We may designate this level of analysis as the *organizational* level. It encompasses aspects of the internal structure and dynamics of organizations as these affect the way in which organizational employees carry out their duties.

A second level of analysis focuses on the perspectives of the employees themselves, but only to the extent that these perspectives are rooted in an occupational or organizational culture. Therefore, it deals with only those aspects of employees' beliefs and attitudes that are acquired on the job, by virtue of their interaction with others who are similarly employed. Thus, these perspectives are not so much aspects of individuals as aspects of occupational groups or an *occupational culture.* How do these occupational perspectives affect individual decision making? Once again we examine research on the police.

As noted in many studies, one aspect of police culture is the belief that officers cannot ignore challenges to their authority; citizens must not be permitted to defy or seriously challenge the police officer's position. In the event they do, police officers are believed justified in using their powers of arrest or even force to coerce respect for their position. Consequently, as this suggests, the way in which police officers deal with citizens, and the decisions they make, will depend to some extent on whether the citizen has been appropriately deferential. When police officers feel citizens have not been sufficiently respectful, they will take action that reflects their belief that such a person deserves harsher treatment than a citizen who is more respectful. In Chapter 6 we briefly discussed some of the differences between correctors and offenders in their *perspectives* and tried to speculate on some of the consequences of these differences. Consequently, in this chapter we will have little to say about the impact of these group perspectives on the carrying out of correctional mandates.

A final level of analysis for examining the nature and outcome of contacts between correctors and offenders is the *situational* level. We use this to refer to what actually transpires during the time when the two are together: what is said, how it is said, what is the offender's demeanor, and so on. Donald Black has shown how important these situational elements can be for an understanding of the police decision to arrest a criminal suspect. He found that a critical determinant of the police decision was whether or not a complainant was actually present when the officer confronted the suspect and, if so, whether the complainant insisted that an arrest be made. "Arrest practices sharply reflect the preferences of citizen complainants, particularly when the desire is for leniency and also, though less frequently, when the complainant demands arrest" (1973: 154–55). An example of how situational and police-attitudinal considerations combine to effect the behavior of police is provided in a discussion of police contacts with juveniles. In these encounters:

> Juveniles who were contrite about their infractions, respectful to officers and fearful of the sanctions that might be employed against them tended to be viewed by patrolmen as basically law-abiding or at least "salvageable." For these youths it was usually assumed that informal or formal reprimand would suffice to guarantee their future conformity. In contrast, youthful offenders who were fractious, obdurate, or who appeared nonchalant in their encounters with patrolmen were likely to be viewed as "would-be-tough guys" or "punks" who fully deserved the most severe sanction: arrest (Piliavin and Briar, 1969: 170).

A NOTE ON ORGANIZATIONAL ENVIRONMENT

Our discussion in this chapter stresses the importance of organizational structure and dynamics in the provision of correctional services. We have chosen to say little about how organizations come to be structured and operated as they are, although this is an important problem for the sociology of corrections. Such a problem necessarily involves questions of the relationship between organizations and their environment. We know that certain types of social settings or environments are required in order for organizations to be structured and operated in certain ways. For example, we would not expect to find rational-bureaucratic correctional organizations in rural areas dominated by feudallike political structures.

We do not know exactly what it is about organizational environments that is most responsible for variations in organizational structures and dynamics in the field of corrections. As Jacobs correctly notes, "prison scholarship is dominated by micro level analyses of the attitudes, values, and roles of prisoners and staff" (1974: 104). Such scholarship ignores the fact that "prisons do not exist in a vacuum: they are part of a political, social, economic and moral order" (1977: 89). Put differently, we lack a clear understanding of how correctional structures and processes articulate with political, economic, and cultural variables in their environments.

Studies of the relationships between corrections and environmental variables could easily be pursued at different levels of abstraction or distance. At one level we could examine how the characteristics of local communities affect the structure and operations of correctional agencies. At a more remote level, we could examine how variations in the political and economic conditions of the various states are reflected in their correctional structures and policies. Finally, we could examine the relationships between overreaching political-economic variables at the national or cross-national level and the structure and functioning of correctional agencies. For example, research of this type could explore differences in the correctional structures and policies of socialist, capitalist, and third-world countries. To date there have been few studies of this type and we will require much more before we can hope for a comparative sociology of corrections. Until we have a better understanding of how environmental conditions affect correctional structures and correctional change, perhaps we should be less optimistic about the prospects for rationally transforming corrections.

CORRECTIONAL APPLICATIONS

Organizational structure and process

In what ways are the provision of correctional services influenced by organizational structures and dynamics? In the remainder of this chapter we will discuss several such processes; however, we emphasize that more research is needed. The importance of such research has been underscored by Martinson et al. (1964: 36) in their discussion of past research on parole and parolee behavior: "An organizational approach would regard the agent-parolee relationship as perhaps changeable, but only within limits set in a much larger canvas. The parole agent has discretion within the complex limits set by operational manuals, by district officer supervision, and by career concerns." More recent research by Takagi and Robison (1969) has shown the wisdom of these remarks. They sought to determine what influences parole officers' decisions to revoke the parole of possible parole violators. They found the decision was affected by the parole officer's perception of her or his superior's likely response. In the decision whether to revoke the parole, a powerful

> . . . influence appeared to be at the district supervisor level, where there is a high degree of correspondence between district supervisors and their subordinates on the case-recommendation task. This finding suggests that the selective enforcement of some rules is as much a characteristic of the officials as selective adherence to rules is a characteristic of the violator (Takagi and Robison, 1969: 85–6).

Similar findings are reported by McCleary (1975), based on his participant observation study in the offices of a parole supervision agency. He notes that "the data show that case decisions are often determined by organizational demands not necessarily related to the rehabilitation of parolees or to the protection of society" (1975: 209). Such research points to the influence of hierarchical interpersonal relationships on the delivery of correctional services. Whenever an overall treatment program is "broken down" into discrete work tasks for individuals, and they are evaluated in terms of how successfully they achieve these discrete goals, they tend to focus on immediate goals and lose sight of the larger program. Observers in the prison (Sykes, 1956) have indicated how this can lead to the "corruption of authority and rehabilitation," and comparable processes have been observed in other correctional agencies; white-collar people-changers appear to spend an inordinate amount of their time on those activities that are most visible to their superiors (that is, the writing of reports). The important point here is that such "distortions" of the service-providing process occur because of its organization in the form of a bureaucracy. The very act of so organizing tends to set in motion forces endemic to the bureaucratic form of organization, forces that often work at cross-purposes with the provision of treatment services in the ideologically or professionally "purest" manner.

Another way in which bureaucratic processes affect the provision of treatment services is seen in organizational competition for offenders who are considered "good risks." The correlative tendency is to search for other agencies on which poor risks can be "dumped." To be sure, such a practice of sloughing potentially embarassing cases can be glossed over as simply eliminating those "unlikely to be responsive to treatment," or those whose "level of motivation to benefit from the program is too low." Through such a process the employees of correctional agencies—especially those agencies whose continued existence is thought to be precarious—attempt to stack the cards in their own favor, in favor of a program's "success." On occasion, the resulting competition between agencies can be rather intense (Miller, 1958). At other times, the process is so skillfully accomplished that it becomes virtually impossible for impartial outside observers to later determine just what happened to all the clients who were originally slated for participation in some program (Lerman, 1975).

A closely related process is observed whenever organizational personnel feel unusual or intense pressure to deliver evidence of the success of some particular program. An excellent example of this is provided by research in the California Department of Corrections. Department officials had been claiming for years that a reduction in the average size of parole caseloads would lead to a reduction in parolees' recidivism.

> During the late 50s and early 60s, the California DC randomly assigned parolees to 35- and 70-man caseloads. Although the DC expected the smaller caseloads to have lower recidivism rates, a preliminary evaluation showed no difference. According to Takagi, high DC officials decided at this point that a no-difference finding would be politically unacceptable. The POs assigned to the small caseloads were consequently told that they would be promoted strictly on the basis of their caseload recidivism rates: the lower the rate, the better the chance of promotion. A subsequent re-evaluation of the program found that the smaller caseloads were more effective than the larger caseloads in reducing recidivism. . . . What happened, of course, is that the researchers did observe a statistical difference but they incorrectly attributed this difference to the effectiveness of the treatment. In fact, the change was due entirely to a shift in the structural dynamic of the parole agency . . . (McCleary, 1975: 224).

This exemplifies a generic process: the tendency of correctional treatment advocates to engage in actions which, even if unintended, assure that their pet programs will be a "success" when they are evaluated.

A final process via which organizational considerations influence the delivery of correctional services flows in yet another direction: from the concern of correctors for the reputation of their agencies and programs to their tendency to premise decisions on the desire to avoid having them held up for public or political ridicule or embarrassment. Parole boards, as we discussed in Chapter 10, are known to be highly susceptible to such pressure (for example, Dawson, 1966). Consequently, they often reach decisions to parole or not parole with an eye toward the net amount of "heat" expected should anything go wrong.

Occupational culture and interactional process

The delivery of correctional services is plagued by several problems that are of such a nature and magnitude as to suggest the extreme difficulty of correctional personnel effectively overcoming them. The origin of these problems is in the structurally given conflict of interest between correctors and offenders, an inherent conflict that cannot be entirely eliminated—even by good intentions and human-relations training.

Correctors reach decisions and recommendations as to the nature and severity of desirable state intervention in offenders' lives, at least in part on the basis of their opinions of what kind of person an offender is believed to be. An awareness of this inevitably leads offenders to accentuate those aspects of their biography, identity, and activities that are most favorable. This is the only rational response in such a situation. Correctors appear to recognize this, which gives rise to the pervasive fear on their part that offenders are trying to "con" them. Thus, we would only partially agree with the following comment on parole board/inmate interaction—which attributes the fear of being conned to the difficulty of determining whether inmates have "really" changed:

> The difficulty which parole board members experience in attempting to determine whether there has been a change in the inmate's attitudes finds expression in a universal fear of being "conned." The parole board shows considerable concern about the inmate who is too glib, who seems to have everything down pat and is so smooth that every detail of his story fits neatly into place. The board members resent inmates who seem to be trying to "con" them or to "take them in" (Dawson, 1966: 255).

Realization of the existence of this "fear-of-being-conned" syndrome places offenders in an awkward and inenviable position; consequently, they do not know exactly how to interact with correctors. Should they appear *too* contrite or changed, they may be accused of trying to perpetrate a "con job." On the other hand, should they be overly candid and forthcoming about their activities —for example, the crimes they committed for which they were never arrested—this information may be used against them. (Lest it be thought that these suspicions are unfounded, research on the actions of parole agents has found that they engage in comparable actions—see Studt, 1973.)

Another locus of interactional difficulties results from disparate perspectives toward the usefulness of correctional services by correctors and offenders. The former imbue these with much more potential importance than do the latter. Indeed, offenders some-

FIRST VISIT TO THE PAROLE OFFICER

Rosenthal stood in a short corridor beyond, framed in a doorway with a pool of sunlight spilling around his legs. He was coatless and his short-sleeved shirt exposed a carpet of coarse black hair on his forearms. "Come on in," he said. "I was worried you'd run. You were pretty nervous last night."

"If I'd known about your electric door I might've skipped. Something like that is frightening. I feel like I'm in a police station."

"Oh, those . . . not my idea. Have a seat."

"I can use that gate money."

Rosenthal shuffled through papers on his desk. "Here we are," he said, handing over the check.

I held it up. "Thirty dollars for eight years. Not much per annum."

"Society doesn't even owe you that."

"It isn't much to start a new life with."

"Try feeling more penitent and less the martyr."

"I'm sorry, I don't feel anything but a little bitter . . . and I'm trying to suppress that."

"So, what'd you do last night?"

I had a lie waiting in ambush for the question. "Visited friends, saw a girl."

"You stay with her?"

"No, in a hotel."

"That's pretty expensive for someone in your position."

"Not this hotel."

Rosenthal tilted his chair and propped his feet on the desk. He laced stubby fingers into a web behind his neck and watched me with candid intensity. He chomped gum placidly. Tension grew with the silence.

"I'm less than satisfied with your attitude," he said, "and about how you're starting out. First you don't want the halfway house, next you run around all night. It isn't a good start, not at all. It's your attitude, your outlook."

I flushed, wanting to protest, but snipped off the hot words. Confrontation with authority was a game I'd played often, and I knew its unfairness. If I argued, Rosenthal could put me in jail (unless I knocked him down and escaped), write a report saying whatever he wanted, and I'd be riding a bus with barred windows back to prison. There would be no hearing, no appeal, and I wouldn't even see what he wrote. So I checked myself, and decided that a plea for reason might get through.

"I'm sorry if you think that," I said. "I'm trying to be forthright and sincere. Tell me what I've done wrong."

"It's your attitude. I keep telling you that. You act like you're free, can do what you damn well please. You're not free. You're still in *custodia legis,* a legal prisoner being allowed to serve part of your term outside on parole. Besides that, you've got a long, long record of mismanaging your life. And you should feel remorse for what you've done."

"Eight years for bad checks should clean the slate." I saw the flippancy in the words after they were out. Rosenthal's face soured. He was obviously a moralist and outraged by my file. He knew more about me than anyone should know about another. Yet the words in the file were less than the whole of me. Nothing there showed that I was human.

Source: Edward Bunker. *No Beast So Fierce.* New York: W. W. Norton & Co., 1973, pp. 53–54.

---

times feel that they are simply exploited by the correctional industry, serving as justification for its continued existence—and, of course, higher budgets—while its personnel in truth have no real control over precisely those resources that offenders need most. Consequently, offenders often feel that the best thing to do is to simply avoid contact with correctors unless it cannot be avoided —since the likelihood of anything positive coming out of their contacts is felt to be low. (Nothing said here denies that people-changers can usually find offenders who are willing to come forward, enthusiastically, with testimonials about how they benefited from the help they received.)

Interactional difficulties in the delivery of correctional services results also from the dissimilar social worlds, and all this represents, from which correctors and their clients spring. Irwin (1970: 157) puts it thus: "In effect, the parole social system has brought into close contact, in an agent-client relationship, two people who represent different social worlds—one, the parole agency, which is unduly influenced at the formal level by conservative segments of society; and the other, a deviant subsociety." Furthermore, parole agents—and here we can generalize to people-changers in other correctional programs—operate on the basis of a meaning of "success" that is narrow, overly technical, and agency-derived; offenders, however, mean something different by success. This disparity often leads to problems between these representatives of two different social worlds. Again, we quote Irwin (1970: 204):

> From the standpoint of the felon a successful postprison life is more than merely staying out of prison. From the criminal ex-convict perspective it must be dignified. This is not generally understood by correctional people whose ideas on success are dominated by narrow and unrealistic conceptions of nonrecidivism and reformation. Importantly, because of their failure to recognize the felon's viewpoint, his aspirations, his conceptions of respect and dignity,

or his foibles, they leave him to travel the difficult route away from the prison without guidance or assistance; in fact, with considerable hindrance. . . .

For the reasons explicated here, as well as those we discussed in the context of the impact of bureaucratic processes on correctional treatment, much of the interaction between offenders and people-changers is shallow and rarely comes to grips with the fundamental concerns or problems of offenders—correctional ideology notwithstanding.

IMPLICATIONS

Apparently, many believe that good intentions and perseverance are all that's needed for correctors to accomplish their goal of changing offenders. Unprofessional or inept behavior by correctors is usually viewed as a commentary on the individuals involved; things would have been different had they been better trained or more committed to their work. Our comments in this chapter suggest other interpretations for such occurrences. The behavior and decisions of correctional personnel are affected by a variety of considerations, only some of which are under their immediate control. Aspects of the structure and dynamics of the organizations that employ them, occupational perspectives learned on the job, and aspects of their interactions with offenders all affect their behavior and decisions. Consequently, if we want to understand why correctors behave as they do, we must have a better understanding of these diverse determinants. We hope that our comments in this chapter have contributed to such an understanding.

EVALUATIVE MODES FOR CORRECTIONS

12

Humaneness and corrections

Despite the deficiencies of psyche, character, or intellect they are believed to suffer from, presumably all would agree that prisoners, as well as probationers, parolees, and any others caught up in the correctional process, are "people." Therefore, we would expect consensus with the assertion that correctional programs must be operated consistent with fundamental standards of humane treatment. Yet, however rare it may be, treatment that violates these standards can still be found in contemporary corrections.

ORGANIZATIONAL DYNAMICS AND TECHNOCRATIC THOUGHT

Bureaucracies are organized on the basis of a division of labor, a hierarchy of authority, formal channels of communication, and the use of both indoctrination and the manipulation of sanctions to secure compliant, predictable behavior from employees. However, the process of breaking down large-scale tasks into smaller ones creates conditions conducive to the kinds of illegal or deviant behavior that individuals perhaps would never commit outside of the work sphere. Stanley Milgram, who has conducted pioneering research on the willingness of individuals to defer moral judgments to higher authorities, has pointed to this tendency with his statement that within bureaucracies there

> . . . is a fragmentation of the total human act; no one man [decides] to carry out the evil act and is confronted with its consequences. The person who assumes full responsibility for the act has evapo-

rated. Perhaps this is the most common characteristic of socially organized evil in modern society (1974: 9).

As a result, the salience and personally perceived relevance of moral and ethical considerations decreases for individual employees.

All bureaucracies, when they divide large-scale tasks into smaller ones, do so under the dominance of organizational ideologies. This is equally true of correctional bureaucracies, where punishment and rehabilitative ideologies suggest that offenders are different from "normal" people. This makes it even easier for correctional employees—indeed for all of us—to overlook the essential humaneness of offenders and to relegate them to the status of inanimate raw material, to be manipulated and processed for the greater good of reducing crime rates or recidivism.

In correctional bureaucracies as in other types of organizations, employees can become so fixated on ultimate objectives, such as punishment or rehabilitation, that short-term ends and means are evaluated only in term of their apparent relationship to and efficiency for achieving these long-range goals. In short, correctional organizations may foster *technocratic* thought. We define this as a preoccupation with means (or techniques) for achieving goals to the exclusion of consideration of the goals themselves and whether they are desirable or appropriate. Richard Korn's poignant reflections on his own correctional employment highlight the nature and consequences of technocratic thought:

> In 1952, at the age of 29, I was appointed to the post of Director of Education and Treatment at the New Jersey State Prison. . . . In our efforts to wrest control of the prison from the inmates, we developed a number of innovations which later became widely emulated. One of these involved building a more secure "prison within the prison" for "persistently recalcitrant or dangerous inmates." I spent considerable time in this prototype of the modern "adjustment center" and, later, after I left the prison, considerable time thinking about it.
>
> The result of this thought was the production of a *Manual for the Treatment of Adaptive Offenders,* by which term I meant the treatment of offenders inaccessible to the treatment strategies I originally had at hand. . . .
>
> At the time I practiced and wrote about these measures, it never occurred to me to question whether I was doing anything that was wrong. I had tacitly accepted a technique for breaking the resistance of my clients as an acceptable means for achieving the goals of eventual release into the community. If anyone had told me that I was collaborating in a process of torture which used isolation and frustration as its weapons, I would have been startled. But I prob-

ably would not have agreed. I had accepted my final goal as valid, and the only question I asked of my means was whether they were efficient (Korn, 1971: 31–2).

Thus, an overriding and uncritical commitment to an ultimate objective of an organization can produce technocratic thinking and morally insensitive behavior by individuals.

A glimpse of some consequences of these processes can be gained from the testimony in a 1966 court case in which an inmate of the California Department of Corrections challenged the conditions under which he was kept in solitary confinement. Testimony and evidence disclosed that he had been confined in a so-called strip cell of solid concrete, six feet by nine feet, almost totally dark, and completely devoid of furnishings except for an "oriental" hole-in-the-floor-type toilet, which could not be flushed by the inmate, and which was sometimes flushed only twice a day by staff. The cell was unheated and was not cleaned during the inmate's 11-day occupancy, even though it was covered with his vomit and other bodily wastes as well as those of its previous occupants. While confined in this cell the inmate was permitted no opportunity to clean his hands, teeth, or the rest of his body. He was kept naked for the first eight days and was forced to sleep on the concrete floor on a stiff canvas mat, which could not possibly be fashioned to cover him, too. During oral arguments and testimony the following dialogue occured between the judge and the department's consulting psychiatrist:

The Court: All right, Doctor, will you pause for a moment and consider yourself inside one of the cells in question with the flaps up. Do you concede that there isn't any light in the cell, Doctor?

The Witness: Yes.

The Court: It is absolutely dark.

The Witness: Not quite, because these are not, as the so-called solitary confinement cells of former years where there was no light. There is a slight seepage of light.

The Court: Very slight.

The Witness: Very slight.

The Court: Mindful of the conditions under which a man is confined in a cell in question, how do you propose he maintain his personal bodily cleanliness, his hands and the like?

The Witness: He is provided with—is provided with the toilet tissue. He is supposed to be removed to be—he is supposed to be removed to be showered.

The Court: When? And how often?

The Witness: I believe at least every five days was the minimum.

The Court: So for a period of five days, at least, his body, if he is stripped, and his hands equally, would be the subject of some degree of contamination. Isn't that correct.

The Witness: Yes, but as——

The Court: Is it correct, Doctor, or is it not?

The Witness: For a period of five days he possibly might be quite soiled.

The Court: Yes. And quite contaminated.

The Witness: Yes.

The Court: Let's confine ourselves to the cell in question, to the degree of light, to the lack of cleanliness, to the lack of apparent facilities for a man to either bathe or wash his hands. I address the question again to you, Doctor, mindful of your constant surveillance over these cells or at least casual surveillance: Did you at any time during the course of your career make a recommendation regarding any device or facility that might be used by the inmate?

The Witness: No devices or facilities. I have made the recommendation that he ought to be taken out and cleaned one way or another.

The Court: That the inmate ought to be taken out?

The Witness: That the inmate ought to be taken out and the cell should be cleaned.

The Court: Was that prompted by a physical observation you made of any inmate?

The Witness: Yes.

The Court: Will you state the name or identity of the inmate.

The Witness: I don't know.

The Court: What was the condition of his body?

The Witness: If I entered a cell and the cell smelled badly, I feel this is an unhealthful situation. . . .

The Court: Is it not true, notwithstanding the stench or smell, many of these inmates were permitted to and forced to eat their meals in that stench and odor?

The Witness: I don't know as they were forced to. It is true that if they were going to eat, that they might have to eat under those circumstances [*Jordan* v. *Fitzharris*, 257 Fed. Supp. 682, 683 (N.D.Cal. 1966)].

Traditionally, technocratic thought has dominated debate over correctional issues. In recent years there are signs of change and, increasingly, questions are asked about the humaneness of alternative types of correctional dispositions. This is an important development, for one of the dimensions on which correctional programs can be evaluated is humaneness. Precisely because of the tendency for moral and ethical considerations to recede in importance in the operation of correctional programs and in the debate over them, it is imperative that we support this renewed interest in humane treatment.

WHAT IS HUMANE TREATMENT?

If correctional practices are to be judged by how closely they conform to principles of humane care and treatment, a problem immediately arises: what is *humane* treatment? How is it to be defined? This is a difficult problem because, presumably, what would be inhumane treatment from the perspective of one individual or group might be considered quite acceptable and within the bounds of humane treatment from the perspective of others. Consequently, humaneness, unlike legality and effectiveness-efficiency— our two other dimensions for evaluating correctional practices— appears to lack the same kinds of objective evaluative criteria. However, there is a way out of this apparent impasse. In the United States, many of the challenges to the humaneness of correctional practices allege violations of the Eighth Amendment to the U.S. Constitution, which prohibits cruel and unusual punishments. Therefore, we can learn something about the more extreme cases of correctional inhumanity by examining litigation and by using the criteria that the courts have established and applied in cases alleging cruel and unusual punishment.

CORRECTIONAL INHUMANENESS: ILLUSTRATIONS AND CHALLENGES

We will briefly review some court cases in which inhumane correctional treatment came to light. No attempt will be made to present an exhaustive coverage of the issues and cases that have been litigated; there is so much consistency in such cases that we can concentrate on a few typical ones. Note, however, that thus far only some of the most shocking practices have come under the scrutiny of the courts; as yet they have not had much occasion to consider conditions in a broader range of correctional programs.

In *Jones* v. *Wittenberg* [323 F. Supp. 93 (N.D. Ohio 1971)] inmates of the Lucas County (Toledo, Ohio) jail challenged in federal district court the conditions under which they were confined. In granting the plaintiffs' request the court stated that

> when the total picture of confinement in the Lucas County Jail is examined, what appears is confinement in cramped and overcrowded quarters, lightless, airless, damp and filthy with leaking water and human wastes, slow starvation, deprivation of most human contacts, except with others in the same sub-human state, no exercise or recreation, little if any medical attention, no attempt at

In December 1970, prisoners in the old Women's House of Detention in New York refused to lock themselves in their cells in protest against the unconscionable conditions they were living in. They were sprayed with water hoses and forcibly locked in their cells for nearly two weeks as punishment for protesting.

Their grievances were reprinted and circulated to New York residents by the Women's Bail Fund, a group of politically active women who had been helping provide bail and legal support for women awaiting trial at the House of D. The inmates had addressed an open letter to *"the concerned people of New York"*:

We the prisoners of the Women's House of Detention wish to inform you of the barbaric conditions we are subjected to by the correction officials here in the House of Detention. The system breeds mental degradation and physical deterioration. The majority of us are Black and Puerto Rican. We cannot afford the ransom the courts call bail. It is apparent to us that you, the public, are not aware of the barbaric conditions that exist here.

Our grievances are:

1.   We do not receive adequate medical attention. We do not have a doctor on duty 24 hours a day although there are 754 women in here. [Maximum capacity was 457.] The doctors we do have are old and senile.

   a.   We ask that all doctors practicing medicine here be required to take a medical Board examination at least once a year.

   b.   We ask for a doctor to be on duty 24 hours a day.

   c.   We ask that it be a requirement that any inmate suffering from any medical problem be permitted to see a doctor at any time of the day or night, and that it not be left to the discretion of the officer on duty or the nurse in attendance.

   d.   We ask for first rate medicine. That it be labeled properly and after it has lost its potency, it be thrown out.

2.   We do not receive an adequate diet. We do not get any fresh vegetables or any fresh fruits. Our diet consists of beans, rice, potatoes, and powdered milk. We get hot cereal twice a weak, one boiled egg once a week. The rest of the days we get cold cereal and powdered milk. The meats that we eat are as old as the building we must live in.

   a.   We ask for our meats to be inspected.

   b.   We ask for at least one glass of fresh milk daily.

   c.   We ask for fresh vegetables and at least one piece of fruit a day.

   d.   We ask for citrus juices once a day.

3.   The House of Detention is infested with mice and roaches. They roam the building freely, carrying filth and disease. We are often bitten by these germ-carrying rodents. There is no extermination system.

   a.   We ask that an exterminating company be allowed to come in twice a month to eliminate these health hazards.

4.   There are four punishment strip cells where we are put if we re-

ceive an "infraction." The cells do not have any toilets, sinks, or mattresses. In them we are stripped of all our clothing. We do not receive any bedding for the cold tile floor. We are allowed to shower only every five days. We ask that these cells be shut down immediately.

5.   We are beaten by the male guards. We ask that male guard brutality be stopped immediately. We are harassed and threatened with an infraction by the female guards. We ask for the harassment to be stopped.

6.   Our funds which are sent and brought to us are misappropriated. We ask for an investigation.

7.   We are unable to purchase in commissary bras, panties, socks or stockings. None of these are given to us by the state as long as we are being held in detention. We ask that we be allowed to purchase bras, panties, socks, stockings, bobby pins for our hair, hair rollers, makeup, large rubber combs for the sisters in here who cannot comb their hair with the very small combs we can now buy, creams for our faces, lotions for our bodies so that we can care for ourselves as women.

8.   We are two in a cell. The cells are 5 feet by 9 feet. Out of a 15 hour day, we are locked up 11 of these hours. We ask for longer recreation periods.

9.   The adolescents are separated from the adults as long as they are on detention floors. Once they have been sentenced, they are put on the same corridors as the adults. We ask that the adolescents be kept separate from the adults after sentencing.

10.   When we are appointed a legal representative by the courts they do not come to us to discuss the facts of our cases. We ask that the courts require a visit to be made by the court appointed legal representative to us, the accused, before we go to court.

11.   We are often brought to court and required to wait in the bull pen five or six hours in order to see a judge only to be told our cases have been adjourned. We ask that when we are brought to court that we see the judge.

12.   There are some of us who have been here 20 months and still have not gone to trial. We ask for speedier court dates. We ask that our court dates be made known to us.

13.   We have been raided at five-thirty in the morning, made to strip off all our clothing and to squat down, our personal belongings being thrown on the floor. The adolescents have been made to go into the kitchen and strip off their clothing in front of everyone.

   a.   We ask that the stripping of inmates be stopped immediately.

. . .We the oppressed women of the New York House of Detention humbly seek your support and help. We who are your fellow human beings need you, the public, to help us in our struggle to eliminate these injustices.

Captive Sisters in the House of D.

Source: Kathryn Watterson Burkhart. *Women in Prison.* New York: Popular Library, 1976, pp. 325–27.

> rehabilitation, and for those who in despair or frustration lash out at their surroundings, confinement, stripped of clothing and every last vestige of humanity, in a sort of oubliette. . . . If the constitutional provision against cruel and unusual punishment has any meaning, the evidence in this case shows that it has been violated. The cruelty is a refined sort, much more comparable to the Chinese water torture than to such cruelties as breaking on the wheel (p. 99).

Several cases originating with convicts confined in Arkansas prisons have shed light on inhuman practices and conditions. *Jackson* v. *Bishop* [404 F. 2d. 571 (8th Cir. 1968)] exposed use of the whip and strap as modes of punishment for alleged infractions of prison rules. Later, in *Holt* v. *Sarver* [309 F. Supp. 362 (E.D. Ark. 1970)], convicts brought a class action suit alleging that the conditions of confinement in Arkansas prisons constituted cruel and unusual punishment. The court found a complex pattern of inhumane conditions in Arkansas, including inadequate supervision of living quarters, which resulted in murders and homosexual assaults; a "trusty" system, which permitted favored inmates to dominate and abuse other inmates; filthy, rodent-infested solitary confinement cells; and an absence of recreational or training programs, which resulted in idleness and violence. The court ruled in favor of the plaintiffs and ordered the state to make extensive improvements in the conditions of its prisons.

The conditions under which convicts are forced to live during solitary confinement have been the basis for a number of challenges. In *Hancock* v. *Avery* [301 F. Supp. 786 (M.D. Tenn. 1969)] the court enjoined officials of the Tennessee State Prison at Nashville from using punishment cells that were found to be dirty and unlighted, and in which inmates were naked and forced to sleep on a bare concrete floor.

That such practices are not confined exclusively to any one section of the United States is obvious from reviewing the cases. In 1967, Lawrence William Wright, an inmate of Clinton State Prison at Dannemora, New York, challenged the conditions under which he was confined in the prison's punishment cells [*Wright* v. *McMann*, 387 F. 2d 519 (2d Cir. 1967)]. Testimony disclosed that Wright had been confined, without any clothing or bedding, in a cell with broken windows that exposed him to the winter temperatures. The court commented that

> We are of the view that civilized standards of human decency simply do not permit a man for a substantial period of time to be denuded and exposed to the bitter cold of winter in northern New York State and to be deprived of the basic elements of hygiene such as soap and toilet paper. The subhuman conditions alleged by

Wright to exist in the "strip cell" at Dannemora could only serve to destroy completely the spirit and undermine the sanity of the prisoner. The Eighth Amendment forbids treatment so foul, so inhuman and so violative of basic concepts of decency (p. 256).

Although we are seeing a plethora of challenges to correctional programs on Eighth Amendment grounds, "it is generally only the abhorrent situation that is afforded judicial cognizance. The courts simply have not had occasion to consider conditions in many, if not most, prisons" (McAninch, 1973: 579). It has been primarily the *physical* conditions of confinement that has received most of the attention; *psychological* consequences of correctional processing have yet to be systematically litigated.

When called to defend the conditions under which convicts are often confined for punishment purposes, prison officials typically cite the need for maintaining security and budgetary limitations that make improvements impossible. Rarely have they challenged convicts' presentations of the facts about their conditions of confinement. Courts have generally held, therefore, that while segregation from the general prison population may be permissible on the grounds of maintaining security, inmates so confined must be treated humanely. "Reasons of security may justify confinement, but that is not to say that such needs may be determined arbitrarily. . . . '[S]ecurity' or 'rehabilitation' are not shibboleths to justify any treatment" [*Landman* v. *Royster*, 333 F. Supp. 621, 645 (E.D. Va. 1971)].

At other times, correctional administrators have asserted that the treatment to which inmates were exposed was not intended as punishment but instead as part of a rehabilitative program. In *Inmates of Boys Training School* v. *Affleck* [346 F. Supp. 1354 (D.R.I. 1972)] the conditions of confinement of boys who were permanently segregated from the remainder of the training school population were successfully challenged. Defendants in the case argued that, since juveniles are confined for purposes of treatment and rehabilitation rather than punishment, the Eighth Amendment challenge was not applicable. The court dismissed this interpretation, stating that

> neither the label which the State places on its own conduct, nor even the legitimacy of its motivation, can avoid the applicability of the Federal Constitution. . . . The fact that juveniles are in theory not punished, but merely confined for rehabilitative purposes, does not preclude operation of the Eighth Amendment (p. 1366).

In *Mackey* v. *Procunier* [877 F. 2d 877 (9th Cir. 1973)] plaintiff Mackey charged that his civil rights were violated when, without his consent, he was administered the drug succinycholine, which acts as a "breath-stopping and paralyzing 'fright drug' " (p. 877). Mackey alleged that as a result of this experience he suffered from nightmares in which he relived the frightening experience and awakened unable to breathe. The district court dismissed the complaint but the Ninth Circuit Court reversed the dismissal and remanded the cases for further proceedings. In *Clonce* v. *Richardson* [379 F. Supp. 388 (W.D. Mo. 1974)] prisoners brought suit challenging their involuntary transfer into a behavior modification program operated by the Federal Bureau of Prisons. Plaintiffs not only alleged violation of due process by their transfer without a hearing, but also that the program itself (S.T.A.R.T.) constituted cruel and unusual punishment. Because the Bureau of Prisons terminated the program before the case was decided the court ruled that most of the issues raised by the inmates were moot. The court did rule that when a prisoner is transferred to a program that involves a "major change in the conditions of his confinement" he must be afforded a hearing. (In a more recent case, *Meacham* v. *Fano*—which we will discuss in Chapter 13—the U.S. Supreme Court seems to have retreated from this position.) Thus, in *Clonce* v. *Richardson* the court considered as immaterial the argument that the program provided treatment designed to benefit the prisoners.

Knecht v. *Gillman* [488 F. 2d 1136 (8th Cir. 1973)] concerned an "aversion therapy" program administered at the Iowa Security Medical Facility. Injections of the drug apomorphine were administered to inmates who had allegedly violated the behavior protocol established for them by staff members. The drug induces involuntary vomiting for a period of 15 minutes to an hour. Inmates brought suit to enjoin further use of the drug, with the court eventually ruling that the act of forcing one to vomit for a 15-minute period constitutes cruel and unusual punishment.

In *Nelson* v. *Heyne* [491 F. 2d 353 (7th Cir. 1974)] several inmates of the Indiana Boys School brought a class action arguing that the institution's use of tranquilizing drugs to control "excited behavior" constituted cruel and unusual punishment. The district court found that the definition of what constituted 'excited behavior' was so loose and the conditions under which the drugs were administered were so poorly supervised, that it ruled in favor of the plaintiffs. The circuit court, in a unanimous opinion, affirmed the district court.

The facts in *Morales* v. *Turman* [364 F. Supp. 166 (E.D. Texas 1973)] revealed that conditions at two Texas institutions for juveniles amounted to what one observer has called "brutality as treatment" (Gilman, 1975). Brutality, terror, and degrading work assignments all were part of the institutional regimen.

As evidenced, knowledge of inhuman treatment is beginning to surface as the result of the court actions of imprisoned victims (Orland, 1975). There have been attempts in the form of standards and codes to rectify the inhumane conditions of imprisonment. These standards, their inadequacies, and some alternatives to them will be delineated and discussed.

FASHIONING STANDARDS

Legal standards

The U.S. Supreme Court has avoided giving a definitive interpretation to the cruel and unusual punishment clause of the Eighth Amendment, holding instead that it draws its meaning from "evolving standards of decency" [*Trop* v. *Dulles*, 356 U.S. 86 (1957)]. Nevertheless, growing out of past appellate litigation, some of which has been referred to here, have been case law standards for the evaluation of penal measures on Eighth Amendment grounds. There is reason to believe the courts will apply these standards to correctional practices labeled "treatment" just as they have been applied to "punishment" measures (Note, 1975). In the U.S., federal courts have generally held that correctional practices are cruel and unusual when (1) they are disproportionately severe for the offense; (2) they are of such character as to "shock the conscience"; (3) although they are applied in pursuit of a legitimate penal objective, they go beyond that which is necessary to achieve their aim (McAninch, 1973); or (4) the method of imposition is arbitrary.

The UN Standard Minimum Rules

The United Nations Standard Minimum Rules for the Treatment of Prisoners represents another approach to the problem of fashioning standards of humane treatment for corrections (American Bar Association, 1974). Developed by the UN's Economic and Social Council in 1957, the UN has sought to induce—or at least has urged—its member states to adopt and implement these standards. In addition to a blanket prohibition on "all cruel, inhuman or degrading punishments" for disciplinary purposes, the rules consist of detailed guidelines broken down in a number of areas, such as discipline and punishment, contact with the outside world, personal hygiene, work, and instruments of restraint.

The Model Act

In 1972 the National Council on Crime and Delinquency issued a Model Act to provide for Minimum Standards for the Protection of Rights of Prisoners (National Council, 1972). The act contains a section that explicitly prohibits "inhumane treatment," which is construed as including, while not being limited to:

1. Striking, whipping, or otherwise imposing physical pain upon a prisoner as a measure of punishment.
2. Any use of physical force by a employee except that which may be necessary for self-defense, to prevent or stop assault by one prisoner upon another person, or for prevention of riot or escape.
3. Sexual or other assaults by personnel or inmates.
4. Any punitive or restrictive measure taken by the management or personnel in retaliation for assertion of rights.
5. Any measure intended to degrade the prisoner, including insults and verbal abuse.
6. Any discriminatory treatment based upon the prisoner's race, religion, nationality, or political beliefs.

National Advisory Commission

The report on corrections issued by the National Advisory Commission on Criminal Justice Standards and Goals (1973) also contains a set of model standards for the protection of offender rights. The commission's standards encompass several different areas of offender treatment, including the following, which would seem to be particularly related to humane treatment: protection against personal abuse, healthful surroundings, medical care, and nondiscriminatory treatment and disciplinary procedures.

DEFICIENCIES OF A "STANDARDS APPROACH"

The preceding indicates efforts to develop and apply standards for humane treatment to correctional programs. But have they actually had a significant impact on the operation of the correctional industry? The merit of a standards approach can be gauged, in the first instance, by determining whether such standards have in fact influenced the operations of corrections. Unfortunately, problems arise in trying to assess the impact of standards.

One assessment approach is to simply inquire to what extent correctional personnel have made a verbal, formal commitment to the adoption and implementation of such standards. In 1974, the American Bar Association, employing a questionnaire developed by the UN, undertook to determine the extent of implementation of the UN minimum standards by correctional systems in the United States. The questionnaire was mailed to the chief administrator of the adult corrections department of the 50 states, the District of

Columbia, Puerto Rico, and the Federal Bureau of Prisons. In the 49 responses there was evidence of considerable lack of knowledge of the very existence of the UN standards. Nevertheless,

> The general profile which emerges from the United States responses indicates substantial and significant implementation of the substance of the Standard Minimum Rules, but at varying levels for different rules, and as a matter of desirable correctional practice and policy rather than any explicit or conscious attempt to follow the Rules as such (American Bar Association, 1974: 2).

The survey found that most state efforts concerning standards are directed to standards issued by the National Advisory Commission on Criminal Justice Standards and Goals.

A more revealing and reliable measure of the impact of such a set of standards can be gained by examining precisely how they have been institutionalized, and whether they have actually influenced the behavior of correctional employees and offenders. Formal pronouncements or standards will mean little (if anything) if all they do is repose in statute books and collect dust. Regrettably, when the mode and degree of implementation of standards is examined, the performance of United States jurisdictions falls far short of the minimum. The ABA study found that "the rules as such are neither available in penal institutions for staff and prisoners nor used as training materials for personnel in the United States" (American Bar Association, 1974: 3). Furthermore, "few reports of experiments or innovative deviations from the rules or suggested modifications were reported by the corrections departments which responded to the survey" (ABA, 1974: 3). Taken together, these findings indicate both a lack of knowledge of and innovative commitment to the UN minimum standards. (The survey did find, however, that a number of states have moved to enact legislatively a set of standards for the treatment of offenders, and other states have modified their administrative codes for the same purpose.)

As yet we have no systematic or reliable data on such questions as whether those states that have formally implemented any of these sets of standards are also states in which offenders are more fully aware of their right to humane treatment, and whether they more often challenge treatment that they consider to be inhumane—without retaliation by correctional employees or agencies. Data of these types are necessary to allow a more thorough assessment of the impact of implementing standards.

There are a number of problems associated with attempts to modify institutional practices on the basis of a set of suggested standards. Taken together, they raise doubts about the reliability or impact of using model standards for promoting and guaranteeing humane treatment for correctional clientele. One of the most serious shortcomings of these standards is that since they have grown out of reviews of some of the most extreme cases of correctional mistreatment—primarily in prisons—they are poorly suited for direct application to the vast majority of routine correctional processes. Most routine day-to-day treatment within correctional regimens is less severe and less patently offensive than the kinds of mistreatment that spawned the standards in the first place. So there is a real danger that the outside observer would see little correspondence between extreme mistreatment and more routinized inhumanity in some correctional regimens.

The point might be better grasped by noting that past court cases have largely dealt with physical mistreatment, and the same is true of the extant sets of standards we have reviewed. Little is said about the psychological suffering or abuse to which correctional clientele might be subjected. When compared with the intolerable physical abuses that gave rise to the issuance of standards, these psychological abuses may seem pale indeed. Consequently, the problem is that, in drafting a set of standards on the basis of particularly extreme cases of abuse, other types of abuse can easily be overlooked and omitted.

In order to effectively influence conduct, a set of standards must spell out precisely what parties are responsible for assuring that they are honored. In short, for such a set of norms to be taken seriously, someone must be explicitly charged with the implementation of them in day-to-day operations. Additionally, procedures should indicate how complaints can be brought, how determinations of violation can be reached, and what kinds of sanctions can be levied against violators. At present, once such standards are issued, responsibility for adopting and implementing them passes to administrators who are free to ignore them entirely or to delay interminably the process of adoption.

Given these shortcomings with model standards, there is little wonder that some states have shown a willingness to adopt them wholesale as part of their "correctional law"; as "law" they are deficient and may represent a minimal threat to existing practices. As they stand, there is every reason to assume that departments of corrections could reap a public relations windfall by "adopting" and then summarily ignoring them. Before these standards would appear threatening to correctional administrators, they would have to be modified to take account of the deficiencies to which we have alluded.

Another deficiency with using model standards to modify correctional practices—and this may appear paradoxical—is that correctional administrators can use support for them as a mechanism for producing their own version of correctional "reform." In this way their liberal-reformist conceptions of "humane" treatment can be grafted onto model standards. These then become part of a package, intended and appropriately titled as a set of standards for "minimum humane" treatment of prisoners. An example of this process is seen by examining portions of the UN Minimum Rules for the Treatment of Prisoners (ABA, 1974). The rules contain a section entitled "Treatment" and another designated "Classification and Individuation," which together comprise a capsule statement of endorsement for the medical model of the preventive ideal. Apparently the drafters of the rules could not adequately differentiate *humane* treatment and treatment *intended to change* offenders.

This illustrates the danger of studying or focusing upon piecemeal correctional reforms instead of viewing them within a context of social, political, and institutional processes. It could be argued, for example, that correctional administrators have been publicly supportive of humane standards in the hopes of driving up the total cost of incarceration, thereby making community corrections programs appear more reasonable by comparison. The more cynically inclined might suggest, too, that by supporting humane standards the correctors can help to insure that these standards are confined exclusively to *prison* programs and conditions, leaving special experimental and community programs unaffected. In other words, they can concede a little in order to avoid losing much more.

In part, this is possible because model standards do not sufficiently state that they are equally applicable to activities intended as "treatment" and to those intended as punishment. By failing to make this application clear, the drafters of model standards leave the correctional administrator and employee free to argue that standards for humane treatment do not apply to treatment programs. Similarly, the standards do not sufficiently argue their applicability to special categories of offenders, especially those whose offenses have previously been divested from the strictly criminal process—for example, to the civil legal process (Kittrie, 1971). Standards will mean little if they are only applicable to correctional practices officially intended to be punitive, or to a category of offenders that has previously been depopulated by actions of the therapeutic state.

Despite the well-known problems with piecemeal reforms of corrections, the serious and obvious shortcomings of a standards approach to assuring humane treatment demands a consideration of alternative means to accomplish the same objective.

MAKING CORRECTIONS HUMANE

We begin with four assumptions. First, of overriding importance, is an understanding of the importance of humane treatment as an end in itself, even if it proves to be inversely related to correctional effectiveness or any other measure of correctional impact. There must be a reordering of the priorities of correctional personnel and programs, with humane treatment receiving primary consideration. Second, standards of humane treatment must be applied to all the experiences to which offenders are subjected—those they would not have experienced had they not been arrested or convicted of crimes. Therefore, how correctional administrators or employees intend or view a program should be irrelevant to the need to evaluate its humaneness; programs labeled as treatment must be scrutinized. Third, real sanction threats and sanctions must be built into efforts to make corrections more humane. We must rely upon more than merely the good faith and intentions of correctional personnel. Finally, making corrections more humane requires administrative commitment and leadership, as evidenced especially by the expenditure of resources. This final point requires more extended comment.

Organizational elites communicate to subordinates their approval or disapproval of behaviors in myriad ways. As a result, when superordinates are not especially committed to and supportive of some policy (e.g., humane treatment), there is no disguising that fact. Consequently, if correctional practices are to become more humane, a fundamental ingredient is a commitment to such a change by administrators, and a willingness to assume a leadership role in promoting and guaranteeing such behaviors by subordinates.

There are two processes by which elites can evidence such commitment. The first is by *expending resources* for: (1) indoctrinating personnel in the value of humane treatment; (2) establishing and operating a procedure for dealing with cases of alleged inhumane conduct either by staff or clientele; and (3) rewarding employees differentially on the basis of their conformity to standards of humane treatment. The second process is by assuming a *leadership role* in all of these activities. By going on record as favoring and boosting such behavior, administrators lend the prestige of their office and person to the task of assuring humane treatment. There is no substitute for this ingredient. In both of these ways, administrators can initiate and maintain conditions essential for dignified treatment for correctional clientele.

13

Corrections and the rule of law

If we were to highlight one occurrence that transformed discourse about corrections during the past decade it would be the increased willingness of correctional clientele to define their situation in legal and political terms. Consistent with this new awareness, they have pressed litigation challenging a wide variety of the conditions of their treatment by police and correctional personnel. Newly cognizant of their rights and of how to seek redress for violations of them, prisoners not only have won decisions from the courts expanding their formal rights but modifications of the administrative laws of corrections in virtually every state.

An indication of the significance of this change is the fact that a decade ago sociological treatments of correctional issues made no significant mention of the legal rights and responsibilities of correctional clientele and employees. Today the same could not occur. Concerned lay citizens, lawyers, and even sociologists have begun to include discussions of such topics as *justice* and *legality* in their writings about corrections. What has become increasingly apparent to many is that correctional practices must be evaluated in the light of how closely they conform to legal guarantees and principles. Therefore, in this chapter we will review the development of concern with the fundamental justice of correctional practices, illustrate some of the practices that have come under scrutiny, discuss the responses to this movement by correctional administrators and legislatures, and discuss the likely impact of the "legalization movement" on the day-to-day operation of correctional agencies and the plight of offenders.

WHY BE CONCERNED WITH JUSTICE AND LEGALITY?

In our technocratic age, discussions of alternative social and political policies tend to be reduced to considerations of *technique*. Attempts to expand the discussion to include questions of values are disparaged as "unscientific," "emotional," or simply "inappropriate." This is regrettable, for as Rawls has asserted: "justice is the first virtue of social institutions," and "laws and institutions no matter how efficient and well-arranged must be reformed or abolished if they are unjust" (1971: 3–4). His statement can be read as both a point of view and a warning. We must insure that corrections becomes more than a fixation with punishment or rehabilitation. However, as Allen (1964: 27, 30) has pointed out, the rise of interest in rehabilitation "has dictated what questions are to be investigated, with the result that many matters of equal or even greater importance have been ignored or insufficiently examined"; the dominance of rehabilitative thinking has created a situation that "not only diverts attention from many serious issues but [has led] to a denial that these issues even exist." For this reason we should not become so preoccupied with the efficiency and effectiveness of correctional programs that we lose sight of more fundamental issues of humaneness and justice.

Following their arrest for a crime, individuals face some of the most severe penalties at the disposal of the organized state. At every step they face severe deprivations and may become subject to discretionary treatment by law enforcement and correctional personnel. When these discretionary deprivations are imposed, every effort must be made to insure that the action is humane, reasonable, and accountable. The importance of this is underscored by the tendency for discrete correctional decisions to "spill over" and affect subsequent ones. These "spill over effects" may be prejudicial and damaging to prisoners' well-being. This is evidenced, for example, in the well-known tendency for inmates' prison disciplinary records to affect their parole prospects (Scott, 1974; Heinz, Heinz, Senderowitz, and Vance, 1976). Consequently, when the prison disciplinary "court" convicts inmates of rule infractions, their chances of making parole may be substantially reduced, thereby resulting in a de facto lengthening of their sentences. Frequently, when parolees are taken into custody and returned to prison for parole revocation hearings, even should they be exonerated, they may already have lost their jobs and the good will of their families, both of which may increase their difficulties when they return to the free world. Therefore, correctional decisions are more than a series of discrete events. Each to some extent is dependent upon and influenced by the others, which makes it important that these decisions and the underlying discretion be scrutinized and controlled.

Additionally, when offenders believe they have been treated unjustly, and that the perpetrators did so with impunity, they may generalize their resentment and alienation to the entire political process. A society that trumpets the virtue of political participation, if it truly values such participation by its citizens, presumably would not want to encourage such a response. For this reason as well, correctional decisions should be subjected to the rule of law.

Related to this as another consideration is the possibility of a relationship between the degree of fairness with which offenders feel they have been dealt and their turning away from subsequent criminal activities. Put differently, dealing with offenders in a fair and just fashion may be a prerequisite to rehabilitation. Thus, two observers have recently noted that "in emphasizing the place of justice in a correctional system, some penologists have argued that rehabilitation in a milieu perceived by the offender as fundamentally inequitable simply is not possible" (Keating and Kolze, 1975: 42). John Irwin has pointed to the "sense of injustice" that pervades offenders' feelings about their experiences at the hands of the criminal "justice" system. He suggests that "if it is believed that an increased commitment to conventional beliefs and values and an increased allegiance to society's institutions and agencies is a desirable and necessary goal in the rehabilitation of felons, then these sources of a mounting sense of injustice should be inspected more closely" (1970: 173).

In the final analysis, since offenders are persons and citizens they should retain all the human and constitutional rights ordinarily due them, excepting those that must necessarily be withheld due to the conditions of their correctional experience. This position, enunciated by a federal court more than 30 years ago [*Coffin* v. *Reichard*, 143 F. 2d 443 (6th Cir. 1944)], has gradually become accepted by many who are informed about correctional issues. Such a change in opinion has not come easily, however. It has required the passage of time, the active intervention of courts and convict rebellions, but it has finally come. We turn now to a discussion of some indications of this change.

THE RENEWED CONCERN WITH JUSTICE AND LEGALITY

In the past decade, as American prisons have been rocked by rebellions, as research has cast doubt on the ability of corrections to truly correct, and as prisoners have mounted an assault on corrections in the courts, increasing numbers of observers have begun to question whether corrections has been permitted to operate in an essentially lawless fashion. Correctional operations have been challenged by a diverse group of persons, ranging from academicians and lawyers to convicts.

Leonard Orland, a law professor and former member of the Connecticut Board of Parole, begins his *Prisons: House of Darkness* (1975: xiii) with the bald recognition that corrections has been permitted to operate in a lawless fashion. Orland recognizes this as truly ironic, given the criminal justice system's existence to uphold the law. John Conrad, a researcher closely identified with the correctional industry, has argued that unless justice is the "first virtue of the public institutions which administer it, none of the other virtues these institutions may possess will matter" (1973: 217). Similar sentiments have been expressed by a working party of the American Friends Service Committee (Bacon et al., 1971), the Committee for the Study of Incarceration (von Hirsch, 1976), and by the members of the Annual Chief Justice Earl Warren Conference on Advocacy in the United States, in their 1973 report on prison reform (Roscoe-Pound, 1973). Nor have law-trained personnel ignored this movement. Norval Morris (1974) and Nicholas Kittrie (1971), both law professors, have argued that correctional programs cannot sacrifice due process and legal considerations in the efforts either to punish or rehabilitate offenders. Finally, we cannot overlook the fact that one of the complaints of rebelling prisoners during the numerous insurrections of the early 1970s was the inhumanity and injustice to which they believed they were subjected. In reciting their complaints, the rebellious convicts expressed a sanguine faith in democratic processes, which can only appear ironic in the light of events such as those at Attica, but the sentiment was unmistakable. For example, on August 11, 1970, inmates in the Tombs prison (New York City) presented a list of grievances to the mayor's office that stated:

> We are firm in our resolve and we demand, as human beings, the dignity and justice that is due to us by right of our birth. We do not know how the present system of brutality and dehumanization and injustice has been allowed to be perpetuated in this day of enlightenment, but we are the living proof of its existence and we cannot allow it to continue (Bacon et al., 1971: 5–6; see also Wicker, 1975).

This broad-based renewal of interest in the issue of correctional justice was a long time coming.

> For a nation that has so consistently boasted of a spirit of benevolence, it is ironic that not until the 1960's did courts rule that star-

vation, isolation in cells without clothes or basic hygenic facilities, and random whippings are cruel and unusual punishments; that prisoners have rights of religion and speech (Rothman, 1973: 9).

Possibly the single most important stimulus to change has been the flood tide of litigation brought by convicts, primarily in the federal courts, during the past decade. Although in Chapter 12 we barely hinted at this movement, some indication of its magnitude can be gained from examining changes in the numbers of suits filed by prison inmates in the federal district courts for each year from 1961 through 1975. These data are contained in Table 13–1. There we can see that in 1961 the rate of suits (per 1,000 inmates in state and federal institutions) was 11.85, and by 1974 this had increased to 84.37 before declining to 80.25 in 1975. Before this movement could proceed very far, the traditional tendency of the courts to defer to correctional administrators had to be reversed. This pattern of judicial conservatism was crystallized in the "hands-off" doctrine.

TABLE 13–1
Prisoner petitions filed in federal district courts, 1961–1976

Year	Total petitions*	Total prison population†	Rate‡
1961	2,609§	220,149¶	11.85
1962	2,948	218,830	13.47
1963	4,254	217,283	19.58
1964	6,240	214,336	29.11
1965	7,888	210,895	37.40
1966	8,540	199,654	42.77
1967	10,443	194,896	53.58
1968	11,152	187,914	59.34
1969	12,924	196,007	62.72
1970	15,997	196,429	81.44
1971	16,266	198,061	82.13
1972	16,267	196,183	82.92
1973	17,218	204,349	84.26
1974	18,410	218,205	84.37
1975	19,307	240,593	80.25
1976	n.a.	263,291	—

* From various issues of the *Report of the Director of the Administrative Office of the United States Courts.*

† From various issues of *Prisoners in State and Federal Institutions,* National Prisoner Statistics.

‡ Per 1,000 inmates.

§ For the fiscal year ending June 30.

¶ For the calendar year ending December 31.

The "hands-off" doctrine

In its 1971–1972 term, the U.S. Supreme Court decided eight cases directly affecting convicted offenders and at least two others with implications for the operation of corrections. In all eight cases directly involving corrections, the offender's contention prevailed. As much as anything, this demonstrates how fundamental the change in the courts' stance was toward corrections, at least until the past two to three years.

An extreme interpretation of the view that courts took toward offenders and their plight during an earlier time is presented without equivocation in an 1871 case [*Ruffin* v. *Commonwealth*, 62 Va. (21 Gratt.) 790 (1871)]. The Virginia Supreme Court declared that a convict has, "as a consequence of his crime, not only forfeited his liberty but also his personal rights, except those which the law in its humanity affords him." The court went on to assert that "he is, for the time being the slave of the state." A more typical case, however, was *Stroud* v. *Swope* [187 F. 2d 850 (9th Cir. 1951)], in which a federal circuit judge declared: "We think it well settled that it is not the function of the courts to superintend the treatment and discipline of persons in penitentiaries, but only to deliver from imprisonment those who are illegally confined" (quoted in Rothman, 1973: 12). This reflected the dominant judicial belief that only disruption and mischief could result from the courts' intervention in prison matters. While there were occasional dissenting views, such as *Coffin* v. *Reichard* [143 F. 2d 443 (6th Dir. 1945)], it was not until 1974 that the U.S. Supreme Court declared unambiguously that "there is no iron curtain drawn between the Constitution and the prisons of this country" [*Wolff* v. *McDonnell*, 418 U.S. 539 (1974)]. It was not until the 1960s that a shift in this direction became clearly perceptible.

The earlier period of judicial reluctance to interfere in correctional affairs was based on three apparent rationales: the theory of separation of powers; an assumed lack of judicial expertise in correctional issues and the corollary assumption of expertise by correctional personnel; and the fear that intervention by the courts would subvert discipline (Goldfarb and Singer, 1970).

Judicial abstention in cases involving community programs (that is, probation and parole) was generally based on an interpretation of them as a "privilege" rather than a "right." In other words, the courts reasoned that the offender's participation in, say, probation was a privilege and need not, therefore, be circumscribed by due process rights or safeguards. Other legal doctrines were similarly fashioned or adapted so as to preclude judicial intervention.

For example, the "constructive custody" doctrine was employed to argue that, even while on probation or parole, offenders actually remained in the custody of prison or jail officials and, therefore, could be removed to those premises should their behavior warrant it (Fisher, 1974).

The erosion of "hands-off"

Although it is difficult to say with confidence just why the courts began to reverse their traditional policy of abstention toward corrections litigation, this change seems to have been part of an emerging critical stance toward criminal justice agencies during the 1960s. Moreover, all seem agreed that social and political events of that decade were partially responsible for hastening the arrival of such a stance. In the context of the civil rights and antiwar movements, a Supreme Court with an already established "liberal" track record on social issues began enunciating a stricter set of standards for criminal justice agencies. Perhaps the rapidly accumulating research literature, suggesting the inability of corrections to correct offenders, made it even more difficult for the courts to continue to ignore correctional injustice (Rothman, 1973). In any case, once the courthouse doors were ajar they were quickly opened all the way. The courts themselves facilitated this opening by broadening their interpretations of the federal civil rights acts, the writ of habeas corpus, and other doctrines providing for federal court intervention. This resulted in an outpouring of litigation, primarily from the prisons. While it may be argued that he exaggerates, Orland's appraisal (1975: 11) of the impact of this is reasonably typical:

> The collective result of this litigation has been nothing less than the achievement of a legal revolution within a decade. . . . To a large extent, the Bastille has been stormed in the quiet of the courtroom. . . . What has emerged is a grass-roots political entity—a people's movement. Significant change has been wrought by prisoners themselves. Such a development is unprecedented in the annals of Anglo-American penal history.

As might be expected, as the courts abrogated their "hands-off" policy and prisoner litigation increased, the volume of literature detailing and discussing it did likewise. One need only compare, under the appropriate headings, the number of entries in recent issues of the *Index to Legal Periodicals* with those from a decade ago to see just how much of an increase there has been. Fortunately, with this growth have come some excellent specialized publications that provide overviews of the most significant developments in correctional law. Among them are the *New England Journal on Prison Law* and the *Prison Law Reporter*. Also, a number of excellent books have been published that provide summaries of the developing case law of corrections (for example, Williams, 1974; Krantz, 1976).

The substance of challenges to corrections

Although convicts have been in the forefront of the legal challenge to corrections, jail inmates and those involved in community programs have also been actively involved in the struggle. The challenge has largely been waged in the federal courts.

The rights that correctional clients have attempted to establish fall into four categories (Goldfarb and Singer, 1970). The first category involves the right to be free from cruel and unusual punishment, and the right to the minimal conditions necessary to sustain life. We have already dealt with this line of challenge in Chapter 12. The second category—and this was the first one recognized by the courts—protects prisoners' access to the courts and to others outside of correctional channels. The third category includes rights usually termed "civil rights" when applied to persons who are not enmeshed in the correctional apparatus: freedom of religion, freedom of expression, the right to vote, and freedom from racial discrimination. Finally are offenders' rights to demand that they be given the benefit of reasonable standards and procedural protections when decisions are made that have a significant impact on them; examples are the denial of parole and revocation of "good time" for violations of prison rules. The First, Eighth, and Fourteenth Amendments to the U.S. Constitution have been the principal avenues by which these claims have been pressed. A brief review of several important cases will serve to illustrate not only the substance of some challenges to corrections but also several significant developments in correctional law.

Black prisoners, especially Black Muslims, were the vanguard of challenges to the actions of prison administrators (King, 1969). *Jackson* v. *Godwin* [400 F. 2d 529 (5th Cir. 1968)] may serve to illustrate the increasing refusal of black prisoners during the 1960s to tolerate racially discriminatory treatment. Herman Jackson, a 24-year-old black inmate under a death sentence in Florida State Prison, charged that his constitutional rights had been violated by the refusal of prison officials to permit him to subscribe to black publications. He argued that since white prisoners were permitted to subscribe to white publications, this restriction on black prisoners amounted to denial of equal protection of the law, which is prohibited by the Fourteenth Amendment. In ruling in Jackson's favor, the appeals court said that as a rule there must be "some substantial and controlling interest which requires the subordination or limitation of these important constitutional rights, and which justified their infringement." In applying that test, the court concluded that Florida prison officials had been arbitrary in their policy on receiving publications. Accordingly, the court held, the "necessary effect and result of such regulations, even if not arbitrary and though even handedly enforced, is racial discrimination in violation of . . . Fourteenth Amendment rights."

Prison officials had long maintained restrictions on the right of prisoners to assist one another in preparing legal petitions or papers. These restrictions, aimed at so-called jailhouse lawyers, were justified on the grounds that such convicts raise unrealistic hopes in other prisoners, use their services to gain sexual favors from other prisoners, exploit the legal naivete of their peers, and simply clog the courts with frivolous and poorly prepared legal petitions. In 1965 the Tennessee State Prison at Nashville had a regulation stating:

> No inmate will advise, assist or otherwise contract to aid another, either with or without fee, to prepare Writs or other legal matters. It is not intended that an innocent man be punished. When a man believes he is unlawfully held or illegally convicted, he should prepare a brief or state his complaint in letter form and address it to his lawyer or a judge. A formal Writ is not necessary to receive a hearing. False charges or untrue complaints may be punished. Inmates are forbidden to set themselves up as practitioners for the purpose of promoting a business of writing Writs (*Johnson* v. *Avery*, p. 490).

In February 1965, Johnson, serving a life sentence in the Tennessee State Prison, was transferred to the maximum security building in the prison for violating this regulation by assisting other prisoners in preparing writs. In July 1965, he filed in the U.S. district court a petition that the court treated as a motion for a writ of habeas corpus. The district court held the regulation void because it had the effect of barring illiterate prisoners from access to federal habeas corpus and portions of the U.S. Code. The state appealed and the court of appeals reversed the district court, finding that the state's interest in preserving prison discipline and in limiting the practice of law to attorneys justified any burden the regulation might place on access to federal habeas corpus. The U.S. Supreme Court reversed the appeals court and remanded the case for further action consistent with its opinion [*Johnson* v. *Avery* 393 U.S. 483 (1969)]. The Court held that in the absence of some provision by the state of Tennessee for a reasonable alternative to assist illiterate or poorly educated inmates in preparing petitions, the state could not validly enforce a regulation that absolutely bars prisoners from furnishing such assistance to other prisoners. To do so, declared the Court, is to deprive "those unable themselves, with reasonable adequacy, to prepare their petitions, of access to the constitutionally and statutorily protected availability of the writ of habeas corpus."

Community correctional programs have not escaped the courts' more critical gaze. *Morrissey* v. *Brewer* [408 U.S. 471 (1972)] involved petitioners who claimed that their paroles were revoked without a hearing; this, they charged, deprived them of due process of law. Both the district and appeals court denied the petitions, declaring that parole is only "a correctional device authorizing service of sentence outside a penitentiary," and concluded that a parolee who is still "in custody" is not entitled to a full adversary hearing such as would be required in a criminal trial. The Supreme Court reversed the appeals court and remanded the case for further action. In reaching its decision, the Court unambiguously rejected the notion that "constitutional rights turn upon whether a governmental benefit is characterized as a 'right' or a 'privilege.'" Instead, "whether any procedural protections are due depends on the extent to which an individual will be 'condemned to suffer grievous loss.'" The Court recognized that "the liberty of a parolee, although indeterminate, includes many of the core values of unqualified liberty and its termination inflicts a 'grievous loss' on the parolee and often on others." And so, "it is hardly useful any longer to try to deal with this problem in terms of whether parolees' liberties are a 'right' or a 'privilege.' By whatever name, the liberty is valuable and must be seen as within the protection of the Fourteenth Amendment. Its termination calls for some orderly process, however informal." The Court declared that termination of a parolee's liberty requires an informal hearing to give assurance that the finding of a parole violation is based on verified facts to support the revocation. Such a hearing should be reasonably prompt, conducted by an impartial hearing officer near the place of the alleged parole violation or arrest, and should seek to determine if there is reasonable ground to believe that the parolee has violated a parole condition. The parolee should receive prior notice of the inquiry, its purpose, and the alleged violations. The parolee may present relevant information and (absent security considerations) question adverse informants. The hearing officer should weigh the evidence to determine whether probable cause exists to believe the parolee violated the conditions of parole, and he or she should state the reasons for holding the parolee for the parole board's decision. At the subsequent revocation hearing, which must be conducted reasonably soon after the parolee's arrest, minimum due process requirements are: (1) written notice of the claimed violations of parole; (2) disclosure to the parolee of evidence against him or her; (3) opportunity to be heard in person and to present witnesses and documentary evidence; (4) the right to confront and cross-examine adverse witnesses (unless the hearing officer specifically finds good cause for not allowing confrontation); (5) a "neutral and detached" hearing body, such as a traditional parole board, members of which need not be judicial officers or lawyers; and (6) a written statement by the fact finders as to evidence relied on and reasons for revoking parole. Thus, for the first time the Court circumscribed the parole revocation process with due process guarantees.

In *Gagnon* v. *Scarpelli* [411 U.S. 788 (1973)] the Court made a limited extension of the provisions of *Morrissey* v. *Brewer* to the probation-revocation process. The petitioner, Gerald Scarpelli, pleaded guilty in July 1965 to a charge of armed robbery in Wisconsin. The trial judge sentenced him to 15 years' imprisonment, but suspended the sentence and placed him on probation for seven years. Later his probation supervision was transferred to Cook County, Illinois. On August 6, 1965, Scarpelli was apprehended by Illinois police who surprised him and a confederate in the process of burglarizing a house. The two men admitted that they had broken into the house for the purpose of stealing merchandise or money. Probation was revoked by Wisconsin on September 1 without a hearing, and Scarpelli was subsequently incarcerated in the Wisconsin State Reformatory. Some three years later he applied for a writ of habeas corpus. As the basis for his petition, he contended that the due process clause of the Fourteenth Amendment had been violated because he had been denied the right to a hearing upon notice and to have legal counsel assist him. The case eventually reached the U.S. Supreme Court, which sought to resolve the issue of whether probationers are entitled to hearings, and whether they are entitled to representation by appointed counsel. Writing for the Court, Justice Powell noted that many of the basic elements of parole are similar, at least in the constitutional sense, to those found in probation. The Court went on to declare that Fourteenth Amendment due process provisions require that probationers, like parolees, be accorded a hearing procedure when they face possible revocation of probation. The Court further declared that while both the probationer and parolee may be represented by counsel at such a hearing there is no constitutionally guaranteed right to counsel. Instead, a decision as to the need for counsel must be made on a case-by-case basis by the state authority charged with responsibility for administering the probation and parole system.

Although the presence and participation of counsel will probably be both undesirable and constitutionally unnecessary in most revocation hearings, there will remain certain cases in which fundamental fairness—the touchstone of due process—will require that the State provide at its expense counsel for indigent probationers or parolees (p. 790).

The cases reviewed thus far represent major extensions of constitutional rights to prisoners, probationers, and parolees during the period of approximately 1965–1975. There is reason to believe that this period of judicial activism is rapidly drawing to a close. The federal courts are drawing back from their interventionist stance of just a few years ago and returning to a "hands-off" policy. A number of recent cases would seem to warrant this assertion. One such case is *Wolff* v. *McDonnell* [418 U.S. 539 (1974)], a case in which prison disciplinary practices were challenged. In deciding the case, the U.S. Supreme Court refused to extend the full panoply of due process rights to convicts who face disciplinary hearings. The primary issue in *Wolff* was the extent to which due process is applicable to disciplinary hearings where prisoners face punitive confinement or loss of "good time." The Court stated that due process demands must be balanced against institutional needs so that prison officials can maintain discipline and institutional security. Stating that due process is a flexible concept, the Court declared that it is applicable to a disciplinary hearing only to the extent that a prisoner (1) must be given written notice of the charges a least 24 hours before the hearing, and (2) is entitled to a written statement of the evidence relied on by the prison officials in reaching their decision, and of their reasons for taking disciplinary action. The Court denied inmates the right to submit documentary evidence, to call witnesses in their own behalf, and prohibited the right to confront and cross-examine adverse witnesses. The Court proclaimed that confrontation and cross-examination are not "rights universally applicable to all hearings."

In *Meachum* v. *Fano* [96 S. Ct. 2532 (1976)] an action was brought to the U.S. Supreme Court by state prisoners who alleged that their transfers to less-favorable institutions without adequate fact-finding hearings deprived them of liberty without due process of law. The Court held that the due process clause of the Fourteenth Amendment does not entitle state prisoners to a hearing even when they are transferred to prisons whose conditions are substantially less favorable to them.

A much more important decision was rendered by the U.S. Supreme Court in the case of *Jones* v. *North Carolina Prisoners' Labor Union, Inc.* [97 S. Ct. 2532 (1977)]. In this case the Court let stand regulations of the North Carolina Department of Corrections that effectively prohibit establishment or operation of a prisoners' union. This would seem to be a case with important implications for the future of American corrections.

Despite this evidence of a return of judicial conservatism, litigation and the attendant publicity have cast the spotlight on just how far traditional correctional practices have been permitted to operate at variance or in conflict with legal guarantees and safeguards. Certainly, the same effect was achieved by the numerous prison rebellions of the 1960s and early 1970s, when inmates dramatically and poignantly portrayed the web of injustice in which they were caught. In the aftermath of both these movements, much time and effort has been expended in attempts to rectify some of the more glaring injustices of corrections. It remains for us to discuss some of these responses, to assess them in the light of both what is known about the impact of such reforms and recognized standards of justice and due process, and to determine whether these structural or procedural reforms have had any significant effect upon the lives of offenders.

INSTITUTIONAL CONSEQUENCES

How have correctional agencies and interest groups responded to these challenges from offenders? It must be noted, first of all, that so long as administrative discretion was unfettered and clients confronted a policy of judicial abstention, correctional administrators made few efforts to assure that their clients were treated consistently with due process and equal protection guarantees. Only when the courts began to look askance at their practices, to return decisions critical of them, and to intervene in the operations of their agencies, did they adopt a strategy that some might see as typical of bureaucracies when faced with a source of environmental uncertainty: they developed programs to routinize the challenges and bring them under their own control.

Model standards

In Chapter 12 we alluded to various sets of model standards developed by groups or individuals interested in the correctional process. Virtually all of these sets of standards contain provisions for establishing and protecting offenders' rights and their access to the courts. Typical of such standards are those presented by Krantz et al. (1973) as *Model Rules and Regulations on Prisoners' Rights and Responsibilities*. A more influential set of standards has been issued by the Commission on Accreditation for Corrections (1977) (affiliated with the American Correctional Association) as part of its program for accrediting correctional institutions.

Similar to model standards, as a response to the legal shortcomings of corrections, is the issuance of policy statements or model legislation by correctional interest groups. In Chapter 12 we referred to the Model Act for the Protection of Rights of Prisoners developed by the National Council on Crime and Delinquency (1972). In addition to this effort, the NCCD Board of Directors has recently issued a policy statement on the Peaceful Settlement of Prison Conflict (1974). This statement proposes a seven-point program for "reducing causes of conflict and for preventing and resolving crises in correctional institutions." NCCD proposes that each state: (1) establish by legislation or administrative order minimum standards for the protection of rights of prisoners that prohibit inhumane treatment; (2) establish in each of its institutions formal procedures for handling individual and collective grievances; (3) enact legislation authorizing prisoners to engage in negotiations as a means of providing peaceful democratic alternatives to violence; (4) provide a means whereby, if an impasse is reached in negotiations, "professionally trained third-party neutrals" could be asked to participate in the negotiations; (5) authorize in each of its institutions a prisoner organization for the purpose of credibly representing prisoners; (6) provide a means whereby, at times of prison crises, a team of specially trained and selected personnel can be brought together for settling the crises without violence; and (7) establish training for both prison personnel and prisoners in techniques of conflict resolution.

Changes in legislation and administrative codes

Until recently, statutes regulating the provision of correctional services and the power of correctors were rare. And the legislative standards that did exist were vague. For example, laws in some states directed that prison food and clothing be "wholesome," "coarse," "cheap," "plain," or "sufficient to sustain health." Seldom were correctional facilities required to be anything more than "clean and healthful" (Goldfarb and Singer, 1970). Legislation regulating community correctional programs was scarcely more detailed. In the wake of the correctional tumult of the 1960s this has changed. Many states, including New Mexico, Kansas, Wisconsin, Illinois, and Connecticut, have modified their statutes or administrative codes to provide more detailed regulations. Simultaneously, in some states these changes have included explicit substantive recognition of of-

fender rights and procedural mechanisms for dealing with grievances. For instance, in Maryland a statutory grievance procedure,
the Inmate Grievance Commission, was established by the state legislature in 1971 (McArthur, 1974). Certainly, one motivation for
making these changes has been the belief that judicial intervention
is an unwieldly or inherently unworkable means for producing correctional reforms (Rubin, 1971). It is possible, too, that such legislative and administrative changes have been motivated in many places
by the simple desire to curtail the flood of prisoner litigation. This
strategy is seized upon as one way of making changes while still re-
taining control within the correctional agency. Orland's discussion
in *Prisons: Houses of Darkness* is illustrative. At one point he belit-
tles the wave of litigation that has poured from American prisons as
a "prisoner's fantasy" (1975: 8). Later he leaves little doubt that he
is largely concerned with stemming "the outpouring of prisoners'
rights litigation which, in ever increasing proportions, is clogging the
courts" (1975: 150).

Grievance mechanisms

Probably the most popular single modification of correctional
practice to result from court decisions and rebellions has been the
establishment of formal institutional grievance mechanisms. Just
how popular is indicated by the fact that a 1973 survey of 253 U.S.
penal institutions found that, of the 209 institutions responding, 160
said they had a "formal procedure for handling grievances of inmates" (McArthur, 1974). Half of these procedures had been
started after March 1972. At least three broad categories of grievance mechanisms have been identified: the "labor," "investigative,"
and "participatory" models (Keating and Kolze, 1975).

The *labor* model is so named because it is analogous to the model
of grievance resolution in industrial labor relations. It builds on the
premise that prisoners should elect their own representatives, who
would function much like shop stewards in private industry. Thus,
prisoners would decide what grievances to accept and pursue. Such
a procedure would probably culminate in binding arbitration, at
least on questions relating to the application of policies and
regulations.

In the May 1973 survey of 209 U.S. institutions, 56 percent reported that they had inmate councils or groups of inmates selected
to represent the inmates' point of view in dealings with corrections
officials. In 107 of these institutions, all or some of the representatives are elected by the prisoners. Presumably, therefore, in many of
the institutions one or more of the council members are selected by

the institutional staff. However, it cannot be determined from the report of survey findings whether these inmate councils are involved in the screening and resolution of particular prisoner grievances (McArthur, 1974).

A special case of the labor model is the representation of prisoners by an organization similar to a union. In addition to the powers discussed above, under the labor model such an organization would be empowered to bargain with correctional management over terms and conditions of correctional policy, prison living conditions, terms of labor, and grievance procedures. Prisoner unions usually have been resisted by correctional administrators as a threat to the internal order and security of prisons, and apparently there is no place in the U.S. at present where such an organization has won the recognized right to function as bargaining agent for prisoners. In a survey of 209 prisons, 44 reported that attempts had at least been made to organize their prisoners into a union (McArthur, 1974). The results of the survey do not report the success of these endeavors or the obstacles typically encountered by prisoners in attempts to organize.

Prisoners' attempts to organize in some states have received considerable publicity (for example, California) while efforts in other places have gone largely unchronicled. Based in part on a review of attempts by Ohio prisoners to form a union, Huff (1974) offered this summary of the legal status of organizing efforts:

1. Any right prisoners might have to unionize is secondary to the state's interest in maintaining orderly and secure prisons. Therefore, before being permitted to organize prisoners would have to demonstrate that a union would be able to control its members and would pose no threat to the prison's order and security.
2. Where there is litigation over the right to organize, the state will have to be able to convincingly argue that there would be undesirable effects in the prison if it hopes to win the case. And,
3. While the state may recognize prisoner unions if it wishes to do so, there is doubt whether prisoners could meet the definition of "employees" under the National Labor Relations Act.

Given the recent U.S. Supreme Court decision in *Jones* v. *North Carolina Prisoners' Labor Union, Inc.*, some of these comments seem prophetic. Nevertheless, there is support for one of the demands that presumably has motivated prisoners to engage in organizing activities. The Board of Trustees of the NCCD, in a policy statement (1972a), has called for extension of the minimum wage to prisoners.

The *investigative* model can take two different forms. It can involve the appointment of an individual to receive and investigate complaints. Such a person then makes recommendations based on the investigation's findings to the appropriate administrators, who may accept or reject them. Such a model places primary emphasis on the investigator, who assumes total responsibility for investigating complaints and formulating solutions. An ombudsperson is the closest approximation to this model, and a number of states have established such a position and grievance process. Alternatively, the investigative model may be a multilevel appeal process, in which a complaint may be appealed to other investigators at other prisons, to different departmental levels, or even to outside reviewers. In either form, this model proceeds from an investigation of the facts to a decision based on the investigator's recommendation.

The third model, the *participatory* model, simply provides that, at some level of the grievance procedure, prisoners and line staff participate directly in the consideration of complaints and formulation of recommended resolutions. This participation usually takes the form of an inmate/staff committee that hears grievances and attempts to devise a mutually acceptable resolution.

All three types of grievance procedures appear to be popular, as gauged by their use in American prisons. For example, 64 of 209 prisons surveyed in May 1973 reported having an ombudsperson. Seven states have statewide correctional ombudspersons: Georgia, Hawaii, Minnesota, New Jersey, Ohio, Oregon, and South Carolina. Thirty-nine of the 64 ombudspersons are in these seven states; the remaining ombudspersons serve specific institutions (McArthur, 1974). We have noted that 117 institutions reported having inmate councils. One-hundred-sixty of the institutions said they have a formal grievance procedure that most closely approximates the second type of the investigatory model. Almost all of these procedures provide for a prisoner's complaint to be submitted first to someone within the prison; most then allow appeals from unfavorable decisions, with the ultimate appeal usually to someone or some group outside the institution (McArthur, 1974).

Legal services programs

Although legal services programs are administered in a variety of ways, law schools provide the services in some institutions (Resource Center, 1974). Under such programs, law students work on prisoners' legal problems either for academic credit or the experience. In many prisons, legal services are provided by legally knowledgeable prisoners. In all, 149 of the 209 institutions from the survey noted above reported having a program that provides legal service to prisoners (McArthur, 1974).

A recent survey of the 143 law schools within the United States

JUDICIAL LIMITS ON INMATE RIGHTS

(Decision of the U. S. Supreme Court in the Case of *Jones* v. *North Carolina Prisoners' Labor Union, Inc.*)
Mr. Justice REHNQUIST delivered the opinion of the Court.

Pursuant to regulations promulgated by the North Carolina Department of Corrections, appellants prohibited inmates from soliciting other inmates to join appellee, the North Carolina Prisoners' Labor Union, Inc. (the Union), barred all meetings of the Union, and refused to deliver packets of Union publications that had been mailed in bulk to several inmates for redistribution among other prisoners. The Union instituted this action . . . to challenge these policies. It alleged that appellants' efforts to prevent the operation of a prisoners' union violated the First and Fourteenth Amendment rights of it and its members and that the refusal to grant the Union those privileges accorded several other organizations operating within the prison system deprived the Union of equal protection of the laws.

* * * * *

Appellant prison officials concluded that the presence, perhaps even the objectives, of a prisoners' labor union would be detrimental to order and security in the prisons. . . . It is enough to say that they have not been conclusively shown to be wrong in this view. The interest in preserving order and authority in the prisons is self-evident. Prison life, and relations between the inmates themselves and between the inmates and prison officials or staff, contain the ever-present potential for violent confrontation and conflagration. . . . Responsible prison officials must be permitted to take reasonable steps to forestall such a threat, and they must be permitted to act before the time when they can compile a dossier on the eve of a riot. The case of a prisoners' union, where the focus is on the presentation of grievances to, and encouragement of adversary relations with, institution officials surely would rank high on anyone's list of potential trouble spots. If the appellants' views as to the possible detrimental effects of the organizational activities of the Union are reasonable, as we conclude they are, then the regulations are drafted no more broadly than they need be to meet the perceived threat—which stems directly from group meetings and group organizational activities of the Union. . . . When weighed against the First Amendment rights asserted, these institutional reasons are sufficiently weighty to prevail.

* * * * *

It is precisely in matters such as this, the decision as to which of many groups should be allowed to operate within the prison walls, where, confronted with claims based on the Equal Protection Clause, the courts should allow the prison administrators the full latitude of dis-

cretion, unless it can be firmly stated that the two groups are so similar that discretion has been abused. That is surely not the case here. There is nothing in the Constitution which requires prison officials to treat all inmate groups alike unless differentiation is necessary to avoid an imminent threat of institutional disruption or violence. The regulations of appellants challenged in the District Court offended neither the First nor the Fourteenth Amendments, and the judgment of that Court holding to the contrary is
    Reversed.

Source: *Jones* v. *North Carolina Prisoners' Labor Union, Inc.,* [97 S. Ct. 2536, 2542–44 (1977)].

found that, of the 97 schools responding, 42 had prison legal services programs in operation. Of the 42 schools with legal services programs, 29 began operations after 1968, and 11 began during the period 1966 through 1968 (Cardarelli and Finkelstein, 1974: 92). A survey of correctional administrators in the U.S. found broad support for the principle of legal services programs. Underlying this support for prison legal services was the belief that "it is consistent with fundamental principles of justice and right and . . . the embodiment of these values is a prime duty of a good correctional system" (Cardarelli and Finkelstein, 1974: 102). The authors of the survey conclude by noting: "Prison legal services for inmates not only are here to stay, but will in the future be seen as a necessary component of a functional correctional system, and not as a luxury of inmates to be resisted by some and championed by others" (Cardarelli and Finkelstein, 1974: 102).

Other procedural changes

In addition to substantive changes in correctional law, to the establishment of grievance procedures, and to legal services programs, many institutions and departments of correction have modified their operating procedures to consider the decisions of courts or to forestall litigation. Prisons have made changes in their manner of conducting disciplinary hearings, parole boards have modified their decision-making and parole-revocation processes, and courts and probation departments have altered their procedures for revocation of probation. Most of these changes, seemingly, have been made in response to actual or pending court decisions. We will mention or review two such changes for illustrative purposes.

In October 1973 the United States Board of Parole put into operation a general reorganization and regionalization plan. Case decision-making authority has now been delegated to panels of hearing examiners, using explicit parole selection policy guidelines established by the Parole Commission—as the former U.S. Board of Parole is now called. The new structure also provides a two-level administrative appeal process for prisoners who choose to contest the decision in their case. Another part of the plan provides for prisoners who are denied parole to be given a written statement of the reasons for their denial (Hoffman and DeGostin, 1974).

The new parole-selection policy guidelines involve a three-step process (Sigler, 1975). When reviewing a prisoner's case, the examiner panel first gives the case a *salient factor score*, ranging from zero to 11; the higher the score, the better the prospects for successful completion of parole. The case receives or loses points on the basis of such factors as prior commitments, education, employment history, and the like. Previous research has demonstrated that each of these factors has some predictability for success on parole.

The case is then given an *offense severity rating*—low, low moderate, high, very high, and greatest. This rating does not depend upon only the subjective rating of the examiners. Instead, they are given a chart that lists offense categories under each severity rating.

Then, with the salient factor score and the offense severity rating, the examiners refer to another chart, which indicates the amount of time an offender with a given background and salient factor score should serve for an offense of a given severity, assuming relatively good prison performance. Table 13–2 is a list of the salient factors. An individual's salient factor scores and offense severity ratings are cross-classified to arrive at averages for the amount of time to be served before release on parole. (Table 13–3.)

The use of these new guidelines is intended to bring about an increased degree of fairness in the parole selection process, by insuring that prisoners with similar backgrounds and offenses serve about the same amount of time. But, in cases in which the clinical judgments of the examiners suggest the prisoners have a much better chance of success on parole than their scores and ratings indicate, the examiners can shorten the amount of time to be served below those specified by the guidelines. Or the examiners can *extend* the amount of time to be served beyond that specified in the guidelines, for those cases where the prospects for success on parole is judged to be worse than that suggested by the score and rating.

When prisoners receive negative decisions (no parole), they are given the reasons in writing.

A second example of procedural change came about as a result of a consent decree in March 1970 following litigation in *Morris* v.

TABLE 13–2
Salient factor score used by U.S. Parole Commission

Case name .... Register No .... ☐
 Item A .... ☐
No prior convictions (adult or juvenile) = 3.
1 prior conviction = 2.
2 or 3 prior convictions = 1.
4 or more prior convictions = 0.
 Item B .... ☐
No prior incarcerations (adult or juvenile) = 2.
1 or 2 prior incarcerations = 1.
3 or more prior incarcerations = 0.
 Item C .... ☐
Age at first commitment (adult or juvenile):
 26 or older = 2.
 18 to 25 = 1.
 17 or younger = 0.
 Item D .... ☐
Commitment offense did not involve auto theft or check(s)
 (forgery/larceny) = 1.
Commitment offense involved auto theft or check(s) = 0.
 Item E .... ☐
Never had parole revoked or been committed for a new offense
 while on parole, and not a probation violator this time = 1.
Has had parole revoked or been committed for a new offense
 while on parole, or is a probation violator this time = 0.
 Item F .... ☐
No history of heroin or opiate dependence = 1.
Otherwise = 0.
 Item G .... ☐
Verified employment (or full-time school attendance) for a total
 of at least 6 mo during the last 2 yr in the community = 1.
Otherwise = 0.
 Total score .... ☐

Source: *Federal Register,* vol. 42, no. 151, August 5, 1977, p. 39815.

Travisono [310 F. Supp. 857 (D.R.I. 1970)]. Officials of the Rhode Island Correctional Institution established comprehensive regulations for handling disciplinary matters (Harvard Center, 1972). The judge's consent decree was based on a proposed set of regulations aimed at insuring fairness in the prison's disciplinary proceedings by establishing a variety of procedural safeguards. This *procedural due process* approach has been a popular one that many courts have taken, *Wolff* v. *McDonnell* being one example. The Rhode Island plan called for written notice to the convict, limited use of prehearing detention in the hole, investigation of the charges by a superior officer, representatives for defendant inmates at the subsequent hearing, a modified composition of the disciplinary board, and explicit limitations on the board's permissible disposition of cases.

TABLE 13–3. Guidelines for decision making in adult cases: U.S. Parole Commission [customary total time to be served before release (including jail time)]

Offense characteristics—severity of offense behavior (examples)	Offender characteristics—parole prognosis (salient factor score) (in months)			
	Very good (11 to 9)	Good (8 to 6)	Fair (5 to 4)	Poor (3 to 0)
Adult				
Low:				
Escape [open institution or program] (e.g., CTC, work release)—absent less than 7 d.				
Marihuana or soft drugs, simple possession (small quantity for own use).	6–10	8–12	10–14	12–18
Property offenses (theft or simple possession of stolen property) less than $1,000.				
Low moderate:				
Alcohol law violations				
Counterfeit currency (passing/ possession less than $1,000).				
Immigration law violations				
Income tax evasion (less than $10,000)				
Property offenses (forgery/fraud/theft from mail/embezzlement/interstate transportation of stolen or forged securities/receiving stolen property with intent to resell) less than $1,000.	8–12	12–16	16–20	20–28
Selective Service Act violations				
Moderate:				
Bribery of a public official (offering or accepting)				
Counterfeit currency (passing/ possession $1,000 to $19,999).				
Drugs:				
Marihuana, possession with intent to distribute/sale (small scale (e.g., less than 50 lb)).				
"Soft drugs," possession with intent to distribute/sale (less than $500).				
Escape [secure program or institution, or absent 7 d or more—no fear or threat used).				
Firearms Act, possession/purchase/sale (single weapon: not sawed-off shotgun or machine gun).	12–16	16–20	20–24	24–32
Income tax evasion ($10,000 to $50,000)				
Mailing threatening communication(s)				
Misprison of felony				
Property offenses (theft/forgery/fraud/ embezzlement/interestate transportation of stolen or forged securities/ receiving stolen property) $1,000 to $19,999.				
Smuggling/transporting of alien(s)				

TABLE 13-3 (continued)

Theft of motor vehicle (not multiple theft or for resale)				
High:				
Counterfeit currency (passing/ possession $20,000 to $100,000).				
Counterfeiting (manufacturing)				
Drugs:				
Marihuana, possession with intent to distribute/sale (medium scale (e.g., 50 to 1,999 lb))				
"Soft drugs," possession with intent to distribute/sale ($500 to $5,000). . . .				
Explosives, possession/transportation . .	16–20	20–26	26–34	34–44
Firearms Act, possession/purchase/sale (sawed-off shotgun(s), machine gun(s), or multiple weapons).				
Mann Act (no force—commercial purposes)				
Theft of motor vehicle for resale				
Property offenses (theft/forgery/fraud/ embezzlement/interstate transportation of stolen or forged securities/ receiving stolen property) $20,000 to $100,000.				
Very high:				
Robbery (weapon or threat)				
Breaking and entering (bank or post office-entry or attempted entry to vault).				
Drugs:				
Marihuana, possession with intent to distribute/sale (large scale (e.g., 2,000 lb or more)).				
"Soft drugs," possession with intent to distribute/sale (over $5,000).	26–36	36–48	48–60	60–72
"Hard drugs," possession with intent to distribute/sale (not exceeding $100,000).				
Extortion				
Mann Act (force)				
Property offenses (theft/forgery/fraud/ embezzlement/interstate transportation of stolen or forged securities/ receiving stolen property) over $100,000 but not exceeding $500,000 . .				
Sexual act (force)				
Greatest:				
Aggravated felony (e.g., robbery, sexual act, aggravated assault)—weapon fired or personal injury.				
Aircraft hijacking	Greater than above—however, specific ranges are not given due to the limited number of cases and the extreme variation in severity possible within the category.			
Drugs: "Hard drugs," possession with intent to distribute/sale (in excess of $100,000).				
Espionage				
Explosives (detonation)				
Kidnaping				
Willful homicide				

Source: *Federal Register*, vol. 42, no. 151, August 5, 1977, pp. 39813–14.

These are but two examples of structural or procedural changes brought about by actual or pending litigation. Because there have been so many changes, it would be difficult to present a comprehensive list of them. It is very important, however, that we discuss and understand some of the limitations of the judicial approach to correctional reform, the ambiguous responses of correctional administrators and employees to suggested or mandated reforms, the social sources of resistance to reform, and the effectiveness of the changes that have been made so far in correctional practices.

LIMITATIONS OF AND RESPONSES TO JUDICIAL ACTIVISM

The abrogation of judicial abstention from the review of correctional practices has produced something akin to a panic reaction on the part of correctional administrators and employees. "The essential and unassailable fact is that the era of unlimited administrative discretion is coming to an end" (Singer and Keating, 1973a). Because even correctional employees have realized the validity of this appraisal, they have adopted a variety of strategies, sometimes making structural and procedural modifications in their operations, and other times truculently resisting any changes at all. We will discuss some of the reasons for these varying strategies, and conclude with an enumeration of some of the inherent limitations on using judicial decisions as a vehicle for reform.

Varied responses and roots of resistance

Previously, we indicated that one response to judicial intervention has been the initiation of substantive, structural, and procedural modifications in correctional operations in many states and institutions. In other states and institutions, however, correctional administrators have engaged in tactics of delay and outright defiance of court directives.

In January 1973, a federal district judge found officials of the Federal Bureau of Prisons in contempt of court for failing to implement religious freedoms earlier found by the court to be constitutionally required. In Virginia, another judge found correctional officials in contempt for their failure to carry out court-ordered reforms of prison disciplinary procedures (Singer and Keating, 1973a). In California, prison employees continued to monitor telephone calls between prisoners and their lawyers even after several court decisions had banned the practice (Project, 1973). In New York, Russell Oswald, while commissioner of corrections, defied a court order by refusing to permit prisoners to receive mail concerning a proposed prisoner union (Singer and Keating, 1973).

Where corrections officials have instituted reforms they have done so—apparently, for mixed reasons. Often they have made changes either in direct response to court orders or because they feared that their procedures would never stand the test of judicial scrutiny. As early as 1968, two observers warned correctional employees against too strident resistance—

> a position of extreme opposition to court intervention is, if only be-cause of its inflexibility, sure to lose. Those who accept no alterna-tive to reposing unlimited discretion in correction would force the courts toward the opposing extreme; namely that no correctional decision is exempt from court review. Merits of the controversy aside, this stand is tactically unwise (Kimball and Newman, 1968: 8).

They went on to suggest that a far better strategy for correctional administrators would be to try and "persuade the courts in a num-ber of ways that [corrections] does not need much external regula-tion" (1968: 10). In urging corrections to make some reforms and concessions, they left little doubt as to the reasons for doing so: "The question is not whether the courts ought to intervene—they will continue to do so anyway, in some degree—but how correction can strengthen its position against undesirable expansion of court supervision" (Kimball and Newman, 1968: 13). Apparently, this desire to forestall more far-reaching judicial intervention has moti-vated many correctional administrators to institute changes, how-ever grudgingly and minimal.

One example of the correctional response to judicial intervention has been the multiplication of rules and regulations circumscribing the conduct of correctional employees and clients. Apparently, in response to their frequent inability to explain or defend discretion-ary decisions, correctional administrators have added to the rules and regulations as a defense against similar problems in the future. For example, recent research has shown that between 1956 and 1969 most states increased their number of parole rules, "perhaps be-cause the courts have become more concerned with the rights of convicted prisoners and parolees. It is now becoming more and more necessary to prove in court that specific regulations have been vio-lated—and the more specific the regulation, the easier it is to prove the violation" (Arluke, 1969: 267).

In many respects, the response of corrections to judicial interven-tion has been similar to police response to court decisions they con-sidered threatening or detrimental to their interests and to "good police work" (Pepinsky, 1970). Charges that the courts are med-dling in administrative matters, that they lack understanding of correctional matters, that they are threatening the stability of the correctional industry, that correctional administrators lack the fiscal resources to make wholesale changes, and that the courts have seriously eroded staff morale, are all reminiscent of police reactions to such decisions as *Mapp, Miranda,* and *Escobedo.* There would seem to be two important reasons for this similarity of response. One reason has to do with the similarity of organizational structure of correctional and police bureaucracies. The second has more to do with the tension between occupational expertise and legal processes.

Sullivan and Tifft (1975) have noted that correctional organizations do not always comply with court directives to change their practices. They suggest a relationship between the way an organization's employees are managed and the way they, in turn, manage their clients. They further suggest that the adoption of court-ordered due process mandates by correctional bureaucracies may be directly related to the presence of managerial due process for their own employees. Organizations that are unresponsive to employee due process rights are unlikely to be receptive to judicial directives that they respect the due process rights of their clients. Since correctional organizations traditionally have been quasi-military in structure and process, they epitomize the type of organization in which we would least expect a compliant stance toward court orders. Such an interpretation is strengthened by an awareness of the similarity of police and correctional responses to court directives (Pepinsky, 1970). Administrators and employees of both types of organizations have reacted with strident charges that the "courts are making it impossible to do our job the way it has to be done." Moreover, judicial intervention seems to be partially responsible for the movement toward unionization by police and correctional employees. Similarities in structures and managerial styles may account for these similarities in response. If indeed there is a relationship between managerial style and responses to judicial intervention, then prompt and sympathetic compliance with court orders may first require internal changes in correctional structure and management.

Correctional resistance to court orders can also be viewed as an example of the more generic conflict between occupational "experts" and what they often claim to be interference by untrained, unknowledgeable outsiders. Correctional employees consider themselves experts in the handling and rehabilitation of offenders. While they frequently recognize and acknowledge the deficiencies of their programs, they attribute these to conditions beyond their control. They believe that they are best qualified to formulate and implement remedial actions to correct these deficiencies. They feel the courts do not fully understand the operations of correctional agencies. The courts, in turn, make what correctional personnel call "unrealistic" or "dangerous" demands upon these agencies. Consequently, the response of correctional personnel to the latest court directive is likely to be cool at best, hostile or indifferent at worst. With such an attitude it is not surprising that correctional administrators sometimes defy court orders.

Limitations of the use of court decisions to modify corrections

President Andrew Jackson reportedly responded to a decision by the U.S. Supreme Court, with which he disagreed, that "Mr. Marshall [Chief Justice] has made his decision. Now let him enforce it." This points up one of the most serious deficiencies of efforts to employ court decisions to reform correctional operations: the absence of a ready, responsive, and reliable enforcement apparatus for court decisions. We referred to this in Chapter 11; here we reemphasize that courts possess very limited powers or abilities to coerce compliance with their decisions in the face of adamant resistance or even procrastination. The essential ineffectiveness of *Brown* v. *Board of Education* in integrating public schools testifies to the validity of this assertion.

The fact that courts proceed on a case-by-case basis also detracts from their effective impact. Having made a decision in one case, the court's seeming intention for similar cases can be ignored by others unless or until their own case is explicitly litigated. Often, correctional officials simply ignore the implications of some court decision for their own agency if it is in their interest to do so. The burden is then placed on other aggrieved parties to begin the difficult and time-consuming process of litigation if they hope to see the earlier decision applied to their situation.

Indeed, the extreme length of time—and the special expertise required to litigate—is itself one of the most serious deficiencies in relying too heavily upon the courts as a vehicle for reform. Many complaints of correctional clients will either become moot or will go unrectified because of the complications presented by these two considerations.

A final problem with using the courts to reform corrections arises from the natural reluctance of the judiciary to engage in confrontations with agencies of the executive branch of government. As a result, it is precisely in cases of administrative defiance that judges are most likely to become timid and fearful of the charge of attempting to usurp the powers and prerogatives of a co-equal branch of government.

It is probably because of the well-recognized deficiencies of depending on court orders to reform corrections that so many writers have turned to the development of grievance procedures as an alternative strategy for insuring the fairness of correctional operations. Singer and Keating (1973) have provided an insightful discussion of the weaknesses of some types of correctional grievance procedures. Their discussion can be read both as an enumeration of the characteristics of a potentially effective prison grievance procedure and as an indirect indictment of using the courts to settle grievances; the effective grievance procedure is very much *unlike* the judicial approach to grievances. An effective procedure must first of all be independent of the system it seeks to change: "If the procedure adopted is totally within the framework of the penal system, in terms of administration and personnel, it is instantly suspect in the eyes of inmates" (1973: 347–48). An effective procedure must also have flexibility.

> Flexibility in the procedures created means that they must respond quickly to inmates' complaints. At the same time, they must be capable of providing, when required, a full-blown administrative hearing, with notice, testimony of witnesses, and right to counsel. The mechanism must be simple to get moving and close to the daily lives of both inmates and staff. It should not have too many steps, for each hurdle adds delay and frustration. And it must be capable of providing a final, decisive resolution, if it is to become anything but another arbitrary, meaningless process to the prisoners involved (Singer and Keating, 1973: 348).

THE IMPACT OF STRUCTURAL AND PROCEDURAL REFORMS

The effective impact of the various structural and procedural reforms discussed thus far is largely unknown. To date, very little evaluative research has examined whether these changes have produced their intended effects, or if any of a number of other possibly worthwhile effects have been evidenced. While we do have several case studies on the impact of changes in particular agencies or programs (for example, parole), there are several areas of needed research that may provide new directions and insights.

Three types of evaluative research are worthy of pursuit. First, research is needed to examine whether procedural reforms are adequate to provide legal guarantees and remedies to offenders. Several excellent case studies have been conducted by law-trained personnel; all of them have suggested deficiencies in the programs they evaluated (Harvard Center, 1972; Project, 1973; Genego et al., 1975). A second type of evaluative research examines the degree of compliance with court decisions or with changing legislative or administrative regulations (e.g., Resource Center, 1974a; Harris and Spiller, 1977). Third, studies of the effects of procedural and structural changes on what actually happens to offenders should be initiated. Does reform result in shorter terms in confinement? Does reform produce fewer cases of parole revocation? When convicts are allowed to be represented by another person at parole hearings, are their chances of a favorable parole decision increased (Beck, 1975)? Finally, we need research on the social psychological impact of the various reforms that have been proposed and enacted. Does, for example, the establishment of grievance procedures produce an increased feeling of fairness about the correctional process in offenders? Does the establishment of such procedures reduce the level of violence within prisons? All these types of research are important if we are to understand the actual impact of the legalization movement.

Finally, however, evaluative research that focuses exclusively on the "internal justice" of correctional operations will ignore the social context in which corrections operates as well as the issue of fairness and social justice that arise there. We dare not become so preoccupied with the internal operations of correctional agencies and correctional due process as to lose sight of more fundamental issues that have to do with the use of criminal sanctions generally.

14

Effectiveness and efficiency:
Evaluative research for corrections

Correctional techniques and programs are developed, promoted, and carried out because someone believes they will be especially effective. To be effective means either to change offenders or to prevent nonoffenders from committing crimes. Clearly, we want to ask questions about every correctional program: Is it humane? Is it legally acceptable? In addition to these crucial questions, sooner or later we will wish to ask also: Do these programs or techniques actually produce the desired results claimed for them? Two separate questions are involved when we ask whether or not the desired goals of correctional programs are realized in practice. The first question is one of *effectiveness;* that is, whether some technique or program improves upon the results achieved by some alternative method(s) of dealing with offenders—including doing nothing at all. The second question concerns the *efficiency* of a technique or program— whether its results are achieved at an expenditure of resources that is defensible in view of the costs of alternative methods of dealing with offenders. *Evaluative research* is the process of collecting and analyzing information about the effectiveness and efficiency of correctional programs. This chapter considers various types of evaluative research, and a variety of issues that arise in conducting it.

EVALUATIVE RESEARCH: CONCEPTS AND DEFINITIONS

The questions about correctional programs asked in evaluative research are of variable complexity. At one extreme are such questions as whether a particular correctional technique (for example, group counseling) is more effective than another method of treatment. A more complex question might ask whether some new program is more effective or efficient than alternative programs and treatment strategies (for example, methadone maintenance versus no programs at all for heroin addicts). The most complex questions probe the effectiveness or efficiency of significant components of the entire criminal justice system, or changes in those components. Illustrative of such a research problem is the seven-year project conducted by the Center for Criminal Justice at Harvard Law School to study the reforms in juvenile corrections in Massachusetts. There the traditional training schools for the juveniles have been closed and replaced by a system of diversified community-based correctional programs. A study such as this clearly involves a more complex set of questions and processes than the fairly simple one of whether a particular correctional technique is effective in modifying the behavior of those offenders who receive the treatment. For purposes of the following presentation and discussion, we shall confine ourselves primarily to questions of the latter type. Our evaluative research techniques have not as yet progressed much beyond this level of analysis, anyhow, and most of the public and policy-related interest has been concentrated at this level.

Traditionally, evaluative research in corrections has examined only the effectiveness of techniques or programs; that is, the degree to which they achieve some appropriate objective (the reduction of recidivism). Only in recent years has research begun to examine the efficiency of correctional programs. An explication of the nature of evaluative research necessitates a discussion of five component concepts: comparison groups, criterion measures, independent variables, efficiency, and follow-up periods.

Comparison groups

By necessity, any minimally adequate assessment of the effectiveness of a correctional treatment program requires a *comparison* of at least two groups: those who received the treatment or who participated in the program, and those from whom the treatment was withheld. In the absence of a comparison, a raw success or failure rate indicates nothing significant about the effectiveness of a treatment or program. For instance, if we are told that a program's "success" or "effectiveness" is indicated by the fact that only 25 percent of those subjected to it recidivated, this claim is meaningless because we are not given the recidivism rate for a *comparable group* of offenders who received an alternative treatment. But even statements about the comparative effectiveness of alternative treatments are only valid when the groups of offenders are actually alike. To the extent they differ, especially on some attribute related to outcome, a statement about the effectiveness of alternative treatments becomes extremely difficult to interpret with confidence. Thus, one of the most difficult problems in conducting correctional research is the construction of truly comparable groups of offenders to be exposed to different treatment techniques or programs.

Criterion measures

The measure of program outcome that is used to evaluate a program is customarily designated the *criterion* (also, the *dependent variable*). *Recidivism* is frequently used as a criterion measure. As a measure of reinvolvement in criminal behavior after correctional intervention, it is variously defined in terms of arrests, convictions, or incarcerations. Short incarcerations, of say, less than 60 days, may or may not be exempted from the definition of recidivism.

Recidivism is not the only measure of effectiveness that has been used in correctional evaluative research. Other measures include changes in attitudes, values, career aspirations, work habits, personality characteristics, disciplinary record within an institution, abstinence from alcohol or drug use, and size of earnings after release from imprisonment. An important problem in evaluative research is how to select and measure the most useful *criteria* for different programs and circumstances. On the basis of past evaluative research, much has been learned about the characteristics of good criteria for evaluating correctional programs. Glaser (1973: Chapter 3) has suggested that good criterion measures should be: (1) "hard" or objective, rather than "soft" or subjective; (2) continuous, rather than discrete statistical variables; (3) relevant to attainable goals; and (4) useful in the determination of appropriate levels of financing for a program.

Too often there has been a tendency to make claims for the effectiveness of a correctional treatment on the basis of subjective evaluations, usually by those who support or administer the program. Similarly, programs sometimes have been indicted as ineffective on the basis of equally unreliable subjective impressions. Reliance upon subjective impressions is often found whenever those "evaluating" a program have some political, personal, intellectual, or career investment in the outcome of the program. The likelihood of subjective evaluations under such biased circumstances is but one of the many reasons why some have suggested that the responsibility for objectively evaluating correctional programs should be lodged in personnel who are independent of the correctional establishment (Ward, 1973). The unreliability of subjective evaluations is the principal reason why we must develop and utilize objective criteria—those that are constructed from externally observable events. Examples of subjective criteria are: staff impressions of the degree of behavioral or internal change by the participants in some special program, testimonials by selected offenders who have taken part in a program, and citations of the alleged improvements shown by one or a few participants in a program. By contrast, examples of objective criteria are: scores on a standardized personality test, the magnitude of parolees' earnings from legitimate employment, and the seriousness of any subsequent crimes committed by offenders. Unlike subjective criteria, these are not only *externally* observable, but they are based upon the actual *behavior* of those who have previously been processed by some component of the correctional industry. Inasmuch as the putative goal of corrections is to change the behavior of offenders, the latter quality of objective criteria is especially desirable. It is on this point that the use of recidivism as a criterion measure can be faulted.

> Not all new crimes or technical violations are discovered, so the official recidivism rate presumably underestimates return to crime. Another difficulty: any measure of recidivism is a measure of how one or more decision-makers (police officers, parole agents, parole board members) respond to information about people's behavior. While this response presumably depends *in some way* on people's behavior, the relationship need not be simple, invariant from one penal system to another, or constant over time (Greenberg, 1972: 4–5). (Emphasis in the original.)

A good criterion measure for evaluating correctional programs should not only be objective, but it should also be capable of continuous rather than simply discrete measurement. A criterion that can assume only a few discrete values or categories (for example, committed new crimes or did not commit new crimes) does not permit the same degree of sensitivity to program impact as does a continuously measured criterion (e.g., total number of days living free of committing new crimes). Moreover, a discrete criterion does not permit the same degree of flexibility in evaluating a program, because it does not enable us to make more exact statements about the degree of impact or improvement shown by those receiving treatment as does the use of continuous criteria.

It usually is desirable to employ multiple criteria in evaluative studies of correctional treatments. As Campbell (1971) has argued, each criterion measure is subject to various types of measurement biases; moreover, experimental programs nearly always produce a variety of potential benefits and unwanted side effects. By building into our research an allowance for multiple criteria, we increase the likelihood of understanding a wider range of consequences from experimental programs. The use of multiple criteria is also helpful when there is the possibility that any one of them might become the object of political conflict. In such a case, alternative measures of a program's impact can be cited.

In deciding upon a criterion measure, consideration should be given to the short-range, or more immediate, goals of a program, rather than to the selection of goals that are more remote and difficult of measurement—if not attainment. Goals of the former type have been referred to by Glaser (1973: 19) as the "most attainable" ones. He has suggested that researchers should avoid using criteria which, on the basis of past experience, are either too far removed from any reasonable expectation of program impact or so global in nature that a wide variety of confounding variables could make it impossible to confidently untangle the impact of the correctional treatment alone.

A final characteristic of a good criterion measure, especially if the results of evaluative research are to have a significant impact on correctional programming, is that it should be useful in the determination of appropriate levels of financing for a program. In other words, on the basis of research results, it should be relatively easy to arrive at an assessment of the degree of financing necessary for the evaluated program or treatment. Such a quality of a criterion measure can be particularly desirable when dealing with administrators or legislators (i.e., those who make budgetary decisions). Partly because of the desirability of developing criterion measures that possess this quality, in recent years, we have seen the emergence and growth of *cost-benefit analysis* in the evaluation of correctional programs.

Independent variable

Following convention, we shall refer to the correctional technique or program that is being evaluated as the *independent variable*. Examples include the assignment to correctional workers of reduced caseloads of probationers or parolees, vocational counseling for parolees, group counseling for incarcerated offenders, or a methadone maintenance program for heroin addicts. As with criterion measures, independent variables (that is, correctional treatments being evaluated) should, ideally, possess certain qualities, and care must be taken to assure that the treatment does not change during the period in which the program is being evaluated. In fact, this latter consideration has proven to be difficult, as Lerman (1975) discovered in his reanalysis of the treatment given to experimental subjects as part of the California Community Treatment Project.

First, an independent variable should be defined in such a way that it is sufficiently operational—so the components of the treatment can be clearly identified. As Logan (1972: 378) has so aptly put it, "it is not enough to know that a particular program ended in success or failure if we cannot determine *what it is* that succeeded or failed" (emphasis in the original). This can be especially problematical if the treatment is so broad that it includes a whole range or variety of different activities. Second, the treatment should be capable of routinization in diverse settings and times. It should not be too dependent for its impact upon any unique personal characteristics of either clients or correctors, or too dependent upon unusual historical or social circumstances. For example, a treatment program, which is successful with clients from minority religious groups and in a setting where that group resides, might prove to be either ineffective or difficult to routinize in a religiously heterogeneous group of offenders or locale.

Efficiency and cost-benefit analysis

When evaluating correctional treatments we generally want to know not only how effective it is but also some indication of the *cost* of the achieved results. Since effectiveness must be weighed in terms of the costs expended, we need to know something about the *efficiency* of alternative types of correctional treatment. *Cost-benefit analysis* (also referred to as *social cost analysis*) utilizes criterion measures that allow us to assess a program's efficiency. Some of the more obvious advantages of attempting to translate the comparative costs and benefits of programs into monetary terms are that (1) it facilitates communication with administrators and legislators, and (2) it makes it much easier to arrive at truly comparative assessments of the payoff from alternative correctional programs (since each has a monetary figure attached to it). Cost-benefit analysis appears to be the "wave of the future" in correctional evaluative research (Martinson, 1976). It is the use of a *monetary* criterion measure that makes possible cost-benefit analysis.

> In its simplest form, the monetary criterion focuses on differences in the costs of processing control and experimental subjects. If post-release behavior is similar, advantage lies with the program in which the processing costs are lower. . . .
> In more elaborate forms, the monetary criterion examines bene-

fits as well as costs. The corrected offender not only reduces his future correctional costs, he also takes his family off welfare, earns wages or salary in regular employment, is a productive worker, and otherwise augments the economic and social condition of the community (Adams, 1974: 1026).

Follow-up periods

Reliable information on the effectiveness and social costs of alternative correctional programs requires that the behavior of offenders exposed to them be monitored for some period of time after exposure to treatment. As Glaser puts it: "The key principle of evaluation is to follow up those persons whom an agency tried to change to see if they do change, and to follow up a control or comparison group to see whether they also change, even if nothing is done to them or if an alternative kind of treatment is given them" (1973: 840). During this *follow-up period*, data are collected on the behavior of offenders that comprises the criterion measure(s). When conducting evaluative research, decisions must be made about the duration of the follow-up period—when it will begin and what offenders will be included in it.

A decision on the length of the follow-up period must take account of the possibility that research results cannot be delayed too long, because they are especially needed by administrators for evaluation of their programs. Also, the follow-up period should not extend beyond what might be termed the *consequential period* for the type of offender being evaluated. By the consequential period we mean that time beyond which it would be unreasonable to expect or to observe any significant amount of additional change in the subjects. At the same time, the follow-up period should be long enough to permit detection of precisely those behavioral changes at which the treatment program is directed. Thus, it is difficult to specify in an ad hoc fashion just how long a follow-up period should be (the decision being made in part on the basis of the hoped-for nature of behavioral change and the type of clientele with which the program deals).

Despite the frequent temptation to delay the start of the follow-up period until after the *completion* of treatment—for example, delaying the evaluation of the effects of confinement until after subjects have been released—the follow-up period should begin just as soon as offenders have been assigned to the experimental and control groups. Regardless of the criterion, any adequate accounting of the results of treatment should begin immediately. The logic of doing so is easiest to grasp when cost-benefit analysis is used, because a complete accounting of the costs and benefits of a treatment program must include *all* the costs (including those associated with the administration of the program itself). But the same logic applies equally well even in cases where recidivism or the commission of new crimes is used as the criterion. To wait until after offenders have been released to the community is to ignore the crimes they might commit while imprisoned; ignoring these crimes can only be justified if we arbitrarily define victimized prison inmates as nonpersons who can be the victims of criminal acts without those acts being considered "crimes."

Despite the best-laid plans and hopes of correctors and researchers, after the experimental and control groups have been constructed there will be some mortality (i.e., dropouts) from each group. In examining the criterion behavior of subjects it is necessary to include all offenders who were original members of the two groups.

> In comparing an experimental and a control group, evaluators have sometimes compared only those who completed the experimental program, on the grounds that the inclusion of others who did not complete the program would be unfair to the program. Yet, if those who are least motivated or least amenable to the program are those who do not complete it, the assumption that the program would have been successful with them had they remained in it may well be in error, and their omission from the comparison a possible source of distortion. When the dropouts considerably outnumber those who complete a program, as is sometimes the case in addiction treatment programs, quoted success rates for survivors can be highly misleading (Greenberg, 1974: 2–3).

To arbitrarily omit dropouts from the analysis is to stack the cards in favor of the "success" of the evaluated correctional treatment. Just how misleading the results of this practice can be is apparent when we consider two different ways of arriving at a success rate for the Highfields study. Highfields, a special residential treatment program for delinquent boys, was inaugurated by the state of New Jersey in 1950. Participants were 16- or 17-year-old males who, following conviction by a juvenile court and agreeing to participate, were screened by the Highfields staff. For those boys accepted by the staff, the program consisted primarily of "guided group interaction," a type of group counseling (Weeks, 1958). In order to evaluate the postrelease behavior of Highfields's boys, a matched comparison group was constructed from boys admitted to the state boys' reformatory at Annandale. Not all the boys who were originally accepted into the Highfields program remained in the program long enough to complete it. Instead, they were eliminated from it and sent to Annandale. When these dropouts are not counted as members of the treatment group, the Highfields success rate is 66 percent (using recidivism as the criterion). However, when these "internal failure" cases are included, the success rate for Highfields drops to 48 percent—as compared to a rate of 48 percent for boys in the control group (Lerman, 1968).

CONSTRUCTING CONTROL OR COMPARISON GROUPS: SOME ALTERNATIVE RESEARCH DESIGNS

Given the need to base estimates of the effectiveness and efficiency of correctional programs on comparisons of the results attained with different but comparable groups of offenders, a variety of strategies have been employed to construct such groups and to examine the effects of correctional treatment. Several of the more common research designs will be discussed here.

The true, or classic, experimental design

In the classic experimental design, an *experimental* and *control* group are randomly selected from the same population of offenders, and a treatment (i.e., independent variable) is administered to the experimental group but withheld from the control group. In every other way, efforts are made to assure that the two groups are treated exactly alike. Since the groups are assumed, subject to the laws of probability, to be equivalent because of randomization, and the occurrence of the independent variable is the only thing that differentiates the two groups, any subsequently observed difference on the criterion can be attributed to the occurrence of the treatment variable. Thus, in the classic experiment, the two groups to be compared are constructed through the process of random assignment. Figure 14–1 is a schematic representation of the structure of the true experimental research design.

FIGURE 14–1
The structure of the true experimental research design

→ Time →		
1	**2**	**3**
Groups constructed by random assignment (therefore, assumed equivalent)	Groups receive identical treatment (except for X)	Both groups measured on the criterion (any difference attributed to X)
Experimental group	Receives experimental treatment (X)	
Control group	Does not receive experimental treatment	

A true experimental research design was employed in a California study that examined the effectiveness of group counseling in a prison setting on both the in-prison and postrelease behavior of convicts (Kassebaum et al., 1971). The medium security institution in which the study was conducted is architecturally divided into quadrants, and this facilitated the conduct of the study. Convicts were randomly assigned to one of the quadrants for their term of imprisonment. In two of the quadrants, convicts received varying types and degrees of group counseling; convicts in another quadrant were used as a control group and received the regular prison program but without any type of group counseling. The study found that the claimed benefits of group counseling could not be substantiated. Waldo and Chiricos (1977) employed an experimental research design to examine the impact upon recidivism of participation in a prison work-release program. Between July 1969 and December 1969 every third Florida convict who met the minimal requirements for work release was placed in a control group, and the other two-thirds were placed in the work-release program. This resulted in 188 experimental subjects and 93 control subjects, who continued to participate in the correctional programs in which they were then involved. In this piece of research as well, the researchers were unable to document the rehabilitative impact of involvement in work release that its supporters have claimed for it.

Although the logic that underlies the classic experimental design is both compelling and simple, such designs have not found a great deal of use in correctional evaluative research, despite the fact they can make available the most persuasive evidence on the impact of treatment programs. The difficulty is that "more often than not, political or administrative constraints make an experimental design with any type of randomization absolutely impossible" (Glaser, 1973: 64). Among the reasons for this are:

1. Sometimes it is necessary to arrive at a decision on the effectiveness, level of funding, or even the maintenance of a program so quickly that time does not allow the conduct of a true experimental evaluation.
2. The treatment program may no longer be in existence, so there is no opportunity to randomly assign subjects to it. At other times the decision to evaluate is made only *after* subjects have already been selected for the program.
3. There may be objections to assigning some subjects to the treatment program if the treatment to be tested is perceived by officials as more lenient than traditional practice.

4. Administrators may resist randomly assigning subjects to the control group because they object to the "denial of treatment" to control group members—seeing this as unethical or unprofessional.

5. Random assignment sometimes conflicts with governmental goals other than changing offenders, for example, with the presumed goal of deterring others from committing crimes (cf. Glaser, 1973: 64–8; Adams, 1975: 60–1).

6. Administrators may fear an objective evaluation because negative results may have serious repercussions for the continued operation of some special correctional.program.

It is largely for such reasons as these, which make a true experiment impossible, that we have seen the use of alternative strategies for constructing comparison groups.

Quasi-experimental designs

Quasi-experimental research designs are those in which a comparison group of offenders is constructed in an effort to assure equivalence; however, due to the lack of randomization, equivalence cannot be confidently assumed. Since the two groups being compared are not *experimental* and *control* groups, in the sense in which these terms are used in discussions of the classic experiment, following convention we will refer to them as *treatment* and *comparison* groups, respectively. Two commonly employed methods for constructing such groups are discussed here: matching, and the use of base expectancy scores.

There are two ways of attempting to *match* a treatment and a comparison group: matching by profile analysis, and matching by individuals. In the former the researcher would, for example, endeavor to assure that the percentage of blacks in each group would be comparable, that the average age of the two groups would be equivalent, or that the percentage of those in each group with previous criminal convictions would be alike. In matching by individuals, the researcher attempts to locate pairs of offenders who are alike in their personal attributes, and then assigns one member to the treatment group and the other to the comparison group.

An illustration of how matching was employed in a situation in which a true experiment was not possible is reported by Eichman (1966). Following the U.S. Supreme Court decision in *Gideon* v. *Wainwright* [372 U.S. 335 (1963)], Florida released from prison those inmates who had not been represented by counsel at their trial. Eichman compared the subsequent behavior of these men released from prison before the expiration of their sentences, as a result of this "right to counsel" decision, with a comparison group of full-term releasees. The two groups were carefully matched on such characteristics as the number of prior convictions, type of offense, age, and occupational skill level. Eichman eventually was able to match only 110 pairs of releasees, because of his rigorous matching procedures. (After a 28-month follow-up period, the rate of reincarceration for the *Gideon* early-release group was 13.6 percent and 25.4 percent for the full-term releases). Clearly, this research could not have employed a random sample of early releasees, because the release decisions were made on the basis of legal criteria. Thus, a quasi-experimental design was the best that could be used under the circumstances.

A matching procedure also was employed in a study designed to evaluate the effectiveness of Southfields, a Kentucky residential treatment program modeled after Highfields (Miller, 1970). Boys were assigned to Southfields on the basis of the court's judgment, and the evaluative research examined the recidivism of the first 191 boys to complete the program. Two comparison groups were constructed by a matching procedure; one comparison group consisted of boys placed on probation, and the other consisted of boys sent to Kentucky Village, a regular correctional institution. The research found that both probation and Southfields were about equally effective in reducing recidivism, and that both were somewhat superior to regular correctional confinement (at Kentucky Village).

Unfortunately, whether groups are matched by individuals or by profile analysis, they may still differ on other attributes than those on which they were matched—and these may be related to the outcome of correctional treatment. Because it is difficult to determine whether this is the case, matching is much less powerful than random assignment in the construction of comparison groups.

Construction of a comparison group by the use of base expectancy scores necessitates some explication of the concept of *base expectancy*. Base expectancy scores are a means of sorting offenders into groups on the basis of the probability of their recidivating, (that is, risk groups). The scores are calculated on the basis of information about offenders available at the time of their admission to a correctional system. Glaser (1973: 142–3) provides the following examples of base expectancy score groups (or B.E. Categories) for California Youth Authority wards released in 1964:

B.E. Category 1, scores over 545 .... 22% recidivists
B.E. Category 2, scores 419 to 545 .... 35% recidivists
B.E. Category 3, scores 337 to 418 .... 41% recidivists
B.E. Category 4, scores 290 to 336 .... 47% recidivists
B.E. Category 5, scores 195 to 289 .... 56% recidivists
B.E. Category 6, scores below 195 .... 68% recidivists

Here we also quote at length from Glaser's description of how these score groups are constructed and then used in California to evaluate prison programs:

> The term "base expectancy rate," applied to a group of offenders, refers to their expected violation rate when they are first admitted. For this reason, all items of information used to calculate [base expectancy rates] for them is restricted to what is known at the time of their admission; deliberately omitted is the additional information available such as their assignments, performance, escapes, and family communications while confined. If those *in a given base expectancy category* actually have a lower recidivism rate after parole from a particular institution or program than the predicted rate for their category from all institutions and programs in California, then the particular institution or program they were in would be credited with reducing recidivism rates. Thus some programs from which releasees had high recidivism rates might be regarded favorably because their expected recidivism rates, according to the B.E. categories of the inmates they received, were even higher than their actual rates. (Emphasis in the original.)

Perhaps an analogy would be helpful: Suppose that at birth individuals were placed in life expectancy groups ("L.E. Categories") purely on the basis of information known about them and their families at that time (that is, birth). Individuals with certain characteristics and family backgrounds would, presumably, have more favorable L.E. scores than those with other characteristics and family backgrounds. If we were interested in examining the impact of various life experiences upon *longevity* (for example, the effect of diet, nonsmoking), we could examine the actual longevity of subgroups of individuals, within particular L.E. categories, who experienced different dietary and smoking habits. If those who had abstained from smoking lived longer than would have been expected from their L.E. scores, we would have some confidence in attributing part of this increased longevity to their not having smoked.

Mannheim and Wilkins (1955) used a procedure similar to base expectancy in their study of the effectiveness of borstal training. (Borstals are English penal institutions, very similar to American reformatories.) They wanted to compare the recidivism rates of boys released from open and closed borstals. They first found that open borstals had a success rate of 64 percent, while the success rate for closed borstals was only 48 percent. Because this difference could possibly have been explained by the closed borstals receiving poorer risks from the courts, Mannheim and Wilkins carried their analysis one step further. A number of personal characteristics of the boys were found to correlate with success after release. Using this information it was possible to classify the boys as good, average, or poor risks. This permitted the researchers to compare the actual success rates of open and closed borstals for boys in the same risk categories. The fact that the success rates for all three risk groups were superior for those in open borstals strengthened the researchers' belief that open borstals may have some special reformative effect (Greenberg, 1972).

Since a quasi-experiment is the best that can be employed in many research situations, it is important to understand why we cannot have as much confidence in the findings from it as we can have in the results obtained from true experiments. This necessitates a discussion of the concept of *validity threats*, and some of the more common types of such threats. As we shall see, nonexperimental evaluative research is much more vulnerable to them than is even quasi-experimental research.

Validity threats

In the conduct of evaluative research we would like to be able to attribute any criterion differences between our comparison groups to the presence of the independent variable in the experimental (or treatment) group. Under ideal circumstances the use of a classic experimental design permits us to make this assumption, that is, to confidently rule out the possibility of there being any other plausible explanation for the observed differences. However, to the extent we depart from the classic experiment, there are a number of possible alternative explanations for observed differences that cannot logically be ruled out. These rival explanations have been designated as *validity threats* by Campbell and Stanley (1966) and Campbell (1971). Here we shall discuss a few that have proven to be especially troublesome in correctional evaluation research. And as should become apparent, not even the classic experiment, as typically conducted in the real world of corrections, is entirely free from some of these problems.

Selection and mortality biases

Whenever groups to be compared are selected by any other process than randomization, we must be alert to the possibility of nonequivalence. The reason to avoid such biases is simply because the comparison groups might differ on some attribute(s) related to outcome (that is, the criterion). Both matching and the use of base-expectancy scores are attempts to construct equivalent groups in the absence of random assignment. But even when these methods are employed, there is still the possibility that the treatment and comparison groups may differ in attributes or in the treatment they receive in other ways than the presence or absence of the program being evaluated. For example, if the treatment group was constructed from volunteers for a treatment program, and a comparison group was constructed by matching from among the general population of offenders, we could not confidently rule out the significance of selection biases as an explanation for any subsequent differences on the criterion.

It is possible that our two groups may be similar "with respect to easily documented variables like age or prior arrest record, but dissimilar in aspirations or strength of motivation to avoid future criminal involvement, attributes which may have a strong bearing on outcome" (Greenberg, 1974: 2). Nevertheless, all one can do is to make every effort at the outset to insure that the treatment and comparison groups are alike on those variables likely to be related to outcome.

Often, comparison groups that were equivalent—or, at least, thought to be—at the beginning of a treatment and follow-up period will become progressively dissimilar during the period of the study, due to differential mortality (dropouts) from the two groups. Those who believe in the treatment program that is being evaluated are tempted to eliminate from the evaluation those cases that did not complete the treatment, and there are several well-known instances where this occurred (in the Highfields study). Such a temptation must be resisted. As noted earlier, "a program to change people should be evaluated on the basis of all those whom it undertook to change. Therefore, those who do not remain in the program must be considered with those who remain; together they comprise the totality that was to be changed" (Glaser, 1973: 71).

Reactive arrangements

Any time offenders are assigned to a special program or treatment we must be alert to the possibility that they will, for that very reason, perform differently on the criterion than would have been the case had they not been part of a special program. The tendency for research subjects to behave differently for no reason other than the realization that they are participating in "something special" has become known in social science parlance as "the Hawthorne effect." (It is so named because it was first noticed during research on industrial work groups some 40 years ago at the Hawthorne works of Western Electric in Cicero, Illinois.) It is possible for experimental subjects to perform better than expected, or worse, depending upon their evaluation of their special status. The lesson for correctional evaluative research is clear: whenever participants in a treatment program are aware of their special status, this fact becomes a potential threat to the validity of the research findings; it becomes a plausible rival explanation for the results of the research.

Further, and quite apart from any changes in the behavior of offenders, something comparable may occur in the behavior of those correctional *employees* who are involved in the program being evaluated. Usually it is all but impossible to hide from employees the fact that some special program is being evaluated; nor is it possible to hide the identity of those offenders who receive the special treatment. As a result, employees sometimes engage in actions that tend to assure the program will prove to be "successful." This does not necessarily mean that they intentionally bias the results of the study; they may do so quite unintentionally. For example, they may try harder in their efforts with experimental subjects than with members of the control group. The problems this can create in evaluative research can be illustrated with data from the California Youth Authority's Community Treatment Project (CTP), which has been in operation since 1961. After commitment to the Youth Authority Reception Center, eligible youths were randomly assigned to either (1) a control group, confined in an institution, and then given regular parole; or to (2) an experimental group and released immediately to probation. Cohort follow-up showed that the experimental subjects had a higher success rate than the control group. However, as we noted earlier, "within certain boundaries, the recidivism rate can be influenced by the decision-making authorities" (Robison and Smith, 1971: 69). This was obvious in the case of the CTP, where parole agents and authorities knew which parolees were members of the experimental group. "In the CTP study, the recidivism rates were managed in such a way as to make the experimentals appear favorable" (Robison and Smith, 1971: 70). In reanalyzing the CTP data, Lerman found that while on parole "the experimentals [actually] had more known delinquent offenses per boy than the controls (2.81 to 1.61)" (Lerman, 1968: 57). His subsequent analysis suggests that the parole-violating behavior of experimentals and controls was reacted to differently by parole authorities, with the experimental subjects receiving some preferential treatment (1975: 60). [Subsequent analyses of data from the CTP have only added to the uncertainty and controversy surrounding the effectiveness of this much-publicized experimental program (Greenberg, 1977).]

Presumably, one solution to this problem would be to obtain measures of the behavior of offenders that are "pure," that is, uncontaminated by the effects of official discretionary actions. Unfortunately, we have not yet developed such measures. An alternative solution to the problem is to so *blind* the special treatment that employees do not know the identity of those offenders receiving it. This would then make it impossible for officials to contaminate the criterion. The potential biases produced by the Hawthorne effect can be controlled by using a *double blind,* that is, a study in which *neither* officials *nor* offenders were aware of which offenders received the treatment. By such a strategy, the tendency for both groups to behave differently because of involvement in something unusual or special can be controlled.

Maturation

Yet another reason for selecting comparison groups by randomization is to avoid the possible biases of maturation differences between the groups. *Maturation* refers to naturally occurring changes within offenders that could, either by themselves or in combination with the treatment, produce results different for our two groups of offenders. In the absence of random assignment, the members of the experimental group could, for example, show a greater spontaneous growth in self-awareness during the period of the evaluation; this then would account for whatever changes in their behavior were subsequently observed, and not the occurrence of the independent variable. Or perhaps the members of the comparison group naturally developed a greater fear of imprisonment during the course of their correctional careers and, as a result, performed *better* on the criterion than the treatment group. In this case, differential maturation effects would make it appear that the treatment was ineffective, when it might have been effective if truly equivalent groups had been compared.

History

History refers to events or occurrences external to a group of offenders after they have been placed in a treatment or control group. Historical differences become a potential threat to validity whenever two groups who have experienced different histories are compared on a criterion. In later discussion we will see that these are a special problem in cohort analysis. But they can similarly contaminate the results of even true experiments if the follow-up period for the experimental and control groups, though the same length for both, begins and ends at different points in time. In such a case, for example, the possibility that one group experienced greater difficulty finding employment because of changes in the unemployment rate could account for their poorer performance irrespective of whatever treatment they received.

Inability to generalize

All the validity threats we have discussed thus far are *internal* threats. By this is meant that they are threats to our ability to confidently attribute any criterion differences between two groups solely to the occurrence of the independent variable in the experimental or treatment group. It is not enough, however, for a study to be internally valid; we also strive for *external* validity (Campbell and Stanley, 1966). Since nearly all research is conducted on *samples* of offenders, we are always interested in generalizing our research findings to extant groups or populations not involved in the research itself. Unfortunately, the nature and characteristics of the population from which our samples (i.e., comparison groups) are drawn become constraints on the ability to generalize the conclusions we draw from our experiments. If this population is atypical, the applicability of the experiment's conclusions for other populations is questionable.

For instance, in the Community Treatment Project a true experimental design was used, but only after 25 percent of the original population had been screened out. Thus, it would be questionable to generalize the study's results to all offenders—since one-fourth were eliminated at the outset (Levin, 1971). Similarly, the Provo experiment in delinquency treatment was conducted in an area heavily populated by members of the Church of Jesus Christ of Latter-Day Saints (Empey and Rabow, 1961). Presumably, too, Mormon youths represented a significant proportion of the experimental group. This fact, if true, makes it very difficult to generalize the study's results to other parts of the United States, and to offenders of other religious backgrounds.

NONEXPERIMENTAL RESEARCH DESIGNS

The foregoing are some of the more commonly encountered threats to validity in correctional evaluative research. It was suggested that the classic experiment and the quasi-experiment are less vulnerable to them than are some of the other types of evaluative "research" employed in corrections. Despite their clear superiority for yielding valid and reliable knowledge about the effectiveness-efficiency of correctional programs, true experiments and quasi-experiments have been employed in a small minority of correctional evaluative studies (Adams, 1975: 53). Instead, *nonexperimental designs* have been used. Thus, in view of the frequency of their use, it is important to understand some of the more common types of nonexperimental research designs and the various ways they are vulnerable to validity threats.

Nonequivalent comparison group designs

We will be discussing several different types of nonequivalent comparison group designs. All are distinguished by making comparisons between the performance of a treatment group and another group that can in no way be considered equivalent to it. Typically, no effort is made to assure their equivalence (by matching). Since not even a minimal effort is made to assure equivalence, the results of this type of research are especially suspect. Occasionally in this type of research the success rate for a treatment group is reported, along with the purported success rate for a larger group of offenders (the entire populations of offenders); the implication is that the performance of the treatment group, had there been no treatment, would have been equal to that of the general population of offenders. But since there is no way to assume the groups' equivalence, such an interpretation is unacceptable. (For example, the treatment group and general population may differ on such attributes as age, offense history, marital status, or race. Further, the members of the treatment group may have volunteered for the treatment, making them different in this way, too.)

Cohort analysis

Cohort analysis is a special type of nonequivalent comparison group analysis. In cohort analysis, comparisons are made between the performance of two naturally occurring groups of offenders (for example, all those released from confinement during 1975 and those released during 1976). Unfortunately, since these groups cannot be considered equivalent, and since the effects of maturation and history may be different, it is difficult to have much confidence in the results of this type of research. Suppose we are comparing the recidivism rates of all offenders placed on probation in a given jurisdiction during 1970 with the recidivism rate of all those granted probation in the same jurisdiction in 1975. There is, of course, no way these two cohorts can confidently be assumed equivalent. It is also likely that the postconviction experiences of the two cohorts differed, for example, in ease of finding decent employment. In other words, history differences could account for any difference in the recidivism rates of the two cohorts. Selection biases could have influenced the results, too. Thus, if the rate at which probation was granted had changed from 1970 to 1975, this probably would make the two cohorts different with respect to background attributes. (Where probation is liberally granted, poorer risks receive it more often than where it is used less. Thus, any difference in the rate of probation *use* becomes, simultaneously, a mechanism by which differences in the risk of recidivism are created or maintained.)

Before-after designs

A *before-after research design* is one in which comparisons are made between a group's performance before treatment and its subsequent performance. In other words, the "comparison group" is really nothing other than the treatment group's pretreatment performance. For obvious reasons, this type of design is inappropriate for examining the effects of treatment on the recidivism rate of a group. However, it is used in examining the impact of a treatment on a host of other criteria (for example, academic functioning, self-concept, level of occupational functioning). An example of such a study would be the administration of standard personality tests to offenders before placing them in a special treatment program. After completion of the program, the offenders are retested and any changes on the personality tests are attributed to the treatment program.

As should be apparent, the validity problems with this type of design are numerous. In the absence of a comparison group of any type, the implicit assumption is made that either no change would have occurred in the treatment group or that the change would not have been as great as was subsequently observed. History, maturation, selection and mortality biases, and reactive arrangements, either singly or in combination, are rival alternative explanations for any changes in the treatment group between the pretest and posttest observations.

Case studies

The results of a *case study* are so vulnerable to validity threats that it is questionable whether such "research" should even be graced by this appellation. In any event, a case study consists of exposing a group of offenders to some treatment and then proclaiming the program a success due to the group's performance on the criterion. Since no criterion performance is reported for a comparison group, we are expected to assume that the treatment group would have performed worse had they not received the treatment program. This type of research design is more vulnerable to rival alternative explanations than any other design we have discussed.

294

Regrettably, despite such obvious design flaws, we continue to see such studies used to support claims for the success of various types of correctional programs.

EVALUATIVE RESEARCH USING STATISTICAL CONTROLS

To this point, the entire presentation has focused on evaluative research that makes use of experimental controls as a means of attempting to rule out alternative explanations of research results. There is another genre of evaluative research, however, that uses statistical controls to accomplish the same objective. Multiple regression, a statistical analysis technique that permits the simultaneous statistical control of a number of different independent variables, is commonly used. Unfortunately, this type of research yields findings that are often difficult to interpret, and we cannot place as much confidence in them as we can in the findings of experimental research. Here we simply take note of statistical controls in evaluative research. A brief discussion of some of the promises and pitfalls of this type of research can be found in Levin (1971).

OBSTACLES TO THE ROUTINIZATION OF EVALUATIVE RESEARCH

The accumulated experiences of social scientists in their attempts to establish the "rule of research" in the correctional industry has, by now, produced a large volume of literature on the recurrent obstacles encountered in the process. Those who lament what they see as the rather inconsequential impact of research on corrections should find useful an explication of these obstacles. The same should be true of those committed to increasing the impact of research.

There might be some analytic utility in distinguishing between obstacles encountered in attempting to induce correctional administrators to permit, sponsor, or *conduct* evaluative research and those obstacles that, seemingly, prevent the *utilization* of evaluative research results by correctional administrators. However, the following discussion does not pursue a rigorous distinction between these two processes, choosing instead to focus on the common elements in them.

Conflicting ideological stances

Correctional administrators and employees, as a result of their training and experiences, tend to have a certain amount of faith in the efficacy of correctional theories, techniques, and programs. Empirical researchers tend, on the other hand, to be skeptics and to be insistent on subjecting statements grounded in faith to the test of research. Moreover, correctional personnel tend to have an immediate practical interest and concern, which makes them impatient with those who seem intent on developing long-range knowledge or with those who seem to be unable to answer practical questions without designing and conducting a lengthy study. These conflicts of ideological predispositions naturally produce a certain wariness and misunderstanding between correctors and researchers. While this may not prevent limited cooperation on occasional research projects, it can militate against the successful institutionalization of evaluative research.

Organizational programs

Historically, there have been two patterns in the organizational arrangements by which evaluative research has been conducted. The first has been for individuals or organizations external to correctional agencies to plan and conduct research projects. Universities have been the origin of most of these ventures. For example, the Ford Foundation funded a study of the federal prison and parole systems, which was conducted by Daniel Glaser (1964), then at the University of Illinois. In recent years, however, the private research organization has become more prominent in research of this type; these organizations conduct research for a fee, on a contractual basis. The second organizational model has been the development of research units within correctional agencies or departments (Ohlin, 1974). Although each of these two types of organizational arrangements for the conduct of research presents somewhat different problems for the routinization of evaluative research, the following comments emphasize the problems that they have in common.

Experience suggests that research units and the conduct of research projects should be closely integrated into the day-to-day operations of correctional agencies—though not so integrated that they become completely dominated by line administrators. A high degree of integration increases the likelihood that correctional personnel will be involved in all phases of research projects, from conception and planning to data collection and analysis. Such a high degree of cooperation and communication decreases the chances of the research unit or project being seen as alien, disruptive, or threatening. An excellent example of this process of close communication with correctors is found in the study by Kassebaum et al. (1971), which evaluated the effectiveness of group counseling in a California prison.

This study utilized criterion measures that were developed in close communication with correctional staff, who were encouraged to list what they thought were the benefits of group counseling.

Minimal research impact is likely when, exclusive of specific research projects, there is little routine communication and coordination between line correctional personnel and research staff. This increases the likelihood that research staff will pursue idiosyncratic or esoteric research projects that have little relevance for the host correctional agency. Glaser (1965) has suggested that this was one reason the early attempt to establish and routinize evaluative research in the Illinois prison system failed. The absence of close communication and supervision by superiors permitted researchers to pursue research related to their own interests and goals rather than those of the correctional agency.

Administrative stance

Organizational problems such as these can be minimized if there is sufficient administrative understanding of and support for evaluative research. Unfortunately, administrators often seem unable to adopt such a stance. After all, implicit in the very notion of evaluative research is the possibility that some program, which has been touted as effective in changing offenders, will be shown to be ineffective. Many times, for correctional administrators and employees, this potential for negative results appears as a threat. It produces feelings of vulnerability and a resistance to permitting or conducting research. Within the agency or department the possibility of negative findings may disrupt the balance of power and privilege, thus creating new problems for the administrator. Various occupational groups may, then, have a vested interest in discouraging any kind of research that could prove to be disruptive of established arrangements. When administrators are differentially sensitive to or dependent upon these groups, they may proceed with extreme caution in the area of research.

Environmental supports

Administrators may resist research if they have developed beneficial relationships with outside groups or organizations that presume the effectiveness of correctional treatment. In such a situation, negative research findings may prove disruptive of these sources of support. Although the legislature is the best example of such an external organization, there are, in addition, various professional and private correctional groups or organizations. Not all of these groups may understand or support evaluative research, and in such a situation the administrator may either veto the conduct of research altogether or else move to isolate the potentially disruptive effects of it by minimizing its impact.

At a more general level, the routinization of correctional evaluative research is probably dependent upon some minimal prior degree of environmental rationalization (that is, support for and understanding of research by key organizations and groups in the environment). It is difficult, for example, to imagine the routine conduct of evaluative research by a correctional agency whose relations with environmental groups are essentially feudal in nature. In commenting on these environmental prerequisites for research, Glaser (1965) has suggested there must be a certain type of "cultural base." This seems an apt way of calling attention to the critical dimension of environmental conditions and relationships.

Divergent interests of researchers

For their part, the personnel of research units often have contributed to their own lack of significant impact on correctional structures and practices. When left to their own devices, they have shown a remarkable tendency to concentrate on research that is calculated to advance their careers in other spheres (for example, the university). Moreover, they may engage in esoteric or idiosyncratic research projects of little demonstrable relevance to agency concerns or problems. This is the basis for the claim, made by correctional personnel, that researchers are too concerned with "impractical" problems or trivial theoretical issues.

Curiously, however, in recent years, with the appearance of the research-for-fee system, has come a new potential problem: the possibility that researchers will become *too* sensitive to the expressed problems and "needs" of correctors, in the hope of doing more business in the future. Under such circumstances, researchers might focus too much attention on extremely insignificant problems, thus failing to assume the role of impartial challenger and innovator.

To summarize, the likelihood of evaluative research becoming routinized in a correctional agency is enhanced when there is a supportive and understanding environment, when administrators understand and are committed to the use of research, when the agency is relatively free of internal conflicts that could be exacerbated by research, and when research focuses on questions of obvious relevance to agency problems, in consultation with agency personnel.

15

The results of evaluative research
on correctional intervention

Although we already have a substantial number of studies that examine the effectiveness or efficiency of correctional treatments and punishments, this literature is of varying quality and studies must therefore be interpreted with caution. Still, a review of this body of research literature can tell us much about correctional programs, processes, and prospects. Before turning to such a review, we must discuss and clarify a fundamental disagreement over the evaluative research process.

> Research which confirms the popular is often popular; that which does not is frequently discredited on emotional grounds. For example, let us assume that research has discovered that whipping men for their misbehavior has a beneficial effect upon the recidivism rate. This conclusion would probably be accepted or rejected upon the basis of whether or not one did or did not believe in whipping, on grounds quite unrelated to its effectiveness as a correctional treatment. There would probably be individuals who would not whip, no matter how effective it might be discovered to be, because they just did not want to whip. This, of course, would not alter the effectiveness of whipping as a correctional device (Schnur, 1958: 773–74).

This statement, which suggests that questions about the effectiveness of correctional treatments can and should be separated from all other questions about them, is probably an accurate reflection of what most social scientists have believed about the correctional evaluative process. However, in recent years we have become aware of two pitfalls for such a position. First, as we pointed out in Chapters 12 and 13, there seems to be an emerging consensus that it is entirely appropriate that correctional dispositions be evaluated on other grounds than their effectiveness; more "emotional" criteria should also be used. In short, there is a growing realization that "technical efficiency cannot be the sole criterion upon which to base a policy that involves the reality of coercion" (Lerman, 1975: 88). Accordingly, questions about the fundamental humaneness and legality of correctional programs are increasingly raised today. Second, there is some question whether disparate groups of even supposedly neutral experts or scientists can come to a common agreement on the effectiveness of any particular correctional treatment. Two different positions on this important issue can be identified.

Objectivists

Devotees of one perspective on evaluative research and the implementation of research findings believe that the social world, like the physical one, is an objective realm of factual realities. The nature of this world, especially the cause-effect relationships within it, can be discovered or laid bare by use of scientific research methods. For this reason we designate their perspective the *objectivist* one.

Social research, like research in physics, biology, or chemistry, is believed to be basically a technical process. It consists of applying sound research methods to empirical problems. "Good" research is distinguished from "bad" research because it conforms more closely to these widely accepted principles of research design.

Because there are objective, independent, and widely agreed upon standards for evaluating the quality of research, persons of diverse backgrounds, professions, personal beliefs, and organizational affiliations can examine the same piece of research or research findings and come to a common evaluative judgment on it (that is, whether it is good or bad research). For this reason, objectivists believe that the social research process is primarily a technical, rational, and cerebral process. Regardless of individuals' personal or organizational commitments, they can evaluate the same correctional program or research findings and arrive at the same conclusions about the program's efficacy. Having done so, they then would be willing and ready to modify their own commitments.

Objectivists believe that, while political or administrative problems might occasionally hinder the conduct of evaluative research, these obstacles are understandable. Problems of this nature also can be researched. And just as there is good and bad research, presumably there are good and bad strategies for implementing evaluative research findings. Once we have identified these strategies they can be used as guides in future efforts to reform correctional practices. Put differently, obstacles to the conduct and implementation of evaluative research are believed to be rationally rectifiable.

Objectivists argue that if only some way can be found to eliminate reliance on any kind of correctional evaluative criteria except those of effectiveness and efficiency, corrections can be improved and reformed. Objectivists draw a sharp distinction between scientific and other kinds of criteria for evaluating correctional programs and treatments. Consequently, they have urged correctional administrators to conduct evaluative research and to use the results of this research to rationally restructure the correctional industry. The evaluative research process has been depicted as the most unbiased and objective means of reforming corrections on the basis of facts and scientific evidence. Glaser (1965), for instance, has referred to such a state of affairs (that is, where evaluative research is routinely conducted and used to modify correctional structures and practices) as an "elusive paradise."

Critics

There is an alternative view of the evaluative research process, a perspective that is rooted squarely in the sociologies of knowledge and science. Its disagreements with the objectivist position are evidenced first in its skepticism of the existence of an objective, factual world, and second in its skepticism about the ability of supposedly objective research findings to win the support of groups of individuals who have accumulated political, intellectual, and career investments in the presumed validity of some set of beliefs—in this case, the efficacy of correctional treatment. This perspective is designated as the *critical* one. It is so named because of its insistence that what is considered to be "good" research, "reliable" research findings, or "reasonable" inferences from research varies with the evaluators' backgrounds, social contexts, and organizational affiliations. Further, this perspective assumes that individuals conceive, conduct, and interpret research as members of groups or communities whose collective standards and perspectives are employed in the process. In sum, the critical position argues that we must adopt a sociological perspective on the entire process of conceptualizing, conducting, interpreting, and implementing evaluative research. Just as we would not be surprised if scientists employed by the tobacco industry disagreed with those employed elsewhere as to the harmfulness of smoking, we also should expect disagreement over the effects of correctional treatment by diverse groups of social scientists.

The work of the historian Thomas Kuhn is consistent with the critical perspective. In *Structure of Scientific Revolutions* (1962) Kuhn argued that scientific theories and research change and progress as a series of revolutionary cyclical transformations, rather than in a linear and cumulative fashion. During these revolutionary periods of change there is very little switching of theoretical allegiances by established scientists, because they have too many stakes in the correctness of some other scientific theory. As a result, it is usually the younger, relatively uncommitted members of a discipline who become adherents of new theories and new types of research. Unlike those who take an objectivist position on the nature of the scientific enterprise, people such as Kuhn are extremely skeptical of the view that scientists, more than any other groups of individuals who differ so much in their backgrounds and organizational allegiances, can somehow put aside the consequences of their differences and agree on one "correct" interpretation of a body of theory and research. Nevertheless, this is precisely what is believed by those who are convinced that evaluative research in corrections can unite those whose initial beliefs and commitments might be radically different.

EVALUATIVE RESEARCH AS A SOCIAL AND POLITICAL PROCESS

The prevailing view of correctional research—the objectivist position—is that research results speak unambiguously and that researchers and administrators will modify their beliefs and programs on the basis of research findings. It is assumed, of course, that the results of evaluative research can and should be used to restructure correctional programs. So the objectivist position celebrates the potential benefits of "correctional science" (Fosen and Campbell, 1966), and the only problem in the entire evaluative research process is persuading correctional administrators to permit or conduct such research. In contrast, the critical perspective views the entire evaluative research process as problematic, a process that is socially negotiated and constructed. Two important areas of further difference between the objectivist and critical positions are distinguished and discussed here: (1) disagreements about the nature and origins of research problems, and (2) the process of interpreting research findings.

Nature and origins of research problems

Advocates of the objectivist position do not adequately acknowledge or confront the issue of whose interests determine and structure the questions to which answers are sought in evaluative research. Although it is recognized that research problems are not distributed in some random fashion across all categories of candidate problems, the reasons behind this constriction of research problems and its consequences have not especially interested supporters of the objectivist position. From their perspective, there is little reason to explore such problems, since the principal objective of all correctional research is to simply develop factual knowledge about correctional processes.

By contrast, advocates of the critical perspective argue that we must understand who defines correctional research problems and the political and ideological biases that are inevitably embedded in these definitions of problems. When research problems are not randomly distributed, they are socially patterned and usually come to be defined in terms sympathetic or experientially relevant to only certain groups or strata. Correlatively, the problems and perspectives of other groups or strata may never be solicited or given serious consideration. Becker (1967) indicates that much social research—and here we include correctional research—has employed an implicit *hierarchy of credibility*. This consists of investing the problems and perspectives of those at higher levels of an organization with more credibility than those of lower-level members. Two implications of this and the constriction of research problems are noteworthy.

First, evaluative research seems incapable of generating proposals or programs that represent truly fundamental or radical alternatives to existing correctional arrangements. In other words, the prevailing tendency is for evaluative research to examine or propose programs that are only incrementally different from existing ones and that do not fundamentally contradict them. Second, there will be little understanding of correctional issues from the vantage point of subordinate groups or strata. Our factual knowledge about corrections will, therefore, be extremely skewed. Now, given the belief that correctional programs can only succeed in treating offenders humanely and changing them if they take account of the perspectives of both line staff and offenders, this is a serious indictment of our research efforts. It suggests a need to democratize the process by which research problems are identified, conceptualized, and investigated.

Interpreting and reacting to research findings

From the objectivist perspective, science is the great arbiter of correctional issues, providing definitive answers—at least over a long enough period of time and research—on the basis of which correctional structures and practices are refashioned. From the critical perspective, however, doubt emanates whether this is the way in which research findings function or the kind of reception they receive in the real world. The case of research on the effects of marijuana smoking is instructive and illustrative in this regard.

In an interesting article, Goode (1969) has pointed to the issue of contention here. He asks how it could be that scientists, after conducting so much "scientific" research, seem unable to agree whether smoking marijuana is harmful, and if so, to what degree and in what ways. After analyzing the debate between advocates of different positions on these issues, Goode (1969: 83) concludes that:

> . . . the marijuana controversy is primarily a political rather than a scientific debate. It is a struggle to establish moral hegemony. Stances toward marijuana use and legalization are largely a manifestation of prior basic underlying ideological commitments. Scientific truth or falsity seem to have little or no impact on the positions taken—although both sides will invoke scientific findings and in fact will actually believe them—and have been preselected to verify a position already taken.

Goode contends that the "objective facts" about marijuana smoking are largely irrelevant to the debate over its effects. Instead, he suggests that it is extremely difficult, perhaps even impossible, for those who have prior ideological commitments to different positions on the issue to lay aside these differences and come to one "correct" interpretation of the research literature.

EFFECTS OF CORRECTIONAL INTERVENTION

Punishment and treatment

A distinction is often drawn between official actions intended to punish offenders and those intended to "treat" them or contribute to their rehabilitation. We indicated in Chapter 4 that, while this distinction can be made hypothetically, in reality it is virtually impossible to maintain. Treatment and punishment usually coexist in correctional programs and cannot be viewed as mutually exclusive.

Deterrent and treatment effectiveness

Nevertheless, corresponding to the traditional tendency, to think of correctional measures as *either* punitive *or* rehabilitative, is a split in the social science literature between research on deterrence-incapacitation and research on correctional effectiveness. Where the former research has looked at the impact of officials actions which seem patently punitive, such as the death penalty or prison terms, the latter has examined the effect of ostensibly rehabilitative measures, such as counseling, job training, or education participation. We have followed this distinction here and will discuss deterrent effectiveness and treatment effectiveness separately. However, community delinquency prevention programs, which usually are not correctional dispositions and include a larger target population, will be omitted.

How effective are correctional treatments?

By now the sheer volume of correctional evaluative research has reached such a magnitude that it has become difficult to keep abreast of it. Fortunately, however, as the volume of research has grown, several articles and at least one book have appeared that summarize and review this research literature (Bailey 1966; Robison and Smith, 1971; Hood, 1971; Logan, 1972; Martinson, 1974; Lipton et al., 1975; Greenberg, 1977). Drawing upon these summary reviews, several tentative conclusions about evaluative research in corrections seem justified:

1. The level of methodological sophistication of most evaluative research in corrections is rather low. One observer claims that no more than 10 percent of evaluative studies have employed true experimental designs (Adams, 1975: 10). Logan (1972: 380) reviewed 100 studies and concluded that "there is not yet one single study of correctional or preventive effectiveness that will satisfy the most minimal standards of scientific design."
2. It is often difficult to identify precisely what independent variable was employed in a study; the nature of the treatment being evaluated is often imprecise or overly broad. "It is not enough to know that a particular program ended in success or failure if we cannot determine *what it was* that succeeded or failed" (Logan, 1972: 379). (Emphasis in the original.) Although it is useful to *know* that probation is at least as successful as imprisonment in reducing recidivism, ideally we would like to know precisely what it is about probation that accounts for this success.
3. The lack of methodological sophistication in correctional evaluative research makes inferences from it an extremely risky venture. Typical are the difficulties we encounter in interpreting the comparative success rate of probation and imprisonment (Levin, 1971). When recidivism is used as the criterion, the

success rate for probation is consistently higher than the success rate for imprisonment. The reasons for this remain unclear, however, since it is nearly impossible to determine the effects of selection biases in the assignment of offenders to either probation or an institution. Perhaps, as Wilson cogently notes, "if probation success rates now appear good, it is only because judges are good at guessing who will be successful" (1975: 168).

Correctional evaluative research has examined a variety of issues and programs. Robison and Smith (1971) suggest that this research has been concerned with answering five basic questions about the effectiveness of alternative correctional procedures:

1. Is probation more effective than imprisonment?
2. Do offenders recidivate less if they are locked up for longer periods of time?
3. Does educating and "treating" offenders while they are in prison reduce recidivism?
4. Does supervising offenders in smaller probation and parole caseloads reduce recidivism?
5. Does it make any difference whether we discharge prisoners outright or supervise them on parole? [Put differently, is parole more effective in reducing recidivism than simply doing nothing with released offenders?]

In addition, there is one other question about the effectiveness of correctional treatment that is increasingly asked today. It is more "global" than the first five:

6. Does community treatment reduce recidivism more than confining offenders in traditional correctional institutions?

Given the diversity and complexity of these questions, it is not easy to summarize the correctional evaluation research literature. Nevertheless, the following are summary statements from several systematic reviews of this body of research:

1. Having examined and reviewed a sample of 100 studies of correctional effectiveness, Bailey (1966: 159) concludes that "evidence supporting the efficacy of correctional treatment is slight, inconsistent, and of questionable reliability."
2. Robison and Smith review the results of several well-known research projects conducted in California. Their review "strongly suggests the following conclusion: *There is no evidence to support any program's claim of superior rehabilitative efficacy*" (1971: 80). (Emphasis in the original.)
3. After his review of correctional evaluative research, Greenberg (1977: 140–41) states that "many correctional dispositions are

failing to reduce recidivism. . . . Much of what is now done in the name of 'corrections' may serve other functions, but the prevention of return to crime is not one of them. Here and there a few favorable results alleviate the monotony, but most of these results are modest and are obtained through evaluations seriously lacking in rigor. The blanket assertion that 'nothing works' is an exaggeration, but not by very much."

4. "While some treatment programs have had modest successes, it still must be concluded that the field of corrections has not as yet found satisfactory ways to reduce recidivism by significant amounts." This is the conclusion from what is possibly the most systematic and ambitious review of the results of evaluative research yet undertaken (Lipton et al., 1975).

5. As yet, there is little if any evidence to suggest that community correctional programs are any more effective than more traditional forms of correctional intervention (Greenberg, 1975a).

The rather tentative and restrained tenor of the conclusions presented in these summary reviews of evaluative research contrasts somewhat with the interpretations of them that others have drawn. Indeed, there is a heated controversy over the effectiveness of correctional treatment and it is very reminiscent of the debate over the effects of marijuana smoking. Surveying the same body of correctional research literature, some feel reason for optimism, while others conclude that correctional treatment seems largely ineffective. Lipton et al. (1975) reviewed 231 different studies on the effectiveness of correctional treatments. In an earlier article based on this review, Martinson (1974) cautiously suggested that correctional treatment has not yet proven to be very effective. Later, Palmer (1975), a researcher closely identified and associated with the correctional industry, leveled a sweeping and detailed attack on the analytic methods and conclusions of Martinson's article. Palmer concludes that there *is* reason for optimism, especially if we concern ourselves with *differential treatment* effects. Wilson (1975: 169–70) suggests that correctional treatment has now been shown ineffective, while Adams (1974: 1021) feels that "an optimistic stance seems warranted."

From the critical perspective on evaluative research there is little reason for surprise over this clash of opinion. In fact, this exchange of views (see Martinson, 1976) is precisely what we would expect, given the high stakes so many have invested in the presumed efficacy of correctional treatment. On the other hand, this is not what we would necessarily expect on the basis of the objectivist position. From this position, we would expect to see at least some members of the correctional community reassessing their formerly held beliefs in the efficacy of treatment—and coming over to the camp of those who believe that treatment has clearly been shown to be ineffective. This does not seem to have happened on any large scale—at least those who have converted have been extremely quiet about their conversion. The entire debate over the validity of evaluative research findings and the findings of summaries of evaluative studies (such as Lipton et al.) is reminiscent of Cressey's (1958) earlier discussion of how correctional personnel have developed and use a *vocabulary of adjustment* to discount or attack the results of research that shows their favorite programs to be ineffective. As Cressey noted, research suggesting that treatment is ineffective presents correctional personnel with a serious dilemma. On one hand, they are presumably committed to the use of evaluative research while, on the other hand, they have a heavy investment in programs to effectively treat offenders. "Fortunately, there is a solution to the dilemma. Stated simply, it is to insure that any research results can be interpreted as 'conclusive' if they favor continued utilization of the technique and as 'inconclusive' if they do not" (Cressey, 1958: 759). Some researchers have recognized such a process at work:

> We expect that policies will be little changed with regard to work release, despite our findings that it does not have the rehabilitative consequences anticipated. We suspect that commitment to the program is so great that policy-makers will point to shortcomings in the research (for example: it involved a sample drawn several years ago, and the present program is different) to denigrate its immediate import (Waldo and Chiricos, 1977: 104).

Such observations should make us question whether evaluative research has been oversold. Perhaps we have accepted an overly naive view of its promise, one that obscures the true nature of its application to the realm of socially and politically negotiated realities.

Differential treatment

In reviewing the results of correctional evaluation research, supporters of correctional treatment basically claim that what has been demonstrated thus far is that no particular correctional treatment works well with *all* types of offenders or in *all* settings. Consequently, they argue, we must move in the direction of trying to determine what *types of treatment* work best with what *types of offenders*. Warren (1971) may be used to illustrate this development and line of thought. She correctly notes that "studies of the impact of treatment of client populations have been generally discouraging" (1971:

245). She suggests two interpretations for this predicament. "One possibility is that, in our present state of knowledge, treaters simply don't know how to bring about changes in individuals via a treatment process" (1971: 245). She opts for the second interpretation, that *masking* has occurred in our evaluative research results.

> By lumping together all subjects, the beneficial effects of a treatment program on some subjects, together with the detrimental effects of the same treatment program on other subjects, may each mask and cancel out the other.
>
> It is very likely that, in many treatment studies, this masking effect has occurred, either because the data have not been viewed in sufficiently complex fashion, or because the crucial dimension, the classification of subjects in a treatment-relevant way was missing (1971: 245-46).

In other words, masking means that while the overall success rate for a treatment might be low, this summary rate probably masks the possibility that certain types of offenders performed much better than did other types of offenders. The belief that masking has frequently occurred in previous evaluative research has reached the point of near dogma in contemporary correctional literature (for example, Palmer, 1975).

This has given further impetus to the movement to develop typologies of offenders that can be used for *differential treatment* purposes. Although the belief in differential treatment has always been an integral part of the medical model of treatment, only recently have serious research efforts to develop offender typologies been undertaken. Warren (1971) reviewed 16 such typologies and suggested that common to all of them are six offender subtypes: (1) asocial, (2) conformist, (3) antisocial-manipulator, (4) neurotic, (5) subcultural identifier, and (6) situational offender. She believes the recurrence of these six types of offenders in the typologies she reviewed is cause for optimism; perhaps correctional researchers and personnel are gradually developing some consensus on fundamental types of offenders. Once this has been done, research can investigate the differential effects of treatments.

An illustration of what many take to be the promise of differential treatment can be seen in the results of the Pilot Intensive Counseling Organization (PICO) (Adams, 1970). PICO, which began in 1955, was designed to study the effects of individual therapy on older delinquents. Treated youths were to be compared with control youths on personality and behavioral changes within a medium security correctional institution and after release on parole. California Youth Authority wards, before admission to Deuel Vocational Institution, were screened for possible inclusion in the PICO program. Those with any of the following characteristics were screened out of the pool of eligibles: a commitment of less than six months' duration, probable out-of-state parole, juvenile court case, psychotic, gross mental deficiency, non-English-speaking, and serious reading difficulty. After screening, subjects were randomly assigned to the experimental and control groups. However, one additional determination was made about each subject—his degree of *amenability* to treatment. This was ascertained through pooled clinical judgments by a team that studied the subjects at their admission into the reception-diagnostic center. Use of judgments about each subject's amenability, along with assignment to either the experimental or control groups, resulted in four groups: (1) treated amenables, (2) treated nonamenables, (3) control amenables, and (4) control nonamenables. For the experimental subjects, treatment consisted of once- or twice-weekly individual counseling sessions. These sessions continued for an average of about nine months for both the treated amenables and the treated nonamenables. During nontreatment hours, the experimental subjects pursued the same program as the control subjects—full schedules of academic training and vocational training.

A variety of criterion variables was used to assess the effectiveness of the treatment. The results were generally consistent for all criteria: treated amenables performed better than any of the other three groups, followed by control amenables, then control nonamenables, and lastly, by treated nonamenables. In other words, those subjects deemed to be nonamenable to treatment actually performed worse than would have been the case had they received no treatment at all.

These findings generally are interpreted as supportive of the need for developing offender typologies and differential treatment. In Hood's (1971: 178) words, "the key to progress in treatment research is the development of typologies, both of offenders and treatments. . . . What kinds of people would respond best to discipline, counseling, therapy, fining, intensive case-work, limited supervision?"

How efficient are correctional treatments?

In addition to calling for more emphasis on differential treatment effects, correctional supporters have taken another tack in response to the gradually accumulating evidence that correctional treatment efforts are not especially effective. Increasingly, they assert that even if correctional treatment is no *more* effective than institutionalization, at least it is *as* effective; in such a situation, preference should be given to types of programs more cost-effective (efficient).

This strategy represents a considerable toning down of the traditional claims for correctional treatment effectiveness, as well as a new claim for increased use of community correctional programs.

Until recently, little if any empirical research was conducted on the cost-effectiveness of alternative correctional programs. It was conventional wisdom in correctional circles that the traditional community correctional programs (probation; parole) were much less expensive than institutionalization. This belief generally was buttressed by citing comparative cost figures for maintaining an offender on probation for one year and in an institution. With the emergence and growth of the community corrections movement, these beliefs became dogma. To be sure, there were those who sounded a cautionary note, suggesting that the greater cost-effectiveness of community correctional programs might be illusory.

> While it is not universally true that the cost of a community disposition is less than that of imprisonment, frequently this is the case. Yet cost arguments can be misleading, for some community alternatives may be less expensive only because of budgetary stinginess. If the goal of making educational and vocational opportunities or individual psychiatric counseling available to those who wanted these services were to be taken seriously, the cost might well increase these costs. In addition, much of the cost of running prisons is fixed and does not vary with a reduction in the number of inmates. For this reason, a diversion of some inmates to community dispositions may simply mean a higher per capita cost of imprisonment for those still incarcerated, with no overall savings. Indeed, the author knows of no Department of Corrections among those where extensive decarceration has taken place that has reduced its overall budget. Given organizational instincts for self-preservation and expansion, the prospects for substantial budget cuts through decarceration seem slight (Greenberg, 1975a: 6).

Correctional cost-effectiveness research has appeared only recently and has generally dealt with this very issue. From all indications, whether community correctional programs are more efficient than traditional institutional ones will be no easier to resolve than was the issue of treatment *effectiveness*. Certainly one reason for this is because some of the reservations and misgivings about community corrections have been borne out in practice. Although it is far too early to offer any summary statements about the efficiency of community treatment, experience in California may prove to be instructive.

Lerman (1975) examined some of the cost-effectiveness claims for two widely heralded California programs: Probation Subsidy and the Community Treatment Project.

The major findings of this study indicate that major goals of the community treatment strategy were not realized in practice. Community treatment was proposed as an effective alternative to traditional institutionalization and proved to be no more effective. . . . And community treatment was supposed to be less expensive, but proved to be associated with cost overruns (Lerman, 1975: 120).

This research strongly suggests that organizational instincts for expansion and self-preservation, coupled with the system effects of moving to increased reliance on community programs, may obliterate their cost-effectiveness advantage.

The deterrent and incapacitative effects of correctional intervention

The issue of the deterrent and incapacitative effects of various types of correctional programs is analytically distinguishable from the issue of their rehabilitative effectiveness. In fact, programs that proved to be ineffective as rehabilitative measures could still have a significant deterrent or incapacitative effect. In the present context, *deterrence* is the inhibiting effect of punishment on the criminal activities of people other than the punished offenders. (In other words, we are restricting our definition to the question of *general* deterrence.) *Incapacitation* is the effect of isolating known offenders from the larger society, thereby preventing them from committing crimes in that society. Now, what can we say about the deterrent and incapacitative effects of correctional programs?

At the end of 1975 the National Academy of Sciences established a Panel on Research on Deterrent and Incapacitative Effects in order "to provide an objective technical assessment of the studies of the deterrent and incapacitative effects of sanctions on crime rates" (National Research Council, 1978: 16). The panel's final report concludes that while existing research does "offer some credible evidence of the existence of a deterrent effect . . . we cannot yet assert that the evidence warrants an affirmative conclusion" regarding such an effect. Still, "the evidence certainly favors a proposition supporting deterrence more than it favors one asserting that deterrence is absent" (National Research Council, 1978: 7). The panel's report makes it clear, however, that more work needs to be done before more conclusive statements can be made about the deterrent effectiveness of various types of correctional dispositions.

Efforts to determine the incapacitative effects of changes in imprisonment policy must necessarily make assumptions about critical, but largely unknown, parameters that characterize individual criminal careers. But "as long as there is a reasonable presumption that

312

offenders who are imprisoned would have continued to commit crimes if they had remained free, there is unquestionably a direct incapacitative effect" (National Research Council, 1978: 9). It is difficult to make more precise estimates of the incapacitative effects of imprisonment and changes in imprisonment policy. The panel concludes, however, that

> the expected incapacitative effect of any change in imprisonment policy is quite sensitive to the current value of the individual crime rate and to the current value of imprisonment policy variables. When the current rate of imprisonment per crime and the individual crime rate are low, the percentage increase in prison population needed in order to achieve a given percentage reduction in crime is large. Since the high-crime-rate jurisdictions that are most likely to be looking to incapacitation to relieve their crime problems also tend to have relatively lower rates of time served per crime, they can expect to have the largest percentage increases in prison populations to achieve a given percentage reduction in crime (1978: 10).

In view of the disenchantment with rehabilitation as a correctional justification, and the rapid ascendance of incapacitation and deterrence to take its place, we will likely see much more research in the next few years on the deterrent and incapacitative effects of correctional dispositions.

CORRECTIONAL REFORM

16

Correctional reform: Substance, process, and problems

In this chapter we return to a topic we touched upon briefly in earlier chapters: the process of correctional reform. In Chapter 3 we discussed three different perspectives on the process of correctional change: the *conservative*, *liberal-pluralist*, and *radical-elitist*. We indicated that supporters of each of these perspectives disagree on how correctional change should be interpreted and promoted. The approach in Chapter 3 was generally retrospective and passive; that is, we discussed how each of the three perspectives interprets correctional changes that occurred at *earlier times*. In contrast, the approach in this chapter is *prospective* and programmatic. We will deal with differences in what each perspective sees as (1) the substance of "true" correctional reform, (2) the nature of the reform process, and (3) how we can account for the fact that reforms are so difficult to make and, once made, often prove to have results either different or less dramatic than their supporters intended.

THE SUBSTANCE OF CORRECTIONAL REFORM

The felt need and desire to reform correctional practices was probably born with corrections itself, because it seems every generation has sought to institute reforms. Thus, it appears that reform is a historical constant. Today we are certainly in the midst of such a period. From all quarters comes the call to reform corrections, and all sides seem agreed that corrections is in a transitional state.

316

Conservatives

As we indicated in Chapter 3, conservatives are distinguished in the first instance by their unsympathetic stance toward offenders and by their identification with the victims of crimes. Further, conservatives are primarily concerned with the maintenance of social order. They believe that correctional measures should be adopted that take social defense, the maintenance of public safety, and peaceful social conditions as a first priority.

To conservatives, crime is an individual phenomenon. Conservatives have no use for theories of crime causation that stress the importance of environmental or social structural variables. On the contrary, crime is socially harmful behavior committed by individuals who either choose to engage in such behavior or who are so defective that they cannot avoid doing so. Conservatives have long held to the belief that some persons are so incurably criminal that they represent a distinctive "criminal class" that necessitates repressive action. For instance, in his presidential campaigns Richard Nixon

> took a rather classical, conservative stand: criminals were immoral
> lawbreakers; whether or not they grew up in slums and poverty was,
> first of all, of doubtful relevance, and second, was certainly no basis
> for issuing a certificate of exemption for the consequences of their
> actions. By these standards of reckoning, there are two classes of
> people, the criminals and the rest of us. The righteous are expected
> —on the basis both of self-righteousness and of self-interest—to put
> the criminals in their place, which is usually in jail (Ryan, 1971:
> 188–89).

In the conservative mind, crime can be reduced—though probably never eliminated—by making the risks of committing it sufficiently high that those who are tempted will abstain. This means having a sufficient number of police officers to make their presence noticed, thereby frightening would-be offenders. It also means giving the police enough fiscal and legal resources to combat criminals. Once offenders have been apprehended, dealing with them swiftly and severely will deter others from following in their footsteps.

Today's conservatives are staunch believers in the preventive ideals of deterrence and incapacitation. Since they do not have a very optimistic view of the human potential, conservatives feel that humans are naturally tempted and imperfectible and must be checked lest their evil impulses break through, resulting in socially harmful behavior. The judicious use of punishment of sufficient severity is calculated and believed likely to prevent widespread criminality. Conservative extremists feel that some criminals are probably so depraved or defective that they should be permanently isolated from society, or executed. In short, "really serious" offenders should be incapacitated.

Unlike liberals and radicals, conservatives rarely speak of the desirability of reforming corrections. In part this is because they believe there are inherent limits on government's ability to accomplish social welfare objectives—which they often see as attempts to make people moral or righteous. Consequently, when conservatives see government sponsored programs fail, their first inclination is to say "I told you so." These failures require little explanation; they are only further evidence of government's inability to achieve welfare objectives. Conservatives are likely, therefore, to argue against too much emphasis on rehabilitation as a correctional objective and in favor of minimal correctional programming. Given their rather pessimistic view of the prospects for governmental action or effectiveness, and their view of criminality as an individual matter treatable by swift, sure, and severe punishment, conservatives see many correctional programs as misguided frills concocted by liberal dreamers. Prisons, for example, should be spartan places, with the emphasis on simple incapacitation, instilling discipline, and the creation of good work habits.

To the extent that conservatives ever speak of correctional reform, they believe it can be accomplished by applying professional expertise and sound business practices to the operation of governmental agencies. What Gibbons and Garabedian (1974: 52) note as characteristic of earlier conservative criminology continues to be true today.

> In general, old-time criminology tended toward *a faith in the ultimate perfectibility of the police and criminal justice machinery.* In this view, if we "throw out the rascals" who currently manage these operations and replace them with "professionals," high-caliber police work and effective correctional therapy would be within our grasp. (Emphasis in the original.)

Today's conservatives believe that public officials should be permitted to do their jobs without "meddling" or interference from liberals or the courts. Since the police, prosecutors, and correctional administrators are the experts, they should be left alone to handle the criminals as only they know how. The rest of us should support their efforts and resist any attempt by outsiders, for example the courts, to make their work any more difficult.

Conservatives believe there is nothing mysterious about the correctional task. All we need to do is to apply the principles of crime control, which are as old as the human experience (that is, retribution, deterrence, and incapacitation). When government fails to make use of this knowledge, the blame is often laid at the feet of liberals and liberal social scientists. It is they who fill the public's mind with muddled, heretical ideas, and who influence politicians and correctional administrators to do the very things that seem to exacerbate the problem of defending social order. Contemporary conservative writers are more gracious than some of their predecessors in attributing these errors to the discipline of sociology rather than to sociologists personally.

> Criminologists and perhaps all sociologists, are part of an intellectual tradition that does not contain built-in checks against the premature conversion of opinion into policy, because the focal concerns of that tradition are with those aspects of society that are, to a great extent, beyond the reach of policy and even beyond the reach of science. . . . Sociology . . . is at heart a profoundly subjectivist discipline. When those who practice it are brought forward and asked for advice, they will say either (if conservative) that nothing is possible, or (if liberal) that everything is possible. That most sociologists are liberals explains why the latter reaction is more common, even though the presuppositions of their own discipline would more naturally lead to the former (Wilson, 1975: 62–3).

Contrary to liberal advice, prisons should not be closed—though perhaps they should be made somewhat more humane. Indeed, conservatives suggest building more if that is what is required to "get the criminals off the streets."

Liberal-pluralists

As compared with liberals, there is a degree of timelessness about conservatives' proposals for correctional reforms. Liberals, however, tend to change their reform package from one generation to the next. But they are never happy with corrections, and there are always reforms to be made. The following are some popular contemporary proposals for correctional reform (Carlson, 1976):

1. Restrictions on plea bargaining, reductions in the length of sentences, more uniformity in sentencing, and elimination or substantial modification of the indeterminate sentence.
2. More "humanization" of correctional practices and further expansion of prisoners' rights.
3. Less reliance on or even the elimination of the prison.
4. Increased use of the community for correctional programs.
5. Decreased use of coercive treatment and greater use of voluntary correctional programs.

6. Limiting the use of the prison—if it is used at all—to those considered too dangerous to release.
7. Reorganization and perhaps less reliance on parole.
8. Greater use of diversion, community programs and probation.

With the resurgence of conservative thought in recent years, many liberals seem to feel a need to sound more conservative in their own proposals. For instance, Carlson is unmincing in stating that

> those who exploit and harm others, regardless of their motivations, can and must be stopped more effectively. More decisive punishment with proven deterrent effects, coupled with sophisticated crime prevention measures, can and will reduce the most destructive offenses and will, as a result, reduce the overall crime rate (1976: 168).

And, Carlson says, "As long as people prey on others, we must stop them—and with more effective punishments than we have been using—even as we frustratingly seek to ameliorate conditions that are conducive to crime" (1976: 168). Many of today's liberals are determined not to be outdone by conservatives in repressing crime. It has not always been such.

Despite their ambivalence today, liberals proudly proclaim that their reform proposals are grounded in humanitarianism and social science research. They tend to view conservatives as barbaric, philosophically atavistic types who want to build more prisons and incarcerate criminals for longer periods of time, all in the name of social defense. Liberals, however, want to help offenders, to rehabilitate them, and to only incarcerate those who "really need it." In sum, liberal-pluralists believe that (1) their proposals are grounded in scientific research, (2) they have a more sophisticated and realistic understanding of the political process and how it effects the correctional reform process, and (3) they want to "help" offenders instead of punishing them.

How do liberal-pluralists account for the failure to follow through on correctional reform? Usually they begin by citing the existence of competing, divergent perspectives on what reforms should be made and how they should be implemented. Opposing the overly crude, moral consensus theories of conservatives, liberals view the political and administrative processes as conflictual ones, in which diverse groups endeavor to influence them to their own advantage or viewpoint. In the process, reforms are either defeated or twisted, distorted, and transformed into something even their promoters would not recognize. As Carlson explains, "Corrections is hardly monolithic; it is tugged and pulled by interest groups with different goals.

These varying and conflicting interests have not achieved any con-
census on the direction of change" (1976: 159).

Of course, liberals assume that the correctional system itself can
defeat reform efforts or, at least, turn them in directions different
from those their framers had intended. Stated differently, liberal-
pluralists understand the importance and the functional role of correctional bureaucracies as interest groups. This can sometimes lead
to the defeat of reform efforts.

> One reason we have too much hospitalization is that we have too
> many hospital beds—supply can create demand. This is demon-
> strably so in medicine and to a somewhat lesser degree in the law.
> But it may also be true of cells, guards, and probation and parole
> officers. The prison is a business, as is probation and parole. An-
> nually $2.7 billion are turned over in the corrections industry. The
> state and federal systems employ 190,000 people. In addition, the
> Federal Bureau's prison industry alone generates $58 million. Fi-
> nally, the federal government and the states combined spend an
> undetermined sum on research and program development related
> to corrections. This isn't exactly Exxon, but it's not insignificant.
> And in many towns dotted across the United States, the prison is
> the staple industry—shut the prison down and you shut down the
> town.
>
> Next, add to these cash flows the swarm of researchers, thera-
> pists, and bureaucrats who are sustained by the correctional busi-
> ness. None of these people, nor those directly employed in penal
> work, would be overjoyed if the system were jettisoned. As a result,
> it is argued, often by offenders and ex-offenders, that the system
> managers are the real blocks to reform. Any reform that might re-
> duce the size of the system is likely to be opposed (Carlson, 1976:
> 167).

Moreover, liberals understand that correctional agencies, as formal
organization, are subject to problems of goal displacement and
others that can defeat intended reform. When examining correctional agencies,

> the sociologist brings to the analysis of these structures the inside
> dopester's awareness that social organizations are often "screwed
> up." That is, he knows about all kinds of complex organizations that
> operate in ways quite different from those sketched in organiza-
> tional charts or manuals of procedure. This growing sophistication
> of criminological analysis has been paralleled by a marked decline
> in the criminologist's faith in the perfectibility of the legal-correc-
> tional machinery (Gibbons and Garabedian, 1974: 55).

For a variety of reasons, then, liberal-pluralists understand that
narrow, parochial interests are sometimes able to manipulate the re-

When I entered the California prison system there were just three prisons. When I was finally discharged, almost 20 years later, there were 13 prisons and more were planned. It's expensive to build and operate prisons and each new unit added to the correctional bureaucracy. More guards—more sergeants, more lieutenants, more captains, more program administrators, wardens, associate wardens and superintendents. More correctional counselors, clerks and storeroom keepers. More vocational instructors, teachers, doctors, dentists and medical techs. More psychologists, psychiatrists, sociologists and psychometricians. More chaplains, librarians, stewards, cooks, and recreational supervisors. And, always more and more prisoners. The jails of every county were packed with the convicted waiting to begin their sentences in one of the state facilities. Sometimes they waited months. And as each new prison opened the relief was only temporary. Soon the jails were crowded again. The Cynic had an idea about this. You ever notice how when they want to build a new prison all of sudden paroles are hard to get and they're busting dudes back on violations for spitting on the sidewalk, and, pretty soon, they've got us warehoused ten deep, then they go to the legislature and cry about the over-crowded conditions which only a new prison will relieve.

Source: Malcolm Braly. *False Starts.* Boston: Little, Brown, 1976, pp. 243–44.

form process to their advantage. At other times, enlightened governmental programs simply lag far behind the obvious needs of the times or the findings of social science. Liberal-pluralism has posited a number of explanations for this.

A misinformed or unsupportive public

Liberal-pluralism does not deny to ordinary citizens the potential for influencing governmental actions, even if they are not organized to pursue their interests. In fact, it generally assumes that on most issues public opinion will reign triumphant, especially as it becomes known to administrators and elected representatives. Thus, a resistive and unsupportive public is blamed for defeating or negating correctional reforms. As Bowker (1977: xii) puts it: "Prison conditions are an expression of the will of the general citizenry, and they will not change significantly until the public develops a different conception of what to do about crime and criminals."

In situations where the public is not sufficiently informed about an issue to make intelligent decisions on the merits, they must be "educated" to the issues involved. It is at just such times, incidentally, when the danger of parochial interests having their way at the expense of the public interest is believed to be greatest. The public needs to be educated, therefore, not only to be able to make intelligent, informed decisions, but also to keep abreast of what is happening lest special interest groups exploit their ignorance and, in a triumph of chicanery, change the governmental structure or policies to their private advantage.

At other times, however, the public is extremely well informed about issues and speaks through its elected representatives with a clear and unequivocal voice. An example of this is said to occur during periods of escalating violent crime. During these "crime waves" the public grows restive and increasingly dissatisfied with rehabilitative approaches to the treatment of offenders. Instead, they inform their legislators, and also make it known through scientific public opinion polls, that they expect a crackdown on criminals. Faced with this united and intransigent front, there is little that prosecutors, judges, and legislators can do but punish offenders more severely, sentencing more of them to prison and, as in some states, even reenacting the death penalty.

Lack of scientific knowledge

A crucial role in the promotion and construction of sound, progressive governmental programs is assigned to the collection of scientific knowledge about existing problems. Unfortunately, there are times when the objective scientific knowledge needed to guide political decision-making seems to be lacking. So if action of some kind seems to be required, a crash effort must be made to collect such information. This process occurred repeatedly during the 1960s as first Lyndon Johnson and later Richard Nixon appointed various presidential commissions to gather "the facts" about this or that "social problem." Among the fact-finding bodies that proceeded, after their appointment, to hire professional social scientists to collect research knowledge, conduct public hearings, and issue final reports were the President's Commission on Law Enforcement and the Administration of Justice, the Commission on Obscenity and Pornography, the National Advisory Commission on Civil Disorders (the Kerner commission), the National Commission on Marihuana and Drug Abuse, the Commission on the Causes and Prevention of Violence, and the National Advisory Commission on Criminal Justice Standards and Goals.

The presidential or congressional mandate to these various commissions reads like a litany of the liberal-pluralist position on the political and policy-making processes. There is never any doubt that "the facts" can be found, adequately summarized, and used to guide informed and progressive policy making. Nor is there any doubt that the facts will appear equally unambiguous to representatives of diverse groups in the population. Thus, most such commissions were stocked with the representatives of all the legitimate interest groups (organized labor, business, law enforcement). Should there not be an immediate consensus among the representatives of these diverse —yet amazingly similar (Platt, 1971)—groups, assumedly they can easily reach a compromise and present a set of facts and recommendations in the public interest.

Because of the special need for objective knowledge about social problems, social scientists and various other experts are believed to have a special role to play in the reform of governmental policies and programs. They are hired as consultants to governmental agencies and commissions and encouraged to conduct research on problems of pressing concern. Likewise, due to their specialized training and expertise, their opinions must be carefully considered in the halls of government when changes or reforms are needed.

Resistance and entrenched interests

Even though the facts about a problem are clear and compelling, public opinion calls for governmental action, and though interest groups are united and strong in urging appropriate reform, the reforms still may not be forthcoming. How, given the assumptions of liberal-pluralism, can this be? In addition to the reasons we have already discussed, the resistance of strategically situated organizations and groups is commonly cited as a reason.

Real or potential reform programs often appear as a threat to individuals, groups, or employees of affected organizations who, correctly or not, feel that it represents a downgrading of their importance, mission, or approach to some problem(s). Frequently they view the changes as not only threatening to them but also as being dangerous or threatening to the public welfare. When these two sets of beliefs are joined, we have the ingredients for resistance to the new program or a rearguard action against it. The recent history of correctional reform is replete with examples of this process. Correctional administrators in several jurisdictions resisted and generally failed to comply with the court directives that they make modifications in the structure or operations of their institutions. Similarly, in some states prison employees have moved to unionize, apparently in response to what they view as the courts' interference in prison operation; unionization has been seen as an effective means of resisting this external "interference."

While liberal-pluralism makes allowances for these resistive actions, they are still viewed as being temporary or of malleable nature. In either case, they are viewed as only short-term obstacles to reform. Nevertheless, the resistance of entrenched interest groups is often invoked to explain why reform efforts seem to lag behind the most enlightened thinking.

Radical-elitists

Radical-elitists have taken a two-pronged approach to the problem of the ineffectiveness of correctional reform. First, they argue that these efforts are really successful, though not in ways that liberals would acknowledge or even understand. And second, they propose their own structural reasons why reforms either cannot be made or are unsuccessful if attempted.

This does not mean, however, that proposals for reform and limited reforms are completely ineffective, only that they're effective in ways that liberals and conservatives do not recognize or acknowledge. In the first place, proposed and limited reforms are helpful in maintaining ideological hegemony about the nature of crime, criminals, and what should be done to correct them. Put differently, the substance and rhetoric of reform are part of the process by which public consciousness and understanding of crime and offenders are manipulated and mystified by elites. Second, correctional reforms, to the extent they are actually adopted, serve to increase the ability of the correctional apparatus to more effectively control the underclass—the 'true' function of the penal system and punishment policies. Combining these two meanings of correctional effectiveness, reform proposals and limited reforms serve to establish and maintain a set of ideas about crime and criminals that obscures their true nature and that serves to more effectively control the surplus population and underclass.

> Prisons are institutions set up to perform a service for capitalist society, and that is the exclusion and elimination of particular groups of people who threaten the system. The process is legitimated by a network of ideas, which provides the ideological fortress supporting the actual physical structure. . . . Prisons and parole were never designed to return people to their family and community better able and equipped to maintain their existence, but, rather, to eliminate the "dangerous classes" (Schmidt, 1977: 112–13).

Given these facts about the "real" uses of corrections, debate over reform proposals are viewed as naive and misleading.

> It is as if we merely had to change our ideas or consciousness to create changes in prisons. [Reformers] do not see that there are objective material conditions that support the process of imprison-

ment as it is. Until those conditions are changed, prisons and parole will not change (Schmidt, 1977: 118).

Thus, radicals criticize liberals and conservatives alike for even supposing that their reform proposals can substantially modify penal practices unless or until there are fundamental political and economic changes in the society as a whole. In the absence of such changes, correctional reform proposals are viewed as exercises in "pure ideology," essentially divorced from and irrelevant to penal practice.

Historically, such beliefs have left radicals in an awkward position regarding liberal reform efforts. Believing that they are ill-fated or worse—used to thwart, mystify, and control the underclass—how could they support them? But if they choose not to support limited reforms, they run the risk of appearing indifferent—or even callous —toward suffering prisoners. Radicals have vacillated in reacting to this dilemma, sometimes openly supporting liberal reforms and sometimes refusing to do so. A recently published radical analysis of parole and the parole-release practices of the U.S. Parole Commission concludes on a typical note:

> It is not the intent here to criticize liberal reforms. Those reforms which help to ameliorate the conditions under which people live are very important and should be supported. However, it is not certain that reforms such as determinate sentences and punishment instead of rehabilitation are liberal reforms or steps forward. . . . It remains to be seen whether such reforms actually do make prison life easier (Schmidt, 1977: 141–42).

WHICH EXPLANATION IS "BEST?"

Which of these views of correctional reform most accurately explains what is known about the process? If we could answer this question we would know how to package and promote correctional reforms to maximize the likelihood of their adoption and implementation. Alas, however, we can give no easy answer to the question, for different observers can agree neither on the kinds of evidence to examine nor on how it should be interpreted.

For many years liberalism was the unifying faith of correctional sociologists. Much of this unity has disappeared in the past 15 years, leaving competing perspectives among social scientists who are interested in correctional structures and processes. Presumably, the members of all of these competing camps are united in accepting scientifically garnered evidence as the final arbiter of the issues that divide them. However, there is a problem: the same substantive disagreements that divide them affect their evaluations of scientific research and its findings. Put differently, as the critics we discussed in Chapter 15 maintain, social scientists are no different from the remainder of the population. All their perceptions and evaluations are affected by deeply held beliefs that are rarely articulated and many times not even recognized. Consequently, when social scientists employ different domain assumptions in their work, the path is clear for them to disagree over the work itself. Until such time as altered historical conditions once again create unity on their domain assumptions, we can expect the disunity among correctional social scientists to continue.

References

Abrahams, Joseph, and Lloyd W. McCorkle
1946 "Group psychotherapy of military offenders." *American Journal of Sociology* 51 (March): 455–64.

Adams, Stuart
1970 "The PICO project." Pp. 548–61 in Norman Johnson, Leonard Savitz, and Marvin E. Wolfgang, eds., *Sociology of Punishment and Correction*, 2d ed. New York: John Wiley & Sons.
1974 "Measurement of effectiveness and efficiency in corrections." Pp. 1021–49 in Daniel Glaser, ed., *Handbook of Criminology*. Chicago: Rand McNally.
1975 *Evaluative Research in Corrections: A Practical Guide.* Washington, D.C.: U.S. Department of Justice, Law Enforcement Assistance Administration, National Institute of Law Enforcement and Criminal Justice.

Administrative Office of the United States Courts
1976 *Federal Offenders in United States District Courts* 1973. Washington, D.C.: Admin. Office of the U.S. Courts.
1977 *Federal Offenders in United States District Courts* 1974. Washington, D.C.: Admin. Office of the U.S. Courts.

Alexander, Myrl E.
1960 "Correction at the crossroads." *Crime and Delinquency* 6 (October): 344–50.

Allen, Francis A.
1964 *Borderland of Criminal Justice.* Chicago: University of Chicago Press.

328

American Bar Association
1974 *Survey of United States Implementation of the United Nations Standard Minimum Rules for the Treatment of Prisoners.* Report Submitted to the Secretary General of the United Nations by the Government of the United States of America. Washington, D.C.: American Bar Association.

Arditi, Ralph R., Frederick Goldberg, Jr., M. Martha Hartle, John H. Peters, and William R. Phelps
1973 "The sexual segregation of American prisons." *The Yale Law Journal* 82 (May): 1269–71 and 1272–73. Reprinted by permission of The Yale Law Journal Company and Fred B. Rothman & Company.

Arluke, Nat R.
1969 "A summary of parole rules—thirteen years later." *Crime and Delinquency* 15 (April): 267–74.

Arnold, William R.
1970 *Juveniles on Parole.* New York: Random House.

Bacon, G. Richard, et al.
1971 *Struggle for Justice.* New York: Hill and Wang.

Bailey, Walter C.
1966 "Correctional outcome: An evaluation of 100 reports." *Journal of Criminal Law, Criminology and Police Science* 57 (June): 153–60.

Balbus, Isaac D.
1973 *Dialectics of Legal Repression.* New York: Russell Sage Foundation.

Barnes, Harry Elmer
1930 *Story of Punishment.* Boston: Stratford Company.

Bartollas, Clemens, Stuart J. Miller, and Simon Dinitz
1976 *Juvenile Victimization: The Institutional Paradox.* Beverly Hills, Calif.: Sage Publications, Inc. © 1976 and reprinted by permission of the Publisher, Sage Publications, Inc. (Beverly Hills/London).

Beck, James L.
1975 "The effect of representation at parole hearings." *Criminology* 13 (May): 114–17.

Becker, Howard S.
1963 *Outsiders.* New York: Free Press.
1967 "Whose side are we on?" *Social Problems* 14 (Winter): 239–47.

Berger, Peter L., and Thomas Luckmann
1966 *Social Construction of Reality.* Garden City, N.Y.: Anchor Books. Copyright © 1966 by Peter L. Berger and Thomas Luckmann. Reprinted by permission of Doubleday & Company, Inc.

Berk, Richard A., and Peter H. Rossi
1977   *Prison Reform and State Elites.* Cambridge, Mass.: Ballinger.

Berman, John J.
1976   "Parolees' perception of the justice system: Black-white differences." *Criminology* 13 (February): 507–20.

Black, Donald J.
1973   "The social organization of arrest." Pp. 154–60 in Earl Rubington and Martin S. Weinberg, eds., *Deviance: The Interactionist Perspective,* 2d ed. New York: Macmillan.

Blau, Peter M., and W. Richard Scott
1962   *Formal Organizations.* San Francisco: Chandler.

Blumberg, Abraham S.
1967   *Criminal Justice.* New York: Franklin Watts. Copyright © 1967 by Abraham S. Blumberg.

Blumer, Herbert
1967   "Threats from agency-determined research: The case of Camelot." Pp. 153–76 in Irving L. Horowitz, ed., *Rise and Fall of Project Camelot.* Cambridge, Mass.: MIT Press.

Bowker, Lee H.
1977   *Prisoner Subcultures.* Lexington, Mass.: D.C. Heath.

Braly, Malcolm
1976   *False Starts.* Boston: Little, Brown. Copyright © 1976 by Malcolm Braly.

Bunker, Edward
1972   "War behind walls." *Harper's* 244 (February): 39–47.
1973   *No Beast So Fierce.* New York: W. W. Norton. Selections are reprinted with the permission of W. W. Norton & Company, Inc. Copyright © 1973 by W. W. Norton & Company, Inc.

Burkhart, Kathryn Watterson
1976   *Women in Prison.* New York: Popular Library.

Caldwell, Robert G.
1965   *Criminology,* 2d ed. New York: Ronald Press. Copyright © 1965 John Wiley & Sons. Reprinted by permission of John Wiley & Sons, Inc.

Campbell, Donald T.
1971   "Reforms as experiments." Pp. 233–61 in Francis G. Caro, ed., *Readings in Evaluation Research.* New York: Russell Sage.

Campbell, Donald T., and H. Laurence Ross
1968   "The Connecticut crackdown on speeding: Time-series data in quasi-experimental design." *Law & Society Review* 3 (August): 33–53.

Campbell, Donald T., and Julian C. Stanley
1966 *Experimental and Quasi-Experimental Designs for Research.*
Chicago: Rand McNally.

Cardarelli, Albert P., and M. Marvin Finkelstein
1974 "Correctional administrators assess the adequacy and impact
of prison legal services programs in the United States." *Journal of Criminal Law and Criminology* 65 (March): 91–102.

Carlson, Rick J.
1976 *Dilemmas of Corrections.* Lexington, Mass.: D.C. Heath.

Carter, Robert M., and Leslie T. Wilkins
1967 "Some factors in sentencing policy." *Journal of Criminal Law, Criminology and Police Science* 58 (December): 503–14.

Cartwright, Dorwin
1951 "Achieving change in people: Some applications of group
dynamics theory." *Human Relations* 4: 381–92.

Casper, Jonathan D.
1972 *American Criminal Justice: The Defendant's Perspective.*
Englewood Cliffs, N.J.: Prentice-Hall.

Cassou, April Kestell, and Brian Taugher
1978 "Determinate sentencing in California: The new numbers
game." *Pacific Law Journal* 9 (January/July): 22, 26. Copyright 1978 by the University of the Pacific, McGeorge School
of Law. Reprinted by permission.

Chang, Dae H., and Warren B. Armstrong, eds.
1972 *Prison: Voices from the Inside.* Cambridge, Mass.: Schenkman.

Chang, Dae H., and Charles H. Zastrow
1976 "Inmates' and security guards' perceptions of themselves and
of each other: A comparative study." *International Journal of Criminology and Penology* 4: 89–98.

Citizens' Inquiry on Parole and Criminal Justice
1975 *Prison Without Walls: Report on New York Parole.* New
York: Praeger.

Claster, Daniel S.
1967 "Comparison of risk perception between delinquents and
nondelinquents." *Journal of Criminal Law, Criminology and Police Science* 58 (March): 80–86.

Clear, Todd R., John D. Hewitt, and Robert M. Regoli
1977 "Discretion and the determinate sentence: Its distribution,
control and effect on time served." Paper presented at the
meeting of the American Society of Criminology, Atlanta,
November.

Clemmer, Donald
   1958   *Prison Community* (originally published in 1940). New York: Holt, Rinehart and Winston.
Clinard, Marshall B.
   1949   "The group approach to social reintegration." *American Sociological Review* 14 (April): 257–62.
Commission on Accreditation for Corrections
   1977   *Manual of Standards for Adult Correctional Institutions.* Rockville, Maryland: Commission on Accreditation for Corrections.
Comptroller General of the United States
   1977   *Probation and Parole Activities Need to be Better Managed.* Washington, D.C.: General Accounting Office.
Conrad, John P.
   1973   "Corrections and simple justice." *Journal of Criminal Law and Criminology* 64: 208–17.
   1974   "The managerial model of criminal justice." *British Journal of Criminology* 14 (April): 117–24.
Cressey, Donald R.
   1955   "Changing criminals: The application of the theory of differential association." *American Journal of Sociology* 61 (September): 116–20.
   1958   "The nature and effectiveness of correctional techniques." *Law and Contemporary Problems* 23 (Autumn): 754–72.
   1965   "Social psychological foundations for using criminals in the rehabilitation of criminals." *Journal of Research in Crime and Delinquency* 1 (July): 49–59.
Currie, Elliot Park
   1973   *Managing the Minds of Men: The Reformatory Movement, 1865–1920.* Unpublished doctoral dissertation, University of California, Berkeley, December.
Davis, Allan J.
   1968   "Sexual assaults in the Philadelphia prison system and sheriff's van." *Trans-Action* 6 (December): 8–16.
Davis, Kenneth Culp
   1971   *Discretionary Justice.* Urbana: University of Illinois Press.
Dawson, Robert O.
   1966   "The decision to grant or deny parole: A study of parole criteria in law and practice." *Washington University Law Quarterly* 1966 (June): 243–303.
Dembo, Richard
   1972   "Orientation and activities of the parole officer." *Criminology* 10 (August): 193–215.

Denfeld, Duane, and Andrew Hopkins
  1975 "Racial-ethnic identification in prisons: 'Right on from the inside.' " *International Journal of Criminology and Penology* 3 (November) : 355–66.

Dershowitz, Alan M.
  1971 "The law of dangerousness: Some fictions about predictions." *Journal of Legal Education* 23 : 24–48.

Duffee, David
  1975 *Correctional Policy and Prison Organization.* New York: Halsted Press.

Durkin, Mary
  1974 *Behavior Therapy as a Paradigmatic Scientific Revolution.* Unpublished master's thesis, University of Tennessee, Knoxville.

Eichman, Charles J.
  1966 *Impact of the Gideon Decision upon Crime and Sentencing in Florida.* Tallahassee: Florida Division of Corrections.

Empey, Lamar T., and Jerome Rabow
  1961 "The Provo experiment in delinquency rehabilitation." *American Sociological Review* 26 (October) : 679–95.

England, Ralph W.
  1955 "A study of postprobation recidivism among five hundred federal offenders." *Federal Probation* 19 (September) : 10–16.

Erickson, Rosemary J., Wayman J. Crow, Louis A. Zurcher, and Archie V. Connett
  1973 *Paroled But Not Free.* New York: Behavioral Publications.

Etzioni, Amitai
  1964 *Modern Organizations.* Englewood Cliffs, N.J.: Prentice-Hall.

Evjen, Victor H.
  1962 "Current thinking on parole prediction tables." *Crime and Delinquency* 8 (July) : 215–38.

Fisher, H. Richmond
  1974 "Parole and probation revocation procedures after *Morrissey* and *Gagnon*." *Journal of Criminal Law and Criminology* 65 (March) : 46–61.

Flynn, Edith Elisabeth
  1973 "Jails and criminal justice." Pp. 49–88 in Lloyd E. Ohlin, ed., *Prisoners in America.* Englewood Cliffs, N.J.: Prentice-Hall.

Fogel, David
  1975 "*. . . We Are the Living Proof . . .*" Cincinnati: W.H. Anderson Co.

Fosen, Robert H., and Jay Campbell, Jr.
  1966 "Common sense and correctional science." *Journal of Research in Crime and Delinquency* 3 (July) : 73–81.

Frankel, Marvin E.
  1973 *Criminal Sentences.* New York: Hill and Wang. Material reprinted with the permission of Hill and Wang (now a division of Farrar, Straus & Giroux, Inc.) Copyright © 1972, 1973 by Marvin E. Frankel.

Galliher, John F., and James L. McCartney
  1973 "The influence of funding agencies on juvenile delinquency research." *Social Problems* 21 (Summer) : 77–90.

Gaylin, Willard
  1974 *Partial Justice.* New York: Alfred A. Knopf.

Genego, William J., Peter D. Goldberger, and Vicki C. Jackson
  1975 "Parole release decision-making and the sentencing process." *Yale Law Journal* 84 (March) : 810–903.

Giallombardo, Rose
  1966 *Society of Women.* New York: John Wiley & Sons.
  1974 *Social World of Imprisoned Girls.* New York: John Wiley & Sons.

Gibbons, Don C., and Peter Garabedian
  1974 "Conservative, liberal and radical criminology: Some trends and observations." Pp. 51–65 in Charles E. Reasons (ed.), *The Criminologist: Crime and the Criminal.* Pacific Palisades, Cal.: Goodyear.

Gibbs, Jack P.
  1975 *Crime, Punishment and Deterrence.* New York: Elsevier.

Gill, Owen
  1974 "Residential treatment for young offenders: The boys' perspectives." *British Journal of Criminology* 14 (October): 317–35.

Gilman, David
  1975 "Developments in correctional law." *Crime and Delinquency* 21 (April) : 163–73.

Glaser, Daniel
  1962 "Prediction tables as accounting devices for judges and parole boards." *Crime and Delinquency* 8 (July) : 239–58.
  1964 *Effectiveness of a Prison and Parole System.* Indianapolis: Bobbs-Merrill.
  1965 "Correctional research: An elusive paradise." *Journal of Research in Crime and Delinquency* 2 (January) : 1–11.
  1971 "Some notes on urban jails." Pp. 236–44 in Daniel Glaser, ed., *Crime in the City.* New York: Harper & Row.
  1973 *Routinizing Evaluation: Getting Feedback on Effectiveness of Crime and Delinquency Programs.* Washington, D.C.: Na-

tional Institute of Mental Health, Center for Studies of Crime and Delinquency.

Glick, Ruth M., and Virginia V. Neto
1977 *National Study of Women's Correctional Programs.* Washington, D.C.: National Institute of Law Enforcement and Criminal Justice, Law Enforcement Assistance Administration.

Goffman, Erving
1962 *Asylums.* Garden City, N.Y.: Anchor Books.

Goldfarb, Ronald
1975 *Jails.* Garden City, N.Y.: Anchor Books.

Goldfarb, Ronald L., and Linda R. Singer
1970 "Redressing prisoners' grievances." *George Washington Law Review* 39 (December): 175–320.

Goldman, Nathan
1963 *Differential Selection of Juvenile Offenders for Court Appearance.* New York: National Research and Information Center of the National Council on Crime and Delinquency.

Goldstein, Barbara
1975 *Screening for Emotional and Psychological Fitness in Correctional Officer Hiring.* Washington, D.C.: American Bar Association, Commission on Correctional Facilities and Services.

Goode, Erich
1969 "Marijuana and the politics of reality." *Journal of Health and Social Behavior* 10 (June): 83–94.

Gottfredson, Don M.
1970 "Assessment of prediction methods." Pp. 745–71 in Norman Johnston, Leonard Savitz, and Marvin E. Wolfgang, eds., *Sociology of Punishment and Correction,* 2d ed. New York: John Wiley & Sons.

Gouldner, Alvin W.
1968 "The sociologist as partisan: Sociology and the welfare state." *American Sociologist* 3 (May): 103–16.

Greenberg, David F.
1972 "The special effects of penal measures (treatment, special deterrence, etc.): A descriptive summary of existing studies." Washington, D.C.: Committee for the Study of Incarceration, staff memorandum.
1974 "Much ado about little: The correctional effects of corrections." New York University, Dept. of Sociology, mimeo.
1975 "The incapacitative effect of imprisonment: Some estimates." *Law & Society Review* 9 (Summer): 541–80.
1975a "Problems in community corrections." *Issues in Criminology* 10 (Spring): 1–34.

1977   "The correctional effects of corrections: A survey of evaluations." Pp. 111–48 in David F. Greenberg, ed., *Corrections
and Punishment*. Beverly Hills, Cal.: Sage Publications.

1977a   "Fixed sentencing: The cooptation of a radical reform."
Paper presented at the meeting of the American Society of
Criminology, Atlanta, November.

Gross, Seymour Z.
1967   "The prehearing juvenile report: Probation officers' conceptions." *Journal of Research in Crime and Delinquency* 3
(July): 212–17.

Guenther, Anthony L., and Mary Quinn Guenther
1976   " 'Screws' vs. 'thugs.' " Pp. 511–28 in Anthony L. Guenther,
ed., *Criminal Behavior and Social Systems*, 2d ed. Chicago:
Rand McNally College Publishing Company © 1976.

Hagan, John
1974   "Extra-legal attributes and criminal sentencing: An assessment of a sociological viewpoint." *Law & Society Review* 8
(Spring): 357–83.

1975   "The social and legal construction of criminal justice: A
study of the pre-sentencing process." *Social Problems* 22
(June): 620–37.

Hakeem, Michael
1961   "Prediction of parole outcome from summaries of case histories." *Journal of Criminal Law, Criminology and Police
Science* 52 (July–August): 145–55.

Haney, Craig, Curtis Banks, and Philip Zimbardo
1973   "Interpersonal dynamics in a simulated prison." *International Journal of Criminology and Penology* 1 (February):
69–97. Copyright by Academic Press, Inc. (London) Ltd.

Harris, M. Kay, and Dudley P. Spiller, Jr.
1977   *After Decision: Implementation of Judicial Decrees in Correctional Settings*. Washington, D.C.: National Institute of
Law Enforcement and Criminal Justice, Law Enforcement
Assistance Administration.

Hartung, Frank E., and Maurice Floch
1956   "A social-psychological analysis of prison riots: An hypothesis." *Journal of Criminal Law, Criminology and Police Science* 47 (May–June): 51–57.

Harvard Center for Criminal Justice
1972   "Judicial intervention in prison discipline." *Journal of Criminal Law, Criminology and Police Science* 63 (June):
200–28.

Hawkins, Gordon
1976   *Prison: Policy and Practice*. Chicago: University of Chicago
Press.

Heinz, Anne M., John P. Heinz, Stephen J. Senderowitz, and Mary Ann Vance
    1976   "Sentencing by parole board: An evaluation." *Journal of Criminal Law and Criminology* 67 (March): 1–31.

Hirschi, Travis
    1969   *Causes of Delinquency.* Berkeley: University of California Press.

Hoffman, Peter B., and Lucille K. DeGostin
    1974   "Parole decision-making: Structuring discretion." *Federal Probation* 38 (December): 7–15.

Hogarth, John
    1971   *Sentencing as a Human Process.* Toronto: University of Toronto Press.

Hood, R. G.
    1971   "Some research results and problems." Pp. 159–82 in Leon Radzinowicz and Marvin Wolfgang, eds., *The Criminal in Confinement.* New York: Basic Books.

Horowitz, Irving L., and Martin Liebowitz
    1968   "Social deviance and political marginality: Toward redefinition of the relation between sociology and politics." *Social Problems* 15 (Winter): 280–96.

Huff, C. Ronald
    1974   "Unionization behind the walls." *Criminology* 12 (August): 175–94.

Hughes, Everett C.
    1971   "Good people and dirty work." Pp. 87–98 in Everett C. Hughes, ed., *The Sociological Eye,* vol. 1. Chicago: Aldine-Atherton.
    1971a "Social role and the division of labor." Pp. 304–11 in Everett C. Hughes, ed., *The Sociological Eye,* vol. 2. Chicago: Aldine-Atherton.

Irwin, John
    1970   *The Felon.* Englewood Cliffs, N.J.: Prentice-Hall, © 1970.
    1974   "Adaptation to being corrected: Corrections from the convict's perspective." Pp. 971–93 in Daniel Glaser, ed., *Handbook of Criminology.* Chicago: Rand McNally:
    1977   "The changing social structure of the men's prison." Pp. 21–40 in David F. Greenberg, ed., *Corrections and Punishment.* Beverly Hills, Cal.: Sage Publications.

Irwin, John, and Donald R. Cressey
    1961   "Thieves, convicts and the inmate culture." *Social Problems* 10 (Fall): 142–55.

Jacobs, James B.
    1974   "Street gangs behind bars." *Social Problems* 21 (Spring): 395–409.

1976   "The Stateville counsellors: Symbol of reform in search of a role." *Social Service Review* 50 (March) : 138–47.
1977   "Macrosociology and imprisonment." Pp. 89–107 in David F. Greenberg, ed., *Corrections and Punishment*. Beverly Hills, Cal.: Sage Publications.
1977a   *Stateville: The Penitentiary in Mass Society*. Chicago: University of Chicago Press.
forth-   "What prison guards think: A profile of the Illinois force."
coming   *Crime and Delinquency*.

Jacobs, James B., and Harold G. Retsky
1975   "Prison guard." *Urban Life* 4 (April) : 5–29.

Johnston, Norman, Leonard Savitz, and Marvin E. Wolfgang, eds.
1970   *Sociology of Punishment and Correction*, 2d ed. New York: John Wiley & Sons.

Joint Commission on Correctional Manpower and Training
1968   *Corrections 1968: A Climate for Change*. Washington, D.C.: Joint Commission on Correctional Manpower and Training.
1969   *A Time to Act*. Washington, D.C.: Joint Commission on Correctional Manpower and Training.

Kassebaum, Gene, David A. Ward, and Daniel M. Wilner
1971   *Prison Treatment and Parole Survival*. New York: John Wiley & Sons.

Keating, J. Michael, Jr., and Richard C. Kolze
1975   "An inmate grievance mechanism: From design to practice." *Federal Probation* 39 (September) : 42–47.

Kimball, Edward L., and Donald J. Newman
1968   "Judicial intervention in correctional decisions: Threat and response." *Crime and Delinquency* 14 (January) : 1–13.

King, Daniel P.
1969   "Religious freedom in the correctional institution." *Journal of Criminal Law, Criminology and Police Science* 60 (December) : 299–310.

Kittrie, Nicholas N.
1971   *The Right to Be Different*. Baltimore: Johns Hopkins Press.

Korn, Richard
1971   "Of crime, criminal justice and corrections." *University of San Francisco Law Review* 6, No. 1 (October) : 27–75.

Krantz, Sheldon
1976   *The Law of Corrections and Prisoners' Rights in a Nutshell*. St. Paul: West Publishing Co.

Krantz, Sheldon, Robert A. Bell, Jonathan Brant, and Michael Magruder
1973   *Model Rules and Regulations on Prisoners' Rights and Responsibilities*. St. Paul: West Publishing Co.

Kuhn, Thomas
1962   *Structure of Scientific Revolutions*. Chicago: University of Chicago Press.

Leger, Robert G., and John R. Stratton, eds.
1977   *Sociology of Corrections*. New York: John Wiley & Sons.

Lemert, Edwin M.
1970   *Social Action and Legal Change*. Chicago: Aldine.

Leopold, Nathan F., Jr.
1958   *Life Plus 99 Years*. New York: Doubleday.

Lerman, Paul
1968   "Evaluative studies of institutions for delinquents: Implications for research and social policy." *Social Work* 13 (July): 55–64.
1975   *Community Treatment and Social Control*. Chicago: University of Chicago Press. © 1969 by The University of Chicago. All rights reserved.

Levin, Martin A.
1971   "Policy evaluation and recidivism." *Law & Society Review* 6 (August): 17–45.

Lipton, Douglas, Robert Martinson, and Judith Wilks
1975   *Effectiveness of Correctional Treatment: A Survey of Treatment Evaluation Studies*. New York: Praeger.

Logan, Charles H.
1972   "Evaluation research in crime and delinquency: A reappraisal." *Journal of Criminal Law, Criminology and Police Science* 63 (September): 378–87.

McAninch, William S.
1973   "Penal incarceration and cruel and unusual punishment." *South Carolina Law Review* 25 (November): 579–603.

McArthur, Virginia
1974   "Inmate grievance mechanisms: A survey of 209 American prisons." *Federal Probation* 38 (December): 41–47.

McCleary, Richard
1975   "How structural variables constrain the parole officer's use of discretionary powers." *Social Problems* 23 (December): 209–25.

McConkie, Mark L.
1975   *Management by Objectives: A Correctional Perspective*. Washington, D.C.: U.S. Dept. of Justice, Law Enforcement Assistance Administration, National Institute of Law Enforcement and Criminal Justice.

McCorkle, Lloyd W., and Richard Korn
1954   "Resocialization within walls." *The Annals* 293 (May): 88–98.

MacIsaac, John
1968   *Half the Fun Was Getting There*. Englewood Cliffs, N.J.: Prentice-Hall. © 1968 by John MacIsaac.

Mannheim, Herman, and Leslie Wilkins
    1955   *Prediction Methods in Relation to Borstal Training.* London: Her Majesty's Stationery Office.

Martinson, Robert
    1972   "Collective behavior at Attica." *Federal Probation* 36 (September) : 3–7.
    1974   "What works?—questions and answers about prison reform." *Public Interest* 35 (Spring) : 22–54.
    1976   "California research at the crossroads." *Crime and Delinquency* 22 (April) : 180–91.

Martinson, Robert M., Gene G. Kassebaum, and David A. Ward
    1964   "A critique of research in parole." *Federal Probation* 28 (September) : 34–38.

Marx, Karl
    1964   *Selected Writings in Sociology and Social Philosophy.* Trans. by T. B. Bottomore, ed. by T. B. Bottomore and Maximilien Rubel. New York: McGraw-Hill.

Matheny, Kenneth B.
    1976   *Conditions of Jails within the United States.* A Report prepared for the National Institute of Corrections, Atlanta, Georgia.

Mattick, Hans W.
    1974   "The contemporary jails of the United States: An unknown and neglected area of justice." Pp. 777–848 in Daniel Glaser, ed., *Handbook of Criminology.* Chicago: Rand McNally.

May, Edgar
    1976   "Prison guards in America." *Corrections Magazine* 2 (December) : 3–49.

Meehl, Paul E.
    1954   *Clinical vs. Statistical Prediction.* Minneapolis: University of Minnesota Press.

Milan, Michael A., and John M. McKee
    1974   "Behavior modification: Principles and applications in corrections." Pp. 745–76 in Daniel Glaser, ed., *Handbook of Criminology.* Chicago: Rand McNally.

Mileski, Maureen
    1971   "Courtroom encounters: An observational study of a lower criminal court." *Law & Society Review* 5: 473–533.

Milgram, Stanley
    1974   *Obedience to Authority.* New York: Harper & Row.

Miller, Lovick C.
    1970   "Southfields: Evaluation of a short-term inpatient treatment center for delinquents." *Crime and Delinquency* 16 (July) : 305–16.

Miller, Walter B.
1958   "Inter-institutional conflict as a major impediment to delinquency prevention." *Human Organization* 17: 20–23.
1974   "Ideology and criminal justice policy: Some current issues." Pp. 19–50 in Charles E. Reasons, ed., *The Criminologist: Crime and the Criminal*. Pacific Palisades, Cal.: Goodyear.

Mills, C. Wright
1942   "The professional ideology of social pathologists." *American Journal of Sociology* 49 (September) : 165–80.

Mitford, Jessica
1973   *Kind and Usual Punishment*. New York: Alfred A. Knopf.

Morris, Norval
1974   *The Future of Imprisonment*. Chicago: University of Chicago Press.

Morris, Pauline, and Farida Beverly
1975   *On License: A Study of Parole*. New York: John Wiley & Sons.

Motivans, Joseph J.
1963   "Occupational socialization and personality: A study of the prison guard." *Proceedings of the Annual Congress of the American Correctional Association*. Washington, D.C.: American Correctional Association.

Murton, Tom
1976   "Shared decision making as a treatment technique in prison management." *Offender Rehabilitation* 1 (Fall) : 17–31.

National Advisory Commission on Criminal Justice Standards and Goals
1973   *Corrections*. Washington, D.C.: U.S. Government Printing Office.

National Council on Crime and Delinquency
1972   "A model act for the protection of rights of prisoners." *Crime and Delinquency* 18 (January) : 4–13.
1972a   "Compensation of inmate labor: A policy statement." *Crime and Delinquency* 18 (October) : 333–34.
1974   "Peaceful settlement of prison conflict: A policy statement." *Crime and Delinquency* 20 (January) : 1–3.

National Probation and Parole Institutes
1976   *1972 Parolees, Three Year Follow-up and Trend Analysis*. Davis, Cal.: National Council on Crime and Delinquency Research Center.

National Research Council, Panel on Research on Deterrent and Incapacitative Effects
1978   *Deterrence and Incapacitation: Estimating the Effects of Criminal Sanctions on Crime Rates*. Washington, D.C.: National Academy of Sciences.

Neithercutt, M. G., William H. Moseley, and Ernst A. Wenk
1975 *Uniform Parole Reports: A National Correctional Data System.* Davis, Cal.: National Council on Crime and Delinquency.

New York State Special Commission on Attica
1972 *Attica: The Official Report of the New York State Special Commission on Attica.* New York: Bantam Books.

Newman, Graeme R.
1976 *Comparative Deviance.* New York: Elsevier.

Note
1975 "Criminal law—emerging rights of prisoners—right to refuse rehabilitation." *Tennessee Law Review* 42 (Summer): 793-803.

O'Connor, James
1973 *Fiscal Crisis of the State.* New York: St. Martin's Press.

Ohlin, Lloyd E.
1974 "Organizational reform in correctional agencies." Pp. 995-1020 in Daniel Glaser, ed., *Handbook of Criminology.* Chicago: Rand McNally.

Ohlin, Lloyd E., Herman Piven, and Donnell M. Pappenfort
1956 "Major dilemmas of the social worker in probation and parole." *National Probation and Parole Association Journal* 2 (July): 211-25.

O'Leary, Vincent, and Daniel Glaser
1972 "The assessment of risk in parole decision making." Pp. 135-98 in D. J. West, ed., *The Future of Parole.* London: Duckworth.

O'Leary, Vincent, and Joan Nuffield
1972 *The Organization of Parole Systems in the United States.* Hackensack, N.J.: National Council on Crime and Delinquency.
1972a "Parole decision-making characteristics: Report of a national survey." *Criminal Law Bulletin* 8 (October): 651-81.

Orland, Leonard
1975 *Prisons: Houses of Darkness.* New York: Free Press.

Packer, Herbert L.
1964 "Two models of the criminal process." *University of Pennsylvania Law Review* 113 (November): 1-68.

Palmer, Ted
1975 "Martinson revisited." *Journal of Research in Crime and Delinquency* 12 (July): 133-52.

Pappenfort, Donnell, Dee Morgan Kilpatrick, and Alba M. Kuby
1970 *Detention Facilities.* Census of Children's Residential Institutions in the United States, Puerto Rico, and the Virgin Islands: 1966, vol. 7. Chicago: University of Chicago, School of Social Service Administration.

Partridge, Anthony, and William B. Eldridge
1974   *Second Circuit Sentencing Study.* Washington, D.C.: Federal Judicial Center, August.

Pepinsky, Harold E.
1970   "A theory of police reaction to *Miranda* v. *Arizona.*" *Crime and Delinquency* 16 (October) : 379–88.

Piliavin, Irving, and Scott Briar
1964   "Police encounters with juveniles." *American Journal of Sociology* 70. © 1964 by The University of Chicago. All rights reserved.

Plamenatz, John
1970   *Ideology.* New York: Praeger.

Platt, Anthony M.
1971   "The politics of riot commissions, 1917–1970: An overview." Pp. 3–54 in Anthony M. Platt, ed., *Politics of Riot Commissions 1917–1970.* New York: Macmillan.

Platt, Tony, and Paul Takagi
1977   "Intellectuals for law and order: A critique of the new 'Realists.' " *Crime and Social Justice* 8 (Fall–Winter) : 1–16.

Portes, Alejandro
1971   "On the emergence of behavior therapy in modern society." *Journal of Consulting and Clinical Psychology* 36 (June) : 303–13.

President's Commission on Law Enforcement and Administration of Justice
1967   *The Challenge of Crime in a Free Society.* Washington, D.C.: U.S. Government Printing Office.
1967a   *Task Force Report: The Courts.* Washington, D.C.: U.S. Government Printing Office.

Project
1973   "Judicial intervention in corrections: The California experience—an empirical study." *UCLA Law Review* 20 (February) : 452–580.

Quinney, Richard
1973   *Critique of Legal Order.* Boston: Little, Brown.
1977   *Class, State and Crime: On the Theory and Practice of Criminal Justice.* New York: David McKay. Copyright © 1977 by Longman Inc. Reprinted by permission of Longman.

Rainwater, Lee, ed.
1974   *Social Problems and Public Policy: Deviance and Liberty.* Chicago: Aldine-Atherton.

Rawls, John
1971   *A Theory of Justice.* Cambridge, Mass.: Harvard University Press, Belknap Press.

Reed, John P., and Charles E. King
  1966   "Factors in the decision-making of North Carolina proba-
         tion officers." *Journal of Research in Crime and Delinquency*
         3 (July): 120–28.

Resource Center on Correctional Law and Legal Services
  1974   "Providing legal services to prisoners." *Georgia Law Review*
         8 (Winter): 363–432.
  1974a *Survey of Prison Disciplinary Practices and Procedures.*
         Washington, D.C.: American Bar Association, Commission
         on Correctional Facilities and Services.

Robertson, John A., ed.
  1974   *Rough Justice: Perspectives on Lower Criminal Courts.* Bos-
         ton: Little, Brown.

Robison, James O., and Gerald Smith
  1971   "The effectiveness of correctional programs." *Crime and
         Delinquency* 17 (January): 67–80.

Rogers, Kristine Olson
  1972   " 'For her own protection . . .': Conditions of incarceration for
         female juvenile offenders in the State of Connecticut." *Law &
         Society Review* 7 (Winter): 223–46.

Roscoe Pound-American Trial Lawyers Foundation
  1973   *A Program for Prison Reform.* The Final Report of the An-
         nual Chief Justice Earl Warren Conference on Advocacy in
         United States, June 9–10, 1972. Cambridge, Mass.: Roscoe
         Pound-American Trial Lawyers Foundation.

Rosenhan, D. L.
  1973   "On being sane in insane places." *Science* 179 (January 19):
         1–9.

Rossett, Arthur, and Donald R. Cressey
  1976   *Justice by Consent.* Philadelphia: J.B. Lippincott.

Rothman, David J.
  1971   *The Discovery of the Asylum.* Boston: Little, Brown.
  1973   "Decarcerating prisoners and patients." *Civil Liberties Re-
         view* 1: 8–30.

Rubin, Sol
  1971   "Needed—new legislation in correction." *Crime and Delin-
         quency* 17 (October): 392–405.

Rusche, Georg, and Otto Kirchheimer
  1939   *Punishment and Social Structure.* New York: Columbia Uni-
         versity Press.

Ryan, William
  1971   *Blaming the Victim.* New York: Vintage Books.

Saleeby, G. F.
  1972   "Five years of probation subsidy." *California Youth Au-
         thority Quarterly* 5: 3–13.

Sarri, Rosemary C.
1974   *Under Lock and Key: Juveniles in Jails and Detention.* Ann
       Arbor: University of Michigan, National Assessment of
       Juvenile Corrections.

Schein, Edgar H.
1962   "Man against man: Brainwashing." *Correctional Psychi-
       atry and Journal of Social Therapy* 8: 91–120.

Schmidt, Janet
1977   *Demystifying Parole.* Lexington, Mass.: D.C. Heath.

Schnur, Alfred C.
1958   "Some reflections on the role of correctional research." *Law
       and Contemporary Problems* 23, no. 4 (Autumn): 772–83.
       Published by the Duke University School of Law, Durham,
       North Carolina. Copyright 1959 by Duke University. Re-
       printed with permission.

Schroeder, Andreas
1976   *Shaking It Rough.* Garden City, N.Y.: Doubleday.

Schwitzgebel, Ralph K.
1971   *Development and Legal Regulation of Coercive Behavior
       Modification Techniques with Offenders.* Washington, D.C.:
       National Institute of Mental Health, Center for Studies of
       Crime and Delinquency.

Scott, Joseph E.
1974   "The use of discretion in determining the severity of punish-
       ment for incarcerated offenders." *Journal of Criminal Law
       and Criminology* 65 (June): 214–24.

Scull, Andrew T.
1977   *Decarceration-Community Treatment and the Deviant: A
       Radical View.* Englewood Cliffs, N.J.: Prentice-Hall © 1977.
1977a "Madness and segregative control: The rise of the insane
       asylum." *Social Problems* 24 (February): 337–51.

Shover, Neal
1974   " 'Experts' and diagnosis in correctional agencies." *Crime
       and Delinquency* 20 (October): 347–59.
1975   "Criminal behavior as theoretical praxis." *Issues in Crimi-
       nology* 10 (Spring): 95–108.

Sigler, Maurice H.
1975   "Abolish parole?" *Federal Probation* 39 (June): 42–48.

Singer, Linda R.
1973   "Women and the correctional process." *American Criminal
       Law Review* 11 (Winter, 1973): 295–308.

Singer, Linda R., and J. Michael Keating, Jr.
1973   "The courts and the prisons: A crisis of confrontation."
       Criminal Law Bulletin 9 (May): 337–48. Copyright 1973,
       Warren, Gorham, and Lamont, Inc., 210 South Street, Bos-
       ton, Mass. Reprinted by permission. All Rights Reserved.

1973a "Prisoner grievance mechanisms." *Crime and Delinquency* 19 (July): 367–77.

Smith, Joan, and William Fried
1974   *Uses of the American Prison.* Lexington, Mass.: D.C. Heath.

Sobell, Morton
1974   *On Doing Time.* New York: Charles Scribner's Sons.

Stanley, David T.
1976   *Prisoners Among Us: The Problem of Parole.* Washington, D.C.: Brookings Institution.

Steadman, Henry J., and Gary Kveles
1972   "The community adjustment and criminal activity of the Baxstrom patients: 1966–70." *American Journal of Psychiatry* 129 (September): 304–10.

Street, David, Robert D. Vinter, and Charles Perrow
1966   *Organization for Treatment.* New York: Free Press.

Studt, Eliot
1973   *Surveillance and Service in Parole.* Washington, D.C.: U.S. Department of Justice, Law Enforcement Assistance Administration, National Institute of Law Enforcement and Criminal Justice.

Sullivan, Dennis C., and Larry L. Tifft
1975   "Court intervention in correction: Roots of resistance and problems of compliance." *Crime and Delinquency* 22 (July): 213–22.

Swigert, Victoria Lynn, and Ronald A. Farrell
1976   *Murder, Inequality, and the Law.* Lexington, Mass.: D.C. Heath.

Sykes, Gresham M.
1956   "The corruption of authority and rehabilitation." *Social Forces* 34 (March): 157–62.
1958   *Society of Captives.* Princeton, N.J.: Princeton University Press.

Sykes, Gresham M., and Sheldon L. Messinger
1960   "The inmate social system." Pp. 5–19 in Richard A. Cloward et al., eds., *Theoretical Studies in Social Organization of the Prison.* New York: Social Science Research Council, Pamphlet no. 15.

Sylvester, Sawyer P., John H. Reed, and David O. Nelson
1977   *Prison Homicide.* New York: Spectrum Publications.

Takagi, Paul
1967   "Evaluation and adaptations in a formal organization." Unpublished dissertation in Sociology, Stanford University. Quoted in John Irwin, *The Felon.* Englewood Cliffs, N.J.: Prentice-Hall, 1970.
1975   "The Walnut Street Jail: A penal reform to centralize the powers of the state." *Federal Probation* 34 (December): 18–26.

1976   "Revising liberal conceptions of penal reform: A biblio-
        graphic overview." *Crime and Social Justice* 5 (Spring-
        Summer): 60–65.

Takagi, Paul, and James O. Robison
1969   "The parole violator: An organizational reject." *Journal of
        Research in Crime and Delinquency* 5 (January): 78–86.

Temin, Carolyn Engel
1973   "Discriminatory sentencing of women offenders: The argu-
        ment for ERA in a nutshell." *American Criminal Law Review*
        11 (Winter, 1973): 355–72.

Tittle, Charles R.
1974   "Prisons and rehabilitation: The inevitability of failure."
        Social Problems 21: 385–94.

Tittle, Charles R., and Charles H. Logan
1973   "Sanctions and deviance: Evidence and remaining questions."
        Law & Society Review 7 (Spring): 371–92.

Toch, Hans
1977   *Police, Prisons, and the Problem of Violence*. Washington,
        D.C.: National Institute of Mental Health.

U.S. Department of Justice, Law Enforcement Assistance Administration
1973   *Sourcebook of Criminal Justice Statistics 1973*. Washington,
        D.C.: National Criminal Justice Information and Statistics
        Service.
1975   *Children in Custody: Advance Report on the Juvenile Deten-
        tion and Correctional Facility Census of 1972–73*. Washing-
        ton, D.C.: National Criminal Justice Information and
        Statistics Service.
1975a   *The Nation's Jails*. Washington, D.C.: National Criminal
        Justice Information and Statistics Service.
1976   *Capital Punishment 1975*. Washington, D.C.: National Crim-
        inal Justice Information and Statistics Service.
1976a   *Census of Prisoners in State Correctional Facilities 1973*.
        Washington, D.C.: National Criminal Justice Information
        and Statistics Service.
1976b   *Criminal Victimization in the United States 1973*. Washing-
        ton, D.C.: National Criminal Justice Information and Statis-
        tics Service.
1976c   *Survey of Inmates of State Correctional Facilities 1974*.
        Washington, D.C.: National Criminal Justice Information
        and Statistics Service.
1977   *Children in Custody: Advance Report on the Juvenile Deten-
        tion and Correctional Facility Census of 1974*. Washington,
        D.C.: National Criminal Justice Information and Statistics
        Service.
1977a   *Expenditure and Employment Data for the Criminal Justice
        System 1975*. Washington, D.C.: National Criminal Justice
        Information and Statistics Service.

1978   *Prisoners in State and Federal Institutions on December 31, 1976.* Washington, D.C.: National Criminal Justice Information and Statistics Service.

n.d.   *Survey of Inmates of Local Jails: Advance Report.* Washington, D.C.: National Criminal Justice Information and Statistics Service.

van den Haag, Ernest
1975   *Punishment: Concerning a Very Old and Painful Question.* New York: Basic Books.

van Dine, Stephan, Simon Dinitz, and John Conrad
1977   "The incapacitation of the dangerous offender: A statistical experiment." *Journal of Research in Crime and Delinquency* 14 (January): 22–34.

Vinter, Robert D., ed.
1976   *Time Out: A National Study of Juvenile Correctional Programs.* Ann Arbor: University of Michigan, National Assessment of Juvenile Corrections.

von Hirsch, Andrew
1976   *Doing Justice.* New York: Hill and Wang.

Wahl, Albert, and Daniel Glaser
1963   "Pilot time study of the federal probation officer's job." *Federal Probation* 27 (September): 20–25.

Waldo, Gordon P., and Theodore G. Chiricos
1977   "Work release and recidivism: An empirical evaluation of a social policy." *Evaluation Quarterly* 1 (February): 87–108.

Ward, David A.
1973   "Evaluative research for corrections." Pp. 184–206 in Lloyd E. Ohlin, ed., *Prisoners in America.* Englewood Cliffs, N.J.: Prentice-Hall.

Ward, David A., and Gene G. Kassebaum
1965   *Women's Prison.* Chicago: Aldine.

Warren, Marguerite Q.
1971   "Classification of offenders as an aid to efficient management and effective treatment." *Journal of Criminal Law, Criminology and Police Science* 62: 239–58.

Weeks, H. Ashley
1958   *Youthful Offenders at Highfields.* Ann Arbor: University of Michigan Press.

Wheeler, Stanton, E. Banouch, M. Cramer, and I. Zola
1966   "Agents of delinquency control: A comparative analysis." Pp. 31–60 in Stanton Wheeler, ed., *Controlling Delinquents.* New York: John Wiley & Sons.

Wicker, Tom
1976   *A Time to Die.* New York: Ballantine Books.

Wilkins, Leslie T.
1965   *Social Deviance.* Englewood Cliffs, N.J.: Prentice-Hall.

348

1971   "The case for prediction." Pp. 375–81 in Leon Radzinowicz
        and Marvin E. Wolfgang, eds., *The Criminal in Confinement.*
        New York: Basic Books.

Wilks, Judith, and Robert Martinson
1976   "Is the treatment of criminal offenders really necessary?"
        Federal Probation 40 (March): 3–9.

Williams, Jeremy S.
1974   *The Law of Sentencing and Corrections.* Buffalo: William S.
        Hein.

Williams, Vergil L., and Mary Fish
1974   *Convicts, Codes and Contraband.* Cambridge, Mass.: Bal-
        linger.

Wilson, James Q.
1968   *Varieties of Police Behavior.* Cambridge, Mass.: Harvard
        University Press.
1973   "If every criminal knew he would be punished if caught."
        The New York Times Magazine, January 28, 1973. © 1973
        by The New York Times Company. Reprinted by permission.
1975   *Thinking About Crime.* New York: Basic Books.

Wooden, Kenneth
1976   *Weeping in the Playtime of Others.* New York: McGraw-
        Hill.

Wright, Erik Olin, ed.
1973   *Politics of Punishment.* New York: Harper Colophon Books.
Young, Jock
1975   "Working-class criminology." Pp. 63–94 in Ian Taylor, Paul
        Walton, and Jock Young, eds., *Critical Criminology.* London:
        Routledge & Kegan Paul.

Zimbardo, Philip
1972   "Pathology of imprisonment." *Society* 9 (April): 6–8.

Zimring, Franklin E.
1977   "Making the punishment fit the crime: A consumer's guide to
        sentencing reform." Occasional paper no. 12 from the Law
        School, University of Chicago.

Zimring, Franklin E., and Gordon J. Hawkins
1968   "Deterrence and marginal groups." *Journal of Research in
        Crime and Delinquency* 5 (July): 100–14.
1973   *Deterrence.* Chicago: University of Chicago Press.

NAME INDEX

350

Connett, Archie V., 332
Conrad, John P., 61, 114, 248
Cramer, M., 95
Cressey, Donald R., 67–68, 84, 166, 307
Crow, Waymen J., 332
Currie, Elliot Park, 35, 37, 45, 65–66, 76

D

Davis, Allan, J., 147
Davis, Kenneth Culp, 332
Dawson, Robert O., 205, 221–22
DeGostin, Lucille K., 264
Dembo, Richard, 129, 211
Denfeld, Duane, 167
Dershowitz, Alan M., 200
Dinitz, Simon, 61, 127–28, 179–81
Duffee, David, 113
Durkin, Mary, 71

E

Eichman, Charles, 200, 284–85
Empey, Lamar T., 291
England, Ralph W., 195
Eldridge, William W., 81
Erickson, Rosemary J., 332
Etzioni, Amitai, 124
Evjen, Victor H., 161

F

Farrell, Ronald A., 97
Finkelstein, M. Marvin, 263
Fish, Mary, 183
Fisher, H. Richmond, 251
Floch, Maurice, 161
Flynn, Edith Elisabeth, 141
Fogel, David, 119
Fosen, Robert H., 301
Frankel, Marvin E., 86, 104–5
Fried, William, 46, 49–50

G

Galliher, John F., 32
Garabedian, Peter, 317, 320
Gaylin, Willard, 81
Genego, William J., 205, 272
Giallombardo, Rose, 181
Gibbons, Don C., 317, 320
Gibbs, Jack P., 63
Gill, Owen, 133, 136
Gilman, David, 238
Glaser, Daniel, 116, 129, 131, 146–47, 197, 200, 207–9, 211, 276, 278, 280, 283–86, 288, 295–96, 297, 300
Glick, Ruth M., 185, 190
Goffman, Erving, 25, 163–64, 181
Goldberg, Frederick, Jr., 181, 184–89
Goldberger, Peter D., 205, 272

Goldfarb, Ronald, 143, 148, 150, 250, 252, 258
Goldman, Nathan, 217
Goldstein, Barbara, 120
Goode, Erich, 303
Gottfredson, Don M., 197
Gouldner, Alvin W., 27, 29–30, 32
Greenberg, David F., 23, 61, 73, 100, 108, 277, 281, 287–89, 304–6, 310
Gross, Seymour Z., 201–2
Guenther, Anthony L., 122–23
Guenther, Mary, 122–23

H

Hagan, John, 97–98
Hakeem, Michael, 198–99
Haney, Craig, 111–13, 164
Hartle, M. Martha, 181, 184–89
Harris, M. Kay, 273
Hartung, Frank E., 161
Harvard Center for Criminal Justice, 265, 272
Hawkins, Gordon, 63–64, 116, 120–21
Heinz, Anne M., 246
Heinz, John P., 246
Hewitt, John D., 107–8
Hirschi, Travis, 64
Hoffman, Peter B., 264
Hogarth, John, 95–96
Hood, R. G., 304, 309
Hopkins, Andrew, 167
Horowitz, Irving L., 20
Huff, C. Ronald, 260
Hughes, Everett C., 10, 12

I–J

Irwin, John, 26, 73–74, 85, 129, 135–36, 166, 168–69, 210, 212, 224–25, 247
Jackson, Vickie, C., 205, 272
Jacobs, James B., 116–19, 121–22, 124, 127, 130, 167–68, 218–19
Johnston, Norman, 197
Joint Commission on Correctional Manpower and Training, 12, 114–15, 117, 120, 126–29, 131

K

Kassebaum, Gene, 69, 181, 211, 283, 295–96
Keating, J. Michael, Jr., 247, 259, 268, 272
Kimball, Edward L., 269
King, Charles E., 202, 211
King, Daniel P., 252
Kilpatrick, Dee Morgan, 152
Kirchheimer, Otto, 45, 47–49
Kittrie, Nicholas, N., 44, 243, 248

SUBJECT INDEX

Evaluative research—*Cont.*
  quasi-experimental designs, 284–87
  results, 298–312
  as social and political process, 301, 303
  statistical controls, 294
  validity threats, 287–91
Experience tables, 196–97
External validity, 291

F

"Fear-of-being-conned syndrome," 222
Federal Bureau of Prisons, 148, 238, 268
Federal Reformatory for Women, 181
Felon, 6
Felony, 6
Feminine sex role, 182–83
First Amendment, 252
Florida State Prison, 252
Follow-up period
  definition, 280
  desirable characteristics, 280–81
  dropouts, 281–82
Formal rationality, 98–99
Fourteenth Amendment, 252–56
Frontera, 181

G

Gagnon v. *Scarpelli,* 255–56
Girl's training schools
  effects of feminine sex role, 182–83
  homosexuality, 180
  inmate solidarity, 180
  pseudo-family structures, 180
"Good time," 87, 107, 256
"Great human being theory," 42
Grievance mechanisms
  characteristics, 272
  popularity, 259
  types, 259–61
Group dynamics
  assumptions of, 68–69
  as preventive ideal, 66–68

H

Habeas corpus, 251, 253–55
Hancock v. *Avery,* 236
"Hands-off" doctrine
  background, 250
  erosion, 251–52
  justifications, 250
Harvard Law School, Center for Criminal Justice, 275
Hawthorne effect, 288
Hierarchy of credibility, 25–26, 302
Highfields, 281–82, 285, 288
Holt v. *Sarver,* 236
Humane treatment
  compliance with standards, 240–41

Humane treatment—*Cont.*
  definition, 233, 239
  promotion of, 244
  standards, 239–40
  "standards approach," 240–43

I

Ideology; *see also* Preventive ideals; Punishment, ideologies of; *and* Rehabilitation, ideologies of
  definition, 57, 75–76
  impact on correctional change, 57–58
  and reform process, 76–77
Illinois Department of Public Safety, 114
Illinois State Penitentiary, 168, 181
  importation model, 166
Incapacitation
  definition, 59
  effectiveness, 311–12
  as preventive ideal, 59–61
Independent variable
  definition, 278
  desirable characteristics, 278–79
  examples, 278
Index to Legal Periodicals, 251
Indiana Boy's School, 238
Individual treatment model; *see* Medical model
Inhumane practices, 233–39
Inmate Grievance Commission, 259
Inmate social system, 163
Inmates of Boys Training School v. *Affleck,* 237
Institutional racism, 32
Internal validity, 291

J

Jackson v. *Bishop,* 236
Jackson v. *Godwin,* 252
Jacksonian period, 44, 46
Jail inspection, 148
Jailhouse lawyers, 253
Jails
  current conditions, 142–47
  historical, 141–42
  inmate characteristics, 142–43
  reform proposals, 147–50
  size and programs, 143–47
  state variation, 143–44
Jones v. *North Carolina Prisoner's Union,* 256–57, 260, 262–63
Jones v. *Wittenberg,* 233–36
Johnson v. *Avery,* 253–54
Judicial abstention, 250
Judicial activism
  correctional response, 268–71
  development, 251–52
  limitations, 271–72

*This book has been set linotype in 10 and 9
point Century Schoolbook, leaded 2 points.
Section numbers are 14 point Optima and
section titles are 24 point (small) Optima.
Chapter numbers are 30 point Optima and
chapter titles are 14 point Optima semi-bold.
The size of the text area is 26 by 45½ picas.*